Individualisation, Marketisation and Social Capital in a Cultural Institution

The Case of the Danish Folk Church

Individualisation, Marketisation and Social Capital in a Cultural Institution

The Case of the Danish Folk Church

Edited by
Hans Raun Iversen, Lisbet Christoffersen,
Niels Kærgård and Margit Warburg

University of Southern Denmark 2019

University of Southern Denmark
Studies in History and Social Sciences vol. 582

© The authors and University Press of Southern Denmark 2019
Graphic design and printing: Narayana Press
Cover by Dorthe Møller, UniSats
ISBN 978-87-408-3232-7

*Individualisation, Marketisation and Social Capital
in a Cultural Institution* is published with support from:
G. E. C. Gads Fond
Jens Nørregaard og Hal Kochs Mindefond

University Press of Southern Denmark
55 Campusvej
DK-5230 Odense M
www.universitypress.dk

Distribution in the United States and Canada:
Independent Publishers Group
814 N. Franklin Street
Chicago, IL 60610
USA
www.ipgbook.com

Distribution in the United Kingdom:
Gazelle
White Cross Mills
Hightown
Lancaster
LA1 4 XS
U.K.
www.gazellebookservices.co.uk

Contents

Foreword   7

1. Introduction: The Danish Folk Church as a Cultural Institution   9
   Hans Raun Iversen

I. Historical Dimensions of the Danish Folk Church

2. From State Church to Folk Church: Origins of a Cultural Institution as Reflected in the Reformation Celebrations in Denmark 1617-2017   37
   Margit Warburg

3. Secular Lutheranism as Common Institutional and Mental Background for the Danish Welfare State and the Danish Folk Church   65
   Hans Raun Iversen

4. From Tithe to Tax. The Economic History of the Folk Church in the 20th Century   87
   Sidsel Kjems and Niels Kærgård

5. Theological Accommodation to Individualisation in the Folk Church   103
   Hans Raun Iversen

II. Inroads and Resistance to Marketisation in the Folk Church

6. New Public Management in the Folk Church   127
   Annette Kruhøffer

7. Legally Supported Marketisation and Individualisation of the Folk Church as a Cultural Institution   147
   Lisbet Christoffersen and Karen Marie Leth-Nissen

8. The Level of Church Income: Different Explanations   174
   Sidsel Kjems and Niels Kærgård

III. Cultural Institutions Facing Individualisation and Market Orientation

    9. Economy in the Folk Church and Other Cultural Institutions   191
    Niels Kærgård

    10. The Quest for Public Value. The Folk Church and the Other Cultural Institutions between Market and Cathedral   208
    Hans Raun Iversen

    11. Occasional Consumers in the Folk Church   235
    Marie Vejrup Nielsen

    12. The Significance of Cultural Buildings: Inventing a Ritual for Church Closures   254
    Jes Heise Rasmussen

IV. Social Capital, Majority Religion and Discrimination

    13. Interrelations between Social Capital and Religion   273
    Ingrid Storm

    14. Rites of Passage and Creation of Social Capital in the Folk Church   292
    Karen Marie Leth-Nissen

    15. Legal Re-Organisation of the Danish Religious Market   302
    Lisbet Christoffersen

    16. The Folk Church and the Public Debate Before and After Individualisation and Marketisation   326
    Niels Kærgård

Summary of Main Points

    17. The Danish Folk Church in the Age of Marketisation and Individualisation. A Challenged Cultural Institution   347
    Hans Raun Iversen, Lisbet Christoffersen, Niels Kærgård and Margit Warburg

    About the Authors   360

Foreword

The aim of this book is to analyse and discuss the consequences and limits of market orientation in old cultural institutions. The primary questions relate to how individualisation and marketisation change old cultural institutions, how institutions maintain their understanding of themselves and how they continue to contribute to social capital. The aim, therefore, is to understand the extent to which changes in societal factors surrounding cultural institutions also change the way in which they contribute to the social capital of that society.

The core example used throughout the book for conducting this analysis is the *Danish Folk Church*. This is an institution which is now undergoing state governed marketisation and is subject to social individualisation (as all cultural institutions in Danish society are). Such pressures are challenging previous ideas of social capital, both within the institution itself, and in the way it contributes to social capital in society as such.

The book is a result of collaborative research within the interdisciplinary research project *What Money Can't Buy. The Dynamics between Market Orientation, Individualization and Social Capital in Cultural Institutions. The Case of the Danish National Church* (University of Copenhagen, 2014-18). The project has resulted in a number of scientific articles, 3 PhD theses, this book, as well as the forthcoming book *The Old National Churches of Northern Europe: The Persistence of Societal Religion* (edited by Linda Woodhead & Hans Raun Iversen). The project was generously funded by The Danish Council for Independent Research/Humanities. To this has been added considerable support from our departments and faculties at the universities of Copenhagen and Roskilde. The Centre for Modern European Studies at the University of Copenhagen has provided two special grants for conferences.

The four editors of this book have been directing *the What-project* as we call the above mentioned project, in close collaboration with the three PhD students sponsored by the project: Sidsel Kjems, Karen Marie Leth-Nissen, and Jes Heise Rasmussen. Danish and international colleagues have contributed with ideas and critiques at various points throughout the working process. Some of these colleagues have also contributed by writing articles for the project. We offer our thanks to all of them, to the anonymous peer reviewer and, not least, to our language consultant Dr Harris Wiseman, who has contributed broadly and patiently, in terms of language use as well as in the editorial work.

For the publication of this book, we have received grants from Jens Nørregaard og Hal Kochs Mindefond and G. E. C. Gads Fond. We herewith express our heartfelt gratitude for all grants, support and collaboration.

Hans Raun Iversen, Lisbet Christoffersen, Niels Kærgård and
Margit Warburg, August 2019

1. Introduction: The Danish Folk Church as a Cultural Institution

Hans Raun Iversen

This first chapter introduces and discusses the basic concepts in play throughout this book. They will be treated in the following order: culture; cultural institutions; religion as culture; and Christianity as culture. Then, I will discuss the reasons for choosing the Danish Folk Church as the subject for our studies of cultural institutions. And, finally, the key concepts to be found in the title of the book – concepts characterising Western societies today – will be introduced: marketisation, individualisation and social capital. I will move on to asking whether there are limits to the market. Can everything, including all aspects of culture, be handled at the market level without being damaged by the conditions of the market? In the final section, the structure and contents of the chapters of the book will be introduced.

Culture

The English word 'culture' (Danish: *kultur*), has its origins in the Latin word '*cultura*' or '*cultus*': growing or making something grow. In its simplest form, culture is the process, and the result, of human beings' work on parts of *nature* (for example, building houses from bricks of clay). Since the time of Cicero, in the 1st century CE, the word 'culture' tends to refer to activities that cultivate the soul or spirit of human beings. Following that track, culture refers to phenomena through which human beings can build up their identity as individuals and citizens. Thus, cultural activity involves more or less the same as processes of formation (*Bildung* in German, *dannelse* in Danish). Culture is the environment in which, and contains the resources by which, education and formation take place. However, understanding culture in this way often results in it being seen as an elitist phenomenon, focusing on culture in terms of the fine arts (Himmelstrup 2016, 30).

The Danish classical philologist, educationalist and politician Hartvig Frisch deliberately used a different definition of culture in his history of culture from 1928, one very well-known in Denmark. He defined culture, simply, as a set of practices or habits (*vaner* in Danish). In that way, culture points to basic traditions and social patterns that secure continuity in the way we live and interact in our societies (Jensen 1998).

Both aspects, that culture belongs to what is specifically human and that it is decisive for the stability of life in our communities, are important. Culture, however, also includes physical work with material from nature (for example, handicraft and sculpture), and it most certainly also includes invention and creation of new thoughts and expressions of human life.

Cultural institutions

Most traditional societies had no distinction between religion and culture. At first glance, it can seem reasonable to regard religion and churches as part of the culture of society in Denmark, too. Looking more carefully at Danish political and cultural practices (as well as at theological arguments), religion, including the Danish Folk Church, is often placed in a category of its own, one different from culture in general. This book argues that it is reasonable and fruitful, and maybe even necessary, to study and understand Danish Christianity as a part of culture in Denmark, seeing the Folk Church as a cultural institution on par with other institutions usually labelled cultural institutions.

As with the concept of 'culture', definitions of 'cultural institutions' are not very sharp. To the contrary, definitions vary with the historical context in which they are placed. In the *Dictionary of the Danish Language*, a cultural institution is defined as 'an institution that forms a framework for the attempts of human beings to create spiritual (*åndelige*) experiences (*oplevelser*) for themselves and for one another'. The concept is 'used about theatres, music houses, cinemas, museums, radio and TV channels, libraries, schools and universities'.

In the time of the sovereign kings, culture was primarily organised as an instrument in the hands of the rulers. The idea of relatively independent cultural institutions emerged around the time of the Enlightenment. The relationship to the state, as well as the extent of the legal and economic dependency on the state, varies among cultural institutions today. Defining criteria, with continued importance placed on belonging to the group of 'cultural institutions', seem to be that there be open access to the services and products of the institutions for everybody (even though usually tickets do have to be paid for). Some cultural institutions have a sort of monopoly in limited areas, for example the National Museum, when they undertake special functions on behalf of the state. In general, cultural institutions must live side by side with 'competing' institutions, working from the principle 'live and let live'.

Until the free constitution of Denmark, 1849, both the church and the emerging cultural institutions were fully state controlled. After 1849, school, church and culture were placed together under the same ministry of 'Cultus' (*Kultusministeriet*). In 1916, Denmark created a special branch of government, the *Ministry of Ecclesiastical Affairs*, dealing with the highest levels of administration for the Folk Church as well as other formal regulations between state and religion. The reason for creating the new Ministry was simply that the politician, Thorvald Povlsen from the Radical Left (*Det Radikale Venstre*), who was to become minister for *Cultus*, did not want to be responsible for church affairs. In 1961, a special Ministry of Culture was established, following the development in France. This happened without even considering the possibility of having culture and church in one ministry (Himmelstrup 2013, 62-64).

Even at that time, the Folk Church (unlike the Catholic Church in France that was separated fully from the state in 1905) had a legal position parallel to the Danish State Railways and the Royal Danish Post, all of which were called state services or departments (*etater*). The idea at that time seems to have been that, on general principle, culture is for everybody, whereas church is only for some (i.e., the church members, although until 1975 95 percent were members). Thus, the state administers the two areas with parallel systems but with separate procedures. The fact that the Folk Church had, and still has, many more members and visitors (or users) than any other single cultural institution was not relevant in that respect. Church and culture were simply considered separate and distinctly different areas.

Politically, and in research projects, the Folk Church is still even now generally placed in a category of its own, as it has an organisation and a legislation of its own. One contributing factor is that the church, seen in strictly legal terms, is still a public law entity, supported by the state through legislation, (royal) leadership and some economic funding. This relies on the constitutional formulations to ensure a Folk Church and is different from all other cultural institutions. On the one hand, this makes the church very special. On the other hand, this puts the church in a position similar to strongly state-related cultural institutions, such as the National Museum and the Royal Theatre. Looking at state-sponsored public surveys, we have only one recent example where the church has been examined alongside other cultural institutions. In a survey of the flow of money and resources in Denmark's music life, it was found that the Folk Church is by far the biggest employer of musicians and the biggest organiser of public musical events in Denmark (Rambøll 2010). Another point worth mentioning is that the congregational boards are the caretakers of 1,500 medieval church buildings and approximately 700 younger churches – containing a core of Danish public cultural heritage in terms of buildings (Christoffersen 2015).

In some respects, church and religion are categorised as a part of culture. At universities, religion is studied alongside other cultural phenomena and *Statistics Denmark* register church activities under 'Culture and leisure activities' or under the common label of 'Culture and church'. When Danish government ministers are invited to and often give a speech in one of the Danish churches abroad, where many pastors' salaries are paid by the Danish Bill of Finance, the government ministers unanimously praise the church for being such a fine expression and promoter of 'Danish culture'. That the churches are more specifically intended to promote Danish Evangelical-Lutheran Christianity is left unsaid; or perhaps that form of religion is simply understood as being a natural part of 'Danish culture'.

Until some decades ago, news media had a special page or program for 'church' matters. Today, such a page only exists in a few papers such as *Kristeligt Dagblad* (The Christian Daily), which is increasingly becoming a magazine for existential and ethical matters, promoting itself under the common heading 'Life and Soul'. National radio and TV in Denmark are currently following the track set by the BBC, where religion and Christianity are integrated into various programs, which are never named 'religion' or 'Christianity', but – to mention two contemporary programs on P1 on the national radio – are called 'Spirit of the Time' (*Tidsånd*) and 'The Higher Powers' (*De højere magter*). This reflects the results of surveys and focus groups among the listeners and viewers.

Religion as culture

In dealing with religion in Denmark, it is necessary to work with a distinct understanding of religion: religion is something cultivated and developed by human beings, not randomly; nor, however, just according to the special wishes of certain people. The patterns of religion in Denmark are highly influenced, and to a great extent determined by, Danish history and the local environment (Gundelach et al. 2008). Thus, religion is not like a given essence or substance that one can dig out as one would excavate minerals from a mine. Nor is religion something people cultivate for fun or to obtain certain benefits, as when you grow vegetables in a tiny kitchen garden, or when you produce entertainment.

A good analogy for religion is an old central park in a major city. In Copenhagen, you may think of the King's Garden or, even better, Frederiksberg Garden. The old park has been there, and has been developed, for many centuries. It has become what it is due to a complicated combination of conditions set by nature and the intelligent (and sometimes hard) work of people and, not least, the will of the rulers. The old park has a degree of existence independent of people, even though they will certainly know about it if they live reasonably close by. People can watch the park from the outside, or take their daily walk in the park according to a certain route arranged by the park authorities, or they can walk around in their own way. They can also use the park for leisure only, as when sunbathing. In all these respects, Danish religion resembles an old city park. Thus, one possible label for religion in Denmark, including Folk Church Christianity, might be *the Danish Park of Religions* (Iversen 2005, drawing on Aldèn 2004)!

Texts and interviews from all of the seven main branches of religion in Denmark reveal a common, religious pattern, which is systematised in Table 1 (updated from Iversen 2005, 109-119). We shall not attempt to estimate the size of the various branches, as most people in Denmark belong to several branches integrating various religious sentiments. The point of the table here is only to show that a somewhat similar religious structure – God, virtue and destiny or destination – can be found in all of the seven dominant branches of the Park of Religions in Denmark. This structure seems to be a major part of the background since Folk Church Christianity, and perhaps other parts of religion in Denmark as well (that have not been examined in this project), can be seen to fit rather easily into Danish Culture in general.

Table 1. Common structure within the Danish Park of Religion: God, Virtue and Destination

	Form of religion	God	Virtue	Destination
1)	**Implicit religion**	Experience of difference	Moral markings	Happiness and a good life
2)	**Folk religion**	God as destiny of the individual	Virtue	Eternal life of the soul
3)	**New religions and spirituality**	Micro-macro cosmology	Karma – balance between cause and effect	Reincarnation
4)	**Church Christianity**	Trinity	Love of neighbour	Resurrection of the flesh
5)	**Culture Christianity**	God as partner	Wish to be good	Prospects and good advice
6)	**Civil religion**	God cares for the nation	Love of the nation	Societal coherence
7)	**Islam**	Allah	Sharia	Allah's provision

Conventionally, with its historically changing forms, it is argued that Church Christianity has been the most dominant and continuous religion in Denmark for more than 1,000 years. There is no doubt that the church has attempted to eradicate or embrace (and thus absorb) other forms of religion. What the church has left the great majority of people in Denmark today with is more Culture Christianity than a Church Christianity. Here, people subscribe to a concept of history and of human beings, plus basic values such as the duty to love one's neighbour, deriving from Christianity. Church Christians are a separate part of the Cultural Christians, and in addition to subscribing to all that, they accept and at least occasionally practise prayer, hymn singing, confession of creed and other church rituals (Iversen 1999).

Even so, less elaborate, more home-grown forms of religion, including *implicit religion*, concealed in all sorts of customs and so on (Bailey 1990), may well have influenced the common religious pattern in Denmark as much as Church Christianity. The most elaborated, and clear-cut connections described in Danish empirical research (i.e. between God as destiny, virtue as 'taking the middle path' morals and eternal life of the soul as destination), can be found in *folk religion* – as, indeed, it could be found rather strongly in agricultural Denmark until 50-100 years ago (Rod 1961).

In recent years, mainly due to immigration, Islam (having approximately four percent of the present population as followers) has become dominant in the debate about religion in Denmark. Incidentally, Islam's core structure, with Allah, the moral values found in Sharia and Allah's decision about the destiny of the individual, looks compatible with the core structure of the other Danish religions. In seems safe to say that this is so with respect to the more widespread Cultural Islam; however, more studies are required to draw the same conclusion for the many other forms of Islam also found in Denmark.

Even though 'God' is an increasingly questioned figure in Denmark, faith in God is still the strongest and most centrally placed oak in the Danish park of religions. In contrast, according to the *European Value Studies*, sin, hell, grace and salvation are Christian concepts that are disappearing from the minds of Danes. 'God' has, however, always been around, and remains, so far at least. From their school and confirmation classes, almost all Danes know about the stories of God, the creator, and Jesus, his son (Højsgaard and Iversen 2013). Recent changes in the forms of life have not been quite as dramatic in Denmark as they have been in Sweden (Bäckström et al. 2004). Industrialisation was much stronger in Sweden compared to Denmark. Still, the basic shifts from an agricultural, through industrial, to a service society and the consequent changes in religion have been basically the same in the two countries during the last 150 years. The sacred canopy that used to embrace common life in agricultural Denmark has disappeared, and so too, therefore, has the secure place and powerful position of God. Some sort of faith in some sort of God is, however, still common. The balance between community and individualism in the mentality of the Danes finds strong expression when we look at faith in God. Incidentally, the situation is portrayed well in the following brief dialogue from Woody Allen, though made without special reference to Denmark:

A: Do you believe in God?
B: I'm not sure ...
A: Well, Kierkegaard says that if you're not sure, then you don't!
B: Okay! Then I guess I do!
(quoted from Warmind 2005, 290)

Another way of expressing a rather average Danish attitude to religion can be found in the following small portion of an interview with a retired army officer:

A: Do you believe in life after death?
B: No, I don't. I believe in the undertaker, and she's already been decided on. She knows the parameters.
A: Would you say that you are a Christian?
B: Yes, I would. It's not a faith, it's primarily a tradition.
(Gundelach et al. 2008, 141)[1]

An illustration of the recent development in the attitudes to the Folk Church in Denmark during the last 50 years can be seen in the following answers to the hypothetical question: *Would you register as a member of the Danish Folk Church if it was required for being a member?* The Danish Institute for Social Research firstly posed this question in the first 'leisure time' survey of 1964. Having been repeated several times since then, we now have the following row of answers (Table 2):

Table 2. Would you register as a member of the Folk Church if necessary? (Percentage)

	1964	1975	1987	1993	1998	2013
Yes	72	58	45	58	56	48
No	16	37	23	26	23	29

(Fridberg, 2000; Højsgaard and Iversen, 2013)

The Danes can leave the Folk Church any day, *and they know it*. They belong to their church, but they do not believe strongly in the importance of this belonging. They are, as they might put it themselves, not 'religious' about their membership. From 1974 to 2015, the general rule has been that less than

10,000 people give up their church membership per year. Although this figure more than doubled in 2016, due to the first organised atheist campaign, there are no indications that members will leave the church in any big quantity – even if approximately 10 percent say that they consider doing so according to surveys. We can conclude that church membership is still rather stable for most people. One way of describing this situation is that Christianity and its organisation, the Folk Church together with the national identity and its organisations, e.g. the queen, work as a common backdrop for the Danish mentality (Gundelach et al. 2008).

Christianity as culture – theologically speaking

From a sociological point of view, Christianity is a part of the culture in Denmark, even more so than religion in general due to the historical interaction between state, people and the church. Phenomenologically, there is no significant reason to deal with Danish religion and Christianity as something different from other sorts of culture. Religion is a special or distinct part of culture. It is, however, not that much more special or distinct than other aspects of culture. Still this notion is highly disputed, especially in the dominating theology of the 20th century. When asking theologians – and probably a considerable number of strong Church Christians – the question of the precise nature of Christianity as a part of religion and culture, the answers becomes much more complicated.

The first major work within Protestant theology on the church as a societal phenomenon was Ernst Troeltsch's *Die Soziallehren der Christlichen Kirchen und Gruppen (The Social Teachings of the Christian Churches)*, published in 1912. Here, Troeltsch operates with two kinds of churches only, 'Church' and 'Sect', and his ideal was for the church as an institution to exist in harmony with state and society. In this way, these societal institutions can form a strong civilising force together. Even so, Troeltsch sees Christianity as a highly individualised religion whose core is the relationship of the individual to Christ. Thus, for Troeltsch – as for Kierkegaard – Christianity in the strict sense is something quite different from culture. Christianity is situated in the will and emotions of the individual human being. On the one hand, church is, or should be, an ordinary part of society, if it is not 'sectarian' (as the free churches are, according to Troeltsch). On the other hand, Christianity is, at its core, something entirely different from culture in general. This position was elaborated in H. Richard Niebuhr's seminal work *Christ and Culture*, 1951, where the author discusses five types of possible relationship between Christianity and culture: *Christ against culture, Christ in culture, Christ above culture, Christ in tension with culture* and *Christ transforming culture.*

Positions like these helped prepare the road for the most influential theological position in Denmark in the 20th century, that of the dialectical theology pioneered by Karl Barth. Here, true Christianity is always contradicting human culture. The message of God is always something else (*was ganz Anderes*), opposing human will, and the church is only a real church insofar as it sticks to proclaiming that message. For decades, dialectical theology, in Denmark too, tried to save Christianity from Freudian critiques (seeing religion as a form of sublimation) and likewise from the Marxist critique of religion as a promise of a pie in the sky. Theological responses to these critiques tended to assert that whatever is criticised is 'only religion'. In essence, Christianity is not a religion, since religion and culture are created by human beings. The reality of Christianity is the work of God alone! As such, the above critiques are only attacking the 'outer shell' of Christianity, as it were, the human construction, rather than the underlying truth itself.

Until sometime in the 1980s, the dominant position in Danish theology held that religion may be part of culture, but Christianity is not as it is basically not a religion. In recent years, this position has been modified so that theologians tend to talk about 'Christianity and other religions' (see, for example, Nørgaard-Højen 1988). Even theologians emphasising that Christianity is based on God's revelation in Christ admit that empirically, and practically, Christianity looks like a religion. Thus, most theologians today regard Christianity as a part of culture. However, as is also often the case with other fields of culture (for example the fine arts), theologians may emphasise that there is a sublime core in Christianity which meets people as a divine gift or revelation in the midst of what is otherwise a product of human work and invention.

The 'meaning of life' as found in Christianity, and promoted by the Folk Church, is the faith that Jesus of Nazareth, who lived and died 2,000 years ago, rose from his grave and continued to live and act as he did in his earthly life. This is a point that cannot be verified empirically, but faith in Christ as the son of God interacts with culture. It takes a cultural shape and is even promoted by a cultural institution, the church. Christianity rests on a non-empirical idea that Jesus of Nazareth rose from his grave to sit and act at his father's right hand. If this is true, Christianity is an invention of God the almighty. Whatever consequences Christians draw from this faith are, however, part and parcel of a culture that can be studied empirically on a par with other cultural activities. Such interactions between ideas that cannot always be verified empirically is common to all cultural institutions. There are, for example, many authors or musical composers, who say that their core inspiration and ideas came to them as revelations. However, by the time these 'revelations' have become available in the form of a book or a piece of music, they have surely become culture.

In 1988, Professor of Systematic Theology at the University of Copenhagen, Niels Henrik Gregersen formulated a comprehensive definition of culture. Drawing on a long list of philosophers, sociologists and anthropologists (including Arnold Gehlen, Edward B. Taylor, T. Parsons, Niklas Luhmann and Jürgen Habermas), Gregersen writes:

> Culture embraces the practices of human life together with the understanding of life, habits and worldviews as they are integrated in the complex entirety of mutual relations of meaning and significance. ... Culture has several layers. Comprising an entirety of practices and understandings of life, culture consists of 'small traditions'[2], where the patterns of meaning are formed closely related to practice when we find orientation in daily life, deal with other people and express ourselves to others and ourselves. ... Culture, however, also embraces 'big traditions' that attempt to collect cultural knowledge into a coherent understanding of life, embracing theoretical-cognitive knowledge about the world, the external side of the knowledge of culture. Moreover, the internal sides of the knowledge of culture include the practical-moral knowledge about how to adapt oneself to the world through action, and the expressive-aesthetic knowledge of how the subject experiences the world and expresses its needs and wishes in relation to the world. (Gregersen 1988, 32f, author's translation)

According to this definition of culture – so too, probably, with most other definitions – Danish religion, including Folk Church Christianity, with its great variety of activities, involvements in and ideas about human existence[3], obviously appears as a part or a dimension of culture in Denmark. If we look at the various forms of expression and action in the church (rituals, music, speeches and so on), they all have their counterparts in other parts of culture. Often, they interact with (or sometimes they are more or less directly taken over from) other parts of culture.

The Folk Church as case for studying cultural institutions

As pointed out above, historically, church and Christianity were incorporated in Danish society to a very large extent. The church was not a cultural institution on par with others. Rather, it was an ideological department of the state, even though of course it had its own cultural means (e.g. music, rituals and textbooks). In the full sense of the word, the Folk Church has only very recently presented itself as an institution for the promotion of Danish Lutheran Christianity, alongside other contributors to culture in Denmark (see Chapter 2).

Today, the Folk Church is the main institution promoting Danish Christianity, primarily Church Christianity, among the Danes (but in reality Culture Christianity, too). Thus far, no less than 70 percent of 14 year old youngsters in Denmark have attended confirmation classes annually (Iversen 2018, Chapter 2). As such, they have practised Church Christianity enough to make them Culture Christians for the rest of their lives. During the first 200 years after the Reformation, the Lutheran church strategy was to trust the family fathers and heads of households to do the basic work of securing Christian knowledge and behaviour, for example teaching Luther's Small Catechism to the household. The pietists, 200 years later, and the rationalists after them, realised that this strategy had failed. Therefore, they introduced compulsory confirmation classes in 1736 and seven years of compulsory schooling in 1814. For two and a half centuries, some sense of Christianity (knowledge of some Bible stories, the Lord's prayer, the Apostolic Creed, a number of central hymns and some moral ideas) was kept alive in the Danish people by means of teaching, and only to a limited extent due to the Sunday services and other rituals in the church. Today, after the school reform of 1975, families and schools contribute to Christian education only to a very limited extent. The only institutions offering access to Christian practice and faith for all sorts of people are the churches, primarily the Folk Church, with 75 percent of the population as church tax paying members. So far, this makes the Folk Church a rather central cultural institution in Danish culture, not as important as the schools, but perhaps as important as all the various museums taken together. Where all Danish museums have a combined 18 million visitors annually, the Folk Church, in all of its more than 2,000 churches, gather 20 million people to its approximately 500,000 annual gatherings (Iversen 2018, 201).

When discussing cultural institutions in Denmark, as indicated above, we conventionally refer to a number of institutions organised with a leading or coordinating national organisation and with local branches, such as the Folk Church. Typical examples are:

1. DR (Denmark's national radio and TV channels), which, like the Folk Church, is formally state-controlled and financed by a special tax (license) to be paid by all users, as DR is supposed to deliver a 'public service'.
2. Art, history and nature museums, each having their messages and material to be shared with people whom they can attract to visit them. Like the Folk Church, they seek new ways of operating today, as they cannot survive on the old styles of standard exhibitions and performances.
3. Libraries have traditionally specialised in lending out books and are currently fighting to find new ways of operating in a digitalised society.
4. Theatres, concert halls, cinema and similar art and entertainment institutions where the performances are usually of a very high, professional standard today.
5. The book market, with its production and distribution of books.
6. The universities.[4]

As is outlined in Section III of this book, there are at least at three points where the Folk Church behaves as any other cultural institution in Denmark facing individualisation and market orientation:

1. All cultural institutions promote certain elements of culture in line with the Folk Church's promotion of (Danish, Lutheran) Christianity.
2. In a society with strong tendencies towards individualisation and marketisation, all cultural institutions (just like many other societal institutions and businesses) are obliged to sharpen their profile focusing on both their public value (see Chapters 9 and 10) and their relationship

with their users. This may lead to numerous changes in the priorities and personnel within those cultural institutions.
3. People, in general, follow the same patterns when using the Folk Church as when using other cultural institutions. They use whatever part of the products (and respond to whichever invitations are issued from the cultural institution) that fit their personal needs and interests, without identifying themselves with all that the institutions stand for and produce.

In this book, our claim is that it is legitimate to label and study the Folk Church as a cultural institution and that it may even be fruitful to use the Folk Church as a case for a project focusing on the reactions of cultural institutions when facing the marketisation, individualisation and the need to contribute to social capital.

Individualisation and marketisation

Individualisation and marketisation are megatrends in Western societies today, and to a great extent globally as well. As pointed out in recent research, these trends have significantly penetrated into cultural institutions as well as churches (Gautier et al. 2013, Moberg 2016).

Individualisation and marketisation have partly separate backgrounds. Often individualisation is connected to predominant features or events in the West such as Christianity, the Renaissance, the Reformation, the Enlightenment and the so-called subjective turn in the 20th century (Siedentorp 2014, Taylor 1991 and 2007). The creation of the modern capitalist market is conditioned by a number of more or less independent historical factors (accumulation of money to capital, availability of raw material and the labour force, and the development of technologies for industrial production, etc.). According to Max Weber, the Protestant ethic, especially in Calvinism, worked as a catalyst for the spirit of market capitalism (Weber 1905).

Today, individualisation and marketisation interact and promote one another in ways that often make it impossible to see which of the two factors is the strongest force behind a certain development. One example is the development in schools where youngsters are being educated to compete on the market as individuals (Pedersen 2011). The wish of many parents to promote their children as unique individuals interacts with the political wish to educate the children to be ready to adapt to societal changes according to the development of the future market. The same mixture of motives is at work behind developments in the public sector, where management procedures from private business are introduced in public administration, demanding new forms of individual performance (Hood 1991). Mixed motives can also be found when the market expands into all sorts of human areas, as if life itself can be handled at the market level without negative consequences (Sandel 2012).

Both individualisation and marketisation can be analysed as something positive, as creating more possibilities for the individual and greater economic wealth in society (Pedersen 2011). Obviously, the meaning of life is something that cannot be bought as such. Even so, meaningfulness may often be found in the midst of the market. One area of the negative consequences produced by marketisation seems to relate to the *social capital* available in society and in the life of the individual. If we are only competing and celebrating alone (e.g. when bowling alone, as Putnam famously put it [Putnam 2000]), there is not much creation of personal social capital or development of societal relations and competences (Putnam 2000, Bourdieu 1986). Another challenge is the growing social inequality that seems to be built into neo-liberal market economies (Piketty 2014). For some people, quality of life is directly at risk, for example when there is no room for 'resonance' but a high risk for stress (Rosa 2016). For individuals, as for society at large, it is risky business if all sorts of culture, including the cultural heritage, are turned into a commodity on the market for entertainment instead of it being a glue for binding the members of society together.

What Money Can't Buy: Limits of Markets?

The main title of our project is borrowed from Michael Sandel's book *What Money Can't Buy? The Moral Limits of Markets,* 2012. Perhaps surprisingly, the book does not forward any suggestions as to how and where to set limits for the expanding market – even though the author is very much aware of the fact that Europe, and certainly the USA, does not only have a market but that they have literally become *market societies.* Nor does the book suggest criteria for setting moral limits to the market. Rather, Sandel keeps on asking the question of whether this or that form of marketisation is morally defensible. As such, Sandel begins and ends with one and the same question: *do we want a society where everything can be bought for money?* Instead of discussing moral limits to the market, Sandel examines a huge number of empirical cases where the market has expanded into deeply human and personal affairs. I have sorted Sandel's material into the following four categories.

In the first category, we find cases where the sense of human honesty and authenticity tend to be spoilt. Of course, the President of the USA may use his speechwriter when he has to deliver his state of the union speech. Something more questionable is going on when a bridegroom can buy a professional speech to deliver to his bride at their wedding. And, if you try to buy a friend for money, you will most surely sense that you are only getting a surrogate friendship, even if the 'friend' has been casted professionally.

The second category of cases has ethical ambivalence built into them. A poor person selling some part of his body, for example a kidney, to get badly needed money will always come away as a 'reduced person'. It may also be questioned whether it is ethically right that the present practice, where firms can sell and buy quota of rights to pollute, has been elevated to a global right.

In the third category, people may feel that they are doing something morally wrong in a given activity, but such activities are nonetheless widespread. You cannot sell your child, or your vote for an election. This is bad! Though perhaps, not quite as bad: you can receive money for naming your child 'Pepsi' or 'Burger King', and so on. In the USA, in particular, you find many investments in death, where the investor only has to wait for – and if possible even promote – the death of another person. This happens when poor people sell the right to benefit from their life insurance to get money for medical treatment. Another case is sponsoring an attractive flat for a dying person on the condition that the sponsor inherit the flat. More or less in the same category, we have bookmakers who set up games where you bet on who out of a group of publicly known persons will die first. The principle is the same inhuman one all over: the death of one will be the gain of another.

In the fourth category, money has been shown empirically to produce consequences contrary to those intended. For example, if you pay boys per book they read, they will most probably never read a book again once you have stopped paying them. If the inhabitants of a certain mountain area in Switzerland are asked to agree to the government depositing some of the waste from the nation's nuclear stations in their mountains they may agree simply to show solidarity with the energy policies of their country. However, if you offer to pay them a sum per family for their good will, they are likely to say 'no' when asked the same question. Experiments also prove that students paid to collect money for a certain humanitarian purpose collect significantly less money than students undertaking the same job voluntarily and without pay.

Money can buy a lot, but not everything. On the contrary, it can spoil important things in life. If we look at the Folk Church, category four is especially relevant. Lately, to mention but one example, the former chairperson of the Union of Congregational Boards of the Folk Church, Inge Lise Pedersen, has warned the congregational boards about buying what could be done by volunteers, for example choirs leading the hymn singing. What is the value of congregational singing if it ends up being left to professionals who do it for money? Dolly Parton puts the point in her own undeniable way:

> Silver and gold might buy you a home,
> but things of this world they won't last you long,
> and time has a way of turning us old,
> time can't be bought back with silver and gold.

The pastor for immigrants in Copenhagen, Niels Nymann Eriksen, points to the value of human encounters as experienced in his work:

> The benefit a human being gains from the encounter with a stranger cannot be exchanged into another currency. There is no market for the blessing from a stranger (Eriksen 2018, 11).

The contents of this book

The research results published in this book aim at contributing to the international debate on the consequences and limits of market orientation in relation to cultural institutions, insofar as this is possible, against the background of studies into the Danish Folk Church as a cultural institution. This is the reason why this book, dealing almost entirely with Danish material, is in English. In the *What-project* description, we formulated the following working hypothesis regarding the function of the Danish Folk Church within present societal trends and developments, which this book aims at testing:

> It is in the ability to accept individualisation as a pre-condition that the Danish National Church as a cultural institution has a position of strength enabling it to contribute to society's social capital while simultaneously setting limits to market orientation.

The reaction of churches and cultural institutions to the current trends of individualisation and marketisation depend on the context and the character of the institutions in question. In the first major collective study in the *What-project*, we carried out a comprehensive comparative analysis of seven old national churches in Northern Europe (Woodhead and Iversen *in preparation*). One major finding was that churches that turned outwards, and integrated themselves within, society at large did better than churches that turned inward. The Danish Folk Church is, in many respects, doing better than churches occupied with internal structures and traditions (e.g. the Anglican Church in England). On the other hand, it is to be expected that a 'societal church', as the Folk Church is, would also be more marked by trends within society, such as marketisation and individualisation, and the consequences attached to this form of development.

Historical Dimensions of the Danish Folk Church
The first section of this book points out how the Folk Church is special inasmuch as it is moulded by its background in Danish history, mentality, economy and Folk Church theology. Therefore, the results of this study of the Folk Church in Denmark should not be taken as applying automatically to churches in general. Every cultural institution has a peculiar structure, identity and profile linked to it, and is most often directly bound up with its history. It is hard to say if the Folk Church is more peculiar, more unique, than other cultural institutions. We leave that discussion aside here and concentrate instead on four areas where the Folk Church is distinct and special as a cultural institution. At the same time, we deal with four areas that are significant for the stability, work and survival of the Folk Church.

In the first chapter of this historical section of the book, Margit Warburg argues that cultural institutions, in the modern sense of the word, are defined by Enlightenment-based criteria. The Folk Church today lives up to such criteria: It serves the commonwealth by offering general access to Danish Protestant cultural and religious traditions to which three quarters of the Danish population belong through their church membership. Warburg uses the historical Reformation celebrations as a prism to draw out the broader changes in the relations between church, state and society during the last 400 years. In this way, she depicts the historical background of the Danish Folk Church as it has developed out of the Lutheran state religion. She argues that it was not evident that this church would develop into a cultural institution. In particular, its anti-Catholic ideology was incompatible with Enlightenment ideals of representing a common national heritage. Warburg concludes that the Folk Church only became *fully* qualified as a Danish cultural institution with the adoption of lenient attitudes among bishops and pastors towards other Christian churches, as was seen, for example, in the 2017 Reformation celebrations.

In the second chapter of this section, Hans Raun Iversen points to Lutheranism in a secular form as providing a common background for the institutions and mentality behind both the Danish welfare state and the Danish Folk Church. Iversen's argument is not that Lutheranism is the historically decisive agent behind the creation of the welfare state. Instead, the argument is that the relatively high degree of stability in the welfare state as well as in the Folk Church depends on a widespread mentality that has a structure similar to Lutheranism and that makes most people in Denmark feel at home in both places.

Without doubt, the progressive tax system is a decisive factor behind the survival of the welfare state. In the third chapter of this section, Sidsel Kjems and Niels Kærgård tell the history of the development in church economy in the 20th century, wherein the Folk Church went from tithe to tax, so that members pay a certain percentage (in 2018 an average 0.87 percent of their taxable income). The changes did not only come about due to political wisdom or church-minded planning, but as a practical solution, which turned out to have fortunate economic consequences for the Folk Church.

In the fourth and last chapter of this section, Iversen analyses the theological accommodation to individualisation and thereby, to some extent, also to market orientation in the Folk Church. He points to three key words or paradigms slowly taking over, one after the other, since the First World

War: Piety, Preaching and Participation. Iversen argues that a church looking inward in order to build its own piety and a church only giving priority to preaching could not have fostered the same widespread contact with the great majority of Danes as the Folk Church of the 21st century managed to achieve with its many participatory and co-creational activities.

Inroads and Resistance to Marketisation in the Folk Church
Since 1983, various New Public Management strategies, taken over from the private sector, have been introduced into the public sector in Denmark. In the second section of the book, an analysis will be carried out of how the Folk Church, with its supreme administration being run by the state Ministry of Ecclesiastical Affairs, has responded to the introduction of various parts of New Public Management. Ironically, such strategies have been partly adopted in order to have more legitimacy in the struggle to set limits for more New Public Management.

Section II's first chapter, by Annette Kruhøffer, explores the ways in which, and the degree to which, parts of New Public Management, for example demands for performance and results in the institutions placed directly under the Ministry of Ecclesiastical Affairs, have been implemented in ways similar to those found in other parts of the public administration in Denmark. This has happened almost without theological debate on the compatibility of the modern managements methods with Christianity.

In the following chapter, by Lisbet Christoffersen and Karen Marie Leth-Nissen, the same topic is explored at the deanery and parish levels. Firstly, the concept 'Churching Alone', taken from Leth-Nissen's PhD thesis, is introduced to characterise an emerging tendency among users of the Folk Church. This is related to recent changes in church law and to current practice where the deans are challenged to function as 'change agents' within the Folk Church. Thus, the deans introduce parts of New Public Management in their work whilst at the same time being critical of New Public Management in general.

In the third and last chapter of this section, Sidsel Kjems and Niels Kærgård analyse the surprisingly different forms of economy, especially the sources of income, in the old national churches of northern Europe. They indicate that the combination of membership following infant baptism and church tax for members taken in by the state is the best way of securing a high and relatively stable level of income for a church. The Danish Folk Church is a strong illustration of this thesis.

Cultural Institutions facing Individualisation and Market Orientation
Direct comparisons between the developments in the Folk Church and other cultural institutions referring to the term 'Public Value' are presented in the third section. Demands on cultural institutions to prove themselves valuable to society, or to segments of society, have always existed. In the time of the sovereign kings, the artist needed to entertain the rulers or deliver dramatic plays to keep the people loyal to the same rulers. Today, cultural institutions stand in a more direct relation to their users as to customers on the market.

Niels Kærgård continues the economic analysis in the first chapter of Section III, providing a basic introduction to the distinctions between private and public goods, and to the economic logics of the private and the public sectors, respectively. To this is added the concept of 'Public Value', used when, say, cultural institutions argue that they offer goods for the benefit of all people who want to use it and who – as far as needed – are willing to pay for cultural experiences.

In the second chapter of this section, drawing on studies and sources from the book market, libraries and museums, Iversen compares the conditions of work, the reactions and priorities of the Folk Church to that of other cultural institutions. The level of accommodation to market conditions differs clearly between the Folk Church and the book market, the museums and libraries, but the basic patterns of conditions and reactions are the same all over.

In the third chapter, Marie Vejrup Nielsen presents a series of empirical case studies showing how users of the Folk Church behave as occasional consumers – in ways similar to consumers in other areas of culture. She finds that the driving factor comes from the 'power from below', where people exercise their freedom to come and go, instead of having to choose between opting-in and opting-out in their relation to the Folk Church.

The fourth and last chapter of Section III deals with the significance of buildings for cultural institutions. In touching an institution's buildings, you are touching people's image of what the institution is all about. Jes Heise Rasmussen illustrates this point by examining the spontaneously developed rituals for the closure of and saying farewell to two of the church buildings that were transformed to be used in new ways in Copenhagen at the beginning of the second decade of the 21ˢᵗ century.

Social Capital, Majority Religion and Discrimination
The fourth section examines the Folk Church's contribution to the social capital in market society, and the consequences for minorities when living with the Folk Church as a politically handled, state-administered majority religion. A final key question in *the What-project* relates to the integrating power that an old majority church historically used to have, for better or for worse. What happens to this power when the church accommodates itself to individualisation and market conditions?

In the first chapter of this section, Ingrid Storm analyses data from the *European Social Survey* and the *International Social Survey Programme – Citizenship* to trace the significance of religion for social capital in Denmark today. In this regard, religion is fostering 'bonding' much more than 'bridging' capital among the users, in Denmark, which remains a country with a comparatively high degree of trust in institutions and among people.

From her survey, Leth-Nissen, in the second chapter, looking at the connections between social capital and participation in rites of passage in the Folk Church, presents results similar to Storm's. One connection is clear: those who have many friends are often invited to many church rituals and thus benefit from participating in them. In addition, the other part of the 'Matthew effect' – well known from other lines of development in neo-liberal societies – is visible in the Folk Church as well: those who have only a small amount of social capital in their daily lives get even less from participating in church rituals as they are not invited to rites of passage.

In the third chapter of this section, Lisbet Christoffersen presents her analyses of the current, legislative changes in Danish laws on religion. Are religious communicators treated in the same way as other cultural communicators in general? Is full freedom of religion respected? And how do the recent legislative changes bring other religious communities nearer to the way the Folk Church is legally defined and politically governed? Is the success of the Folk Church as a state-privileged, state-governed and state-subsidized cultural institution used politically as a model for how to keep religious communities within the borders of politically 'acceptable politics' at a time of growing nationalism?

Finally, the question about the role of the Folk Church in the public debate is discussed by Niels Kærgård. The church was a political power in Catholic times. After the Reformation in 1536, the church became a political instrument in the hands of the kings, especially after the introduction of sovereign kings in 1660. After the free constitution of 1849, the Folk Church has acted as a normative cultural institution alongside others, even though there have always been and still are political disagreements among leading church people. Kærgård points to individualisation and marketisation as factors that tend to diminish the role of the Folk Church in public debates in recent decades.

The need of studying majority culture

The Danish majority study *At the Heart of Denmark* (Gundelach et al 2008) was carried out at the time of the infamous *Danish Cartoon Crisis* (which was, in Denmark, labelled the *Muhammad Crisis*). Here, it is was made clear just how much the Danes need to understand their own culture, including the Folk Church, in order to understand their impact on others, too. This point was recently framed by the author and musician Kristian Leth when arguing for male circumcision as a legitimate part of a legal culture in Denmark:

> That cultures are different is nothing new. What is new in Denmark is that we don't know our own culture and its history, and take Danish culture to mean freedom from culture (Feature article in Politiken April 27, 2018).

The overall purpose of this book is to explore the Danish Folk Church as an important part of mainstream, majority culture and thus to see how it works as a cultural institution. In doing so, we also point out that being mainstream and Danish is almost the opposite of being free of culture – as if the minorities were alone in being 'peculiar people' with 'strange cultures'. Giving priority to the Folk Church is not standing on neutral ground. It is prioritising a distinct sort of culture and using it, for example to promote politics of national identity.

In the final chapter, we bring together some general conclusions on the Folk Church as a cultural institution on a par with other cultural institutions. Our study is the first of the Folk Church as a cultural institution. As we have learnt a lot about the Folk Church by studying it in the light of other cultural institutions, we assume that our study of the Folk Church may also shed light on the conditions of cultural institutions currently facing market orientation and individualisation with the consequent changes in social capital.

References

Aldèn, Anne 2004. *Religion in Dialogue with Late Modern Society*. Lund: University of Lund.

Bäckström, Anders, Ninna Edgardh Beckman and Per Pettersson (eds.) 2004. *Religious Change in Northern Europe. The Case of Sweden*. Stockholm: Verbum.

Bailey, Edward 1990. 'The Implicit Religion of Contemporary Society: Some Studies and Reflections', *Social Compass* 37/4: 483-497.

Bourdieu, Pierre 1986. 'The Forms of Capital', in J. E. Richardson (ed.), *Handbook of Theory of Research for the Sociology of Education*. New York: Greenwood Press, 241-258.

Christoffersen, Lisbet 2015. 'From Previous Intertwinement to a Future Split in Governance Structures in Cultural and Religious Use of Buildings: On Danish Funding of Religious Heritage.' In Anne Fornerod (ed). *Funding Religious Heritage*. Farnham, Surrey: Ashgate/Routledge (in collaboration with RELIGARE), 75-102.

Christoffersen, Lisbet, Kjell A. Modéer and Svend Andersen 2010. *Law and Religion in the 21st Century – Nordic Perspectives*. Copenhagen: DJØF Publishing.

Christoffersen, Lisbet, Hans Raun Iversen, Niels Kærgård and Margit Warburg (eds.) 2012. *Fremtidens Danske Religionsmodel*. Copenhagen: Anis.

Eriksen, Niels Nymann 2018. *Gæstfrihed*. Copenhagen: Akademisk Forlag.

Fridberg, Torben 2000. *Kultur- og Fritidsaktiviteter 1975-1998*. Copenhagen: Socialforskningsinstituttet.

Frisch, Hartvig 1928 [1952]. *Europas Kulturhistorie 1-4*, Copenhagen: Politikens Forlag.

Goodson, Ivor (ed.) 2013. *Developing Narrative Theory: Life Histories and Personal Representation*. Abingdon: Routledge.

Gregersen, Niels Henrik 1988. *Teologi og Kultur. Protestantismen Mellem Isolation og Assimilation i det 19. og 20. århundrede*. Aarhus: Aarhus Universitetsforlag.

Gauthier, François, Linda Woodhead and Tuomas Martikainen 2013. 'Introduction: Consumerism as the Ethos of Consumer Society', in François Gauthier and Tuomas Martikainen (eds.), *Religion in Consumer Society. Brands, Consumers and Markets*, Farnham: Ashgate, 1-24.

Gundelach, Peter, Hans Raun Iversen and Margit Warburg 2008. *I Hjertet af Danmark. Institutioner og Mentaliteter*. Copenhagen: Hans Reitzels Forlag.

Himmelstrup, Kristian 2013. *Kulturformidling. Grundbog i Kulturens Former og Institutioner.* Copenhagen: Hans Reitzels Forlag.

Hjarvard, Stig 2005. 'Medialisering af religiøse forestillinger', in Morten Thomsen Højsgaard and Hans Raun Iversen (eds.), *Gudstro i Danmark*. Copenhagen: Anis, 163-182.

Hood, Christopher 1991. 'A Public Management for All Seasons'. *Public Administration* 69/2, 3-19.

Højsgaard, Morten Thomsen and Hans Raun Iversen 2013. *Danskernes tro Anno 2013 – Spørgsmål og Svar*. https://teol.ku.dk/cfk/yougov-undersoegelse/.

Iversen, Hans Raun 1999. 'Kulturkristendom, kirkekristendom og karismatisk kristendom'. *Kirke og kulturkristendom. Ny Mission 1*. Copenhagen: Unitas Forlag.

Iversen, Hans Raun 2005. 'Gudstro i den Danske Religionspark'. Morten Thomsen Højsgaard and Hans Raun Iversen (eds.), *Gudstro i Danmark*. Copenhagen: Anis, 103-123.

Iversen, Hans Raun 2018: *Ny praktisk teologi. Kristendommen, den enkelte og.* Copenhagen: Eksistensen.

Jensen, Carsten 1998. 'Kultur'. *Den Store Danske Encyklopædi*, 11, 267-72.

Moberg, Marcus 2016. 'Exploring the Spread of Marketization Discourse in Nordic Folk Church Context', in Frans Wijsen and Kocku von Stuckrad (eds.). *Making Religion. Theory and Practice of the Discursive Study of Religion.* Leiden: Brill, 239-259.

Niebuhr, H. Richard 1951 [2005]. *Christ and Culture*. Malden Mass.: Blackwell.

Nørgaard-Højen, Peder (ed.) 1988. *Kristendommen og de Andre Religioner*. Århus: Anis.

Pedersen, Ove Kaj 2011. *Konkurrencestaten*. Copenhagen: Hans Reitzels Forlag.

Piketty, Thomas 2014. *Capital in the 21st Century*. Harvard: Harvard University Press.

Putnam, Robert D. 2000. *Bowling Alone: the Collapse and Revival of American Community*. New York; London: Simon & Schuster.

Rambøll Company 2010. *Analyse of Pengestrømme og Ressourcer i Dansk Musikliv*. Report to Statens Kunstråds Musikudvalg.

Redfield, Robert 1973. 'Peasant Society and Culture'. *The Little Community and Peasant Society and Culture.* Chicago: The University of Chicago Press.

Rod, Jakob 1961. *Folkereligion og kirke*. Copenhagen: Gad.

Rosa, Hartmut 2016. *Resonanz: Eine Soziologie der Weltbeziehung*. Berlin: Suhrkamp Verlag.

Sandel, Michael. 2012. *What Money Can't Buy? The Moral Limits of Markets.* New York: Farrar, Straus and Giroux.

Siedentop, Larry 2014. *Inventing the Individual. The Origins of Western Liberalism.* London: Allen Lane (an imprint of Penguin Books).

Taylor, Charles 1991. *The Ethics of Authenticity*. Oxford: Harvard University Press.

Taylor, Charles 2007. *A Secular Age.* London: The Belknap Press (of Harvard University Press).

Troeltch, Ernst [1912] 1965. 'Die Soziallehre der Christlichen Kirchen und Gruppen'. *Gesammelte Schriften I*. Tübingen: Mohr.

Warmind, Morten 2005. 'Ateisme i Danmark'. in Morten Thomsen Højsgaard and Hans Raun Iversen (eds.), *Gudstro i Danmark*. Copenhagen: Anis, 279-292.

Weber, Max 1904 and 1905. *Die Protestantische Ethik und der Geist des Kapitalismus.* Archic für Scialwissenschaften und Sozialpolitik, Bd. XX und XXI.

Woodhead, Linda and Hans Raun Iversen (eds.). *The Old National Churches of Northern Europe: The Persistence of Societal Religion.* (in preparation).

Notes

1. Unfortunately, the book *I Hjertet af Danmark. Institutioner og Mentaliteter* (At the Heart of Denmark, Institutions and Mentalities) has not been edited in English. A digital version of its English translation (called *Institutions and Mentalities in Denmark, Backdrop to the Cartoon Crisis*) can be obtained by writing to hri@teol.ku.dk. Some passages of this chapter are elaborated versions of the English translation of the book. I thank Peter Gundelach and Margit Warburg for allowing me to use these passages.

2. For an elaboration of the anthropological concept of 'little and big traditions', see Redfield, 1973.

3. For a comprehensive description and analysis of the variations in Danish religion and Folk Church Christianity, see Chapter 2: 'Troen, sekulariseringen og religionens beskaffenhed' in Iversen, 2018.

4. Kristian Himmelstrup's basic reader on the forms and institutions of Danish culture works with a similar list of institutions, although he leaves the church out without even discussing the omission (Himmelstrup 2013).

I. Historical Dimensions of the Danish Folk Church

2. From State Church to Folk Church: Origins of a Cultural Institution as Reflected in the Reformation Celebrations in Denmark 1617-2017

Margit Warburg

In this chapter, I will analyse the historical development of the Evangelical Lutheran church in Denmark using the Reformation celebrations as empirical foci. In the course of this exposition, I will show that the church gradually acquired the characteristics of a Danish cultural institution.

Cultural institution – a broad concept

The term institution, in connection with culture, has a double meaning comprising physical assets, in the form of buildings and collection of artifacts, as well as the traditions carried on by the institution (Himmelstrup 2013, 251-253). The institutions under the Ministry of Culture are state institutions such as the Royal Theatre, the National Museum of Denmark and a range of major art museums (but also, for example, the Danish Language Council). Furthermore, the ministry financially supports many institutions classified as cultural institutions. They range from Aalborg Symphony Orchestra to Anti-Doping Denmark, showing that the ministry has a very broad perception of what a cultural institution is. In short, what is included within the purview of the ministry at any time is, by definition, culture (Himmelstrup 2013, 19).

However, despite the breadth of the concept, it is noteworthy that museums and exhibition sites concerned with natural sciences and technology, which are considered cultural institutions in, for example, the USA, are not within the purview of the Ministry of Culture. For example, the Natural History Museum of Denmark is part of Copenhagen University and the science centre Experimentarium is a self-governing institution partly supported by private funding. So, the fact that the Folk Church is governed by the Ministry of Ecclesiastical Affairs, and therefore is not listed on the home page of the Ministry of Culture, does not in itself speak against the church being a cultural institution.

Of course, the term cultural institution can also be stretched so much that it disrupts a common perception of what such an institution is; for example, when the traditional beer pub *Jernbanecafeen* close to Copenhagen Central Station describes itself as being a 'Copenhagen cultural institution', presumably not everybody will accept the validity of such a title! Cultural institutions in their common perception probably must live up to a kind of *decorum* and be seen as serving the commonwealth.

Cultural institutions are a heritage of the Enlightenment, and their basic rationale is to offer people access to knowledge in its broadest sense in order to promote free thinking and free choice (Himmelstrup 2013, 37). This is also why it is obvious that natural museums, zoos and science parks be included in the category of cultural institution, as, say, the Smithsonian Institute is (Doering 1995). In the vein of the Enlightenment tradition, public access must be on a voluntary basis and with no discrimination among its audience. This is also a consequence of being part of a democratic society.

The Folk Church today lives up to the above Enlightenment-based criteria. The Folk Church serves the commonwealth by offering access to Danish Protestant cultural and religious traditions, to which three quarters of the Danish population belong through their church membership. There is also public access, because everybody has the right to attend a Sunday service, whether they are members or not, and nobody is forced to attend.

The path to becoming a cultural institution

Accepting that the Folk Church today can be considered a cultural institution does not imply that it has always been one. It is not evident that the Danish Evangelical Lutheran church, from its historical origins in a nationalised Catholic church, would develop into a cultural institution. There is no straight path leading from the religious dictatorship that followed in the wake of the royal take-over of the church in 1536 to the present position of the Folk Church as a cultural institution based on voluntary participation in a democratic society. To understand how and why the Folk Church has reached this position, I propose that we must look at the dynamics between *four entities*, the *state*, the *church*, the *nation* and the *citizens*, starting with the Reformation and looking onwards from there. This is the theme of the present chapter.

The topic is obviously immense and I will therefore apply an analytical lens including the range of historical Reformation celebrations at the major jubilees, including the one in 2017, to provide focused snapshots of the dynamics between state, church, nation, and citizens. The Reformation celebrations are particularly well-suited to serve as analytical lenses for two reasons. The first is that the Reformation itself laid the foundation for the prime characteristics of the Folk Church as a national, Evangelical Lutheran church administered by the Danish state. The second is that historical jubilees are natural occasions for considering the continued relevance and meaning of such events: shall the jubilee be officially marked or not, and for what purpose? Jubilees tend to highlight particular past events and particular historical places as part of a politics of memory, where interpretations of the past serve as guidance for the present (Aagedal 2017). This was also the case during the Reformation celebrations in Denmark (Bach-Nielsen 2015: 13).

In this chapter, I will show that the Danish Reformation jubilees, in particular from 1717 onwards, form a neat string of expressions of a politics of memory characterised by a strong state involvement and a continuous perception of the *national* significance of the Reformation. The celebrations during Absolutism brought the two institutionalised actors, the state and the church, into concerted actions where the citizens were mobilised and the king and nation were hailed. As a purveyor of religious legitimisation, the church had a crucial role in forging a divinely sanctioned, ideological coherence between state, nation and citizens. In short, the church spawned an emerging Danish civil religion. This meant that the church came to promote something beyond Lutheran Christianity, namely *Danishness*. This was in line with the Lutheran principle of providing access to the scriptures in the vernacular, and the publication of Christian III's Bible in 1550 was already a major cultural leap which established Danish as a full written language.

To call the church during Absolutism a cultural institution in the modern sense would, however, be misleading. The church was not an option available to the citizens on a voluntary basis. For this, one had to wait until the compulsory state church became the Folk Church with the free constitution of 1849. How the Folk Church succeeded in becoming a cultural institution will be discussed further in this chapter – many different factors were significant for this development. However, much of the ground was laid before the free constitution, and some of the important and decisive, special characteristics of the Evangelical Lutheran state church were formed already in the first century after the Reformation.

Several of the concrete examples in this chapter have been presented earlier in Danish and/or English and are given with only a few changes (Warburg 2017a; Warburg 2018a; Warburg 2018b). The idea of seeing the Reformation celebrations as expressions of a Danish civil religion was developed there. However, the scope of the present chapter is different, and the proposal to explicitly consider the interplay between state, church, nation and citizens in an analysis of the Reformation celebrations and of the historical development of the church into a contemporary cultural institution is novel.

The European Reformation celebrations of 2017 and the special Danish national angle

Denmark was, of course, not the only country where the 500th anniversary of the Lutheran Reformation was celebrated in 2017. However, when looking closer at the explicit motives for the celebrations and the degree of state involvement, there were distinct differences between the politics of memory in Denmark compared with Norway, Sweden, Germany and other European Lutheran countries (Warburg 2018a).

In Norway and Sweden, the celebration of the Reformation jubilee was arranged by the Norwegian and Swedish churches, and the emphasis was on the confessional significance of the Lutheran Reformation. For example, the main theme of the Norwegian church was *nåde* (grace) which was expounded in three sub-themes: *Frelsen er ikke til salgs* (God's salvation is not for sale), *Mennesker er ikke til salgs* (human beings are not for sale) and *Skaperverket er ikke til salgs* (God's creation is not for sale). The choice of these sub-themes may be a token of the political activism of the Norwegian Church after its bonds with the state were loosened in 2008 (becoming fully effective in 2017). In Germany, the federal government supported the celebration, stressing that it must be open (ecumenical) and international, as opposed to the national and confessional framework of the former jubilees (Warburg 2018a).

In contrast to the above, the Reformation celebration in Denmark distinguished itself by its official emphasis on the *national* significance of the

Reformation in Denmark and by the strong state involvement. In 2010, the Danish government and parliament decided that there should be an official celebration of the Reformation in 2017, and the government then appointed a committee for the celebration with 12 members, which included *one* member from the Danish Folk Church. The other members came from different universities, media and cultural institutions. The Ministry of Ecclesiastical Affairs was given the secretarial function and Her Majesty Queen Margrethe II accepted the role of patron of the Reformation jubilee.[1]

The committee was given the following mandate:

> The Presidium of the 500th Reformation Anniversary in Denmark has overall responsibility for the celebration of the anniversary with the goal of increasing understanding of the impact of the Reformation on society, the church, identity and consciousness in Denmark.

Particularly noteworthy are the words 'the impact of the Reformation on society, the church, identity and consciousness in Denmark'. The mandate thus specifies that the special Danish approach to Reformation celebration was an emphasis on the broad societal and cultural significance of the Reformation *in Denmark*.

This special national emphasis on the Reformation celebration in Denmark may be remarkable in a European comparative perspective. However, it continues a trend set by the historical Reformation celebrations in Denmark, where a recurrent theme in the celebrations was the claim of a special relationship between Denmark and God (Warburg 2017a; Warburg 2018a). Such a claim is a core element in civil religion, and I have identified many concrete expressions of a Danish civil religion in the Reformation celebrations (Warburg 2017a; Warburg 2018a). The below short discourse on civil religion serves as a highly condensed exposition of those central aspects of civil religion which are relevant to the analyses of the Reformation celebrations.

Civil religion in brief

In brief, civil religion is a conglomerate of myths, rituals, symbols and texts, which hallow the people or the nation by reference to a transcendental power, usually called God (Hammond 1976; Cristi and Dawson 2007; Warburg

2008; Warburg 2015). By this reference to an unquestionable authority, rulers have often legitimised the particular social order of a given country. When philosopher Jean-Jacques Rousseau proposed the concept of civil religion in 1762, this top-down use of civil religion was salient in his writings (Gourevitch 1997, 142-151).

The concept of civil religion was reinvigorated in an American setting by Robert N. Bellah in 1967 to explain why Americans of all creeds seemed to accept the special religious legitimacy of the American nation and the American constitution that their Presidents consistently claimed in their speeches. Bellah referred to Rousseau, of course, but he also argued for considering American civil religion as a Durkheimian religious dimension of society in concord with popular sentiments about the characteristics and destiny of the United States (Bellah 1967). The Durkheimian dimension represents an interpretation of civil religion as sustained by bottom-up processes in civil society.

Both top-down and bottom-up processes are at play in many examples of civil religion. These two expressions of civil religion are not opposites, but should be seen as *complementary* ideal types (Warburg 2008; Warburg 2015). Typically, when nationhood is officially celebrated and civil religion is involved, there is a combination of top-down and bottom-up processes, and both are likely to be present for the celebrations to be successfully completed. Organization from above is often administratively and economically necessary, while participation from below is necessary to give the manifestation of civil religion popular legitimacy. This is also clearly seen in the Danish celebrations of Reformation anniversaries throughout history and, not least, today.

From Reformation to Absolutism

The Reformation in Denmark was rather early and happened swiftly. But it was also a politically complicated process which involved power struggles between king, nobility and the bourgeoisie, peasant uprisings in Jutland and a civil war with interference from the outside (Lausten 1995; Møller and Østergaard 2013). Luther's reform ideas had already become widely popular among the citizens of Denmark by the 1520s and in several cities Lutheran church services were regularly conducted in the churches (Lausten 1995). This development was encouraged by the Danish king, Frederik I (reigned

1523-1533). On the one hand, he opposed the Catholic majority in the Council of the Realm (*Rigsrådet*) by doing this; on the other hand, he repeatedly claimed that he was still a supporter of Catholicism.

Frederik's shrewd policy of balance resulted in an ecclesiastical split in 1526-1527. The Catholic Church was still the official church of the country, but the Lutheran clerics and their adherents were now free to form their own parishes with Lutheran priests and church services (Lausten 2002, 97-100). This split gave the king a chance to gain considerable power over both churches, and it also gave him an opportunity to dispense with the right of the Pope to confirm the appointment of new bishops (Lausten 2002, 97-98).

The final steps of the process towards the ultimate break with the Papal church was ruthlessly carried through by Frederik I's son and successor, Christian III (reigned 1534-1559), who had already become a convinced follower of Luther as a young prince. When he was elected king in 1534, Denmark was in the middle of a civil war.[2] Christian III and his party emerged victorious after finally conquering Copenhagen in the summer of 1536.

Christian III successfully blamed the Catholic bishops for the miseries of the civil war and quickly imprisoned them (Lausten 1995). He therefore met little resistance when he called for a general assembly of the estates on October 30th 1536. Here, he announced that Catholic services were forbidden from that point onwards and that services were to be conducted according to Lutheran principles (Lausten 2002, 108-110). The assembly of the estates approved and signed a bill which called for a general peace, confiscated the bishops' properties, allowed the monks and nuns to leave the monasteries and addressed a number of conflicts over taxation and other issues in the wake of the civil war (Kolderup-Rosenvinge 1824, 157-171). The bill provided the legal basis for a thorough (but not always peaceful) religious and social transformation process which had far-reaching consequences for Danish society.

Establishment of the Evangelical Lutheran state church

By 1537, a new church ordinance had already been introduced and the king let himself be crowned as head and protector of the church (Lausten 2002, 110-111). This established a particular unity in Denmark between church, state and king under the grace of God.

In this trinity, the king was by no means a distant power, and Christian III interfered heavily in the administration of the church (Lausten 2002,

110-111). This royal power policy was perpetuated and even strengthened during the reign of King Frederik II (1559-1588). The king feared confessional splits in the Danish church between the different competing branches of Protestantism, and he succeeded in maintaining his authority in having the final say in church matters (Lausten 2002, 121-123). The period from the reign of Frederik II until the late 1600s was characterised by the strong enforcement of religious conformity and orthodoxy. All variants of Christianity other than state church Lutheranism were outlawed. These measures followed the principle of *cuius regio, eius religio* ('Whose realm, his religion'). This principle was one the compromises of the Augsburg peace settlement of 1555 which forced the German-Roman emperor to accept the existence of Lutheran duchies across the empire.[3]

Even foreigners residing in Denmark were not allowed religious freedom but were made to subscribe to the contents of the 'foreign articles' of 1569 (Lausten 2002, 121). These articles summarised the Lutheran creed of the Danish church and disobedience was heavily punished – in principle even by death. The control of foreigners and their possible subversive influence was not only a matter of internal security but, from the 1560s, Denmark and other Protestant powers also feared Catholic Spain as an increasing threat (Jensen 1993).

The strong position of the king in church matters was upheld during the reign of Christian IV (1588-1648). In close agreement with the top cleric, the bishop of Zealand, the king created a strong state church administered by the Danish chancellery (Lausten 2002, 127-128). Nevertheless, the king was also *primus inter pares* in his relation to the confessional matters of the church, and this was stressed ceremonially during the first Reformation celebration of 1617.

The Reformation celebration of 1617

The initiative to celebrate the centenary of Martin Luther's posting of his 95 theses against indulgences came from Wittenberg, the epicentre of the Lutheran Reformation in the years from 1517 onwards. This inspired Hans Poulsen Resen, the bishop of Zealand to arrange a similar event in Copenhagen. Resen was also the rector of the university, and he was eager to use the feast to promote his own version of Luther's teachings which would become the orthodox and only true variety of Christianity in Denmark (Lausten

2002, 129-130). It was with good reason that Resen gave the celebration feast the title *Lutherus triumphans* (Lausten 2002, 130).

The overarching theme of the feast was to thank God for his 'nåderige førelse af landet og folket' (graceful conduct of the land and the people) (Bach-Nielsen 2015, 27). This thought, which at its core is civil religion, was salient in this and all subsequent Reformation celebrations thereafter.

October 31st, the day of the theses being posted, was commemorated by the university. The following day, the king, along with the members of the Council of the Realm and other higher nobility, walked in procession to the Copenhagen Cathedral. Bishop Resen preached and concluded by reciting a thanksgiving prayer written by him. This prayer, which was to be said in all churches within the king's realms and countries, asked God to protect King Christian IV and bless the royal family, the members of the Council of the Realm, other members of the nobility and high-ranking officials. 'Alt med henblik på kirkens vel og rigernes og landenes velfærd og rolighed' (All this for the good of the church and for the welfare and peace of the realms and countries) (Bach-Nielsen 2015, 26). After this blessing, the king and the members of the Council of the Realm went *together* to take Communion, symbolising that the king was on a par with them (Bach-Nielsen 2015, 26). The idea that the king represented God on Earth was first introduced with Absolutism.

Christian IV also began to mark important state events in the church calendar; for example, he ordained a prayer of thanksgiving for the rather mild Lübeck peace settlement of 1629, which concluded Denmark's unsuccessful engagement in the Thirty Years' War 1618-1648 (Bach-Nielsen 2015, 47). It is, indeed, a civil religious idea to thank God for the results of prudent Danish diplomacy.

In summary, the period from the Reformation to Absolutism saw the following trends which had long term effects on the later development of the church as a cultural institution: religious conformity, state centralisation and the emergence of a Danish civil religion. Religious conformity was one of the factors that promoted the remarkable religious homogeneity which characterised Danish society well into the second half of the 1900s.[4] This meant that Folk Church Christianity overwhelmingly dominated the religious culture in Denmark up until that time.

The state centralisation of the Danish church in the wake of the Reformation was crucial for the development of the church after 1849, too. As the only national Lutheran church, the Danish Folk Church has no head cleric, neither does it have an archbishop (as in Sweden and Finland), nor a first bishop or *preses* (as in Norway), who could represent the church as such.[5] The lack of a central clerical authority is important for the popular conception of the church as a *folk* church with a broad acceptance.

Finally, the emergence of a Danish civil religion linked the church with Danishness in a broad sense. This is evidently a significant factor in the development of the Folk Church as a *Danish* cultural institution.

Absolutism and the king as head of the church

The transformation from an elective kingdom (the king was elected by the Council of the Realm) to Absolutism in 1660 was a consequence of the lost wars against Sweden and concurrent trends in continental Europe. The relations between state, church, nation and citizens were re-ordered in the Danish Royal Law of 1665, which became the constitution of the Absolute monarchy of Denmark-Norway (Ekman 1957). The law specified the powers and duties of the king in its first seven paragraphs (*Kongeloven*):

§1 stated that it is best to begin with God. Therefore, the king has ordered that he and his descendants for a thousand generations will worship God according to the Augsburg Confession of 1530 and ensure that every citizen follow these teachings, which are to be protected from all 'heretics, zealots and blasphemers'.

§2 stated that the king is above every citizen (subject) and above all laws, and that there is no one above him in all religious and secular matters except for God alone.

§3 gave the king the supreme power to issue all kinds of laws as he wishes.

§4 gave the king the supreme power to appoint and dismiss all state officials.

§5 gave the king the command over the armed forces and monopoly on waging war and entering into alliances with foreign powers. It also gave him the monopoly on levying taxes and customs.

§6 gave the king the supreme power in all clerical matters, including how church services were conducted.

§7 stated that all governmental matters are only valid with the king's personal signature.

The Danish Royal Law was remarkable for its time with respect to it being a written constitution at all (Ekman 1957). Together with the then still valid 'foreign articles', it established what a modern public might call a religious dictatorship, which more than matches Saudi Arabia today – permitting such an anachronistic comparison, of course.

From 1674, non-Lutherans were allowed to settle and establish religious communities in the Danish city of Fredericia, provided they did not proselytise. Jews, Catholics and Reformed Protestants dominated the city, which in principle was the only place in the Danish realm where a kind of religious liberty existed until the free constitution of 1849 guaranteed universal religious freedom. However, from the 1680s, the Jewish, Catholic and Reformed religious communities were generally acknowledged by royal decrees, although they did not yet enjoy full rights as citizens.[6]

The Royal Law was only superseded by the free constitution in 1849, but parts of it, namely the paragraphs concerning royal succession, were only abolished in 1953 with the present constitution.

Of special interest in the present context is the king's detailed involvement in church matters – is it perhaps a relic of §6 that the reigning monarch still has to approve the liturgy and hymn book of the Folk Church?

I shall now move onto the next Reformation celebrations, which clearly expressed Danish civil religion.

The Reformation jubilee celebration of 1717

The Reformation jubilee celebration of 1717 is a prime example of the thinking about king, country and God after Absolutism was introduced in 1660. It was carefully orchestrated with all the pomp and circumstances of the baroque style.

The individual events were consistently framed as a salute to the king, Frederik IV (who reigned 1699-1730), as well as being a thanksgiving to God for the liberation from the corruption of Catholicism and all the other benefits that the Reformation endowed upon Denmark. Speeches and musical compositions had frequent quotations from biblical texts about the deliverance of Israel from Babylon and other allegorical references to God's care for Denmark. An ode written to the main jubilee church service was in the same vein; it began with the lines:

> Danske Sion! Vær nu glad
> Ved Lutheri Morgenrøde ...
> (Bach-Nielsen 2015, 60)

In English:

> Danish Zion! Now rejoice
> in the first morning blush of Luther ...

In stanza 7, the author of the ode let God send out a prophet, Martin Luther, who sowed a manna grain. As it sprouted in Denmark's soil, at the intervention of King Christian III, the land was cleansed of the Roman sourdough – that is Catholicism.

The distinct anti-Catholic thread running through the celebration was in line with Danish legislation since the Reformation which emphasised the Lutheran character of the state and was remarkably anti-Catholic on certain points (Møller and Østergaard 2013).

The Reformation celebration in Copenhagen of 1717 was organized top-down to the smallest detail, while the celebrations in the big provincial towns were locally organized by city councils and bishops in collusion. The city of Aalborg was especially active; speeches, declarations, church services and festivals were held throughout the week where nobility, citizens and craftsmen celebrated the Reformation (Bach-Nielsen 2015, 70). All in all, in Aalborg and several other cities, there was a significant Durkheimian dimension in the otherwise Rousseauian self-celebration of the Absolute king, and this civil-religious manifestation seemed successful in gathering the people – at least in the cities.

The Reformation jubilee celebration of 1817

In 1817, the bishop of Zealand, Friederich Münter, took the initiative to the celebration and had King Frederik VI (who reigned 1808-1839) announce it with a royal decree. Here, the king made it known to all men – acknowledging the good that the pure evangelical teachings had given the Fatherland – that the Almighty should be thanked with public hymns of thanksgiving and extolled 'fordi han giorde saa vel mod Landets Slægter' (because he did so well by the generations of the country) (Bach-Nielsen 2015, 110). This was a clear civil-religious statement from the king. A detailed manual was prepared for the three festive days, and it was stated that it was important for the common man to become acquainted with the Reformation. This was brought into effect by, for example, ensuring that all primary schools received a short script on the Reformation for distribution (Bach-Nielsen 2015, 111-116).

All in all, the Reformation celebration of 1817 turned out to be more popular than the previous Reformation jubilees, and the main ceremonies in Copenhagen attracted big crowds. While the celebrations in Copenhagen and other major cities were centrally planned, the celebrations in the towns and villages were arranged by the local parishes, as requested in the royal decree (Bach-Nielsen 2015, 131-133). Thus, the Durkheimian component of the Reformation celebrations was strengthened in the later period of Absolutism and indicated a stronger popular identification with the church as a national institution. This was in line with the first half of the 1800s, which also saw the growth of a number of popular revival movements which were dissatisfied with the official way in which the priests explained the current cathechismal textbooks (Lausten 2002, 200-205). There is a difference between internal religious disagreements, even in terms of how strong they might be, and a lack of identification with the Evangelical Lutheran church as such. The fact that nearly all the major revival movements remained within the church later on when it became the Folk Church meant that confessional disagreements in general did not threaten the function of the church as a bearer of a unifying Danish civil religion.

The Danish civil religion implied that being Danish and being (Lutheran) Christian were aspects perceived as being part of the same identity. This imagined bond between nation and Christianity was further strengthened by the influence of the pastor, poet and church reformer N. F. S. Grundtvig (1783-1872). Grundtvig is an inescapable figure in the Danish nation-building process during the nineteenth century (Lausten 2002, 206-219, 238-242). He emphasised the key role of the common man in society and he was a leading figure in the folk high school movement with its goal of enlightening the people. He was a prolific writer, and through his historical-theological essays on and compilations of Nordic mythology ran a vein of a somewhat heterodox belief in a special relationship between God and Denmark – a belief that was also expressed in his many sermons (Vind 1999, 155-203). Such civil-religious ideas were sowed in Denmark's fertile soil during a critical period of nation-building, and the strength of the Grundtvigian movement delivered a widespread message to the Danes that their nation was special to God.

The free constitution of 1849 and the re-ordering of the relations between state, church, nation and citizens

In 1849, Denmark attained its first free constitution. Of special significance to the topic of this chapter is the fact that the constitution perpetuated the unity between church, state and king under the grace of God. The king's role as head of the church was abolished with the constitution. However, the reigning monarch must be member of the church and still has some important functions within the church, such as approving the liturgy and hymn book. The clauses concerning the monarch's relation to the Folk Church can be seen as a symbolic continuation of §1 and §6 of the Royal Law. Regarding 'the grace of God', even into the present day, all Danish law texts begin with the words: 'VI MARGRETHE DEN ANDEN, af Guds Nåde Danmarks Dronning, gør vitterligt ...' [WE MARGRETHE THE SECOND, Queen of Denmark by the Grace of God, make known to all men ...].

The constitution guaranteed religious freedom, but the lawgivers had no intention of disrupting the special ties between the state and a church to which the great majority of the population belonged (Lausten 2002, 230). To mark that decision, the state church was simply renamed the Folk Church, following the arguments made by H. N. Clausen, a prominent member of the intermediary assembly, who drafted the new constitution (Lausten 2002, 230). The intention was to give the Folk Church a statute of governance, but this was never accomplished. Therefore, the church continued to be administered by the state, except now with the Parliament and the government as the highest authority in the church, not the king. Legally and financially speaking, the Folk Church was to be seen as a governmental branch of the state (Christoffersen 2015). This arrangement is still in effect today.

However, the free constitution also meant a major re-ordering of the relations between state, church, nation and citizens. This re-ordering is illustrated in Figure 1 which shows a sociological model of the changing position of the

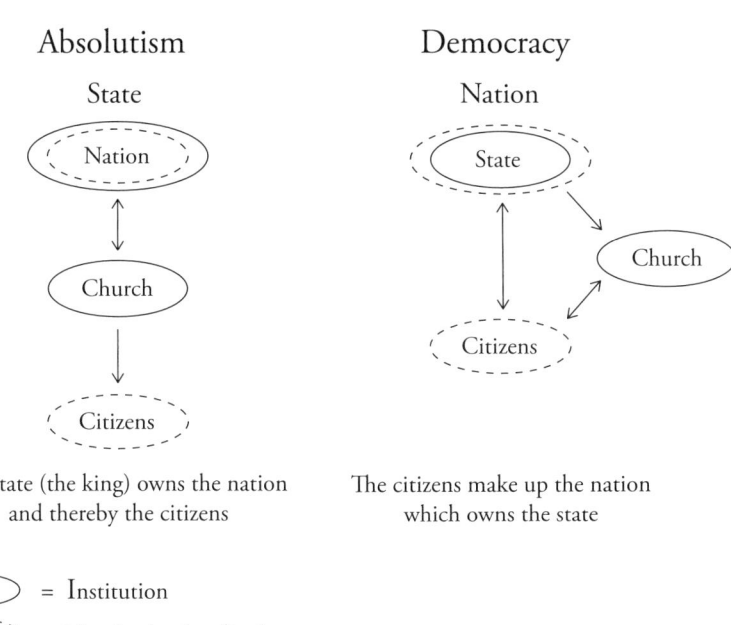

Figure 1. The transition from Absolutism to democracy in Denmark and the re-ordering of the relations between state, church, nation and citizens (Figure translated from Warburg 2005a)

Evangelical Lutheran church in relation to nation, state and citizens. The model covers the period from late Absolutism in the final years of the 1700s up until today. The terms 'citizen' and 'nation' were only firmly established in this period.

The model shows the relationship between citizens, nation, church and state in matters relating to the dissemination of authority in supporting the state, the ruling social order and its norms. During Absolutism, the church was the main vehicle for instructing the population in public morals and obedience to the authorities (see the left side of the model). However, the church was not just a part of the state administration. It had its own theological agenda, and the pastors had closer contact with the population than the rest of the state apparatus (Ingesman 2000; Knudsen 2000).

With the free constitution and religious liberty, the church stepped aside from the previous line of command between state and citizens (see the right side of the model). This rearrangement was later of crucial significance for the Folk Church and meant that it gained legitimacy as a cultural institution based on *voluntary* participation.

The arrows in the model show the paths that influence the different social actors: the church had great influence on the government during Absolutism with regard to questions of public morals, while the Folk Church has no formal influence today.[7] The citizens had no influence on the church during Absolutism and, after the introduction of the free constitution in 1849, they only gradually acquired influence on the administrative matters of the church.[8]

During Absolutism Danish civil religion was exclusively expressed through the state church. With religious liberty after the free constitution of 1849, the church no longer had a monopoly on expressing civil religion. Today, Danish civil religion and the Folk Church are only partially overlapping, as I have demonstrated in studies of several national rituals and manifestations in Denmark (Warburg 2005b; Warburg 2006; Warburg 2008; Warburg 2009; Warburg 2013; Warburg 2017b). This is also the case with the Reformation jubilee in Denmark 2017, which was launched and marketed as a broad cultural and educational event, not just as a churchly event (Warburg 2017a; Warburg 2018a).

The historical Reformation jubilees after the free constitution of 1849

The tradition of celebrating the Reformation on suitable anniversaries continued, and so did the traditional thanksgiving to God for protecting the nation as well as the anti-Catholic bias. For example, when the 400th anniversary of Luther's birth was celebrated in 1883, a prayer, intended to be said in churches in Copenhagen before the reading of the biblical text, ran as follows:

> Almægtige, himmelske Fader!
> Vi takke dig, at Du har ladet Morten Luther fødes til et Vidne mod Pavedømmets Forførelser og sendt ham og hans Medstridere som Ørne over Aadslet!
> (Bach-Nielsen 2015, 212)

In English:

> Almighty Heavenly Father!
> We thank you for letting Martin Luther be born as a witness to the seductions of the Papal regime and for sending him and his co-fighters as eagles over the carrion!

As we shall see, this particular and not very ecumenical facet of the historical Danish Reformation celebrations has been abandoned today in favour of a more tolerant, even friendly attitude among most clerics in the Danish Folk Church. The tendency towards more ecumenical stances in inter-church relations is, in my view, also one of the factors that contribute to regarding the church as a cultural institution which does not emphasise divides.

The Reformation jubilees of 1917 and 1936

The 400th anniversary of Luther's theses posting coincided with a critical phase of the World War I. In Germany, the overstressed war economy and the attrition of the German army on the Western front put a severe dampener on society, and the German government eventually decided to cancel all planned Reformation celebrations (Bach-Nielsen 2015, 237). In Denmark, the official attitude towards a possible celebration was hesitant to begin with, considering the need to neither offend German opinion, nor to embrace it too much out of concern for the relations with Britain and France (Bach-Nielsen 2015, 235). The German decision to cancel the Reformation celebrations thus paved the way for a modest Danish celebration on October 31st 1917. This was prepared by the bishop of Zealand and the Ministry of Ecclesiastical Affairs and it was largely a churchly affair, except that the day was also marked as a public school holiday (Bach-Nielsen 2015, 236-237).

The celebration of 1917 never became a broad national and public attraction (Bach-Nielsen 2015, 247). Such an attraction was, however, achieved in 1936 (the 400th anniversary of the Danish Reformation), not least thanks to initiatives from the municipality of Copenhagen in collaboration with the bishop of Copenhagen (Bach-Nielsen 2015, 269-292). The Ministry of Ecclesiastical Affairs supported the celebrations financially on the explicit condition that the celebration should be a '*folke-* og kirkefest' (a popular as well as a churchly celebration) (Bach-Nielsen 2015, 274; his italics). This condition emphasised, of course, that the church was no longer a state church, and at the same time it signalled that the celebration had a broader cultural and national scope than a churchly celebration alone.

In the years after World War II, the 450th anniversary of the Reformation of 1517 was marked in 1967, in 1983 it was the 500th anniversary of Luther's birth and in 1986 it was the 450th anniversary of the Danish Reformation of 1536. Festivities were held in all three years, there was quite a bit of press coverage and various books and pamphlets were published (Bach-Nielsen 2015, 316-325). Compared with previous celebrations – not least during Absolutism and the celebration of 1936 – these jubilees were not big, wide-ranging events. That was, however, precisely the ambition with the Reformation celebrations of 2017.

The Reformation jubilee of 2017

From the outset, the committee had the goal that the Reformation should be celebrated with many local events all over the country and not only through the major celebration events involving the Danish state. The planning and implementation of the various local anniversary events took place in the dioceses, in the deaneries and in local parishes. Most of the events aimed for a broad participation from other institutions and civil society. The committee assisted in this by establishing an interactive internet portal (Luther2017.dk) where the various events could be systematically advertised and updated. The committee also engaged the People's University at Aarhus University to arrange different nationwide dissemination activities. Along with the Danish Parliament, the committee planned both a ceremonial event on the Reformation Day (October 31st) and a public conference the day before. The special Reformation program of the national broadcasting institution, DR (more on this later), also received assistance from the committee (*Afrapportering* 2018: 36-37, 46-48, 52). Finally, it should be mentioned that the committee generated initiatives for Reformation events along with a number of other cultural institutions, for example an art exhibition with new art created by 26 invited artists and displayed at different art museums, a special exhibition at the Royal Library and a festive concert in Aarhus Concert Hall with a new Luther opera *Schlagt sie tot* (*Afrapportering* 2018: 32-38). Of the many official events, I will only discuss here the official Reformation service which constituted a peak in the interplay between state, church, nation and citizens.

In April 2018, the committee issued a final report on its activities and thereby concluded its function (*Afrapportering* 2018).

The official Reformation service at Pentecost, June 4th 2017

Denmark held its official Reformation service on Pentecost, June 4th 2017 in Haderslev Cathedral in Southern Jutland. It was shown on the national television so that all of Denmark could attend. Haderslev is an important site of remembrance for the Reformation, because the Reformation was actually introduced here in 1526 when Christian III was the duke of this region.

The service was attended by the Queen, the prime minister and several other members of the government, the president of the Parliament, the Danish bishops as well as a host of invited honorary guests. The event was a clear continuation of the festive services of the earlier anniversaries of 1617, 1717, 1817 and 1917, and the service marked the same national unity of monarchy, church and authority.

The service was, of course, a Pentecost service in its basic structure, but with direct and indirect references to Luther, both in the selected hymns and in the sermon read by the bishop of Copenhagen Diocese, Peter Skov-Jakobsen.[9] Unlike previous Reformation celebrations, this service was more inclusive, giving room for, among others, the leaders of the Baptists and the Catholic Church in Denmark each to recite a prayer as part of the church prayer (the intervention prayer).

Inviting these two historical archenemies of the Evangelical Lutheran church was a remarkable turn from earlier curses over the Pope and Catholicism and in view of the religious persecutions of the Baptists in Denmark in the 1840s. As two Danish historians concluded in their analysis of historical anti-Catholic currents in Denmark, the Danish Folk Church and the Danish national identity do not seem to include an open anti-Catholic stance any longer (Møller and Østergaard 2013).

In addition to the representatives of other Christian churches, the Danish head rabbi and the national chairman of Danish Muslim organizations attended the service by invitation. This confessional inclusiveness further emphasised that the Danish Reformation service was staged in a Rousseauian process as a unifying, national-religious event. One of the characteristics of civil religion is that it aims to gather the nation across different creeds by using an inclusive frame of reference to both divinity and nation. The Evangelical Lutheran Danish Folk Church here clearly fulfilled an important role in Danish civil religion.

After the service, the prime minister held a speech in which he expressed Luther's significance to Danish society. He concluded by paraphrasing the first line of Grundtvig's Pentecost hymn which has become almost a standard hymn at Pentecost services in the Folk Church even to this day: 'I Grundtvigs salme stråler solen på os i al sin glans. Med kærlighed. Oplysning. Frihed og ansvar' [In Grundtvig's hymn, the sun shines on us with all its brilliance. With love. Enlightenment. Freedom and responsibility]. With the words enlightenment, freedom, responsibility – which are not part of the original hymn – the Prime Minister indicated that these were important characteristics of the Danish nation and that they were God-given (in Grundtvig's hymn, the sun is a symbol of Jesus). These concluding words were, indeed, an expression of Danish civil religion.

The Prime Minister ended his speech with the following closing words (in Danish): 'Congratulations to the Folk Church. Congratulations to Denmark'. This marked the unity of church and nation and the close relationship between these two pillars of the Reformation celebration.

A local Reformation celebration

More than fifty events were announced on Luther2017.dk as taking place on the Reformation Day itself, October 31st 2017, and several other events were never announced on the official portal but only in the local media. An example of a local Reformation celebration is one that took place in the city of Kolding in Jutland. It was arranged by Sanct Nicolai Parish in collaboration with the museum of Kolding Castle (Kolding Provsti 2017). It began with a conversation salon about Luther's thoughts on learning and education. The salon was introduced by the theatre troupe Mungo Park. This was followed by a worship service in Sanct Nicolai Church that claimed to be 'entirely in Luther's spirit'.[10] About 300 people participated.[11] After the service, the participants walked together up to the illuminated Kolding Castle to the opening ceremony for a new Reformation exhibition in Christian III's Chapel. The exhibition was developed in a collaboration between Kolding Gymnasium and the museum of Kolding Castle and showed, among other things, video films produced by the students of the gymnasium.[12] This ended the event in which about 150 people participated, which was three times as many as expected by the planning committee.[13]

The Reformation celebration in Kolding combined a church service with a walk to an important national monument, Kolding Castle, where the Reformation king, Christian III, died in 1559. The conversation salon set the religious and historical-national part of the event into a modern Danish context of culture and identity. This is clearly civil religion, and it was organized locally in a combination of top-down and bottom-up processes. As a cultural institution, the Folk Church was the driving force behind an event which was broader in its historical and societal scope than a mere church service in remembrance of the Reformation.

The many local initiatives and arrangements celebrating the Reformation jubilee year of 2017 were the result of widespread, bottom-up processes at work.[14] There are no consolidated data to assess the extent of the reception. However, the data from the celebration of Reformation Day in Kolding indicate that it was possible for some of the local celebrations to achieve a considerable public reach.

Nationwide dissemination

During the days surrounding October 31st 2017, the national broadcasting institution, DR, offered a range of programmes dealing with Luther and the Reformation. This included historical re-enactments, debates and films. The peak was a festive concert on October 31st in DR's concert hall, which was attended by the royal family. Luther's theology and the significance of the Reformation for Danish society were interpreted in music, choir singing, performances and a young, popular actress recited monologues on God, Luther and the individual human being.

The committee engaged the People's University (*Folkeuniversitetet*) at Aarhus University with the responsibility for a nationwide dissemination of the significance of the Reformation for Danish society. The overall idea in many of the events arranged by the People's University was to 'revive' Luther and his thoughts within a contemporary context. One of the most interesting initiatives was to use the Reformation and Luther's posting of the 95 theses as a springboard for a discussion of what the Protestant heritage has meant for Danish society and to the individual Dane today. The participants gathered in workshops to formulate 95 modern theses with visions of the future:

> The idea is to give all citizens of Denmark the opportunity to contribute to a reconsideration of our society, our lives and our hopes for the future through the formulation of new theses for Denmark in 2017.[15]

The goal was to establish 10 workshops – in the end there were 17 workshops.[16] On the evening of October 31st, selected theses were projected onto the facade of Aarhus Theatre during a light show which also illuminated the cathedral with animated light patterns.

The basic idea of the workshops was to re-enact the beginning of the Reformation in 1517, ranging from the intellectual work of formulating modern theses to a ritual posting in public on exactly the same date as Luther posted his theses. As such, the event had the dual purpose of reminding the people about Luther's 95 theses as well as focusing on the future of Danish society. The framing of the workshops and adopting the thesis format of Luther's theological claims – now dealing with current Danish social issues – mark out the workshops as civil-religious.

Luther in focus

The official Reformation service in Haderslev was preceded by a local festival arranged jointly by the diocese, the parish and the municipality. In different tents around the cathedral, people could attend speeches, lectures, performances and music. Spectators could also buy various Luther merchandise, and the hungry could choose a special Luther hot dish or a piece of Luther layer cake produced by the local bakery. The cake was decorated with the Luther rose.

Many other of the arrangements announced on Luther2017.dk dealt with Martin Luther, his life and thinking. Luther also appeared on the labels of special beers brewed for the occasion (Warburg 2017a). The Danish popular interest in Luther as a person was, however, a dim reflection of the personality cult and all the Luther merchandise that could be observed in Wittenberg (Vejrup 2017).

The focus on Luther in the Reformation celebrations also gave rise to criticism in the press (Warburg 2018a). Several academics emphasised, among other things, that it should not be forgotten in the course of the celebrations that Martin Luther stood for a crude anti-Semitism, and that he also publicly supported the mass killing of rebel peasants. Two of the leading voices of this message expounded their critique in books (Herbener 2017; Stjernfelt 2017).

The establishment of the Folk Church as a cultural institution – a proposal

In this chapter, I have argued that some early factors in the 1500s and early 1600s were important for the development of the Folk Church as a cultural institution, namely religious conformity, state centralisation and the emergence of a Danish civil religion. The Danish civil religion was strengthened by the ideology of Absolutism, which placed the king as a divine ruler of the nation and its citizens in his capacity as head of both state and church. Late Absolutism also saw a popular identification with the church as a national institution, despite growing resistance among the citizens to its doctrinal practices and demands for religious conformity.

With the free constitution of 1849, the church was no longer the illiberal state church, which was compulsory for the great majority of citizens and which did not tolerate deviations from its current orthodoxy (Lausten 2002, 229). This change was a prerequisite for the church becoming a democratic cultural institution servicing the commonwealth by offering the public access to Danish Protestant cultural and religious traditions on a non-discriminatory basis. These characteristics of the Folk Church were expounded in the introduction to this chapter.

In the planning of the Reformation jubilee of 2017, the committee engaged with a range of cultural institutions and the Folk Church to make the celebration a national-cultural event. The more than one thousand different jubilee events taken together reached a considerable part of the Danish population, and according to the chairman of the committee, this was not least thanks to the many local initiatives within the Folk Church (Henriksen 2017). However, the extent of the popular reception of the Reformation celebrations in 2017 is not in itself an argument for considering the Folk Church a cultural institution – just as the sheer number of people attending a particular Bournonville ballet in Copenhagen does not settle whether the Royal Theatre is a cultural institution or not.

Among Danish politicians there is a widespread reluctance against giving the Folk Church an activist voice in religious and social matters. This was illustrated by the recent failure to get broad acceptance in the Danish Parliament for a proposed statute of governance of the Folk Church, as promised in the constitution.[17] Other established cultural institutions do not have a public voice beyond that of their strict professional specialisation.

During the Reformation celebrations of 2017, it was furthermore obvious that the previous, harsh religious confrontations with other Christian churches, particularly the strong anti-Catholic stances in the historical Reformation celebrations, were gone. Religious polemics are probably conceived of as incompatible with the position and *decorum* of a cultural institution which is to serve the commonwealth without discrimination.[18] These considerations lead me to conclude that the Folk Church only became *fully* qualified as a Danish cultural institution with the adoption of more lenient attitudes among bishops and pastors towards other Christian churches.

References

Afrapportering Vedrørende Reformationsmarkeringen i 2017 [Final Report on the Marking of the Reformation in 2017] 2018. Præsidiet for Reformationsjubilæet i Danmark. Accessible at luther2017.dk.

Aagedal, Olaf 2017. 'Innleiing: Å Feire Fortida', in Olaf Aagedal, Pål Ketil Botvar and Ånund Brottveit (eds.), *Kunsten å Jubilere. Grunnlovsfeiring og Minnepolitikk*. Oslo: Pax Forlag, 11-22.

Bach-Nielsen, Carsten 2015. *Fra Jubelfest til Kulturår. Danske Reformationsfejringer Gennem 400 år*. Aarhus: Aarhus Universitetsforlag.

Bach-Nielsen, Carsten, Niels Henrik Gregersen and Niels Kægård 2018. *Hvorfor Holder vi Reformationsjubilæum? Om Reformationen og Erindringen*. Copenhagen: Eksistensen.

Bellah, Robert N. 1967. 'Civil Religion in America', *Dædalus* 96: 1-21.

Betænkning 1544. *Folkekirkens Styre. Betænkning fra Udvalget om en Mere Sammenhængende og Moderne Styringsstruktur for Folkekirken*. Copenhagen: Ministry of Ecclesiastical Affairs, April 2014.

Christensen, Liselotte J. 2012. 'Ideologier bag den Politiske Håndtering af Religionsforholdene i Danmark 1849-1922', in Lisbet Christoffersen, Hans Raun Iversen, Niels Kærgård and Margit Warburg (eds.) *Fremtidens Danske Religionsmodel*. Copenhagen: Anis, 199-215.

Christoffersen, Lisbet 2015. 'A Long Historical Path towards Accountability, Transparency and Good Governance: On Financing Religions in Denmark', in

Francis Messner (ed.) *Public Funding of Religions in Europe*. Farnham: Ashgate, 125-147.

Cristi, Marcela and Lorne L. Dawson 2007. 'Civil Religion in America and in Global Context', in James A. Beckford and N.J. Demerath III (eds.), *The Sage Handbook of the Sociology of Religion*. Los Angeles: Sage, 267-292.

Danmarks Statistik 1977. 'Kirkestatistik 1974' [Church Statistics 1974], *Statistiske Efterretninger* 69/4, 97-111.

Doering, Zahava D. 1995. *Who Attends Our Cultural Institutions? A Progress Report*. Based on the Smithsonian Institution Marketing Study. Washington D.C.: Smithsonian Institution.

Ekmann, Ernst 1957. 'The Danish Royal Law of 1665', *The Journal of Modern History* 29: 102-107.

Gourevitch, Victor (ed., trans.) 1997. *Rousseau. The Social Contract and Other Later Political Writings*. Cambridge: Cambridge University Press.

Hammond, Phillip E. 1976. 'The Sociology of American Civil Religion: A Bibliographical Essay', *Sociological Analysis* 37: 169-182.

Henriksen, Johannes 2017. 'Debat: Skal, skal ikke. Reformationsjubilæet, som Lykkedes – Efter Omstændighederne', *Kristeligt Dagblad* 27 October 1:10.

Herbener, Jens-André P. 2017. *Luther. Antidemokrat og Statsidol*. Copenhagen: U Press.

Himmelstrup, Kristian 2013. *Kulturformidling. Grundbog i Kulturens Former og Institutioner*. Copenhagen: Hans Reitzels Forlag.

Ingesman, Per 2000. 'Kirke, Stat og Samfund i Historisk Perspektiv', in Tim Knudsen (ed.), *Den Nordiske Protestantisme og Velfærdsstaten*. Århus: Aarhus Universitetsforlag, 65-86.

Jensen, Frede P. 1993. 'Frederik II og Truslen fra de Katolske Magter. Linjer i Dansk Udenrigs- og Sikkerhedspolitik 1571-88', *Historisk Tidsskrift* 16/2: 233-278.

Knudsen, Tim 2000. 'Tilblivelsen af den Universalistiske Velfærdsstat', in Tim Knudsen (ed.), *Den Nordiske Protestantisme og Velfærdsstaten*. Århus: Aarhus Universitetsforlag, 20-64.

Kolderup-Rosenvinge, J. L. A. (ed.) 1824. *Samling af Gamle Danske Love, Udgivne med Indledninger og Anmærkninger og Tildeels Oversættelser IV*. Copenhagen: Gyldendalske Boghandlings Forlag.

Kolding Provsti 2017. *Luther Arrangementer i Kolding Provsti*. Pamphlet issued by Kolding Provsti, Ejlersvej 6, 6000 Kolding.

Kongeloven, 14th November 1665. Accessible on http://danmarkshistorien.dk/leksikon-og-kilder/vis/materiale/kongeloven-1665/.

Lausten, Martin Schwarz 1995. 'The Early Reformation in Denmark and Norway 1520-1559', in Ole Peter Grell (ed.) *The Scandinavian Reformation from Evangelical*

Movement to Institutionalisation of Reform. Cambridge: Cambridge University Press, 12-41.

Lausten, Martin Schwarz 2002. *A Church History of Denmark*. New York: Ashgate.

Møller, Jes Fabricius and Uffe Østergaard 2013. 'Lutheran Orthodoxy and Anti-Catholicism in Denmark 1536-2011', *European Studies* 31: 165-189.

Stjernfelt, Frederik 2017. *Syv Myter om Martin Luther*. Copenhagen: Gyldendal.

Vejrup, Marie 2017. 'Fortid, Nutid og Fremtid – Hvorfor kan Martin Luther Gøre Folk så Glade og Vrede i 2017?', *Religion. Tidsskrift for Religionslærerforeningen for Gymnasiet og HF*, 1: 8-15.

Vind, Ole 1999. *Grundtvigs Historiefilosofi*. Copenhagen: Gyldendal.

Warburg, Margit 2005a. 'Dansk Civilreligion i Krise og Vækst', *Chaos. Dansk-Norsk Tidsskrift for Religionshistoriske Studier* 43, 89-108.

Warburg, Margit 2005b. 'Gudspåkaldelse i Dansk Civilreligion', Morten Thomsen Højsgaard and Hans Raun Iversen (eds.), *Gudstro i Danmark*. Copenhagen: Anis, 125-141.

Warburg, Margit 2006. 'Fra Sørgemarch til Sejrsmarch: Slaget ved Fredericia og Dansk Civilreligion i en Globaliseringstid', *Chaos. Dansk-Norsk Tidsskrift for Religionshistoriske Studier* 45, 129-147.

Warburg, Margit 2008. '*Dannebrog*: Waving in and out of Danish Civil Religion', *Nordic Journal of Religion and Society,* 21, 165-183.

Warburg, Margit 2009. 'Graduation in Denmark: Secular Rituals and Civil Religion', *Journal of Ritual Studies*, 23, 31-42.

Warburg, Margit 2013. 'Gud Bevare Danmark. Dansk Civilreligion i det Store og det Små', Margit Warburg, Signe Engelbreth Larsen and Laura Maria Schütze (eds.), *Civilreligion i Danmark, Ritualer, Myter og Steder*. Højbjerg: Univers, 7-53.

Warburg, Margit 2015. 'Civilreligion', Armin W. Geertz and Tim Jensen (eds.), *Religionsforskningen før og nu. Nyere Tid*. Copenhagen: Gyldendal, 605-615.

Warburg, Margit 2017a. 'Reformationsjubilærne i en Civilreligiøs Fortolkningsramme', *Religion. Tidsskrift for Religionslærerforeningen for Gymnasiet og HF*, 1, 16-28.

Warburg, Margit 2017b. 'Much Ado about a Christmas Tree: A Conflict Involving Danish Civil Religion', *Implicit Religion,* 20, 127-148.

Warburg, Margit 2018a. 'The Danish Reformation Celebrations as Civil Religion', *Journal of Church and State* (in press doi.org/10.1093/jcs/csy030).

Warburg, Margit 2018b. 'Reformationsjubilærnes Iscenesættelse af Samhørighed Mellem Stat, Kirke og Folk i Danmark'. *Religionsvidenskabeligt Tidsskrift* (in press).

Notes

1. All the general information about the Reformation celebration and role of the committee can be accessed on the committee's website https://luther2017.dk. This website will continue to be accessible and its contents will be preserved, see the committee's final report (*Afrapportering* 2018, 58-59).
2. This civil war (*Grevens Fejde*) was primarily fought between supporters and opponents of the former Danish king, Christian II (reigned 1513-1523, predecessor to Frederik I). Christian II, who was a cousin of Christian III, was deposed from the throne by the Council of the Realm after a widespread rebellion against his harsh rule. Christian II died in captivity in Denmark in 1559. Except for the nobility of Jutland, both parties in the civil war were already largely Protestant.
3. From 1474, the Danish king was also Duke of Holstein which was a duchy in the German-Roman Empire.
4. In 1901, 98.8 percent of the Danish population belonged to the Folk Church, and even as late as 1974, 95.2 percent of the population were members of the Folk Church (Christensen 2012; Danmarks Statistik 1977).
5. There is one historical exception: Bishop Hans Svane was promoted to archbishop by Frederik III in return for his prominent role in introducing Absolutism in 1660 (Lausten 2002, 132-133). The title was in reality empty, because Hans Svane was never given the authority to preside over a college of the bishops (Lausten 2002, 132-133).
6. For example, it was only in 1814 that the Danish Jews were allowed most of the rights that prevailed for other subjects of the Danish king.
7. For a long period, the Folk Church had a direct influence on the teachings in elementary school, and education in Folk Church Christianity was compulsory until 1975. Even today, the public school recognises that pupils' preparations for confirmation in the Folk Church can take place during the scheduled teaching periods.
8. Parish councils could already be formed on a voluntary basis from 1856, but it was only from 1903 that the general establishment of parish councils was stated by law. By 1912, they were obligatory (Lausten 2002, 278-279).
9. www.folkekirken.dk/aktuelt/nyheder/folkekirken-festede-for-reformationen.
10. http://www.koldingprovsti.dk/wp-content/uploads/2016/11/LutherKatalog.pdf.
11. Interview with Pastor Martin Rønkilde, Sanct Nicolai Parish, Kolding, November 10th 2017.
12. *JydskeVestkysten Kolding*: 2, 4, November 2nd 2017.
13. Interview with Pastor Martin Rønkilde, Sanct Nicolai Parish, Kolding, November 10th 2017.
14. By mid-November 2017, I counted about 1250 events registered on https://luther2017.dk. Some of the registered events were temporary exhibitions stretch-

ing over a period of a month or more, but by far the largest number (I estimate about 1,100) were one-day events arranged locally. Many of these events were repetitions of performances and lectures offered nationwide by organizations and individuals. In line with my estimate, the committee reported 1,050 events in the event calendar (the difference in numbers is probably due to slightly different methods in counting repetitive events) (*Afrapportering* 2018, 56). In addition, there were local events that were not announced on the homepage, for example the above-mentioned event in Kolding. Many public lectures given by university researchers were also not announced on https://luther2017.dk. To give an example, I know from e-mail correspondence 25-26 March 2018 with church historian Martin Schwarz Lausten, economist Niels Kærgård and economist Jørn Henrik Petersen that they held a combined 234 lectures in connection with the Reformation celebrations of 2017. I could retrieve less than 20 of these lectures from https://luther2017.dk.

15 Translated from http://luther2017.dk/arrangementer/arrangementer-paa-vej/national-folkeoplysning/.

16 Status report by September 2017 from the People's University (unpublished). Sent by Anne Engedal, project leader at the People's University, November 8th 2017.

17 A white paper from a governmental committee (Betænkning 1544) was presented to the political parties in the autumn of 2014, but after some internal debate within the parties, the Minister of Ecclesiastical Affairs concluded that there was no broad political support for making the proposed changes, so she decided to shelve the proposal (www.folkekirken.dk/aktuelt/nyheder/aftale-om-styringsreform-opgivet).

18 In line with this, the authors of a booklet on the Reformation celebrations attempt distilling the essence of the 2017 celebration. They concluded that, in the presently more multi-religious society, the celebrations showed that church, culture, religion and society are not clinically separate entities (Bach-Nielsen et al. 2018, 78).

3. Secular Lutheranism as Common Institutional and Mental Background for the Danish Welfare State and the Danish Folk Church

Hans Raun Iversen

The Danes' social attitudes are remarkable with respect to two areas: the majority of Danes – independent of the economic situation of the country – persistently prefer communal welfare to tax reductions. In addition, they stay on as members of the National Evangelical-Lutheran Church (*the Folk Church*), significantly more faithfully than is the case with folk churches in the four other Nordic countries, even though they have a similar Lutheran background. This chapter argues that secular Lutheranism seems to provide a significant part of the institutional and mental background that sustains the Danish Welfare State as well as the Danish Folk Church in both their ongoing processes of transformation.

Danish mentality, as it interacts with basic societal institutions, obviously has a multifaceted historical background. The Lutheran share can, however, be traced across at least six dimensions: the sovereignty of the individual, the universalism of the welfare state, egalitarianism among people at, for example, workplaces and public squares, the collectively-oriented individualism in everyday life, the social ethics behind the welfare state and the central position occupied by work and close personal relations.

It will be argued in this chapter that there is a *structural similarity* between modern Danish mentality and Lutheranism transformed into a secular form. Following the style of argument in Iversen and Pedersen 2017, the author's assertion is that features central to Lutheran theology can also be found in secular mentality in Denmark today. The 500-year history behind this observation is difficult and perhaps impossible to trace. The result is, however, that the Danes feel at home and secure when they live in their welfare state with its flexicurity. Similarly, they feel at home when they visit the Folk Church as 70-75 percent do annually, being among the total of 20 million visitors pr. year. With both the welfare state and the Folk Church, Danes come to 'their own' societal institutions that have the same mentality as they have themselves.

For the structure of this chapter, I employ a simplified version of the so-called I-D-I-O-T model created by the Danish professor of Political Science, Ove Kaj Pedersen (see, for example, Pedersen 2011, 34-36). I follow the development of secular Lutheranism from Luther's *Idea,* via the time of a monopolistic Lutheran *Discourse,* its central *Institutions* and the *Organization* of the modern Folk Church, to the ongoing process of *Transformation* of church and society today. Only a sketch of Luther's theology will be presented here, I refer primarily to the magisterial overview in Bayer 2017. For the history of Christianity in Danish society, I refer to Lausten 2002, and the first chapter in Iversen 2018.

The Idea

The key idea in Luther's reformation theology is the salvation of the individual by faith alone. Studying the Bible, in particular the Psalms and the first chapter of Romans, the monk Martin Luther developed a feeling of certainty in this new belief: God will graciously (*sola gratia*) grant people with open hearts the faith in God's work in Christ (*solus Christus*). That alone (*sola fide*) can provide the form of salvation that we know about from the Bible (*sola scriptura*). A key point is that human beings can do absolutely nothing to produce or perform the saving faith in God. However, as a gift from God, faith does work through the faithful to do the good deeds needed for a good life in family and society. This portion of Luther's theology was connected to at least the following six anthropological stipulations with potential consequences for society:

1. A central precondition for Luther's concept of salvation is that the individual, who became a living soul by the spirit of God (Genesis 2:7), stands alone before God. No powers, kings or popes, can come between the individual and God in matters of the salvation of the human soul, as it belongs entirely to God. This is so from the side of God the creator who, in his divine love, will save his human creatures from sin and death. This is, however, also so from the side of the individual, as only the faith that the individual has received from God as some-

thing personal (*pro me*) is real faith. Here, a germ of a new form of *individualism* was introduced.
2. The conditions for salvation are fundamentally the same for all human beings independent of their positions in church and society. Even the clergy, including the pope, has no privileged position before God (*coram Deo*), as the real priests, those who can come near to God, are the people who belong to the common priesthood of all believers. Thus, a germ for a new form of *universalism* was introduced.
3. At the same time, Luther emphasised that all people of faith are justified, but still sinful – people of faith are also sinful (*simul justus et peccator*). Thus, a germ for a new form of anthropological *egalitarianism* was introduced.
4. Furthermore, Luther emphasised that a Christian person is fully free and subdued before no one, and at the same time called to serve everybody in need. Thus, a germ for a new form of *balance between the individual and his relation to his neighbour* was introduced.
5. This balance was elaborated in the work ethics of Luther: one must work hard, not primarily for one's own benefit, but to be able to serve one's neighbour and contribute to society. Thus, a germ for a *new social order* was introduced.
6. As the individual can contribute nothing to his own salvation or to his service for fellow human beings by isolating himself in a monastery, the true monk's life is found in the vocations and social positions of everyday life. Thus, a germ for an ethics strongly emphasising the *call to work and the responsibilities in personal relations* was introduced.

These six germs in Lutheran Reformation theology might only have come to work at a spiritual and highly individual level. Or, they might also have potential to work as catalysts for a new form of society, such as the one we have in Denmark today. For more than 300 years from the Reformation in 1536 to the first free constitution in 1849, the signs of this transformation being about to happen were only few and weak, as political and economic conditions in society did not allow these germs to flourish.

The discourse

The Danish kingdom emerged from the time of the Viking chiefdoms literally supported by, and drawing on, Christianity in its Medieval Catholic form (Iversen 2018). Up until the Reformation, there were two swords, that of the king and his state, and that of the bishops and their church. The Lutheran Reformation removed the bishops from power, as they were put into jail after the civil war concluding in the Reformation in 1536.

The West-Nordic Reformation (in Denmark-Norway) was quick and radical in two important respects: the basic theology common to Luther and his companion Philip Melanchthon was taken over, word by word (no more, no less), as found in Luther's *Small Catechism* and *Confessio Augustana* from 1530. At the same time, the two swords were reduced to one, that of the king and the state, as the church was fully integrated into the state – being at one and the same time a servant of God and the king. The king governed the church from above, initially as the first among lay people or as the father of the bishops, and later on, during in the theocratic state of the sovereign Kings 1660-1849, as a combined Caesar and Pope.

Before the Reformation, important parts of societal life were regulated by the Catholic Canon Law, which Luther set on fire. As such, almost all parts of society were regulated by biblical ideas and rules, including those found in the Law of Moses. This was enshrined in King Christian V's *Danish Law* of 1683. On paper, Danish Christianity has been strictly Lutheran throughout the centuries since the Reformation. Strong church discipline, partly inspired by Calvin, as well as the use of force and suppression in all sorts of matters, including faith, became part of this form of combined Church State and State Church Lutheranism in what might well be described as a 'Lutheran Sharia State'.

Did all of this make Danes into Lutheran Christians? Probably not in the modern, or the early Lutheran, sense – which was very personal: the individual's trust in God. During the times of orthodoxy (approximately 1550 to 1700), pietism (1700-1770) and rationalism (approximately 1770-1849), Lutheran Christianity had the monopoly on framing common people's worldview. It was a sort of civil religion that it was almost impossible to escape from. From 1736, youngsters had to be able to memorise Luther's *Small Catechism* in order to be confirmed, and without being confirmed, they could not be married or count as full citizens with any possibility of taking up work with responsibility. Confirmation and, from 1814, seven years of compulsory school education made the Danes obedient citizens in their Lutheran state. At the same time, they had basic knowledge of Lutheran Christianity from Luther's Catechism that was taught to all up until approximately 1950. In many respects, the preconditions of modern Denmark were laid before the free constitution of 1849 (e.g. the cultural homogeneity and, during the later stages of absolute monarchy, the permissive freedom in local matters inside a strong state). It can be argued that it was only during the time of the revivals (approximately 1850 to 1950) that one third of the population became touched by Lutheran Christianity in a sort of modern, personal way.

Institutions and mentality in interaction

Institutions

Discourses, such as the ones found in Danish Lutheranism from the times of orthodoxy, pietism and rationalism, need to rest in institutions in order for them to be internalised among ordinary people. To introduce the Danish landscape in terms of basic institutions and (later on) mentality, I draw on an empirical based study from 2008, co-authored by three colleagues from sociology, sociology of religion and practical theology, at the University of Copenhagen. In this study, the authors demonstrate that the institutions of Danish society today are closely interwoven, building on a common history, and that they are overlaid with a common pattern of mentality (Gundelach et al. 2008)[1].

The 'tribal and almost communist' economic, welfare, culture and mentality-related tendencies in modern Danish society are striking (Mellon 1992). This has a special historical background (e.g. the fact that the former small Danish empire was cut down to the narrow area of the Danish-speaking 'ethnic' Danes in 1864 after the defeat to Germany). Even so, Danes since 1864 have managed to imagine that Denmark is, has always been and must always be, one and the same state of the (ethnic) Danes. This sense of national unity is being upheld today by at least seven strong institutions which are common to almost all Danes, as all Danes have been socialised by them, and are continually strongly influenced by them. The 2008-study points to the following seven institutions as 'basic' in Denmark:

1. Families and childcare institutions with rather common norms for primary socialisation.
2. A fairly egalitarian comprehensive folk school system.
3. A labour market with flexicurity, based on the special 'Danish model' of negotiations between the workers' unions and the employers.
4. A common structure of daily life with a stable rhythm of work, family life and leisure.
5. A strong tradition for many volunteers organized in civil society governed by consensus democracy.
6. A common Park of Religions structuring the religious outlook as well as the flow of the year for most Danes (Iversen 2005).
7. A nation that makes the Danes feel that they belong to it, without knowing what it means and without doing anything to be the Dane they feel they are (Gundelach et al. 2008).

Despite many exceptions and variations in Denmark, as in Nordic countries in general, from an international perspective it is the common factors, denominators and patterns, which are the most dominant. This goes for Denmark in particular: several studies have, for example, pointed to the strong coherence and high degree of trust among people in Danish society as major factors behind Denmark's economic success in recent decades (Campbell et al. [eds.] 2006, Hall et al. [eds.] 2015 and Svendsen and Svendsen 2016).

The institutions overlap in Denmark, and it can be difficult to distinguish public from private. This is true of many areas. The labour market organizations are, for example, deeply involved in public policies, and the (in principle) private unemployment funds are heavily supported by the public purse. For the individual, there can be a problem differentiating between transfer incomes supplied by the state and unemployment funds. The labour market and social benefits interact in the so-called flexicurity-system. Similarly, on the school front, where it is relatively easy to set up independent schools in Denmark, since the state finances most of the expenses to keep them running. Still, the great majority of children attend the municipality schools, called 'folk school', like the Folk Church, the folk libraries and so on. A large amount of the common ground between the institutions is formed and mediated by what was called in the 2008-study the background carpet:

religion and the nation, which themselves are so interwoven that they are well-nigh inseparable.

Mentality

Mentality contributes to, and to a certain extent determines, people's identity. But there is more at play than mentality in one's identity. Mentality is primarily something held in common, whereas identity is primarily something individual and personal. The concept of mentality is majority-oriented, inasmuch as emphasis is on what is shared by the majority. There is nothing wrong with this; but one should be extremely conscious of it!

Mentality is a problematic term if understood as indicating stable, fixed qualities in people or population-groups, for such qualities do not exist. Mentality is developed historically and and bears the stamp of its historical context – like everything else. Since the concept of mentality has often been misused, it is not an easy one to employ, and it says a great deal that *The Great Danish Encyclopedia* carries informative articles about mental hygiene, the history of mentality, mental reservation and mental examination, but nothing on what mentality actually *is*.

Etymologically, the word derives from Latin *mens*, which can be translated as soul, mind or reason. Mentality can refer to a particular mind-condition, or it can carry a psychological or spiritual stamp. In this connection, we look at that part of spirituality that is reflected in people's attitude to other people in practice and to existence in general. Here, an expression such as a 'spiritually distinctive stamp' would come close to covering what we understand by mentality. Philosopher Richard J. Bernstein's definition of mentality is in line with our understanding of the concept:

> ... a general orientation – a cast of mind or way of thinking – that conditions the way in which we approach, understand and act in the world. It shapes and is shaped by our intellectual, practical and emotional lives. Mentalities can take a variety of concrete historical forms. We never encounter a mentality in the abstract, but only in a particular historical manifestation. To fully understand a specific historical manifestation of mentality, we need to locate its context, its distinctive character, and its sources (Bernstein 2005, 18).

Robert Bellah and co-authors (1985), use the phrase 'Habits of the heart' as a description of an existing motivation structure behind social action. In a Danish context, it is moreover thought-provoking that the professor and politician Hartvig Frisch, in his work *The Cultural History of Europe* from 1928, regarded culture as a 'set of habits'. The word 'habit' contains both an emphasis on action, and on the partially instilled and unconscious feelings about what one does and how one does it, as well as about what is right and what is wrong. Following this definition of culture, mentality can be seen as cultural norms integrated in individuals.

There is a certain sluggishness about 'mentality' – nothing new is immediately accepted – but in the course of time, mentality changes. It creates continuity in society, yet there is also room for changes. People reflect constantly on their own and on their associates' mentality, and this creates the capacity to transcend former borders (Wuthnow 2006, 58). In the 2008 study mentioned above, the authors were inspired by the sociolinguist Joshua A. Fishman (1980), who in a theoretical discussion of the concept of 'ethnicity' worked with the terms 'knowing', 'doing' and 'being' as three dimensions of ethnic/national identity (Gundelach et al. 2008). These terms were used to sharpen the understanding of Danish mentality. Some people emphasise that being Danish is best expressed through, for example, historical and cultural knowledge about Denmark and the Danes. Others, if they are asked about Danishness, say that they do voluntary work or do something for the fellow-feeling within the community in some other way – and that is, in fact, typically Danish. Most people, however, do not refer to knowing and doing, only to being. They 'feel' that they are Danish and thus that they are Danes. In the same way, 'feeling' is at the core of belonging to a common mentality.

Coherence in Denmark depends heavily on a common mentality that interacts with the seven institutions. According to the empirically based 2008 study, such coherence includes the following seven dimensions:

1. Joy in Denmark. Danes are extremely happy about Denmark. As affluent people living in a rather small country, Danes travel more than other people do, for example as tourists. When coming home, they unanimously say that the best thing about their travels was coming home to Denmark again.

2. Security, trust, happiness and (self-)satisfaction. For a number of years, Danes have been rated the happiest people in the world. Happiness goes together with a high degree of security, trust and satisfaction about life, including self-satisfaction.
3. Collectively-oriented individualism. Danes are individualists, especially when it comes to existential and ethical questions. They are, however, not utilitarian, nor are they expressivists, whose only target is to express themselves. In Denmark, it is only good to be me if others are around as well.
4. Freedom, equality and low power-distance. Freedom comes first, but only in the sense that all are equally free. If using your freedom makes you think that you are more valuable than others are, you have a problem. The sense of equality means that that even the lowest paid employee can tell the boss that things ought to be done in another way.
5. Fellow-feeling and the differences. There have been numerous rewritings of the old revue song *We're all in the same boat*. What a single group or decision-maker says or does in Denmark often has consequences for everybody in such a small country. The image of the boat can therefore be used to make an appeal for unity, and to urge moderation in attacking others while we are on the collective voyage.
6. Being yourself. In a competition society, where you have to be ready for change all the time and ready to face assessments based on this or that criterion, people look for places where they only need to be themselves, being present and having basic needs met without having to achieve some merit. If Danes share 'being themselves' together with others, they have Danish *hygge*.
7. Danish in many ways. 'To a folk they all belong/whose land their hearts desire,/who sing the mother country's song with patriotic fire'. This stanza from a 160 years old song by N.F.S. Grundtvig, for better or worse, hits the nail on the head even today. You have all the freedom you can wish to be different from the rest the Danes, but do not question Danishness (whatever that is), if you want to live in Denmark.

The Danish orientation towards both the collective and the individual can be traced to the intertwining of public and private in a society which has only been able to develop through political compromises. This creates, at the same time, a demand for freedom and diversity and a willingness to submit to a widespread public system. Experiential centrism has powerful roots in the background carpet of a close link between religion and the nation. The subdued, passive view of Christianity is no longer alone. There are not many Muslims in Denmark – a mere 4 percent – but their presence has given rise to considerable political clashes. Nor are there that many foreign citizens in Denmark – some 10 percent – but they present a challenge to a nationally homogeneous society, and this is happening even as the state is increasingly involving itself internationally on both military and political levels. This is creating change – in both Danish institutions and its mentalities. Much depends now on how Danes react to these changed circumstances.

Organization and transformation

Two things happened simultaneously after the free constitution of 1849, particularly in the first part of the 20th century. The church had to be developed as a somehow independent organization and the new state of the people was gradually transformed into a welfare state. From being fully integrated into the theocratic state, the Lutheran church was slowly transformed into a more or less integrated organization providing spiritual welfare to the citizens and sometimes to the nation in the welfare state of the 20th century (Iversen 2018).

In terms of national leadership, the Danish people's church, *folkekirken*, with 75 percent of the people as members, is still a *state church*. Denmark, however, is no longer a *church state* but a moderately *secular state*. The Sunday opening law has been almost totally liberalised, and the popularity of national holidays on church holy days (e.g. on Great Prayer Day, a Friday in April or May, and Ascension Day) has nothing much to do with the church. Nevertheless, according to a number of modern historians (e.g., Østergaard 1998, Knudsen [ed.] 2000, and Christiansen et al. 2006), it is to a considerable extent through the influence of Lutheran Christianity that the Danish welfare state has evolved. At the very same time, Lutheran teaching has been transformed into parts of the secular mentality of the people.

Religious faith and creeds in their doctrinal forms have become rare. So, too, have regular prayer, Bible reading, Sunday morning church practice and knowledge of Christianity to a lesser extent, too. Still, the basic understanding of the uniqueness of human beings, the continuing development of history and the use of Christian language when it comes to important matters prevail. This is often called 'cultural Christianity', and is almost equivalent to secular Lutheranism in Denmark (Iversen 2005).

One way of arguing about the origin of secular Lutheranism as embedded in Danish institutions and mentality runs as follows. At the time of the Reformation (1536), the victorious King Christian III, and thus the state, expropriated three important things from the former Catholic Church: its property (one third of the land) its infrastructure (parishes, pastors, deans and bishops) and its social vision (primarily as found in the Bible). The comparatively strong Danish state was built up economically on the expropriation of church property, and until 100-150 years ago, society was to a high degree governed via church infrastructure. Geographically, the boundaries for local public and church authorities coincided until the local authority reform of 1970.

The construction of a universalist welfare state corresponds with the Christian vision of social equality in the form of a project for Christian enlightenment and education (the two words are coterminous and can both be covered in the Danish word *oplysning*). This appears to hark back to the comprehensive church package with its social vision that the state expropriated at the Reformation (Ingesman 2000). It took, however, 400 years to find the means to realise it in the form of the welfare state.

There are some historical links between Lutheranism and the development of the welfare state. We shall mention only one: in 1645, King Christian IV made it compulsory to register basic information about all citizens, and thereby all Christians, in the Church Books. Because of this, Danes were already used to being registered when the electronic CPR-register was introduced in 1968, and the Church Book data on the citizens were transferred to the CPR-register – as they still are today. Without that instrument, and the agreement among the Danes about having it, it had not been possible to make the universalist welfare state function. Obviously, the welfare state did not evolve because of the CPR-register, it was only one of many preconditions. Generally speaking, it is next to impossible to trace 500 years of development historically. What we are left with is a structural similarity between the present day's Danish mentality and basic features of Lutheranism as outlined by Martin Luther. This is visible in at least the six points corresponding with the above-mentioned germs in Lutheran Reformation theology.

The sovereignty of the individual

We begin with the basic understanding of the integrity and sovereignty of the individual. In a privileged Western country, it is easy to forget that millions of people around the world are kept as slaves and trafficked as prostitutes while others, especially women, are abused and suppressed in all sorts of ways. Even in Denmark, less than 200 years ago, it was far from taken for granted that people had the right to control their own bodies and the fruits of their own work. The right to be treated as a sovereign individual with your own physical and psychological integrity is basic to all sorts of rights for human beings. It is of little help to have, say, freedom of expression if bosses and rulers around you can take control of your body, work and mind. The story of the development towards sovereign individuals, from un-propertied, walking bodies working under duty into employees with rights to have a contract on their work and to keep their own property, is long and complicated (Pedersen 2011, 2017). A significant step in Denmark was the agreement between workers' unions and employers in September 1899, where workers got the right to organize themselves and go on strike according to the contracts between workers' unions and the employers.

Recently, the debate on the origin of the fundamental sense of individual freedom we have today, including the absolute right to our own bodies and the fruits of our own work, has been taken up again. In subtle ways, studied by historians of ideas, this freedom seems to have been promoted by the Lutheran idea about the freedom of the individual before God (Siedentop 2015; Iversen and Pedersen 2017). Researching this development, Larry Siedentop presented two assumptions in his magisterial work *Inventing the Individual – the Origins of Western Liberalism*:

> The first is, that if we are to understand the relationships between beliefs and social institutions – that is to understand ourselves – then we have to take a very long view. Deep moral changes, changes in belief, can take centuries to begin to modify social institutions. It is folly to expect popular habits and attitudes to change overnight. The second assumption is that beliefs are nonetheless of primary importance, an assumption once far more widely held than today (Siedentop 2015, 2).

Concluding his long view through 2000 years of history, Siedentop finds the beginning of the invention of the individual in St. Paul, whom he describes as being perhaps 'the greatest revolutionary in human history':

> For Paul, the love of God revealed in the Christ imposes opportunities and obligations on the individual as such, that is on consciousness. The Christ becomes a medium of a new and transformed humanity. In one sense, Paul's conception of the Christ, introduces the individual, by giving conscience a universal dimension ... The Christian conception of God provided an ontological foundation for the individual, first as moral status, and then, centuries later, as the primary social role ... the defining characteristic of Christianity was its universalism. It aimed to create a single human society, a society composed, that is, of individuals, rather than tribes, clans or casts ... Hence, the deep individualism of Christianity was simply the reverse side of its universalism (Siedentop 2015, 352-54).

The universalism of the welfare state

The Danish welfare state is universalistic, that is, it supports a major redistribution mechanism on the principle that everyone pays in, and everyone has the right to receive social and health benefits from the public purse. When pressure mounted from the socialist movement towards the end of the 19th century, and again after the Second World War, the welfare state was built up on a compromise between Christian-inspired, social-conservative and social-democrat forces (Christiansen et al. 2006). Instead of the communism that the vast majority feared, the Danes got their welfare state (Knudsen [ed.] 2000) with more equality than any of the communist states ever had. There are hardly any real anarchists in Denmark, as Danes take the state for granted – and have great confidence in it, even when it fails. In principle, all individuals stand alone and as equals, in direct relation to the state, even though today there are an increasing number of people who, for security's sake and because of self-interest, are joining interest groups that can defend their rights in relation to the state.

Fighting the Roman Catholic Church hierarchy of his time, Luther strongly emphasised that all people stand equal as individuals directly before God. Here, no human authority can interfere. The Gospel of the love of God is only valuable when it is received by the individual, *pro me*, in his or her personal relation to God. As indicated by Siedentop in the above quotation, the deep individualism of Christianity corresponds to a strong universalism. Not only was God equally God for all, but the principle of universalism also found its way into society and its institutions, not least in the universalist Danish welfare state.

The egalitarianism among people – workplaces

From the sovereignty of the individual and the universalism of basic institutions such as the state, we move to the third dimension of the same complex: the deep-seated egalitarianism found in Denmark. Strong and rich people who do not hold their weaker and poorer fellow citizens in respect are regarded as showing hubris. Such a view is responded to, as if by saying: 'After all, what kind of person are you, who does not count other people as equals? – only because you had a better fortune? You yourself could have been in the situation of your neighbour whom you despise'. Among the practical consequences of this egalitarianism we also find that the sense of equality means that even the lowest paid employee can tell the boss that things are not good enough and ought to be done differently. This low distance to the power has a positive influence on productivity at Danish workplaces (Gundelach et al. 2008, 208-10).

In theory, the Lutheran teaching about the equality of all in the priesthood of all believers might well have contributed to the widespread egalitarian ideas in Danish mentality. Yet historically, the church has not practised real egalitarianism – there has often been more hierarchy than equality, and even oppression and discrimination of the poorer of the lay people. If the Danish Folk Church is compared to other churches, we see what might be interpreted as a practice of the priesthood of all believers today: the church listens to its members and users – it is not primarily sticking to its internal rules and hierarchy but is eager to be 'close to the people'. The Danish church is not an 'ecclesial' but a 'societal' church (Woodhead and Iversen). To a great extent, lay people rule the church via the congregational boards (though it is debatable whether that can be seen as a legitimate expression of priesthood of all believers). It is, however, more likely that Lutheranism has contributed to the development of egalitarianism in another way: the Lutheran teaching of *simul justus et peccator* has been strong. In principle, all are equally made righteous and saved by faith, by the grace of God. More importantly, all are sinners and the self-righteous are even more sinful by their self-righteousness. The story of the Pharisee and the publican has most often been understood as underscoring just that point (Luke 18:10-13). The Pharisee who thinks he is superior to the humble publican should be happy if he could be counted as his equal.

The collectively-oriented individualism in everyday life

The subjective turn, as Charles Taylor (1989) calls it, is making its presence felt throughout Western society. The Danish form of individualism is collectively oriented (Gundelach et al. 2008). Even though Danes are thinking more and more from a position of the individual, they know very well that being individualised is no good without the well being of others. The proportion of adults living alone is on the increase, around one-third of all citizens. For everybody, it can be a challenge to keep your friends, especially if you have been alone and without work for many years. This requires you to be good at finding the balance in the collectively-oriented individualism. The national poet Benny Andersen has written a song which Povl Dissing pathetically sings about the core of the Danes' collectively-oriented individualism:

> It's nice to be alone – but
> it's best to have a friend!
> ......
> forget about your lust,
> just someone you can trust.

It is crucial to have close relations with your fellow-Danes, preferably family members and good friends. In this way, we see that individualism and the collective norms must be integrated. The Danes' particular brand of collectively-oriented individualism stands in contrast to the American mentality. *Habits of the Heart* (Bellah et al. 1985) shows that individualism is a very central value in American society. The authors demonstrate that American individualism takes at least two different forms: *utilitarian* and *expressive individualism*. The former regards life as a struggle to realise your own interests to the utmost, possibly at the expense of others. Typically, this means that individualism is linked to an economic understanding of humankind. The latter, expressive individualism is a form of self-realisation, where the aim is for the individual to unfold his or her own inner human core. This can be done without coming into conflict with others. This form of individualism leads to, among other things, the use of therapy and other kinds of techniques to nurture and cultivate the self. Together with the evaluation culture, expressivism has also been on the march in Denmark in recent years.

Therefore, even though there are signs of both the expressive and the utilitarian individualism among the Danes, they are typically different from what we – with what sounds like an oxymoron – call the Danish collectively-oriented individualism. This is a mentality that is also found in other parts of Scandinavia. In her interviews on people's life histories, Inger Furseth found what she calls *relational individualism* (Furseth 2006), and Marianne Gullestad (1989) has pointed out that individualism and conformity are closely bound up in Norway. This is also true of Denmark. Emphasis is placed on personal independence, but also on the individual being part of a collective, be it a family, workplace, school or local community and nation. In general, the Danes not only hold the world record in trusting one another, according to the European Values Survey they also exhibit a high degree of trust in 'the system': the state and the municipality, to which they pay their record-high taxes.

In the USA's cultural imagery, a detective who ostensibly saves society through his bloody-minded violation of its rules can be the hero (Bellah et al. 1985). This form of hero represents central individualist values. Through his personal efforts, he ensures that the system works justly, but even though this narrative is also found in Denmark, the typically Danish hero is different. She is the nurse or the kindergarten teacher. Alternatively, he is Hans Christian Andersen's *Jack the Dullard* – challenging the system by being unimpressed, trusting himself and not signalling his knowledge or his cunning – the apparently awkward character who nevertheless beats the system and who gets the princess before all the other better qualified suitors. There is reason to fear that the new evaluation culture will correct Jack or even kill him off. And who will then get the princess? Jack's evaluation-oriented brothers have no chance, according to the fairy-tale.

The social ethics behind the welfare state

In a convincing major study, Jørn Henrik Petersen has pointed to the structural similarity between the social ethos in Luther's theology and the ethical argument behind the introduction of the welfare state. In both places, the core message is this: 'you must work hard, not for your own sake, but to be able to help others in need, and to pay to the common pocket of the state that helps everybody'. That was Luther's core social idea, it was the idea bridging the social classes and making them come together in support of what became the welfare state in Denmark (Petersen 2016). Petersen makes it very clear that he is not indicating that there should be a direct link, as if Danish welfare politicians simply took over Luther's teaching. Most likely, they probably did not even know about it. Petersen is referring to the fact that many church leaders in Scandinavia (e.g. in Sweden) originally opposed the welfare state. Petersen quotes the Swedish sociologist Hans L. Zetterberg, who gives the following description of the relations between Lutheran ethics and the welfare state:

> It is not likely that the welfare state would flourish in civilizations where the love of the neighbour and charity had not been preached for generations. Even so, the establishment of the welfare state in Scandinavia is mainly due to the work through generations by atheists and lukewarm believers. It is a product of the political fight about the distribution of income and privileges, not a gift from heaven (Zetterberg translated from Petersen 2016, 13).

The Lutheran Reformation was not a gift from heaven, nor was the welfare state. The question, therefore, is this: what sort of *mentality* paved the road? Certainly, church people did not generally take the lead. That does not prove that Lutheran ethics in secular form were not involved. The politicians promoting the welfare state probably knew Kant's categorical imperative: acting in such a way that one's actions could serve as a rule for everybody. In modern times, Kant has been more convincing and thus more influential that Luther. At the same time, his categorical imperative does appear to be a secular, universal representation of what Luther says in his social ethics, as it was taught in the schools for almost 450 years after the Reformation.

The central position occupied by work and close personal relations

Danes focus on work and close relations with family and friends much more than other people (Gundelach et al. 2008). The Protestant work ethic was partly developed through the monasticism of the Middle Ages, but it was not until after the Reformation that work became the primary identity-giver for the people and their religion (Lindhardt and Uhrskov 1997; Kærgaard 2007). It is only during the last 200 years that Danes have identified themselves through their chosen work. In the recent past, family businesses and smallholdings in connection with agriculture, fishing and industry have undoubtedly promoted the importance that has been attached to work and close relations. Taking a longer perspective, the link is more complex: the religious vacuum into which the Reformation threw people (given that they could no longer secure their own salvation by religious works) had as its first result the formation of the Protestant ethic of industry. In the next phase, Danes were socialised into having a job and some close relations. Without precisely these two elements, they would have experienced an existential vacuum. In Danish Lutheranism, it has been sung into the national consciousness that:

> I in my call and rank
> my God and father thank
> and duly worship.
> (Kingo 1674)

So, Danes thrive today primarily on work and in close relations, but certainly also on the sum total of what church and state have sought to educate them with since the Reformation:

> As good, secularised Protestants it is in our genes that we must not waste time … We must not be fooled [by the many that take early retirement], for if we look more closely, people work more in their leisure than ever before. Almost every retired person says they have never been busier. The gremlins have moved in with them – and they are as industrious and creative as ever before (Lindhardt and Uhrskov 1997, 67).

Conclusion

In this chapter, it has been argued that the widespread secular Lutheran mentality in Denmark is a basic condition of work, of politicians promoting the Danish welfare state as leaders of the Danish society and of *folkekirke* pastors promoting their church and its folk church Christianity. If we go back to the time of absolute kings, the political outlook of the teaching of pastors was very similar to that of the king. Basic views of society in the teaching of the church today are also probably converging with that of the majority of politicians. The six interacting features of Danish mentality introduced above, all with some common roots in Lutheran theology, are rather deep-seated in church as well as in society. Therefore, both politicians and pastors must appeal to them. These mental patterns tend to support the welfare state as well as the Folk Church – and vice versa! Obviously, there are deviating politicians (e.g. neo-liberals and ultra-nationalists), as well as deviating pastors (e.g. extreme existentialists and orthodox Biblicists) who say something different. Likewise, it must be admitted that the many features in the present development draw the nation away from the secular-Lutheran-welfare-and-Folk-Church-society. So far, however, there seems to be a stable part of Danish mentality corresponding to secular Lutheranism.

The argument in this chapter echoes Max Weber's, when he pointed out that the ethics of Protestantism was at work in – but did not 'cause' – the spirit of capitalism as a direct effect. The lack of security regarding salvation among Calvinists believing in predestination seemed to Weber to have made some Calvinists see success in business as a sign from God indicating that they had the good will of God. In that way, Calvinist Protestantism may have been a catalyst for the development of Western capitalism, which was more directly caused by a dozen other factors. Arguing in the style of Weber, it can be hypothesised that the universal monk's life, now to be envisaged as being in the call and rank of daily life where people can no longer save themselves by good deeds, may have turned Danish Lutherans towards gaining support for their identity in basic societal institutions, such as family, school and work. In this way, integration in the social institutions may have become a part of Danish Lutherans as they have internalised the mentality attached to the institutions. Attempting to find a secure place to remain in a Lutheranism that does not offer many exact instructions on what to do as a Christian, Danes have felt more secure and at home in daily lives structured by social institutions and a common mentality. This may be the reason why Danes are also, even today, comfortable with the two institutions, the welfare state and the folk church, that support and bless them in their daily lives.

References

Bayer, Oswald 2017. *Martin Luther's teologi. I nutidigt perspektiv*. Copenhagen: Eksistensen. (In German: *Martin Luthers Theologie. Eine Vergegenwärtigung*. Mohr Siebeck 2016).

Bellah, Robert et al. 1985/1996. *Habits of the Heart. Individualism and Commitment in American Life*. Los Angeles: University of California Press.

Bernstein, Richardt T. 2005. *The Abuse of Evil. The Corruption of Politics and Religion since 9/11*. Cambridge: Polity.

Campbell, John L., Hall, John A. and Pedersen, Ove K. (eds.) 2006. *National Identity and the Varieties of Capitalism. The Danish Experience*. Copenhagen: DJØF Publishing.

Christiansen, Niels Finn and Åmark, C. 2006. 'Conclusions', in Niels Finn Christiansen et al. (ed.) 2006. *The Nordic Model of Welfare. A Historical Reappraisal*. Copenhagen: Museum Tusculanum Press, 355-380.

Fishman, J. A. 1980. 'Social Theory and Ethnography: Neglected Perspectives on Language and Ethnicity in Eastern Europe', in P.F. Sugar (ed.), *Ethnic Diversity and Conflict in Eastern Europe*, Santa Barbara, ABC-Clio, 69-99.

Furseth, Inger 2006. *From Quest for Truth to Being Oneself. Religious Change in Life Stories*. Berlin: Peter Lang.

Gullestad, Marianne 1989. *Kultur og hverdagsliv: på sporet af det moderne Norge*. Oslo: Universitetsforlaget.

Gundelach, Peter, Hans Raun Iversen and Margit Warburg 2008. *I hjertet af Danmark. Institutioner og mentaliteter*. Copenhagen: Hans Reitzels Forlag.

Hall, John A., Ove Korsgaard and Ove K. Pedersen (eds.) 2015. *Building the Nation. N.F.S. Grundtvig and Danish National Identity*. Aarhus: Aarhus University Press with McGill-Queen's University Press.

Ingesman, Per 2000. 'Kirke, stat og samfund'. Knudsen, Tim (ed.), *Den nordiske protestantisme og velfærdsstaten*. Aarhus: Aarhus University Press.

Iversen, Hans Raun 2005. 'Gudstro i den danske religionspark', in *Gudstro i Danmark*. Morten Thomsen Højsgaard and Hans Raun Iversen (eds.), Copenhagen: Anis, 103-123.

Iversen, Hans Raun 2010. 'Background of the Cartoon Crisis in Danish Mentality' *Religion in the 21st Century. Challenges and Transformations*. Lisbet Christoffersen, Hans Raun Iversen, Hanne Petersen and Margit Warburg (eds.). Surrey: Ashgate, 191-206

Iversen, Hans Raun and Ove Kaj Pedersen. 2017. 'Teologi og politik bag individets opkomst. Luthers og Grundtvigs bidrag', in Ove Korsgaard and Michael Schelde (eds.), *På afstand. Forskydninger mellem Grundtvig og Luther*. Copenhagen: Eksistensen, 37-58.

Iversen, Hans Raun 2018. *Ny praktisk teologi. Kristendommen, den enkelte og kirken*. København: Eksistensen.

Knudsen, Tim (ed.) 2000. *Den nordiske protestantisme og velfærdsstaten*. Aarhus: Aarhus University Press.

Kærgaard, Niels 2007. 'Lyst og pligt til arbejde. Kald og incitament i velfærdsstaten', in Kristen A. Lange. *Den danske friskole: En historisk skildring*. Copenhagen: Udvalget for Folkeoplysning.

Lausten, Martin Schwarz 2002. *A Church History of Denmark*. Aldershot: Ashgate.

Lindhardt, Jan and Uhrskov, Anders 1997. *Fra Adam til robot. Arbejdet – historisk og aktuelt*. Copenhagen: Gyldendal.

Martin, David 2010. 'The settled Secularity of happy Denmark', in Lisbet Christoffersen et al. (eds.), *Religion in the 21st Century. Transformations. Significance and Challenges*. Surrey: Ashgate, 183-190.

Mellon, Sir J. 1992. *Og Gamle Danmark. En beskrivelse af Danmark i det Herrens år 1992*. Copenhagen: Centrum.

Pedersen, Ove Kaj 2011. *Konkurrencestaten*. Copenhagen: Hans Reitzels Forlag.

Petersen, Jørn Henrik 2016. *Fra Luther til konkurrencestaten*. Odense: Syddansk Universitetsforlag

Siedentop, Larry 2014. *Inventing the Individual. The origins of Western Liberalism*. London: Penguin Books.

Svendsen, Gunner Lind Haase and Gert Tinggaard Svendsen 2016. *Trust, Social Capital and the Scandinavian Welfare State: Explaining the Flight of the Bumblebee*. Northampton: Edward Elgar Publishing Incorporated.

Taylor, Charles 1989. *Sources of the Self. The Making of the Modern Identity*. Cambridge MA: Harvard University Press.

Weber, Max 1904 and 1905. *Die protestantische Ethik und der Geist des Kapitalismus*. Archiv für Sozialwissenschaften und Sozialpolitik, Bd. XX und XXI.

Woodhead, Linda and Hans Raun Iversen (eds.). *The Old National Churches of Northern Europe: The Persistence of Societal Religion.* (in preparation).

Wuthnow, Robert. 2006. *American Mythos. Why Our Best Efforts to Be a Better Nation Fall Short.* Princeton: Princeton University Press.

Østergaard, Uffe. 1998. *Europa. Identitet og identitetspolitik.* Copenhagen: Munksgaard-Rosinante.

Notes

1 Unfortunately, the book, *I hjertet af Danmark. Institutioner og mentaliteter* (At the Heart of Denmark. Institutions and Mentalities) has not been edited in English. A digital version, called *Institutions and Mentalities in Denmark. Backdrop to the Cartoon Crisis,* of its English translation is available when writing to hri@teol.ku.dk. Some passages of this chapter are elaborated versions of the English translation of the book. I thank Peter Gundelach and Margit Warburg for allowing me to use these passages.

4. From Tithe to Tax. The Economic History of the Folk Church in the 20th Century

Sidsel Kjems and Niels Kærgård

Introduction

The arrangement of church and religion in Danish society is rather complicated, which shows in a number of conflicting rules and attitudes. In the Constitution, §4 states that 'The Evangelical Lutheran Church shall be the Established Church of Denmark, and as such it shall be supported by the State', while §68 declares: 'No one shall be liable to make personal contributions to any denomination other than the one to which he adheres'.

The former head of the liberal party (Venstre), Anders Fogh Rasmussen, declared as Prime Minister that religion should solemnly be a private matter and not be present in the public sphere, while a recent government headed by the same political party stated in its introductory declaration that Denmark is a 'Christian country'.[1]

This can only be explained by a history that has a high degree of *path dependency*.[2] Denmark created a democratic constitution in 1849, which determines that the established church should have a constitution determined by law, but the Danish Parliament has never succeeded in formulating such a law. A number of attempts have failed (the latest in 2014), partly because of disagreements in the Folk Church, and partly because of disagreements in the political system, see Udvalget (2014). This means, unintentionally, that the monarch is still the governing head of the established Church. In effect, this means that the Minister of Ecclesiastical Affairs[3] has a number of responsibilities which would seem better suited to the hands of the parliament or the Folk Church.

These complications are also characteristic of the economy of the established church (and, in this chapter, the economy will be the sole focus). There are rather few analyses of the Folk Church's economy in Denmark and these are rudimentary, most of them are in Danish (see Christoffersen [2010 and 2015] Finansministeriet [1995], and Christensen [2006] for shorter surveys). The strange part of this economy is that the established church has the responsibility of carrying out certain tasks that benefit the whole of society while also bearing the costs. The Folk Church undertakes the civil registration of the births and deaths of the whole population, and it takes care of the many medieval church buildings, which can be seen as national cultural heritage. The state, for its part, pays 40 percent of the wages of priests, the full wages of the bishops and some other costs. How this complicated intertwinement of the state's economy with that of the Folk Church came about wherein the state pays a considerable part of the wages of the priests – and, in particular, why Denmark has a 'church tax' (a member fee collected together with the ordinary taxes, but only paid by the members of the church) – are the topics of this chapter.

A number of problems can be discussed in relation to this intertwinement. Who benefits the most from these arrangements, the state or the Folk Church? What might constitute a more logical and modern form of organization and how might it be arranged? While valid questions, none of these shall be analysed in this chapter. The aim of the chapter is only to describe why Denmark has acquired such a structure.

The economy of the Folk Church was developed through political negotiations, and as long as the state and the church are legally, administratively and economically intertwined, it must remain so. Political decisions can only be understood through a careful consideration of the history of the church from the late 19th century until today, paying particular attention to the period 1903-1958. The main conclusion seems to be that the church was, for the most part, economically independent of the state at around 1900 (mainly taking its income through the tithe); but in the following decades, the church's economy was transformed to the situation, described above, wherein the church became highly intertwined with the state.

The situation around 1900

The most significant change of all in the history of the Danish church was, of course, the change from being a Roman Catholic church into being a Lutheran church headed by the king in 1536. Previous to that, the big, independent Roman Catholic church owned about one third of the land in

Denmark. The main tax was the tithe; it was divided into three equal parts, one for the priest, one for the church building and one for the bishops.

In 1536, the properties of the church were transferred to the king who became the head of the national Lutheran church. The church was organized in local parishes and they kept two thirds of the tithe, one for the priest and one for the church building. The bishops' third was transferred to the king, hereafter called 'The King Tithe'. The role of the bishops was also transformed. From being independent Catholic clergy, the bishops became officials of the king. Beside their ecclesiastical affairs, they acted as judges and local administrator on behalf of the king and were paid by the king. Besides paying the bishops, the king's tithe was used, among other things, to pay school teachers and university professors (Dübeck, 2004). Today, the bishops are still paid by the state, but the role of the bishops was transformed long ago and now they are only high ranking clergy of the established church.

Typically, the local priests in the rural areas had a farm, they got their third of the local tithe and also some offerings from the local church members, a considerable part of it not in monetary form, but in kinds. The tithe was mainly a tax on farming and therefore, in the cities, the offerings from church members were more important. Gradually, first in Copenhagen and later in other cities, these offerings were transformed into a member fee or a local 'church-tax'. For a survey of the history before 1900, see Stenbæk (2003) and Severinsen (1920).

During the following centuries, the local church buildings, with their tithe and costs, were sold to private individuals (typically local landowners). These contracts meant that the church owners had to take care of the maintenance of the church building, the churchyards and so on. For this, the owner got the church's part of the tithe and other possible income from the church. If there is a net surplus, it becomes his private income as with all other businesses. In 1900, Professor Harald Westergaard conducted an investigation into the income of the churches in the rural areas.[4] He found a total gross income of 5.2 million DKK, distributed as shown in Table 1.

Table 1: Total income for priests in rural areas:

Type of Income	Total amount in million DKK
Tithe	2.30
Farming	1.24
Offerings	0.75
Capital income	0.44
Other	0.47
Total	5.20

Source: Stenbæk (1999, 20-21)

From these figures, it is possible to get a good indication of the total church's income. We know that the church tithe was the same as the priests' tithe; so, the total tithe in the rural area must be around 4.6 million DKK. The tithe was capitalised in relation to the tithe replacement in 1903 to a capital of 133 million DKK. It was capitalised by a factor of 25 in relation to the annual tithe. This means that the annual tithe in 1903 can be estimated to have been 5.3 million DKK. This suggests a tithe in the cities of 0.7 million DKK. This seems small, but the tithe was mainly an agricultural tax.

We know little about the costs of the church in the cities, but let us assume that the cost to priests and buildings per inhabitant was the same in the cities as in the rural area. The average wages for the priest were probably higher in the cities, and the churches more luxurious, but there was also a bigger number of members per priest and church. Around 60 percent of the population were living in the rural area[5], and if we wanted to estimate a total budget for the Folk Church, we could calculate the total cost by multiplying the figures from the rural area with 100/60 = 1.67. According to the Ministry of Ecclesiastical Affairs, the bishops and their administration today cost about 2 percent of the total cost of the church.[6] It seems reasonable to assume that this figure would have been considerably higher in 1900 (the different non-clergy staff has grown considerably since 1900), so let us assume it was 4 percent.

We know what the total tithe amounts to, and we can easily assume that there was no farm income in the cities. If the budget is balanced, we can calculate other income sources in the cities as a residual. The result is shown in Table 2.

Table 2: The total account for the Church around 1900, in million DKK:

Costs	Rural area	National
Priest	5.2	8.7
Building	2.3	3.8
Bishops	0.0	0.5
Total cost	7.5	13.0
Income		
Tithe	4,6	5,3
Farming	1,24	1,24
State paid bishops	0,0	0,5
Other income	1,66	5,96
Total income	7,5	13,0

Source: Calculations explained in the text.

Table 2 is, of course, very approximate, and such estimations are far from showing the exact figures. Nevertheless, two main conclusions seem obvious. The Folk Church had, at that time, little economic interaction with the state, and farming was far from being a dominating source of income (only 15-20 percent in the rural area, and less than 10 percent for the total church). The tithe is an important source of income, therefore, composing more than 40 percent of the total income. And, no doubt, the tithe had been even more important in earlier periods. However, by 1900, urbanisation had already been taking place for a number of decades.

The 1903-1919 period

The situation changed dramatically in the first few years after the turn of the century. The political regime in Denmark changed in 1901, and this was also followed by drastic changes in the organization of the economy of the established church. The farmer's party, Venstre, got political power in 1901, and in 1905, Det Radikale Venstre (the left wing of Venstre), which represented the rural smallholders, was established and gained considerable influence.

This means that taxes like the tithe, and land taxes (mainly paid by farmers), came to lose their good standing.

The tithe had already been considered an outdated form of tax for quite some time. It was originally a tax in kind, but by 1810, the first regulation of how to change it into a money payment had come about, but the rules were relatively unattractive. However, a law passed in 1852 made the change into paying the tithe as a monetary transaction mandatory. The translation of the volume of commodities into monetary value was set through an official list of prices ('Kapiteltakster'). In 1894, a process was started with the aim of abolishing the tithe. Instead, the farmers paid the monetised value of the future tithes. This was made mandatory by law in 1903 (see, for example, Warming 1930, 85-87).

The total value of the monetised tithe was, as mentioned, calculated as 25 times the annual tithe on the basis of the prices for the period 1892-1901. It means that the value is calculated on the assumption that the interest rate is 4 percent. The total amount was calculated to be 133 million DKK, corresponding to an annual tithe of 5.3 million DKK. The church recieved the amount, the farmers paid 18/25 of the amount and the state 7/25. The farmers could pay in cash, or with an interest rate of 4 percent for the following 55½ years (Larsen 1937, 252-253; Warming 1930, 86, Milthers and Christensen 1925 and many others).

This means that the church, in principle, got the full value of the tithe. Nevertheless, it was a problematic issue for the church. The calculation of the annual tithe was, as mentioned, calculated on the basis of the prices in 1892-1901 and, as can be seen in Table 3, this was a period with very low prices. In his textbook from 1885, the economist Professor William Scharling calculated the monetised value of the tithe on the basis of 1861-70 prices, and found them to come, not to 133 million DKK, but to 167 million DKK (Falbe-Hansen and Scharling 1885, 692).

The problem with the low prices was already known at the time when the reform was completed. The union of the clergy protested against using the price level for 1892-1901 (see Stenbæk 1999, 38-44 and 52-52).

Another indication of the fact that the elimination of the tithe was unattractive to the Folk Church can be seen in the church owners' reaction. Almost all the owners of the privately owned churches came to regard their ownership as unattractive, gave up the responsibility for the churches and changed the church's status so as to make them independent institutions. It was no longer good business to be a church owner (see Dübeck 2004, 210).

Table 3: Prices for the three main sorts of cereals (kapitaltakster). Kroner pr. tønde.

Period	Barley	Rye	Oats
1871-75	12.48	14.32	8.24
1876-80	11.88	13.21	7.85
1881-85	10.36	11.86	7.52
1886-90	9.56	9.88	6.88
1891-95	9.30	10.11	7.11
1896-00	9.41	9.92	6.92
1901-05	9.80	10.28	7.29
1906-10	10.80	11.31	7.40
1911-15	14.70	14.69	10.69

Source: Larsen (1937, 232).

The change of the tithe to a monetary capital started in 1907 and finished in 1918. This means that the amount which was fixed in nominal values was strongly hit by inflation, and as seen in Figure 1, the inflation during the World War I period of 1916-1920 was between 15 and 20 percent. This means that 100 DKK in January of 1915 was only worth 38 DKK by the end of December 1920.

P.G. Lindhardt describes the process in very vivid language, not underestimating the effect in the least:

> In Denmark, it was not a Marxist revolution but rather a liberal reform policy in relation to almost 400 years of tradition which, led by the farmers, liquidated the Church as an economic power – in favour of the actual rulers. In 1903, when the farmers won the principal victory over the Church, nobody could foresee the serious inflation of the next 60 years, nor could they have foreseen that the democratic and economic policy, starting with the law of Church councils and the elimination of the tithe, would make the separation of State and Church difficult. (translated from Lindhardt 1966, 30-31)

The other major change was the land reform of 1919, where the state tried to secure arable land from large landowners, and from the church, to distribute among the farm workers (Kærgård and Henriksen, 2014). For the priests and the state, this seemed like a win-win situation. The priests were less and less interested in farming, and the state needed farmland for smallholders and farm workers.

Figure 1: Danish Inflation Rate (1900-1930):

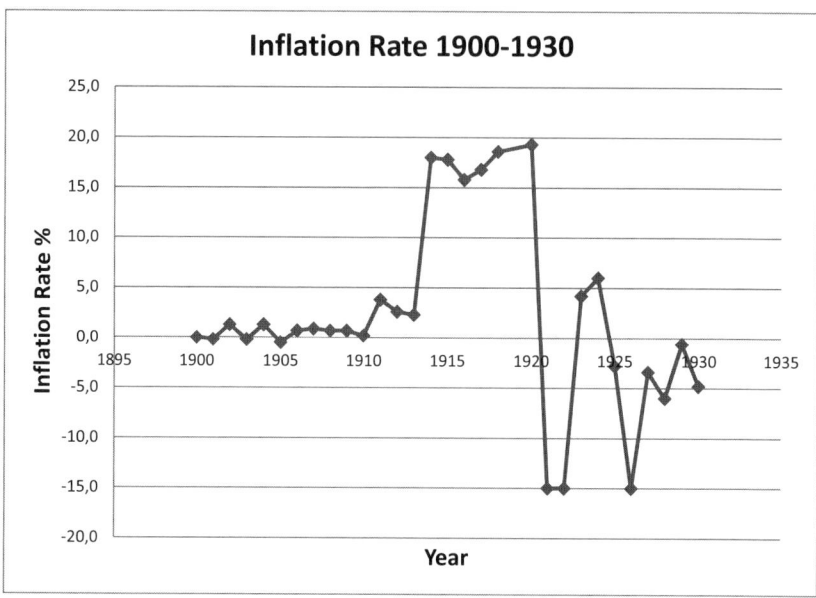

Source: Statistic Denmark (Consumer Price Index).

Around 1900, the system resulted in a considerable difference between the best and worst paid priests – Stenbæk (2003) suggested a range from 1,700 to 10,000 DKK a year. In 1878-79, a reallocation system was introduced, transferring resources from the wealthiest parishes to the poorest. Furthermore, many priests in the increasingly urbanised Denmark were neither qualified for nor interested in farm work; income for priests coming from farming was outdated. In fact, a number of priests and the chairman of their union expressed a wish to sell off the farmland, see Stenbæk (1999, 82-85). The consequence was a law being passed relating to priests' wages in 1913, so they came to be paid a wage according to objective criteria, such as seniority, independent of the income from the local farm and other local income, see Stenbæk, (1999, 63-69; 2003, 440).

The state was, by contrast, strongly interested in farmland. Since the late 1890s, securing some arable land for the farm workers was a political aim and, in 1909-1910 and 1913-1920, *Det Radikale Venstre* (the smallholders' party) took leadership of the government. They were strongly committed to gaining areas for smallholdings for farm workers. This was done through a number of laws culminating with the land reform of 1919.

In relation to the land from the priests' farms, the law determined that the Folk Church was forced to sell any land exceeding an area of 7 hectares per church farm for the first time, the position as priest was vacant. The money was given to the church council and the administration of the transactions was taken care of by the Ministry of Ecclesiastical Affairs.

How big an area these transactions deal with is questionable. Warming (1930, 200) estimates: 'about 20,000 hectares of good quality land from the big landowners and almost the same, but of slightly lower quality, from the priests' farms'. Stenbæk (2003, 441) suggests: 'In total 26,000 hectares of land on which a total of 3,825 smallholdings were established in 1928, of which 1,140 were on church areas; this included about 8-10,000 hectares of the priests' farms'. Møller (2006, 164-65) wrote: 'In 1934, when the transactions were almost finished, 10,122 hectares of priests' farmland were transformed into smallholdings'.

It is difficult to see that these transactions were in clear conflict with the interests of the Folk Church and the priests. Perhaps the price per hectare was a little too low because the sale was forced to take place at a given point in time, but the sale was demanded by a number of priests even before the law, and by the chairman of the union of the priests in 1910. The argument that the new monetary capital, in contrast to farm land, was hurt by inflation does not hold up; according to Figure 1, there was a rather high rate of deflation between 1921-1930.

In the public debate, and even sometimes in the scientific literature, the present system of state support for the established church – where the state pays 40 percent of the salaries of the priests – is seen as compensation for the public expropriation of church farmland. Two Danish bishops and also, it seems, the Minister of Ecclesiastical Affairs, presented this argument recently in the newspaper *Jyllandsposten* (Vibjerg 2016). This is, as explained in details above, wrong.[7]

An important law regarding the wages for priests was also adopted in 1919. This system with *fixed wages* and different wage groups, first introduced in the 1913 law, was then made permanent for the first time. A *national church tax* paid by all members of the church was introduced, and the different local payments for the members of the church were collected in a *local church tax*.[8] This system, along with a collectively agreed wage for priests, combined with a national and a local church tax, is still the backbone of the established Church in Denmark.

The 1920-1958 period

Even though the basic economic structure was determined with the law of 1919, a significant problem persisted. The priests' wages were relatively low. The phasing out of what was historically the main source of income for the church, the tithe, resulted in a drastic cut to the income of the church, as described above. Furthermore, the need for income was growing. The population was growing from 2.18 million inhabitants in 1890 to 3.54 million in 1930, a growth of 62 percent; and there was emigration from the rural to the urban areas. The number of inhabitants in Copenhagen was, for example, 367,262 in 1890 and 771,168 in 1930. There was a considerable need for new churches and priests.

The priests' union fought for 'reasonable' wages. The union argued that university-educated priests should have wages at the same level as other academics (for example university educated teachers in high schools). The wages for priests in the rural areas and young priests, in particular, were relatively low and the 'distress in the home of the priests' was a theme in the public debate. A clothes collection for poor priests' children was arranged in 1944-45, and a couple more such collections were arranged in the following years (Stenbæk 2003, 443).

Solving the problem was not seen as a matter of supporting the church in particular, nor was it seen as a part of ecclesiastical policy. Rather, it was a matter of supporting a group of inadequately paid people, whose wages had not followed the general economic growth of Danish society. The result was that even the communists (who were very critical of the established church and argued for a separation of church and state) voted in 1946 for the law to increase the wages of the priests. However, the issue of relatively low wages and the ailing economy of the Folk Church persisted.

The end solution, which was the completion of a process of development, starting with the temporary law determining priests' wages in 1913, was settled with a 1958 law for the priests' wages. For more about the developments between 1958 and 2013 to 1958, see Stenbæk (1999) and Christoffersen (2017). At that time, the Minister of Ecclesiastical Affairs was the social democrat, Bodil Koch (1903-1972). She became an educated theologian in 1929 and was married to a professor of theology, Hal Koch, a central figure in the Danish debate in the 1940s. They had five children in the 1930s, and she was a housewife in this period. Bodil Koch, however, became increasingly involved in the public debate as a spokesman for women's involvement in public life, among other things. She was elected to Parliament in 1947, and became a member of the government and Minister of Ecclesiastical Affairs for the first time in 1950, but the government lost power a few months later. Koch was made Minister of Ecclesiastical Affairs again between 1953-66 and Minister of Culture between 1966-68. She had strong feelings in favour of an open and liberal Folk Church, and was known worldwide for smoking cigars and for frank discussion with both the American Foreign Minister John Foster Dulles as well as the President of USSR, Nikita Khrushchev. This strong lady enacted a radical solution to these economic problems. She got a wage law passed in the Parliament in 1958, which placed the priest in the general public wage system of academic officials. Herein, the state paid 60 percent of their wages. This is still the system in Denmark today, albeit with some amendments. The 60 percent was changed to 40 percent in 1984, and the number of priests was increased instead, see Stenbæk (2003, 443).

One relevant question is why this arrangement was settled upon in favour of a more logical system, where the state pays for the maintenance of national cultural heritage and the wages of the clergy are paid by the church members. If the church needs money (as it did in the period between 1903-1958), it seems logical that church taxes be raised instead of giving publically funded support financed by the general taxes. This alternative arrangement seems not to have been discussed at the time. The reason might be that, even if there were a more principal discussion of the relation between church and state (a number of the political parties, for example the dominating Social

Democrats, supported a separation of state and church in their program), it would have had very minor economic implications in a society where almost everybody was a member of the Folk Church, see Table 4.

Table 4: Share of the population being members of the established Church

Year	Membership %
1870	99.2
1880	99.1
1890	98.4
1901	98.7
1911	98.5
1921	97.9
1974	94.3

Source: 1870-1921 Danish Census, 1974 calculated from number of Folk Church tax payers.

The issue of whether the wages of the clergy should be financed by the church tax or by the general taxes might not have been an issue at a time when 98 percent of the population were members of the established church. Since 97-98 percent of the population paid church tax, very few were interested in whether that tax was a general or a church tax. The social democrats were afraid of conflicts with the religious part of the population. This fear came to be known by the saying: *'if we get into trouble with the sanctimonious, hell breaks loose'*. Why risk 'hell breaking loose' for a principal position with small practical implications? Indeed, a Folk Church without a governing board and with an economy entwined with the public budget can be seen as a guarantee against a politically active Christianity.

A number of attempts since 1958 to shift the Folk Church's economy towards a more logical structure (for example with fixed public support of the Folk Church's cultural activities) failed for the same reason, see Kirkeministeriet (2009).

Conclusion

The economy of the established church and the Danish state are intertwined in a complicated and obviously illogical way. Church members pay, for example, for a considerable part of the conservation of a national cultural heritage and the state pays for a significant part of the Christian services. This can only be explained by historical traditions. But the historical reason for this intertwinement is not – as is often suggested – the expropriation of farmland belonging to the Folk Church in the early 20th century. The state did take over farmland from the church, but that was not contrary to the wishes and interests of the church, and it is unlikely to be the cause of the economic distress of the established church in the first half of the 20th century.

In contrast, the monetisation of the tithe in 1903 turned out to be very important – and unfortunate – for the church. The economy of the church was already in distress before the turn of the century. Monetisation was put into legislation when the farmers' party, *Venstre*, come to power. The monetised sum was to be paid by *Venstre's* voters and by the state, which gave *Venstre* an incentive to set a fairly low monetisation conversion sum. This was done by using prices ('kapiteltakster') from crops in a ten-year period where the crop prices were at their lowest. And finally, the monetisation of the tithe was hit by inflation in 1914 to 1920. In contrast, the monetisation of farmland in 1919 was positively affected by deflation.

However, neither the monetisation of the tithe in 1903, nor the selling of the farmland from 1919, can explain the current intertwinement of the state and the established church. The historical explanation for the illogical intertwinement must instead be drawn from the fact that the Folk Church drew its membership from 98 percent of the population. This was a situation where it was unimportant in practice whether the member fee of the church or the general taxes was footing the bills.

In this system, priests were seen as but one of many kinds of public officials. In the long process of change from 1913 to 1958, when fighting for giving this group of academics a reasonable wage, the politicians across almost all parties seemed to have considered it easier to support the priests' wages through taxes than to enact a complicated change in the church taxes. A rise in the local Folk Church taxes could be complicated, it would involve many decision makers and a relatively big rise in the national church tax would be necessary, because the tax is relatively small. In contrast, the necessary changes to the general taxes were very small. In 1958, Bodil Koch preferred to let the Danish parliament decide to give public support to the priests' wages instead of letting the rise in wages be financed by a rise in the national church tax (as Minister of Ecclesiastical Affairs, she could actually have enacted this unilaterally, by her own authority). On the other hand, a situation where the church alone paid for everything – paying fully for the priests and for the conservation of the cultural heritage, for the official registration of inhabitants and for all the cemeteries – would also seem unjust. So, a logical separation of the state and the Folk Church's budget might have seemed a complicated and unnecessary process in 1958.

References

Christensen, Peter 2006. 'Folkekirken og Finansloven', in Jens Holger Schjørring and Jens Torkild Bak (eds.) *Udfordringer til Folkekirken; Kirken – Staten – Folket*, Frederiksberg: Anis, 53-78.

Christoffersen, Lisbet 2010. 'State, Church and Religion in Denmark', in L. Christoffersen, K.Å. Modéer and S. Andersen (eds.), *Law & Religion in the 21st Century – Nordic Perspectives*, Copenhagen: DJØF Publishing, 145-161.

Christoffersen, Lisbet 2015. 'A Long Historical Path towards Transparency, Accountability and Good Governance: On Financing Religions in Denmark', in Francis Messner (ed.), *Public Funding of Religions in Europe*, Surrey: Ashgate, 125-147.

Christoffersen, Lisbet 2017. 'Kirken i Samfundet – Fri og Lige Adgang til Vorherre. Kirken og Retten 1901-2017', in Niels Henrik Gregersen and Carsten Bach-Nielsen (eds.), *Reformationen i Dansk Kirke og Kultur*, vol. 3 1914-2017, Odense: Syddansk Universitetsforlag, 195-228.

David, Paul A. 1985. 'Clio and the Economics of QWERTY', *American Economic Review*, 75/2 332-337.

Dübeck, Inger 2004. 'Den Retslige Regulering af Kirkernes økonomi i de Nordiske Lande', *Kirkeretsantologi 2004*, Selskab for Kirkeret, København and Århus, earlier published in *Zeitschrift für evangelisches Kirchenrecht* 47 (2002), 369-393.

Falbe-Hansen, V. and Will. Scharling 1885. *Danmarks Statistik*, Copenhagen: Forlagsbureauet i Kjøbenhavn

Finansministeriet, Kirkeministeriet, Stiftsadministrationen, Danmarks Provsteforening, Landsforeningen af Menighedsrådsmedlemmer og Kommunernes Landsforening 1995. *Folkekirkens økonomi*, Copenhagen: Schultz Information.

Kirkeministeriet 2009. Omlægning af Statens Tilskud til Folkekirken til Bloktilskud, Betænkning 1511, Copenhagen: Kirkeministeriet.

Kjems, Sidsel *Church Tax: Tax or membership fee?* (in preparation)

Kærgård, Niels 1997. Tre økonomiske Professorers Teologi, *Kirkehistoriske Samlinger 1997*, 129-197.

Kærgård, Niels and Thorkild Davidsen 1998. 'Harald Westergaard: From Young Pioneer to Established Authority', in Warren J. Samuels (ed.) *European Economists of the Early 20th Century*, Vol.1, Cheltenham: Edward Elgar, 347-365.

Kærgård, Niels and Ingrid Henriksen 2014. 'Jordreformer som Socialpolitisk Instrument: Landarbejderne og Husmandsbevægelsen', in Niels Finn Christiansen, Jon Kvist, Niels Kærgård and Klaus Petersen (eds.), *På kryds og tværs i velfærdstatens univers – Festskrift til Jørn Henrik Petersen*, Odense: Syddansk Universitetsforlag, 197-215.

Larsen, O.H. 1937. *Landbrugets Historie og Statistik*, 3. Copenhagen: Den Kgl. Veterinær- og Landbohøjskole.

Lindhardt, P.G. 1966. 'Tiden 1901-1965', Vol. VIII in N.K. Andersen and P.G. Lindhardt (eds.), *Den Danske Kirkes Historie*, Vol. I-VIII, Copenhagen: Gyldendal.

Milthers, Vilhelm and Otto Christensen 1925. *Det Danske Landbrugs Historie I: Danmarks Jord*, Copenhagen: G.E.C. Gads Forlag.

Møller, Jes Fabricius 2006. 'Folkekirkens økonomi og Staten – et Historisk Rids', *Dansk Kirketidende* 2006/10, 162-167.

Severinsen, P. 1920. *Folkekirkens Ejendoms-Historie*, Copenhagen: Selskabet for Danmarks Kirkehistorie, G.E.C. Gad.

Stenbæk, Jørgen 2003. 'Folkekirkens Ejendomsforhold og økonomi – Historisk Belyst', *Kirkehistorieske Samlinger 2003*, 123-148, reprinted in L. Christoffersen, H. Gammeltoft-Hansen and T. Jørgensen (eds.), *Kirkeretsantologi 2004*, København and Århus: Selskab for Kirkeret.

Stenbæk, Jørgen 1999. *Præsternes Forening Gennem 100 år*, Copenhagen: Den Danske Præsteforenings Forlag.

Udvalget om en mere sammenhængende og moderne styringsstruktur for folkekirken 2014. *Folkekirkens Styre*, Betænkning 1544, Copenhagen: Kirkeministeriet.

Vibjerg, Thomas 2016. 'Ny minister åbner for et opgør med 100 års praksis'. *Jyllandsposten,* december 6th 2016.

Warming, Jens 1930. *Danmarks Erhvervs- og Samfundsliv*, Copenhagen: G.E.C. Gads Forlag.

Notes

1. The Government Program 'Sammen for fremtiden', June 2015, see the Prime Minister's web-page. http://www.stm.dk/_p_14164.html
2. Path dependency indicates that actual phenomena are caused by passed events. A very simple example is the layout of letters on a modern computer keyboard (QWERTY ...) which can only be explained by the early history of mechanical typewriters more than a hundred years ago, see David (1985).
3. Who do not need to be members of the Folk Church.
4. Harald Westergaard (1853-1936) was an internationally known economist and statistician with a considerable ecclesiastical engagement. He was a central figure in establishing *The Copenhagen Church Foundation* in the 1890s; a foundation which built a considerable number of churches in the new working class districts in Copenhagen, see Kærgård and Davidsen (1998) and Kærgård (1997).
5. http://danmarkshistorien.dk/perioder/det-unge-demokrati-1848-1901/befolkningsudviklingen
6. The Danish National Budget of 2014 (Finanslov for 2014), indicates that the total costs of The Ministry of Ecclesiastical Affairs is 81.9 million DKK, and the wages of the bishops 9.9 million DKK. Of the account of 'Fællesfonden' (the Folk Church's central foundation) for 2013, it follows that the bishops' administration ('stiftsadministrationen') cost 76.1 million DKK. Taken together, all this comes to approximately 168 million DKK and constitutes about 2 percent of the church's total budget of around 8 million DKK.
7. Even if the state has simply confiscated the area in 1919 without paying for it, that would constitute an insufficient argument to justify the actual state support to the wages of the priests. We are talking about 10,000 hectares. If the Folk Church still had this area today, it would be worth about 1.5 billion DKK (Statistics Denmark), since the most recent price of farmland is 143,000 DKK/hectare. Compare this with the public support for ecclesiastical service-oriented activities which amounted to 724 million DKK (Ministry of Ecclesiastical Affairs 2017). This means that, in order to justify the public support, the land capital needs to yield a return of about 50 percent, or 10 times above what is normal.
8. The *national* Folk Church tax ('Landskirkeskatten') and the *local* Folk Church tax ('lokal kirkeskat') have always been called 'taxes' even though the payment is not mandatory and only paid by members of the Folk Church. The church taxes are calculated and collected by the national tax authorities, along with all other taxes, such as the municipality tax. The church tax revenue is then transferred to church parishes and to the national ecclesiastical affairs. Whether it is better to call it a 'tax' or a 'member fee' is a complicated question, which shall not be discussed here. But this is mainly a matter of how to define a 'tax', see Kjems (in preparation).

5. Theological Accommodation to Individualisation in the Folk Church

Hans Raun Iversen

The core of this chapter will be an analysis of the theological development of the Danish Evangelical Lutheran Church (the Folk Church) in its process of adaption to individualisation. This analysis builds on research and documentation formerly published in Danish, most comprehensively in Iversen 2018. It has two main parts. Firstly, there is a brief outline of the main features of the work and theology of the Folk Church in relation to the existential dimension of current Danish culture with which the Folk Church must cope. To this is added an account of some of the negative aspects of the organization of the Folk Church, being bound to the state. This is followed by an outline of the missional dimensions that are, more or less firmly, built into the self-understanding of the Folk Church today and its forms of work. The second part is a historical analysis of the three theological paradigms that have taken over, more or less sequentially, during the course of the last century.

The work and theological self-understanding of the Folk Church

The Folk Church and its kind of Christianity

The Dutch professor of missiology, Stefan Paas, correctly notes:

> Some Christianities […] have developed a high degree of resistance and self-confidence, allowing them to maintain a distinct identity, even in a changing world. Others have proven to be capable of spreading their own kind of Christianity around the world, thus becoming actors in the process of globalisation. Eastern Orthodox Churches may be examples of the first category, while evangelical Protestantism is a clear example of the second. (Paas 2015, 25)

The Folk Church belongs to a third category of churches: those who develop new forms of work as part of an old national church in a new world, even though they may not contribute a lot to world Christianity. Being an outstanding example of this type of church, the Folk Church is much better at molding itself to fit the Danish context than at making an impact worldwide.

Historically, state and society in Denmark have built on Christian ideas and norms, as there was no Denmark before the arrival of Christianity. Today – after secularisation – these ideas are still at work, albeit in secularised forms, in the basic attitudes of important institutions of society as well as in the mentality of the Danes (see Chapter 3). From a historical point of view, you can say that we have a 'Christian society' where a majority of the people tend to label themselves 'Christians', while a growing minority do not do so. However, there is an unfortunate form of intimidation directed at minorities when the right wing government of 2015 labelled Denmark 'a Christian society' in its basic policy document. In this way, Christianity is used as a political hostage in pressing for secular, nationalist politics.

An important step in the secularisation of Denmark is the continuing dissolution of the triangle between state, people and church. One sees this in the modernisation of Denmark, away from an absolute monarchy with a fully state governed church. A decisive turning point was obviously the free constitution of 1849, granting formal freedom of religion to all citizens. Today, freedom of religion without social, or other forms of, pressure is realised almost all over Denmark. Yet, Denmark is still far from treating religious communities equally. The state Ministry of Ecclesiastical Affairs is still the supreme administrator and Parliament is the legislator of the Folk Church. In its daily life, however, the Folk Church works as a free church, a part of civil society, run by its employees, boards and members. The nationalist-minded majority within Parliament want to keep the established bonds between church and state, whereas a majority of the people (according to the most recent surveys) want the state to introduce not only freedom of religion, but also a more reasonable equality of status between the religions in Denmark (Christoffersen et al. 2012). Christianity in and around the Folk Church is therefore not what, for example, Americans label 'Christendom' with a merger between state power, culture and religion. Danish Christianity is a combination of Culture Christianity and Church Christianity, kept alive by the work of the Folk Church (Iversen 2018).

The Folk Church obviously has the basic Lutheran signs of a church (preaching of the Gospel and administration of baptism and the Lord's

Supper). To better understand the Folk Church's work it is, however, more fruitful to consider it as a working model of Christian mission among the Danes. In its theological and Biblical sense, Christianity is found in Denmark in the form of an orientation towards Christ and, even, Christ dwelling in the hearts of people through their faith (Ephesians 3:17). When this orientation towards Christ in its many forms is found in many people who meet together, you can begin to talk about a church in terms of concrete gatherings (using a better word than 'congregation'). You will find such fluctuating gatherings everywhere in and around the 2,354 church buildings of the Folk Church in its 2,123 parishes. Annually, there are approximately 500,000 gatherings in the Folk Church with approximately 20 million participants. 70-75 percent of the people of Denmark participate in one sort of church gathering or another each year, most often attending funerals, baptisms, confirmations or weddings. Only ten percent participate in a Sunday service for the sake of doing so on an annual basis. two percent (approximately 100,000 persons) may be in church on a given Sunday, whereas ten percent will attend in various activities throughout a week (Iversen 2018).

The Folk Church gladly accepts that anybody can come and take part in its practices and rituals. People are not asked to change or convert in any way before participating in the life of the church. This is due to three basic characteristics of the Folk Church: 1) The historical relations between church and people, where church attendance was a formal *duty*, has been changed to participation being a right for everybody, only with restrictions for non-members on weddings and sometimes funerals; 2) 75 percent of the population are paying members of the church, thus they have already paid for any service they may receive when they come to the church and the pastor; and 3) The theological heritage, especially from N.F.S. Grundtvig (1783-1872), means that the Folk Church has a uniquely strong theology of creation (Iversen 2017b), meaning that all human beings are literally created in the image of God as much as any Christian person can ever be. Therefore, everybody must be received in the same way with no forms of discrimination at the doorstep.

The Folk Church has a special function as the main (and often the only) provider for Danish people of possibilities for participation in – and learning from – Christian practices. Even so, from the basic theological perspective of the Folk Church, Church Christianity has no superior status compared to Cultural Christianity or other forms of culture found in the country.

While still living with at least the illusion of a uniform culture until 50 years ago, the Folk Church was characterised by tolerant roominess, often practised as repressive tolerance, as if to say: 'When my group wants its freedom to do and express what we like in the church, we have better let you and your group do the same, even though we don't like you'. Today, in a culturally and religiously pluralistic situation, more and more Folk Church Christians have come to value the theological multiplicity found in the Folk Church. Realising that there are many ways of pointing to and living with Christ, Gregersen (2015) talks about this as 'generous orthodoxy'. Increasingly, it is being accepted that the Folk Church is a part of culture. This means that all sorts of cultural forms can be used in the Folk Church, as long as this is done in a qualified way that points to Christ. Thus, the Folk Church is, at one and the same time, culture and mission work.

Matters of confession and church order are becoming – in a good Lutheran manner – more and more secondary to the mission of the Folk Church. We might say that the Folk Church, like the best of missionaries from the 20th century (cf. Kastfelt 2013), is firm in terms of moral and human attitudes (e.g. standing for equal treatment of all people), but dogmatically flexible (e.g. open to new expressions of Christianity fit for the culture of the present people).

The people in a post-secular society
The process of secularisation has left the Danes with a post-secular society. On the surface, Danes live 'Between a Rock and a Hard Place' (Graham 2013). That is, between old confessional Lutheranism and an equally dogmatically anti-religious public space, where religion is supposed to be kept out of politics, social work, education, the press and so on. There is, however, a religious dimension in most areas of society because it is embedded in Cultural Christianity. And, at the same time, Denmark has a number of very different minority religious groups fighting to make themselves visible. Most importantly, Danes are existentially and religiously alert whenever faced with questions and challenges that go beyond the rhythm and horizon of their privileged daily lives.

The vocabulary of Charles Taylor can be used to summarise ample quantitative and qualitative surveys and indicators of the development. Secular life in Denmark – as in much of the Western world – means living with cross-pressuring horizons of existential meaning in life. Danes, according to, for example, ten recent interview-projects involving cancer-patients[1], are at one and the same time various combinations of naturalists (e.g. believing in Darwin's theories) humanists (putting the individual at the centre) new spiritualists (going for whatever may help) and Cultural Christians (with cultural norms from Christianity). Some are even Church Christians at times! Whatever Danes go for or believe in, they do so in ambivalent or conditional ways. And this is really, as Taylor argues, the core of what secularity means (Taylor 2007). At the same time, Danes feel strongly about being authentic to themselves. To be true to oneself has become the first ethical demand (cf. Taylor 1991).

Furthermore, Danes are more focused on what they think of as their personal experiences than on what science and other authorities may tell them. That means that Danes easily close themselves off to the messages of doctors and preachers if these do not support their feelings of what is authentic and what they have experienced themselves. If Danes are believers, they are weak believers. Most Danes (75 percent) are Folk Church members and pay their church tax. Church membership is important not only to the economy of the Folk Church and its ways of working. To the individual, being a member, or not, of the church is an identity marker. Danes, however, belong to the church without believing much in that belonging. Most Danes continue being members as they are most at ease with that.

'For Anything to be real it must be local' said the famous English author and journalist Gilbert Keith Chesterton early in the 20th century. There is still a lot of sense to that sentence. At the same time, it is to a considerable extent becoming modified. It is not just globalisation, the internet and virtual reality that are corroding Chesterton's rule, but also the fluctuating lives we live. The German theologian Uta Pohl-Patalong, in 2006, edited an important book called *Von der Ortskirche zu kirchlichen Orten* (From the church of the place to churchy places), pointing out what has become increasingly evident in Denmark, too: that people do not only 'church' *when* they 'church', but also *where* they 'church'. Two thirds of the church visits in Denmark take place outside the parish of the visitors. Moreover, when asked, only one third can see a special quality in visiting or using their local church and congregation, or having a special relation to their local pastor. Danes visit churches in the same way as other cultural institutions, such as theatres, cinemas, museums and concert halls. You do not just go to the local place, but rather to the place where you expect there to be something of special interest for you. This tendency is not found only in towns, but also in rural areas where regional churches with more resources than the village churches attract much of the activity within the area (Felter 2015).

The overall development is clear: the remnants of the feudal and early democratic times emphasising the local place are fading out. Along with the English historian Graeme Smith (2008), we can argue that Danes have come 'back to normal', where people seek the great temples while leaving the small synagogues behind. In Denmark, until the Reformation, parish borders did not matter as much as they came to matter during the time of the Lutheran State Church 1536-1849, where people were bound to their local parishes, as pastors and parishes worked as a means of controlling the people, which the king wanted to have. During the time of the revivals in the late 19th century, the ideas of local congregations and the local fellowship of believers were fused with the parish system. That ended up with the idea that a real church must be a building where the same people sit in the same seats Sunday after Sunday, as in a synagogue in the diaspora. This sort of church practice is soon to disappear. Today, people – as in Medieval times – come whenever they feel a need to and wherever it is most fitting for them.

Danes live with an apparent contradiction: we have more people today coming into churches at various occasions than ever during the last 50 years. At the same time, the so-called core congregations are dying out. This is visible in the European Value Studies and confirmed by local observations. Stable core congregations are only found in a minority of the churches. That does not necessarily leave the churches without volunteer co-workers. A key illustration here is the 33 newly opened night churches, where people come and go. Some persons do volunteer for a time to do what needs to be done for the night church to work.

More people come to church occasionally just as they attend cultural events occasionally. They may come with spiritual desires and a wish for meaning in their lives. They also may come to gain a little spiritual support and practical accompaniment at certain, often difficult phases in their lives. The Folk Church sees its ministry today as being a church with and for such people. Let us conclude by illustrating this with reference to some of the empirical evidence collected by Christine Tind Johannessen-Henry for her PhD thesis (2013). In a survey among (former) cancer patients undergoing rehabilitation, Johannessen-Henry asked candidates: 'Do you agree with this: "It makes me feel secure that I can come to the church if I need it."' She got the following answers:

Answers	Not at all	A little	To some extent	Quite a bit	A lot	No reply
Percentage	17	17	18	15	19	14

In her interviews, Johannessen-Henry got statements like these:

> 'The church is where you do not have to explain about yourself. It is a free room. Just knowing that the church is there is having a free room. It is a consolation for me. It means something to me'.

> 'It makes the small hairs on my neck stand up when the organ goes wild, and the choir, yes the choir that makes me sing out loudly – it is wonderful when I can hide myself in the singing crowd, I am crazy about singing'.

> 'We went to listen to Messiah in Our Lady of Copenhagen. We came into the church and I looked up to Thorvaldsen's Christ. All right, then there was this prayer to Our Lord: "Thank you that I am here." That was wonderful, that was the only thing that I managed to focus on – and then all that beautiful music'.

Weaknesses of the Folk Church

The similarities in attitudes between church and people does not mean that the Folk Church has no weaknesses. In important ways, a national leadership elected by the church members could make the church more fit for its mission than state politicians and bureaucrats are capable of. It is always a potential disadvantage for a church to be linked to powers and authorities, as the church is called to mission among the weak and the poor. Even though the slogan among politicians is that the church should not interfere with politics, the same politicians, not least the nationalists, often take the church hostage to promote their politics, attempting to control rebellious churches and pastors (Lindberg 2015).

Many discussions are difficult to carry on with the state as supreme church leadership. Here are some examples of the lack of inflexibility of the former state church with its supreme state administration: 1) church taxes cannot be legally spent outside the borders of the diocese (e.g. in foreign mission); 2) a much-needed reform of the relationship between church membership and baptism does not seem to fit the state; 3) an alternative robe for pastors in services, replacing the now 400 years old black bourgeois dress, cannot be negotiated by the state leadership; and 4) a renewed formulation of the church's basic teaching, which has not been altered since the 1536 adoption of Melanchthon's *Confessio Augustana* from 1530, is unthinkable, as the secular state cannot agree on a creed.

Since 2003, when parliament decided that the state cannot interfere with the use of 85 percent of the church tax-based budget, which is administered by the local congregational boards, many possibilities for local church development have opened up. Furthermore, two direct advantages of the present state-church relations are apparent. First, hard decisions that have to be taken (e.g. regarding female pastors and homosexual marriages) are solved rather quickly as Parliament, following opinion surveys, cut through the theological fights. Such fights would be harder to bring to an end in churches led by a synod, church council or a bunch of bishops. Second, church taxes collected together with state and municipality taxes are the most stable and secure system of church funding, as all budgeted money is automatically available each year (see Chapter 3). Certainly, both of these advantages might continue to work after a reasonable negotiation of new relations between state and church. Disadvantages such as the ones mentioned above might, however, disappear.

Strengths of the Folk Church

It can be argued that the Folk Church is a church in mission, or better, an appropriate model for mission in Denmark (Iversen 2008). I shall elaborate this through seven points that have emerged from comparative studies of seven old national churches in Northern Europe (Woodhead and Iversen, in preparation).

1. The Folk Church is to a great extent a kenotic, self-emptying, church. Throughout its history, the Folk Church has been exploited and/or exhausted itself contributing to the building of society. During the last 150 years, the Inner Mission as well as the Grundtvigian revival movements are clear examples of that. Due to the church tax, the Folk Church is among the most well-off churches in the world. The Folk Church has, however, no major fortune; almost the entirety of its 'property' is the self-owned buildings used for its work; therefore the Folk Church did not become poorer because of the financial crises following 2008, as was the case with churches having investments in banks and businesses. The Folk Church only has what it gets from its members from year to year. Moreover, it spends this money to serve the people. It is not easy to prove, but it may be hypothesised that a church whose economy depends on 75 percent of the population is bound to treat the people very well, in order that people feel they get what they pay for and thus stay on as members. This may be an important background to the fact that the Folk Church is at the forefront among the most trusted churches in Europe, according to European Value Studies (Andersen and Lüchau 2011).
2. The kenotic style is in line with the church's theological view of itself as a church. The church is nothing in itself, it is only a church in so far as it offers the best possible access to Christian practices that can bring people closer to Christ. The church is by no means a mediator between the individual and God. The church, however, offers members and non-members a way of orienting their lives. This is so across all church dimensions (even, quite literally, from the way in which church buildings are facing east, where Paradise was placed and from where Christ shall return). In all that it does, the Folk Church invites people to join in with Christian practices and reflections and to take home in their hearts, minds and bodies whatever they can. That is so with: hymn singing, liturgy, prayers, scripture reading, sermons, baptism, the Lords Supper, blessings, rites of passage services, teaching in churches and schools, coffee fellowships, communal dinners, baby hymn singing, hymn singing with persons suffering from dementia, God and spaghetti services, children's work, choirs for all ages, gospel singing, pilgrimage, pastoral care for soldiers, those admitted to hospitals and prisons, preg-

nant women and new mothers, religious dialogues, social and diaconal work for many sorts of groups with special needs and so on.

3. The Folk Church has a rather firm theological foundation. As it is with the Trinitarian God, so things must be with the church: everything is shared in unity in the life of the Trinity. What is for some is for all. Words and deeds are two sides of the same life of Jesus Christ. So it is with the church. The Folk Church must be transparent in its theology as it is in its administration. There are no (or only few) bureaucratic secrets hidden from the people. Using a biblical term, churches must be present in society as both salt and light (Matthew 5:12-15). The Folk Church prioritises to being a light with a good message to the people. Moreover, it strives to be present among and for people, not limiting itself in any way to caring for those who already have good contact to the church.

4. The Folk Church first and foremost wants to be the 'salt' in its society. It goes for being present all over in society and especially in existentially-open situations (e.g. rites of passage, national and local celebrations, personal, local and national catastrophes and so on) and common places (e.g. schools, universities, hospitals, jails, armies, festivals and so on). Therefore, the Folk Church is open to join and cooperate with all sorts of bodies and agencies in society in order to be present in the existential dimensions of the life of people in Denmark. The Folk Church is open to all sorts of people, and willing to come to all sorts of people whenever possible and needed. The Folk Church has open boundaries towards society. Theologically, the Folk Church argues that the whole world is God's, Christ died for all, and God's work is done outside church as well as within it. Regular church attendance is not necessary for all. For those doing God's work in the world, the church may act as a filling station during occasional visits. In this way, the Folk Church may be labelled a societal church rather than an ecclesial church (Woodhead and Iversen, in preparation).

5. When studying the Folk Church as part of Danish church research, we do not pay special attention to congregations or to church Christians. We study church and people and the relationship between the two. What matters in the Folk Church is the living interaction (*vekselvirkning*) between church and people, to use the expression of the 19th

century church father Grundtvig. Working on development in the Folk Church is not about congregational formation but about local church development. When the Danish Church Fund (*Kirkefondet*) offers programs of Local Church Development, it does not include a survey of the local people as if they were the target group for the mission of the church. The emphasis is on focus groups – or so-called listening round tours – where the people who are themselves members of the church can consider what they want to do with and in their own church. The tendency today is that if people are not taking part as active participants and co-creators, then there is no church. If people do not feel at home in the church, if they do not experience the church as *their* church as much as the church of the parish board and those employed by the church, then the church is not a Folk Church in a proper way. A Folk Church like the Danish one aims to be a church by the people, for the people, towards the people, in support of the people, on the premises of the people and driven by the people.

6. The church is performing mission, whatever it does, i.e. it is crossing frontiers and borders. Like Jesus, the Folk Church is always moving against borderlines, between faith and non-faith, between rich and poor, healthy and sick, supposedly good people and supposedly bad people, weak and strong – as a gift as well as a challenge to everybody. At its best, the Folk Church is a host for everybody, and at the very same time a guest in the lives of all sorts of people. People coming to the church as guests may soon experience themselves as hosts who take care of others. People acting as hosts are doing very little if they do not listen to the lives of other people, thereby becoming guests in their lives and homes. Literally speaking, Denmark's 78 year old queen, Margrethe, with her bad knees will kneel at the Lord's table next to most ill-smelling drunkard in town and they will help one another to get up on their feet again after having received the very same blood and body of Christ. This is a witness to the essence of Christianity.

7. After some decades of tension between the revivalist groups and the majority of non-revivalist Danes, the Folk Church has had an increasingly fruitful interaction between Cultural Christians, Church Christians and Charismatic Christians (revivalists and other burning souls), especially since the Second World War. At almost all events in the

church, from funerals to board meetings, you will find the three groups represented, and most often in respectful cooperation and exchange. Denmark has 300 migrant churches with all sorts of backgrounds, mostly African and Asian. Many are charismatic, including some with strong prosperity theology, where faith is believed to be rewarded with progress in your personal life. In 2012, 50 Folk Churches, 10 Lutheran Mission houses and 53 free churches hosted a migrant church. One migrant church has so far obtained status as an electoral congregation inside the Folk Church. The discussion for the time being focuses on whether the non-Lutheran migrant Christians in Denmark should be invited to be members of the Folk Church. This would be in line with the principle of the Folk Church being open to and embracing everybody who wants to stay in contact with the Folk Church.

Of course, these seven points of strength are not always practised all across Denmark, nor in all parts of the life of the Folk Church. Still, the Folk Church, its 13,000 lay board members and 10,000 employees are, united in seeing these points as ideals for its work. In addition, this is to a great extent also what the Danish people, members and non-members, expect from their church – and the reason why they have such high trust in the Folk Church (Iversen 2018).

Three theological paradigms in the Folk Church 1914-2017: Piety, preaching and participation

In volume III of the new history of the continuing significance of the Lutheran Reformation in the Danish church and society, covering the period 1914-2017 and focusing on the basic theological self-understanding of the Folk Church during the last century, I portrayed the paradigms of the Folk Church in the following terms: communication, democratisation and church life (Iversen 2017a). Analysing various sources, including the main contributions on ecclesiology and priorities within church life in the ten most important church periodicals and yearbooks, I came to see three radically different theological paradigms: piety, preaching and participation; with one, little by little, taking over from the other sequentially during the period. At the same time, remnants of the former paradigms are always kept alive – and allowed – around the country.

During and between the two World Wars, the theological emphasis was on personal piety. To be a real Christian, you must feel the seriousness of your conversion, revival and your fellowship with other congregational Christians. This is the centre from which you can approach the Bible and the church, and perhaps everything. The revival movements touched less than one third of Danes, who were at that time practically all members of the church. Even so, these movements did set the tone for theology and church life for some decades thereafter. The word 'congregation' (*menighed*) was not used in Denmark before the revival in the 19th century (and among the few pietists in the 18th century). The word 'church' meant a building, and Christianity was labelled 'the Religion of the King' (e.g. in the Danish Law from 1683). By 1912, revival terminology had taken over and the new law on permanent parish boards of 1912 introduced the practice wherein new board members promise to work for the 'life and growth of the congregation', which at that time meant the living (revival) congregation. During the same year, in a new ritual for baptism, the baptised babies were said to be 'incorporated into the believing congregation'. This ritual, which has many other problematic aspects, was only revised at one passage in the bishop's liturgy reform from 1992, as the word 'believing' was deleted! To illustrate the core point of the theological paradigm in the Folk Church operating until World War II, I shall quote from the leading Grundtvigian free congregation pastor Morten Larsen (1851-1936):

> What makes a man a groom? A bride, if he can win her. What makes a man a pastor? A congregation, if he can win one ... A pastor becomes pastor when the congregation becomes congregation for him ... the more intimately he lives together with the congregation and the better the living interaction between him and the congregation, the better a pastor he will be. (Larsen, in Iversen 2017a, 129)

Where the key word in the first period was piety, the decisive word after the Second World War and until the turn of the millennium was preaching (*forkyndelse*). In that period, Danish theology in general learnt more from Rudolf Bultmann than from Karl Barth[2]. Nonetheless, the most quoted slogan during the period was provided by Karl Barth: 'Theology must be conducted because of the need to preach next Sunday'. Approximately half of the pastors of the Folk Church in this period would stick to their work of duty: Sunday services, church rituals, teaching for confirmation and some pastoral care. Their claim would be that churches or pastors doing more than this are 'activists', who have no understanding of the Gospel as articulated in preaching and – even worse – seem to attempt to save themselves by doing 'good deeds'.

A special Danish edition of Luther and Karl Barth's theologies of the Word of God became the centre of everything – pointing to the Sunday sermon as the one important thing within the church. Put more positively, the pastors of this generation were busy relating the gospel to the new secular era, which took over quite speedily after the Second World War. This eradicated many forms of more or less exclusively piety-based church activities. This, however, also contributed to the creation of an aura of (self-)expectation around the sermon that made life difficult for a number of pastors. Today, pastors are entirely happy to borrow large parts of their sermons from one another and from the internet. In the decades after the Second World War, the pastor had to repeat the one and only Gospel in the form of a splendid new sermon every Sunday. In his book on being a pastor today from 1974, Rev. Jørn Jørgensen describes his experience as follows:

> The pastor can feel very bad about himself before, under and after a Sunday service. He may easily feel most inclined to run away from his ministry. If he sees few people in the church, he may think that he is the one who is crazy, together with this narrow flock. If he sees many, he can have his doubts about the truth and honesty of his sermon. In one of my small churches, in the sacristy where the pastors dress up, there are two small windows through which a human being might be able to escape. Since ancient times, there are, however, bars before the windows as in a prison, and I interpret these bars as having been installed to prevent the pastor from running away, when he has absolutely no desire to climb the pulpit. (Jørgensen 1974, 84)

An advantage provided by the preaching paradigm was that people – in principle – were placed and treated on an equal footing when coming to the church. This practice is continued around and after the turn of the millennium in the participatory paradigm. The Folk Church today, in its many activities, is working to make all the approximately 500,000 gatherings per year into a good experience, humanly speaking. And, at the same time, using those gatherings as an opportunity to make Christ known, believed and followed in as far as the church can contribute to this. The Folk Church today tends to subscribe to a theology of experience as formulated, for example, by Svend Bjerg (2006). His theory on the development of the Christian faith is based on distinctions in the Danish (and German) language, not articulated so easily in English. Faith, Bjerg says, is a matter of experience. There are however at least two steps in building experiences. The first step is having a sensation (perception) coming to you and thus gaining a certain certitude via the senses. In this way, you have an 'experience' meaning that you have sensed something *(oplevet, erlebt)*. For it to be a full experience *(erfaring, Erfahrung)*, however, what you have sensed must be reflected upon. When you think about what has been sensed, relating it to insights from human life (e.g. a story or a traditional saying), you can understand and keep your sensation as an experience, which belongs to you. Christian faith, Bjerg continues, is a new experience given alongside your former experiences, reflecting on them in relation to the Christ story (Iversen 2012).

The epistemology behind this understanding of Christian faith comes close to 'learning by doing'. That is, 'You must feel, what you shall learn', as Grundtvig puts it.[3] We do not become Christians without our own involvement. It does not happen behind our back, for example, when the pastor stands on the pulpit. On the contrary, when we are involved with nature, social life or God, we learn about what we are involved in. The world comes into our senses when we participate in this or that part of it. Only then, when having a sensory experience of what we are dealing with (e.g. in a song, role-play or a meditation), can we reflect on our experiences in relation to the Christian story.

This way of thinking about learning and formation has come into the Folk Church via work relating to pedagogical development with regard to children and confirmation. Today, the new forms of activity in the Folk Church have become participatory and co-creational in one or more of several senses:

1. You are invited to participate in planning as well as conducting a role-play or a service (e.g. as youngsters or parents in confirmation preparation);
2. You participate by moving around in the church, kneeling at the alter or writing a personal prayer to be included in the common church prayer in night churches;

3. You participate by identifying with others who participate actively (e.g. by being lay readers in the service);
4. You participate by conversing personally and intensely with others in a theological or philosophical salon or singing out together in a gospel choir;
5. Or you participate by meditating according to a directed schedule (e.g. in Church Yoga and Taizé liturgies [c.f. Modéus 2011, 138-147]).

The participatory way of working represents a new paradigm in terms of the forms of communications but also in theological terms. Theologically speaking, people are invited to meet God in their own way – not only in the one-way communication from the pulpit. New forms of work go together with new or old forms of theology, often with new images of God (Iversen 2016). At the moment, there is a lot of discussion about this in the Folk Church. Some claim that the paradigm of participation is turning back to the paradigm of piety, putting the emotions of people higher than the truth of and about God. Others are happy to leave the paradigm of preaching behind (or leaving it to those who still embrace it), seeing the participatory paradigm as the proper form of synthesis of the best from the two former paradigms. The Folk Church, being now more or less the only producer of opportunities for Danes to enter into Christianity, has never invested as much in teaching as it does today, when it has become very clear that classes on religion in school are far from being a Christian baptismal education. The Folk Church is changing from being an institution for Christian preaching and upbringing to a cultural institution for Christian experience and reflection.

What matters most is always what matters at the personal level, e.g. at a funeral. The important thing is the ability of the Folk Church to accept individualisation among people as a precondition for its work. One example might be when a widow asks to have a sailor's song ('En sømand har sin enegang': A sailor always walks alone) sung at the funeral of her husband, who loved the sea so much. In this situation, the pastor can encourage the widow to replace the (sad) sailor's song with a more joyful Christian hymn that reflects the significance of the ocean ('Se, nu stiger solen': See, the sun rises from the ocean). In that way, the pastor can be serious about the wish for a funeral 'in the spirit of the deceased' in such a way that both the widow and the pastor feels that this an authentic (church) funeral.

This chapter does not leave room for a full presentation and analysis of the tendencies within the theological reflections and expression of the Folk Church during recent years. The following short – and deliberately poetical – baptism introduction from the liturgically-free church, Lindevang at Frederiksberg 20th of August 2017, may illustrate some of these tendencies, emphasising a (Danish) theology of creation and using the language of modern Danes:

> We baptise our children in the name of the Father,
> In gratitude for what we have received and for the wonder of life.
> We baptise our children in the name of Jesus,
> That they may have the courage to live and desire life every day of their lifetimes.
> We baptise our children in the name of the Holy Spirit,
> So that this will not fade away and be at a distance only,
> On the contrary, that it must always stand clearly for us,
> That our children are children by the grace of God.

As they are people, so they are church members

Development in society contributes to significant changes in what often seems to be a static, theological self-understanding in the Folk Church. Admittedly, development in theology usually appears only after some delay. The existential, cultural and political tendencies of the time penetrate into the church from below through it users. It also enters from the side through its parish boards' members knowing about modern things from their daily lives, from the inside through pastors and other church workers who are also modern people and from above, through government and bishops, unions and national church institutions who want to implement this or that modern idea and practice.

The theological development within the Folk Church during the last 100 years can be understood in terms of internal theological arguments, where theologians develop their theology by studying and discussing theology with one another (cf. Gregersen 2017). Any full analysis must, however, include the societal influence: people, whoever they are, come into the church with existential needs as well as cultural and political ideas that they live with in their society. It is not just in Grundtvig's theology, but also in real life, that Christians are human beings first! This is the most important background element for explaining what has happened to Danish theology during the last 100 years.

Conditions of life were tough and uncertain in many respects in the time between the wars. Social democrats were fighting to have a self-supporting workers' culture, strengthening their position in the class struggle. Farmers and fishermen were anxious about the changes that seemed to come from new technology and the growing power of the working class. All were scared in the 1930s by the deepest economic crisis ever seen. None of the political parties were eager to support the Folk Church. The conservatives still had the old idea from the 19th century that church and state should be separated for the sake of the church, whereas the social democrats wanted the same – for the sake of the people! Most church leaders had their background in some part or other of the revivals, which they therefore tried to preserve in a dangerous world with an unsure future.

A more comprehensive change occurred in 1934 when the social democrats launched the new program 'Denmark for the People' (*Danmark for folket*). The political idea was now that the workers should not only have their own 'workers' culture', they should have their full share of all social goods in terms of culture, education and social security. This meant that the social democrats slowly also accepted that the Folk Church could keep its relation to the state – provided that social democrats took power in the parish boards and in the Ministry of Church Affairs, plus taking positions as pastors and church workers. The Folk Church was, after all, a part of Danish culture! This was the background against which the new theological paradigm of church as preaching was developed – or taken over – from new studies of Luther and the special Danish interpretation of Karl Barth.

In the modern society after the Second World War, society was organized not so much in classes, but increasingly in terms of social systems, each with its societal purpose and segments of people with more or less similar profiles. As the state now seemed to support strong state-church relations, the pastors' union, formed in 1898 to protect the pastors against the increasingly secular state, began working for the pastors to be employed as full-scale state civil servants. That wish was fulfilled in 1969 when the pastors joined the central organization of academically trained people. During the same years, the idea that the welfare state could manage all social and human problems held strong sway. As such, if the church attempted to do a great deal to help people besides preaching the gospel and the other traditional church things, it would appear as a form of disloyalty to the welfare state. Accepting this, the Folk Church also accepted being a niche institution in modern society, not actively involved with the other social systems and cultural institutions in society.

After the turn of the millennium, the Folk Church increasingly came to think and talk about itself as a church in mission, knowing (as has become obvious during many years of political development) that the church stands alone when it comes to promoting Christianity among the Danes. Given this situation, the church has become quicker to learn from the ways of operating used by the cultural institutions of the surrounding society, and quicker to learn from all sorts of experiences about how to communicate and practise church culture today. At the same time, the theological development in the Folk Church also reflects a society moving from 'Denmark for the people' and the welfare state towards a neo-liberal competition state, modified a little by social politics, but mostly by the growing nationalism of our times. No doubt, the new development in church and society brings more significant challenges to the church. During the first 50 years after the Second World War, the Folk Church generally survived in its societal niche, not interfering with politics. Today, the church is integrating itself and cooperating with other agencies and institutions in society wherever possible. A major question arises as to whether the Folk Church can stick to the old doctrine of no interference with politics knowing about the social and ethnic marginalisation at work in the Danish society?

Conclusion

The Folk Church is a cultural institution accommodating itself to present societal conditions in line with other cultural institutions. The Folk Church has therefore turned to 'the user', and is busy formulating its purpose in new ways (see Chapter 10). New forms of professionals are now employed in the church and new forms of activities or services are offered. This is, to a high degree, conditioned by the historical and theological background of the church and, not least, by the recent relatively rapid shift in the paradigms of work and self-understanding in the church.

References

Andersen, Peter B. and Peter Lüchau 2011. 'Individualisering og aftraditionalisering af danskernes værdier', in Peter Gundelach (ed.), *Små og store forandringer. Danskernes værdier siden 1981.* Copenhagen: Hans Reitzels Forlag, 76-95.

Bjerg, Svend 2006. *Tro og erfaring.* Copenhagen: Anis.

Christoffersen, Lisbet et al. (eds.) 2012. *Fremtidens danske religionsmodel.* Copenhagen: Anis.

Felter, Kirsten Donskov and Ruth Sønderskov Bjerrum 2015. *Hvad forventer folket af kirken?* Det Teologiske Fakultet: Centre for Kirkeforskning.

Ferrer, Jorge N. and Jacob H. Scherman (eds.) 2008. *The Participatory Turn – Spirituality, Mysticism and Religious Studies.* Albany: State University of New York Press.

Graham, Elaine 2013. *Between a Rock and a Hard Place. Public Theology in a Post-Secular Age.* London: SCM Press.

Gregersen, Niels Henrik 2015. *Den generøse ortodoksi – konflikt og kontinuitet i kristendommen.* Copenhagen: Anis.

Gregersen, Niels Henrik 2017. 'Dansk teologi 1914-2017', in Niels Henrik Gregersen and Carsten Bach-Nielsen (eds.), *Reformationen i dansk kultur og kirkeliv 1914-2017.* Odense: Syddansk Universitetsforlag, 253-300.

Gundelach, Peter, Hans Raun Iversen and Margit Warburg 2008. *I hjertet af Danmark. Institutioner og mentaliteter.* Copenhagen: Hans Reitzels Forlag. (English translation available from hri@teol.ku.dk).

Iversen, Hans Raun 2006. 'Secular religion and religious secularism. A profile of religious development in Denmark since 1968'. *Nordic Journal of Religion and Society*, 2/119: 75-92.

Iversen, Hans Raun 2008. 'How can a Folk Church be Missional Church?' in Tormod Engelsviken et al. (eds.), *Mission to the World. Communicating the Gospel in the 21st Century. Essays in Honour of Knud Jørgensen.* Oxford: Regnum, 67-84.

Iversen, Hans Raun 2012. 'Tro og erfaring genovervejet', in Christine Tind Johannesen-Henry et al. (ed.), *Livskraft. Studier i kristendom, fortælling og erfaring.* Copenhagen: Anis, 255-266.

Iversen, Hans Raun 2016. 'Participationens teologi og praksis. Deltagelse som vilkår for kirkeligt arbejde. Teser juni 2015', in Birgitta Sarelin and Mikael Lindfelt (eds.), *Den kommunikativa kyrkan. Festskrift till Bernice Sundkvist på 60-årsdagen.* Skellefteå: Artos, 229-242.

Iversen, Hans Raun 2017a. 'Kommunikationsformer og medier', 'Kirken og demokratiseringen: Teologisk og kulturelt belyst' and 'Kirkelivet og dets forgreninger', Niels Henrik Gregersen and Carsten Bach-Nielsen (eds.), *Reformationen i dansk kultur og kirkeliv 1914-2017*. Odense: Syddansk Universitetsforlag, 125-154, 195-228, and 331-358.

Iversen, Hans Raun 2017b. 'Theology of Creation as Position of Strength in an old National Church in Modern Society', in Coenie Burger et al. (eds.), *Cultivating Missional Change. The Future of Missional Churches*. Wellington, SA: Biblecor, 320-335.

Iversen, Hans Raun 2018. *Ny praktisk teologi. Kristendommen, den enkelte og kirken.* Copenhagen: Eksistensen.

Iversen, Hans Raun 'Denmark: A people and its Church', Linda Woodhead and Hans Raun Iversen (eds.), *The Persistence of Societal Religion. The Old National Churches of Northern Europe*. (in preparation).

Johannessen-Henry, Christine Tind 2013. *Hverdagskristendommens polydoksi. En empirisk-teologisk undersøgelse af tro i cancerrejsens kontekst*. PhD thesis, Faculty of Theology, University of Copenhagen.

Jørgensen, Jørn 1974. *Præst i dag*. Copenhagen: Chr. Erichsens Forlag.

Kastfelt, Niels 2013. 'Missionærer, kulturformidling og den moderne verden'. *Ny Mission No. 25*. Copenhagen: Danish Missionary Council, 8-27.

Lindberg, Jonas 2015. *Religion in Nordic Politics as a Means to Societal Cohesion. An Empirical Study of Party Platforms and Parliamentary Debates 1988-2015.* Dissertation. Uppsala Universitet.

Modéus, Martin 2011. *Menneskelig gudstjeneste. Om gudstjenesten som relation og ritual.* København: Alfa.

Pohl-Patalong, Uta 2006. *Von der Ortskirche zu kirchlichen Orten*. Göttingen: Vandenhoeck & Ruprecht.

Paas, Stefan 2015. 'Mission from Anywhere to Europe. Americans, Africans and Australians Coming to Amsterdam'. *Mission Studies,* 32: 4-31.

Smith, Graeme 2008. *A Short History of Secularism*. London: I.B. Tauris.

Taylor, Charles 1991. *The Ethics of Authenticity*. Oxford: Harvard University Press.

Taylor, Charles 2007. *A Secular Age*. London: The Belknap press of Harvard University Press.

Woodhead, Linda and Hans Raun Iversen (eds.). *The Old National Churches of Northern Europe: The Persistence of Societal Religion*. (in preparation).

Notes

1 See http://faith-health.org/.
2 Leading existential and dialectical theologians, respectively.
3 In a book on participatory epistemology in religious studies, the authors argue as follows: 'This participatory epistemology ... incorporates the post-modern understanding of knowledge and yet goes beyond it. The interpretive and constructive character of human cognition is fully acknowledged, but intimate, interpenetrating and all-permeating relationship of nature to the human being and human mind allows the Kantian consequence of epistemological alienation to be entirely overcome. The human spirit does not merely prescribe nature's phenomenal order; rather, the spirit of nature brings forth its own order through the human mind when that mind is employing its full complement of faculties – intellectual, volitional, emotional, sensory, imaginative, aesthetic, epiphanic ...' (Ferrer and Shermann 2008).

II. Inroads and Resistance to Marketisation in the Folk Church

6. New Public Management in the Folk Church

Annette Kruhøffer

Introduction

New Public Management is a term first dealt with in 1991 (Hood 1991). Professor Christopher Hood created the name to describe a tendency he had observed in the public sector: management had become more visible, with clear demands on both performance and output. Large units were divided into smaller organizational sections with clearly defined tasks, which could then be measured. In both market orientation and management strategies, he saw a strong influence from the private sector on the public. Hood found New Public Management's theoretical origin in economics, and his descriptions of New Public Management diffused through both academic research and public administration throughout the West. It became synonymous, not only with the administrative and institutional reforms that governments and municipalities around the globe have adapted to, but also with the techniques and methods used for the exercise of management. Among these are New Wage (a salary system based on performance rather than seniority), performance and contract management (a way of governing organizations by entering into contracts with them, indicating which goals they are supposed to achieve and what Key Performance Indicators should be used to measure the results), digitalisation, controller functions and so on. As such, the term 'New Public Management' covers an idea, an institutionalised practice and a management toolbox of methods and ideas.

Public administration in Denmark was equally influenced by these ideas and management tools. But, even though the Folk Church can be defined as an institution of public administration (Espersen 2000, 24-26; Christoffersen 1998, 316-317; Knudsen 2007, 392; Andersen and Lindhardt 2010), even by 2002, the Ministry of Ecclesiastical Affairs (*Kirkeministeriet*) had only introduced methods of New Public Management in its administration to a limited extent. However, a serious economic crisis caused by poor management led the Ministry to transform its management over a relatively short period of time. Many of the efforts were directed towards performance management, but other aspects and tools of New Public Management also came into use. This chapter describes the reform process in order to identify which institutions were affected by the process, how changes came about and what effects these changes had.

New Public Management derives from economic theory and is therefore strongly related to material considerations. One could have asked whether the introduction of New Public Management in the Folk Church is part of a secularisation process and, if so, to what extent this is the case. However, the question does not make much sense. The activities of the Folk Church are, and were, regulated by law – both before and after the introduction of New Public Management. Before 2003, only the Ministry of Ecclesiastical Affairs used the same kind of public administration that was used in the other ministries 10-20 years earlier. Therefore, questions of secularisation could not have been reflected in this early stage of the implementation of New Public Management. There was no interest among church officials to influence the process.

The systematic change to Performance Management began with a reorganization of the Ministry of Ecclesiastical Affairs and an implementation of Performance Management in the administration of the Common Fund (*Fællesfonden*) – an account used when financing salaries and some expenses of common interest for the Folk Church.[1] The Administrative Unity of the Folk Church (*Folkekirkens Administrative Fællesskab*) was then founded in 2006 to support the reform of the institutions organizationally linked most closely to the Common Fund: the dioceses, the IT department of the Folk Church (*Folkekirkens IT*) and the educational institutions of the Folk Church.

The primary sources for this chapter are the annual reports (AR) of the Common Fund (submitted from 2004 onward) and of the above-mentioned institutions. As the implementation of New Public Management progressed, several of the institutions under the Common Fund also began to publish annual reports, and these reports identify the priorities of the reform strategy for the various parts of the organizations. By comparing all performance contracts, a picture of the reform strategy for the Folk Church is drawn. As such, the timeframe that will be considered in this chapter covers 2003-2013.[2]

It is to be noted that the Common Fund finances the IT department, the Administrative Unity of the Folk Church, the dioceses and the educational organizations. Each of these institutions are treated separately in the main part of the text to identify the reform process during the chosen period.

In the concluding part of the chapter, the reform process will be considered as a whole. The means of reform will be described and the consequences discussed.

Implementing Performance Management

The Common Fund – organization of the administration of the Folk Church.
The economic crisis of the Ministry of Ecclesiastical Affairs was followed by reports from the Danish National Audit Office (*Rigsrevisionen*) and a project group from the Ministry of Finance (*Finansministeriet*). In 2004, these reports led to a reorganization of the Ministry of Ecclesiastical Affairs into four new offices to improve and streamline administration by creating more transparency and consistency in the allocation of responsibilities. These offices were directed towards Economics (*Folkekirkens Økonomi*), Governance (*Folkekirkens Styrelse*), Human Resources (*Folkekirkens Personale*) and the creation of an IT department (*Folkekirkens IT*).[3]

The annual reports from the Common Fund were modelled on instructions from the Agency for Economics (*Økonomistyrelsen*). They were submitted from 2004 onwards and were economic statements – from 2005 the signature of the accountant was provided and the transition to cost-based accounts was made. The main stakeholders for the reports in the first two years were the Danish National Audit Office and the Ministry of Finance. Therefore, the reports only focused on church life to a small extent. Furthermore, the need to restore the Common Fund's finances made its financial problems a high priority in the ministry's portfolio of tasks.

In the first two years, the focus was on the ministry itself, aiming to improve business procedures and regulations, to consolidate the whole process, to get the Folk Church's IT system integrated in the reform plans and – at a slightly slower pace – to prepare for the reform of the diocese's administration and the educational institutions. The reasons for choosing this reform strategy were undoubtedly to concentrate on the institutions most central to the overall operations of the Folk Church. Besides, these institutions are fully and directly financed by the Common Fund and thereby easier to communicate with than the decentralised parishes and priests.

One of the tools used to facilitate the transition to Performance Management was the collection of information about activities in the various parts of the Folk Church (AR The Common Fund 2004, 13). In 2005, a new IT-strategy was decided upon, pointing to a full digitalisation of administration in the Folk Church from the end of 2006 (AR The Common Fund 2005, 16). The Ministry of Ecclesiastical Affairs closely followed and documented these efforts in its annual reports.

Some of the necessary administrative skills and procedures had been implemented by the end of 2005, which provided a basis for broadening the reforms. The need for reorganizing the workflow across all parts of the Folk Church required a carefully planned process which could then be deducted from the annual reports in retrospect. To meet the criticism raised in the 2003 reports from the Danish National Audit Office and the Project Group from the Ministry of Finance, the benefits of placing certain administrative functions in a central office were considered. This resulted in the formation of the Administrative Unit of the Folk Church in 2006 – an institution to pay out general grants to the churches on the local level, levy taxes, and so on (Law No. 210, 20th March 2006). Other centres for managing common administrative tasks for the dioceses were considered, but in order to form such institutions it was necessary to document the amount of work done so far across the dioceses. Preparation and execution of this analysis was an important focus point for the Ministry of Ecclesiastical Affairs from 2006 onwards and can be detected in the annual reports for the dioceses from 2009 onwards.

At the same time, the educational institution began to submit annual reports. They were administered regionally by the diocese in which they were located, and their administrations were not digitalized. Thus, the Ministry of Ecclesiastical Affairs lacked sufficient knowledge about them to be able to harmonise their governance and set their budgets.

The formula by which all these annual reports are modelled is rather strict. It is therefore quite easy to compare the institutions with each other, and it is clear to see how developments occur in the individual institutions over the years considered. This makes it easier for the Ministry of Ecclesiastical Affairs to supervise their performances as well as making it possible to benchmark their performance against other comparable institutions.

From 2009, the evaluation and communication of the year's financial results in the annual reports were tightened and focused. However, the thorough treatment of the economy did not block space for the inclusion of elements which were the main interest in the administration of the Common Fund before 2003 – namely the acquired professional results. In the annual reports from the Common Fund, focus is on the extent to which the institutions are meeting their Performance Management requirements. These requirements were formulated in cooperation with the institutions and the Ministry of Ecclesiastical Affairs who were supervising and evaluating the results.

The Administrative Unity of the Folk Church was gradually taking over the common financial management and accounting tasks for the institutions under the Common Fund, thereby relieving the dioceses (among others) of some administrative duties. The Ministry of Ecclesiastical Affairs prepared for the foundation of five new centres to take over other joint tasks. For this purpose, the dioceses were given Key Performance Indicators concerning both the identification of tasks to outsource and the mapping of staff competences. In 2012, the new centres were launched, each of them operated by one or two dioceses together.

The reason for choosing this model instead of creating a large (efficient and cheap) administrative centre was to maintain the continued proximity between the dioceses and the local levels (i.e. the parish councils). The decision makers made clear that this was a political (rather than an economic) choice (summary No. 36246/14, from a meeting of the budgetary group of the Common Fund, March 18th 2014). Thus, the ecclesiastical interests made a small mark on the process in this way. According to the annual reports for 2013, the transition from regional case processing to the central administrative solution was hard, and the difficulties were mainly attributable to administrative challenges.

Looking now at the priests and the deans, we can see that they were economically significant to the Common Fund, since wages and pensions totalled almost 60 percent of the Common Fund's expenses (AR The Common Fund 2009, 6). However, they remained almost untouched by the reforms until the introduction of New Wage principles in 2012. In the conclusion, this aspect of the reform will be commented on briefly since New Wage and the reforms of the educational institutions show intentions of extending the

New Public Management reforms to these levels of the Folk Church, too, even though these changes unfolded mainly after 2013.

The IT Department

The poor economy of the Common Fund in 2002 was partly due to poor management of its IT activities. Budget and accounts for the Common Fund's IT expenses showed that the budget was regularly exceeded – in one year by more than 50 percent. The Danish National Audit Office could further confirm that the Ministry of Ecclesiastical Affairs budgeted too low despite their knowledge of the wrong figures. Consequently, during the years 1997-2002, the Ministry of Ecclesiastical Affairs showed budgets much below the actual expenditures (except for one year). Furthermore, they stated that the decision to reduce budgets below the expected level of activity was a political decision relating to the government's general policy of budget cutting (The Danish National Audit Office 2003, 60).

New business procedures for the approval and accounting of invoices in the IT area were quickly introduced (The Danish National Audit Office 2003, 7). The IT department was insourced, and the budgeting was based on the estimated level of activity, instead of just being an extrapolation of the previous year with minor adjustments (The Danish National Audit Office 2003, 36). The annual report of the Common Fund 2004 concluded that the results of the first year of reform had been satisfactory (AR The Common Fund 2004, 13). And, during the years 2003-2013, the economy was stabilised and the major fluctuations in the accounts previously seen disappeared. Leased commitments were settled and the electronic church book (DNK, *Den Ny Kirkebog*) – a major digitalisation project – was consolidated, which contributed to reducing costs.

The IT department generally had more Key Performance Indicators than other institutions within the Folk Church. Emphasis was placed on accessibility, reliability and efficiency, modernisation or implementation of new systems and services, as well as user satisfaction. E-learning courses, risk analyses and new demands for digital services were also among the Key Performance Indicators. The main goal was to facilitate the digitalisation of the Folk Church in general.

The Administrative Unity of The Folk Church

Until 2003, the financial administration of the dioceses had been characterised by a lack of knowledge and oversight, which was expensive and had led to the violation of rules. It was therefore necessary to regulate the administrative practices.

Law No. 210, March 20th 2006, was passed by the Danish Parliament and allowed the establishment of an administrative unit which could carry out administrative tasks in collaboration with the dioceses. This was a unit with a large operating volume, thus making more efficient use of human resources and competencies. The new centre was placed under the Diocese of Lolland-Falster, since this diocese was not otherwise considered sustainable due to its size (*Beslutningsoplæg* 2006, 10). Thus, the Administrative Unity of the Folk Church became an integral part of the Diocese of Lolland-Falster (AR Lolland-Falster 2009, 4), although it had its own budget, submitted separate accounts and was given dedicated tasks. The number of man years[4] for these tasks was estimated based upon a study of the workload in three dioceses.

Some doubts were expressed as to whether the new institution would meet the criterion of a professional 'critical mass', meaning that the number of tasks should match an equivalent number of professionally skilled people. Therefore, a list of services, that needed eventually to be bought by the Ministry of Ecclesiastical Affairs or the dioceses, was made (Ministry of Ecclesiastical Affairs 2006, 8).

The adopted objectives for the Administrative Unity of the Folk Church closely followed the expectations of an economically justified structural change: economies of scale, quality improvements through intensified professionalism, greater operational reliability and fewer errors. The centre was expected to be economically sustainable, and this was to be achieved by voluntary agreements between the centre and its customers, and by objective pricing based on the actual costs.

In addition to this, the users were to be involved in the founding process and later, during its operation, through dialogue on task solutions and the willingness to improve. Finally, increased digitalisation was encouraged, because there were too many manual workflows, far too large a set of differences between the administration of the dioceses' procedures and a lack of standardisation of the budget follow-up processes (Ministry of Ecclesiastical Affairs 2006, 6).

In 2007, the Administrative Unity of the Folk Church took up financial management tasks from the educational institutions, the IT department and, in part, from the ministry (AR The Common Fund 2008, 6). During the following years, the Administrative Unity of the Folk Church gradually took over the accounting and the cash management of the dioceses. In addition, the institution implemented new accounting systems and offered consultant services (see, for example, AR Lolland-Falster 2009, 8; or AR Lolland-Falster 2010, 19-20).

Despite the activity level, there was a problem in making the new organization sustainable. The Diocese of Lolland-Falster had to contribute economically towards various overheads (AR Lolland-Falster 2009, 19-20), and additional grants from the Common Fund permitted the employment of more staff (AR Lolland-Falster 2010, 8). In its annual report to the Common Fund, the Diocese of Lolland-Falster stated that, due to the strained economy and inadequate resources, the Administrative Unity of the Folk Church prioritised more customers and therefore downgraded the basic tasks (AR Lolland-Falster 2013, 13-14). Even so, in 2013, when the Administrative Unity of the Folk Church was fully implemented, neither the monetary nor the staff resources proved to be quite sufficient (AR Lolland-Falster 2013, 5-8). This was mirrored in the (only partly met) Key Performance Indicators for the Administrative Unity of the Folk Church, which related to a greater productivity and rentability of the centre itself as well as to the innovation or implementation of products with the customers.

Many of the elements from New Public Management can be found in the development of the Administrative Unity of the Folk Church, but there are also significant deviations. First, there was no competition, and the new organization could therefore not be said to operate under market conditions and neither could it be benchmarked. Next, the Administrative Unity of the Folk Church was placed under the Diocese of Lolland-Falster, wherein the management took care of both their own diocese and a supposedly independent centre. This brought benefits in terms of flexibility on the staff side, but at the same time, this was also a significant weakness of the project. In the case of problems with the externally funded tasks, priority was given to servicing the paying customers – and that tended to affect the day-to-day operations. There was thus a risk that the diocese and the centre transferred their focus away from the traditional tasks without funding towards the new tasks honoured by the customer.

The dioceses

The 2003 report found that the accounting of the dioceses was satisfactory, but the return of the capital was less than could be expected (The Danish National Audit Office, 10-11). In addition, there were minor deviations from guidelines (The Danish National Audit Office 2003, 43-44). The project group from the Ministry of Finance recommended an adjustment of budget procedures to ensure an unambiguous connection between the economy and the dioceses' activities to allow benchmarking between them. Furthermore, this control should be more consistent across the dioceses to increase quality and efficiency of expenditure (Ministry of Finance 2003, 36).

Staff administration is important to the dioceses, and the division between priests and other employees reflects the structural division of the Folk Church: The parish council is in charge of the administration of staff (all but priests), budgets and buildings, while the priest is independent in the performance of his pastoral duties, which include services, teaching and other kinds of pastoral care. From 2004 onwards, the annual reports from the Common Fund listed and commented on the number of employees of both kinds in each of the dioceses. Wages for priests are partly financed through a grant on the Finance Act while all other employees of the diocese are financed fully from the Common Fund. This may be part of the reason why the two groups are registered differently. The priests are subdivided according to who pays their salary, while the non-theological staff of the dioceses are subdivided according to their various administrative tasks.

From 2009, the dioceses began to submit their own annual reports. Here, they emphasised that an important part of the professional achievement of the year consists of what the priests do. However, it is quite consistent that focus remains on working hours and different kinds of employment contracts rather than the results of the work (see, for example, AR Helsingør 2013, 10). In some dioceses, it is predominantly the bishop's activities which represent the institution's professional achievements. (see, for example, AR Viborg 2013, 11), while there are virtually no statements of the contents of the theological work, possibly because it is not systematically described. Theological values are absent from the annual reports and, until 2013, it was only the Diocese of Ribe which, as an exception, included visions for its ecclesiastical work.

On the other hand, the administrative results for the year include a specification of the time consumption on different tasks as well as the Key Performance Indicators for the year in question. The time spent on the different tasks varies a great deal from one diocese to another, which indicates that the principles for registering time consumption are not clear (thus rendering benchmarking pointless). However, there is an overall increase in the number of administrative staff in the dioceses. It is striking that the resources spent on operating the dioceses tripled between the years 2009-11, even though the costs fell a little in 2012 and 2013. Furthermore, with the foundation of the centres in 2012, the dioceses began to use the term 'external clients' to refer to parishes and parish councils. The use of the word 'external' implies a certain alienation between dioceses and parishes.

The dioceses' Key Performance Indicators were introduced for the first time in 2009. It was a rather prudent beginning. The Key Performance Indicators related to internal workflows (The Danish National Audit Office 2010, 3) and the modest Key Performance Indicators might indicate that the dioceses did not possess the appropriate skills or sufficient resources to perform their tasks both quickly and flawlessly. The annual report of 2009 did not communicate the success rate, but the results of the year were published in the annual report of the Common Fund and supported this assumption, since only 37 percent of the Key Performance Indicators were met, and the dioceses had failed to meet the same number (AR The Common Fund 2013, 22).

The following years saw a slight improvement in the total results (see, for example, AR The Common Fund 2010, 17), but the dioceses' indicators remained modest in both number and extent in the period 2009-2013. The Annual Report for the Common Fund 2013 presented an overview of the Key Performance Indicators for the first five years and emphasised that the requirements in the indicators had remained constant. It was added that there had been progress in the performance across all the dioceses in the 2009-2013 period, which prompted an invitation to consider whether the indicators should be increased in the future (AR The Common Fund 2013, 22). Such a consideration of active management in relation to the Key Performance Indicators is mentioned here for the first time in the annual reports.

Looking at the chosen indicators and the order in which they are introduced over the years, a picture is drawn of a new administration introduced at a steady pace to Performance Management according to the standards issued by the Ministry of Finance in 2001: strategic overall thinking, focus on results, cost awareness, learning and dialogue with the users (Ministry of Finance 2001).

The process of developing the diocese administrations and the establishment of centres followed a plan beginning with incorporating Key Performance Indicator skills and result awareness. Next came a description of the dioceses' functions and future expectations, while concurrently preparing the competence development for employees. Then the distribution of tasks between the dioceses and the centres was established. A new model for the yearly 'employee development interview' between employer and employee (MUS *MedarbejderUdviklingsSamtale*) could then be used to make plans for employees to meet future requirements (AR The Common Fund 2013, 22; AR Dioceses 2009-2013).

The dioceses have been affected in many ways by the management reforms. The number of full-time employees has risen; however, the nature of their activities has changed due to the centre formation. The demands represented by the Key Performance Indicators express an expectation of increased professionalisation of administrations. But more importantly, the dioceses seem to have been more closely linked to the Ministry of Ecclesiastical Affairs while the distance to the parishes has increased.

However, the priests who represent the professional achievements in the annual reports, next to the bishops, were not significantly involved in the dioceses' reform process during the period until 2013. This changed from 2014, where a Key Performance Indicator requested that the dioceses prepare a New Wage policy for priests and ensure that it was presented and adopted by the bishops. The Key Performance Indicator might touch on a significant theological question here since a wage policy correlating work with wage may affect the freedom of the priest in the performance of his pastoral obligations. However, I have not found any signs of a discussion of this problem anywhere.

The Educational Institutions of the Folk Church
The 'Educational Institutions' (*Folkekirkens Uddannelser*) is a term used in the Common Fund's annual reports for those institutions that provide education for current and future priests, deans and church musicians. They were originally managed by the dioceses in which they were located, which meant that their management, finances and courses were not coordinated between the dioceses. Their activities are regulated by law (Law No. 309,

May 16th 1990; and Decree No. 1132, December 13th 1996). They are funded by the Common Fund and have submitted annual reports since 2007, and the *Teologisk Pædagogisk Center* (TPC) and the Church music schools since 2006. Since 2009, they have been assigned Key Performance Indicators.[5]

It is mandatory for priests in the Folk Church to have a Master's degree in theology from a Danish University (with a few rare exceptions). Additionally, they take a semester of pastoral education at the Folk Church's own institutions. These are the schools for pastoral education in Copenhagen and Aarhus: the *Folkekirkens Institut for Præsteuddannelse,* FIP Copenhagen and FIP Aarhus. These two institutions are supplemented with the TPC in Løgum Kloster, whose purpose was to offer courses to the staff employed (mainly priests).[6] Since 2009, these institutions have been subjected to Performance Management and therefore got their own, only partially shared, Key Performance Indicators.

It is striking that the collection of activity data apparently did not affect the institutions' activity level, and the Key Performance Indicators did not affect the choice of data collected. Like the dioceses, the results of the first year of Performance Management were not published in the annual report.

In summary, the *Teologisk Pædagogisk Center*'s performance goals have shifted from analysing and qualifying its own course business and administration to actively professionalising its activity with market investigation, digitalised communication efforts and an economic development of future business models.

FIP Copenhagen and FIP Århus partly shared Key Performance Indicators, focusing on upgrading the institutions' own administration and management, but they were also given their own tasks, too. For instance, the organization of internship appeared in the Key Performance Indicators for both institutions, but it occurred in a staggered fashion and experimented with different perspectives on the chosen outcome. Thus, the Key Performance Indicators were actively used to gather experience in order to reorganise the educational structure for future priests.

In general, the Key Performance Indicators were used to professionalise the pastoral institutions and to develop means and ways of streamlining or creating change from a broader perspective. Several indicators were continued for more years, and the results were thus used to promote longer-term efforts. In some cases, common indicators with a harmonising effect were imposed on the formerly independent institutions before their merger in 2014. The individual indicators for FIP Copenhagen and Aarhus can also be said to fit well into a consolidation of the Performance Management process, focusing on internal collaboration in larger units and a central set of standards and goals.

Like the other educational institutions, the three church music schools were of interest to the Ministry of Finance Project Group, who recommended user payment in 2003, partly to ensure an appropriate incentive structure directed towards the parishes, and partly to harmonise the educational institutions' courses with local wishes and needs (Ministry of Finance 2003, 19). This proposal was not adopted.

A thorough gathering of data concerning the institutions' activities began from 2003 onwards. These data showed a fluctuating and declining number of participants on the courses, but this did not result in the closure of institutions. Neither the pastoral education institutions nor the church music schools had to close down educations because of a decline in the number of students. Furthermore, the data collection and the Key Performance Indicators do not seem to correlate for the church music schools.

The church music schools have had shared and individual Key Performance Indicators concerning their administration and their teachings. According to the Annual Report for the Common Fund 2013, an evaluation was made for the period 2009-2013. The three church music schools had a total of 59 goals. Of these, 32 (equivalent to more than 50 percent) were only partially met. In the annual, report it was nevertheless noted that 'The achievement of objectives is overall satisfactory' (AR The Common Fund 2013, 25).

Conclusion – how and where did the reforms go?

In 2015, Hood and Dixon evaluated New Public Management after 30 years of reforms and changes in Britain. Originally, it was expected that New Public Management would generate a public sector that worked more efficiently and cost less. The two researchers conclude that these results cannot be discerned. Quite the contrary, in fact, operating expenses have risen, and the number of complaints has also risen (Hood and Dixon 2015, 178). The fact that the person who first described New Public Management was the one who articulated such a serious criticism of the reforms, based on a thorough investigation of 30 years of history, has triggered a debate. Some are ready to dump New Public Management while others defend the positive results which, they argue, are not included in the Hood and Dixon investigation (see, for example, Torfing 2016; versus Klausen 2016).

Concerning the introduction of Performance Management in the Folk Church, the unpleasant economic state in the Ministry of Ecclesiastical Affairs in 2003 was partly ascribed to a lack of Performance Management in the ministry (Ministry of Finance 2003, 2-3) which may have eased the transition process. Initially, there was a strong focus on economy, efficiency and results; and this continued from 2009 onwards when other aspects were included in the management. Looking at the whole period, there seems to have been a plan for the reform process since actions are prepared years in advance, but such a plan has not been published.

Tools

The first two years of reform were spent on reforming the Ministry itself by acquiring tools and updating the professional skills to handle the future demands, in accordance with ways and methods that were generally used in the rest of the public administration. The process was internally driven in the sense that there were no Key Performance Indicators or other New Public Management tools mentioned by the Common Fund when the annual reports conveyed the results of the year.

The IT department was mobilised to assist in the digitalisation process, and the economy was restored. But most importantly, the ministry began to expect and coordinate performance from the institutions under the Common Fund.

From 2006, Performance Management was extended to the next level – that is, to the dioceses, the educational institutions and the Administrative Unity of the Folk Church which were established in 2006. The institutions were prepared to meet future requirements by collecting data on their activity. The focus was on effective and uniform management with benchmarking as a tool for managing the institutions as well as an opportunity for the institution's self-regulation. Other tools in reforming the Folk Church were the centralisation (in the form of centres) and the decentralisation (by delegating tasks, and placing the costs where the decisions were made). This facilitated fast and efficient case processing by qualified and specialised staff.

For example, the centre formations were prepared in good time, as were the analyses of the dioceses' workflow, and staff qualification pointed towards the establishment of the new centres with task separation from the dioceses and increased flexibility in human resources.

With the submission of annual reports from 2008/9 onwards, the institutions began a direct and systematic dialogue with the Ministry of Ecclesiastical Affairs regarding the daily operations and the institutions' goals. Thus, they were organizationally linked closer to the Common Fund. The educational institutions in particular were managed more tightly by placing them directly under the Ministry of Ecclesiastical Affairs instead of their former administration by the dioceses. The dioceses were also pulled closer to the Ministry, which may have distanced the parishes and thereby led to some alienation internally within the church.

New Wage is not mentioned in the annual reports until 2014, because it was not an issue decided by the Ministry of Ecclesiastical Affairs, nor by the institutions under the Common Fund. But the introduction of New Wage heralded some changes affecting the local levels. Special duties or skills, increased responsibilities, or a very big parish population, all became criteria for raising the wage. The creation of a profile of competencies for priests and deans was a Key Performance Indicator for FIP Copenhagen in 2012, and in 2014 the dioceses and bishops had a Key Performance Indicator on deciding a New Wage policy. The introduction of New Wage was, and still is, supported by the development of the education of priests. In 2016, a report summarising the projects and studies made by the Board of Directors of the institutions was able to recommend a model for further work on reform of the education of priests (*Folkekirkens Uddannelses- og Videnscenter* 2016). Because of the choice and set-up of Key Performance Indicators, educational institutions qualified and consolidated a revised education for priests – a deed which had previously failed for commissions, committees and reports for many years (Larsen 2014). In this way the institutions were made to cooperate towards defining the priorities of the priests in maintaining the job.

Results

The reforms have been rolled out at a calm but steady pace and with some caution and understanding. The thorough preparations of major changes, such as the formation of centres or the omission of the results from the first year when Key Performance Indicators were implemented, show consideration. There have been no redundancies, and the many unfulfilled performance targets have not resulted in punishments in the form of reduced budgets or staff. This may have facilitated the later achievements of the desired goals.

The results of the reforms have been a qualification of the day-to-day operations in the Common Fund's institutions – especially when it comes to efficiency and competence. At the same time, the institutions have been involved in preparatory work laying the foundation for continued reforms – all motivated by the establishing of Key Performance Indicators in cooperation with the Ministry of Ecclesiastical Affairs. In this way, a centralisation of means and goals is already on its way.

The institutions, which formerly had not systematically coordinated their work, are now inspired by Key Performance Indicators to focus on compatible areas. Competition between institutions does not seem to have been spurred on. To the contrary, the educational institutions were encouraged to try out two different ways of organizing the revised obligatory courses for newly employed priests in order to find the best overall solution.

Experience brought a recognition in the Ministry of the fact that dialogue about expectations, and a follow-up on these conversations, contributed to better results (AR The Common Fund 2012, 19). The reform also had costs. The number of administrative staff in the dioceses has increased (see, for example, AR The Common Fund 2008, 6), which means that more of the church's resources are spent on administration rather than directly on the members and church life. Moreover, during the period considered, expenditure rose a little for all educational institutions even though the general trend was a decrease in the number of students as well as courses and student-courses days.

Until 2013, the reform was mainly limited to the institutions mentioned earlier in this chapter, with the introduction of New Wage in 2012 as an exception. The parishes and the priests were not affected except through the changed workflows in the corporate functions and their derivative effects. But, New Wage has extended the reform plans to the local level and more may be expected. Structural considerations on parish sizes have taken place in most dioceses since at least 2009 but have not resulted in many pastoral changes. This may be different in the future if the priest's salary for handling a big parish comes to be equal to the salary for handling a smaller parish. The competence profile for priests include elements that are well-matched with teamwork, larger parishes and ecclesiastical units, and a more professional approach to the priests as a labour resource. The growing numbers of priests dedicated to a function instead of a parish fuel this development. Individual congregations will be affected by this and in other ways too.

It may also be noted that the theological competencies have not been involved in the reform process. This is paralleled by the fact that theological results are not recorded anywhere in the annual reports. The so-called professional results (*Faglige resultater*) are dominated by the question of how many fulltime employees there have been among the priests and what kind of contracts they have had. Only the bishop's activities are mentioned, but the bishops have not got any Key Performance Indicators personally.

The silence concerning theological consequences and values may stem from a general reluctance to embrace New Public Management in the priesthood. For example, the former bishop Drejergaard regarded New Public Management as an object alien to the Folk Church and therefore something to be fought (Drejergaard 2008). Moreover, New Wage was already suggested to the priests in 2001, but was rejected several times before its introduction in 2012. However, it was possible to introduce New Wage by making a payroll system that accommodates the young priests, while letting the older priests remain on the old system. Similarly, the prospect of collegial cooperation and greater freedom in the organization of work may encourage bigger pastorates and extended cooperation combined with more specialised functions for priests. How these changes may affect the ecclesiology and the theology regarding the nature of priesthood in the Folk Church cannot be deduced from a spreadsheet or an annual report.

References

The following Annual Reports (AR) are available on the respective institutions' websites, or upon request to the Ministry of Ecclesiastical Affair.:
- The Common Fund – from 2004
- The dioceses – from 2009
- The Educational Institutions – from 2009
- The Administrative Unity of The Folk Church (*Folkekirkens Administrative Fællesskab*) – from 2008
- The IT department *(Folkekirkens IT)* – from 2009

Andersen, Erling and Mogens Lindhardt 2014. *Kompetenceprofil – Provsteembedet*. The Ministry of Ecclesiastical Affairs.

Andersen, Erling and Mogens Lindhardt 2010. *Ledelse af Tro. Folkekirken som Virksomhed og Netværk*, Copenhagen: Gyldendal Public.

Beslutningsoplæg til Styregruppen of 21st March 2006, document no. 280643.

Bregn, Kirsten 2006. Resultatmåling i den Offentlige Sektor, *Nordisk Administrativt Tidsskrift*, Nr. 2, October 2006, Jurist- og Økonomforbundets Forlag.

Christoffersen, Lisbet 1998. *Kirkeret mellem stat, marked og civilsamfund*. Copenhagen: Jurist- og Økonomforbundets Forlag

Drejergaard, Kresten 2008. *Smålighed eller Lidenskab?* Feature article, *Jyllandsposten*, 7th November 2008.

Engdahl, Anita Hansen and Mogens Lindhardt 2014. *Kompetenceprofil – for Præster*, The Ministry of Ecclesiastical Affairs.

Espersen, Preben 2000. *Kirkeret. Almindelig del. 2. revicerede og forøgede udgave*. Copenhagen: Jurist- og Økonomforbundet.

Folkekirkens Uddannelses- og Videnscenter 2016. *Præst i Morgen – to Forslag til en Integreret Uddannelse af Nye Præster*.

Greve, Carsten 2012. *Reformanalyse. Hvordan den Offentlige Sektor Grundlæggende er Blevet Forandret i oo'erne*. Copenhagen: Jurist- og Økonomforbundets Forlag.

Hood, Christopher 1991. 'A Public Management for All Seasons'. *Public Administration* 69/2, 3-19.

Hood, Christopher and Ruth Dixon 2015. *A Government that Worked Better and Cost Less? Evaluating Three Decades of Reform and Change in UK Central Government*. Oxford: Oxford University Press.

Klausen, Kurt Klaudi 2016. '*Kritikken af new Public Management er forfejlet,* Feature article, *Politiken*, 23th May 2016.

Knudsen, Tim 2007. *Fra Folkestyre Til Markedsdemokrati. Dansk Demokratihistorie Efter 1973*. Copenhagen: Akademisk Forlag.

Kruhøffer, Annette 2015. *Målstyring i den Folkekirkelige Organisation. Dokumentation og Analyse af Implementeringen af Nye Styringsformer i Perioden 2002-2013*. Thesis from the Faculty of Theology, University of Copenhagen.

Larsen, Christian 2014. 'Et Institut for Pastoralvidenskaberne: Pastoralseminariet 1809-1990'. *Kirkehistoriske Samlinger 2014*.

Law (LBK) No. 537 of June 24th 1997 (økonomiloven).

Madsen, Jørgen Steen, Jesper Due and Søren Kaj Andersen 1998. 'Historien om Nye Lønformer i den Offentlige Sektor. Fra Lønformudvalget Forud for OK87 til Gennembruddet i Forhandlingerne om Nye Lønformer i den Offentlige Sektor Under OK97'. *Samfundsøkonomen*, 4/5: 12.

Ministry of Ecclesiastical Affairs 2001. *It-Strategi: Kirkeministeriet & Folkekirken i Netværkssamfundet 2001.*

Ministry of Ecclesiastical Affairs 2006. *Projektbeskrivelse: Etablering af Administrativt Fællesskab*, document marked 4/5/2006

Ministry of Finance 2001. *Ledelse på Dagsordenen. Perspektiver på Bedre Ledelse i den Offentlige Sektor.*

Ministry of Finance 2003. *Udvikling af økonomistyringen på Kirkeministeriets Område.* Report from the Ministry of Finance Project Group, 16th December 2003.

Præsteforeningen 2008. *Hovedbestyrelsens årsberetning 2008.* Særtryk.

The Danish National Audit Office 2003. *Beretning fra Rigsrevisionen til Statsrevisorerne om Folkekirkens Fællesfond*, April 2003, doc no. RB A203/03.

The Danish National Audit Office 2006. *Notat til Statsrevisorerne om den Fortsatte Udvikling i Sagen om Folkekirkens Fællesfond,* (beretning 10/02) of 14th March 2006.

The Danish National Audit Office 2008. *Notat til Statsrevisorerne om Beretning om Folkekirkens Fællesfond. Opfølgning i sagen om folkekirkens Fællesfond (beretning nr. 10/02 af 25th April 2008,* May 2008.

The Danish National Audit Office 2010. *Notat til Statsrevisorerne om Beretning om Folkekirkens Fællesfond. Opfølgning i sagen om folkekirkens Fællesfond (beretning nr. 10/02) of 9th April 2010,* April 2010.

Summary, No. 36246/14, from a meeting in *Budgetsamrådet for Fællesfonden* of 18th March 2014.

Torfing, Jacob 2016. *Bombe under 30 års Styringstænkning: Hood og Dixon Lægger New Public Management i Graven,* www.denoffentlige.dk, 21st November 2016.

Notes

1. The Common Fund's purpose and revenue basis are determined by law (LBK No. 537, June 24th 1997).
2. The chapter mainly presents the results of the reform process based on my MTh thesis (2015): 'Målstyring i den folkekirkelige organisation. Dokumentation og analyse af implementeringen af nye styringsformer i perioden 2002-2013'. The thesis is available from the University of Copenhagen. It contains a more detailed description of the process of introducing New Public Management into the Ministry of Ecclesiastical Affairs.
3. The IT department was set up in 1996, but it was outsourced as part of the attempt to keep the economy afloat. It was then insourced to link it closer to the ministry's other activities.
4. These were (and are) counted in fulltime employees (in Danish ÅRSVÆRK = year-of-work).
5. By 2009, the education of church officials had already been transferred to other educational systems outside the authority of the Ministry of Ecclesiastical Affairs. Thus, they will not be further discussed in this chapter.
6. On January 1st 2014, the three institutions were merged into one educational institution under the name *Folkekirkens Uddannelses- og Videnscenter* (FKUV); and *Folkekirkens Konfirmandcenter* was included in FKUV at the same time.

7. Legally Supported Marketisation and Individualisation of the Folk Church as a Cultural Institution

Lisbet Christoffersen and Karen Marie Leth-Nissen[1]

Introduction

Cultural institutions adapt to changed conditions and changes in the demands of the consumers of culture. Approaching the Folk Church from the perspective of cultural institutions, this chapter examines dimensions of how the Folk Church likewise adapts to a market of cultural goods, influenced by religious consumers.

In this chapter, we argue that the Folk Church currently has adapted both leadership practices and the Danish legal framework in order to meet new demands, due to increasing individualisation among its users. We also argue that this development is smoothed by a strong tradition of legislation adapting to demands from groups and individuals within the church (the so-called *frihedslovgivning,* the legal framework of freedoms and rights within the church[2]). At the same time, we argue that neither the Folk Church nor the individual actors within the church can be evaluated solely through the lenses of theories of marketisation. Thus, we describe a limited, state-supported marketisation of the Folk Church as a cultural institution.

Our notion of individualisation within the Folk Church comes from the theoretical concept of 'churching alone' (Leth-Nissen 2018).[3] With this concept, Leth-Nissen demonstrates how use of the Folk Church has increasingly become a matter of making individual sense of one's own life. The church has responded to this by providing many different target group activities, thus rendering individuals able to participate in church activities together with people like themselves.

In this chapter, we track such individualisation in the Folk Church in three steps. Step 1 consists of an overview over how exemptions from the general rule of churching together in the geographical parish are legalised, and contribute to the changing life of the Folk Church (from 1849 until now). This legislation affords groups and individuals a freedom of choice *within* the church in more and more areas, and thereby supports not only the existence of minority groups, but also an internal individualisation within the church. Step 2 focuses on the collective level in the parishes by presenting an overview of recent legal changes. These changes give more influence to the lay members of the organization at parish level regarding the ecclesiastical work of the local church. This is an influence which, in practice, is used for making local decisions concerning the welcoming of the individualised church goers. Step 3 then focuses on how changes in recruitment processes and training of the leadership of the churches at a regional level, represented by the deans, also impact marketisation and individualisation of the local churches to some extent.

Marketisation and Individualisation in the Folk Church: Churching Alone

Kruhøffer (Chapter 6) and Rasmussen (Chapter 12) have shown how New Public Management (NPM) is present in the Folk Church in the form of performance management and as an argument in decision-making processes. To explain such changes in large majority churches, Gauthier, Woodhead and Martikainen (2013) have looked to the mega-trends that are changing all societies across the world. They have described how post-war economics have altered our culture and introduced neo-liberalism and consumerism (Gauthier et al. 2013, 1-2.15). The market economy now permeates all social realities, all social life and human action in what is called the 'neoliberal age' (Gauthier et al. 2013: 13). The consequences at organizational and institutional levels have been the generation of an increasing 'management focus' in church organizations (Gauthier et al. 2013:16). Thus, as Martikainen has stated, when the state changes its underlying paradigm, the organization of the national church is likely to change, too.[4]

We see the recent legal changes in the Folk Church as part of this general turn to NPM in the Folk Church, coming about most clearly from 2003 onwards (Leth-Nissen 2018, 81-108). This followed the changes in the Danish state's governance paradigm (Pedersen 2011, see here chapter 6). In Denmark, the legislative framework has always (or, at least, since the Folk Church was developed after the constitution of 1849) allowed for the inclusion of dimensions of what could be called state-driven marketisation (Christoffersen 1998). Likewise, the church structure and administration have always changed with the state, adapting within the framework of the state, due to the intertwinement of state and church (Christoffersen 2006).

The changes in governance towards NPM happen in an interplay between the different Folk Church actors. Through hearings and committee work, Folk Church actors are included in the legislative process of the changes. This seems to be a specifically Danish model of NPM (Ejersbo and Greve 2013, 16). Such reforms and changes in general could be seen as suffering from a democratic deficit in terms of formulating the mandate for reform committees and in selecting the stakeholder organizations or representatives. Within the Folk Church, the main stakeholders tend to be the Ministry of Ecclesiastical Affairs, the bishops, the National Association of Parish Councils and the Parish pastors' union (which is also the deans' union). The result of the changes is an *introduction of* NPM within the Folk Church at the deanery level as well as at congregational level.

At the individual level, there is an ongoing transformation, parallel to what Grace Davie (in regard to European Christianity) has characterised as a move 'from obligation to consumption' (Davie 2013, 2006, 1994). Davie highlights how religion used to be imposed or inherited, but is now increasingly a matter of consumption or choice (Davie 2013, 284). Talk of duty or obligation is tied, as Davie sees it, to notions of tradition, generation and duty to religion. In contrast, talk of consumption points towards individual choice. Davie describes the processes relating to such choice with the concept of consumption. As such, her concepts describe a shift away from a non-market-based way of relating to religion towards a consumerism of religion and its marketisation.

Leth-Nissen incorporates Davie's theoretical concepts in her own concept of *churching alone* (Leth-Nissen 2018). Leth-Nissen argues that the consumption of religion is a way of connecting to the meaning of life (2018, 25-29). There is no way to be religious today other than to be a religious consumer. However, this does not necessarily mean that every religious person has merely shopped for his or her faith in the way that one chooses a car or groceries. 'Meaning of life' is something deeper and more essentially personal than what can be bought at the market, even if people living in a market society may behave as though they were at a market when they look for meaning in life.

Leth-Nissen (2018) shows, using an empirical basis, how the shift from 'obligation to consumption' is happening in the use of the Danish Folk Church (see also Chapter 11). In Denmark, the shift takes place within the framework of the institutionalised national Folk Church. The concept of *churching alone* describes the tendency to use the Folk Church based on an individually motivated choice.

Churching alone is not, however, necessarily about being alone; it is about making individual choices that make sense to oneself, but not necessarily to one's family or in terms of other traditional ways of belonging. The choice of using the Folk Church makes meaning at an individual level when, for example, a bride chooses a certain church for her wedding because she passes it every morning on her way to work, not because that church was the one traditionally used by her family. Another example of *churching alone* comes from individuals taking part in target group activities, such as baby hymn singing. Here, the use of the church makes sense for the parent at an individual level, and it takes place together with other individuals who are in the same situation or at a similar stage of life.

All this contrasts with using the Folk Church as a way of connecting to family, tradition and a sense of duty, which can be described as *churching together*. So, in fact, churching alone does not refer to all the churching that is done in the Danish Folk Church. There is still a lot of churching together going on, lots of gatherings taking place, marked by tradition and marked by connecting to family, history, generations, culture and national identity.

That being the case, the shift towards churching alone *is* happening, and the role of the individuals in church is changing from being part of a passive collective towards becoming active individuals, choosing whether, where and how to church.

Embedded in the concept of churching alone is a reference to Robert Putnam's influential work *Bowling Alone* (Putnam 2000) on social capital. The shift from a collective to an individual focus in the Danish Folk Church follows the development Putnam describes in his analysis of parallel changes in the USA, of how people increasingly bowl alone, whenever it makes sense to them, free of memberships to bowling unions or other ties. Also, for church use, individuals want less obligation, less long-term commitment and more individual sense making. Within use of the Folk Church, this refers to the rise in target group activities such as baby hymn singing and family services with meals, demanding no obligation and usually free of charge for parents and their infants, or families with young children. These are just a few examples of target group activities. Such widespread target-oriented activities accelerate the shift towards churching alone (Leth-Nissen 2018, 3).

To conclude, the 'churching' in churching alone refers to an individual's relation to the Folk Church, with respect to practice, belief and affiliation. 'Alone' refers to the individual's urge to feel free from obligations and being free to choose from a selection of Folk Church activities and services. It is not about being alone, but it is about feeling free to act on an individual basis.

Churching alone brings a new use of the word 'church' to the Danish language. In Danish, 'church' can only be a noun, not a verb as it is used in English.[5] Using 'churching' as a verb emphasises another shift captured in the idea of churching alone, namely the shift of roles between the church and the people. In a society with obligations to or traditions for taking part in church activities, the church seemingly played the active part, aiming to 'church' the people and make them come to church (originally through legal obligations, later through educational impact). Now, 'the people' has turned into individuals who, legally speaking, can freely choose their relations to the church; also culturally, they can now actively make individual decisions about this relation, choosing whichever activities and services they wish to participate in, based on what makes sense to them as individuals.

Relating churching alone to this chapter's context of legal changes for individuals, parish councils and deans, our analysis points to how the legal changes and the changed practices support more churching alone by the parishioners and church members.

Legal changes at the individual level 1849-2013

The Danish Folk Church is, as other full-covering majority churches in Europe, parochially organized according to a geographical structure in congregations, dioceses etc.[6] This was the case from when the church structure was organized by the kings around the year 1000 and up until just after the constitutional reform of 1849. The parochial structure still represents the general rule in Danish ecclesiastical law, meaning that all baptised individuals have a right to church services (including a right to have marriages performed, to baptism and confirmation of their children and to get a church service at their funeral) in their geographical parish and by the parish priest (Christoffersen, in preparation).

With the Freedom of Religion clauses in the constitution of 1849, Danish citizens received the right to change to another religious community or to opt out of any religion. These ideas of the individualisation of religious identity also influenced ecclesiastical law in the Danish Folk Church. Following these ideas, the first long period of individualisation within the church was an individualisation into sub-groups, upholding what could be termed 'churching together', albeit in family groups and in smaller congregations across the various geographical areas.

The first legislation that developed these ideas is found in the law from 1855, giving parishioners the right to dissolve their ties to the geographical parish (*sognebåndsløsning*)[7] and move their spiritual life to another parish pastor in a different geographical congregation, provided the new parish pastor is willing to accept the citizen as a member of his congregation. By using this instrument, the spiritual movements of the 19th century remained and developed within the Folk Church, since the parish pastors from any of these movements could gather a congregation of individuals. As such, we have churching alone in terms of choosing the pastor and thereby becoming parts of a new group, whilst churching together across geographical areas.

Not only could the individual change to another parish church pastor (and thus become members of a different congregation from the one where he or she lives), from 1868 it was also possible for lay members of the Folk Church to organize entire congregations that were not based on the parish structure, the so-called *congregations of choice* (*valgmenigheder*).[8]

A small village congregation could thus be the framework of two different Folk Church congregations. The parochial congregation remained, based on the geographic structures to which all members belonged if they did not choose differently. Alongside the geographical congregation in such a village, a congregation of choice could develop, based on individual belonging amongst people who remained members of the Folk Church (but not of the local, parochial congregation). The members of the congregation of choice choose the new congregation based on individual or family choices to belong to the free congregation. The choice is most often theologically based. From the beginning, these congregations were a protest against state involvement in the choice of the parish priests as well as the choice of liturgy, impacted by Grundtvigian thinking (see Chapter 5). A new wave of congregations of choice has appeared with periods of liturgical as well as (semi-fundamentalist) theological influence, especially coming from the USA.

These congregations of choice are based on individual membership. The members of the congregations of choice remain members of the Folk Church, albeit not of their local parishes. The congregations of choice must, in order to be approved, build a new church for themselves (or at least have regular access to a church building). They choose their own parish pastor, pay for him, for board and lodging, and so on.

The dissolution of parish bonds and membership of congregations of choice while remaining a member of the Folk Church were two developments that both supported an old form of marketisation within the church, establishing the foundation for churching together, but on an individualised basis.

A third element in the old laws of free choice within the church also contributes to not being tied to the parochial system and to being able to choose for yourself. That element is the legislation concerning the use of the local church building which, for more than a century, has given an individual church member the right to use his or her church for weddings and burials with a parish priest from another congregation (for example, the parish priest to whom new parish bonds have been established).[9] In addition, minor groups from the parish congregation can require the use of the parish church for an ordinary church service with a parish priest *of their choice* from a different congregation. Thus, there is a tradition of individual choices established within Danish ecclesiastical law (see also Christoffersen 1998; Christoffersen 2017).

Finally, it is part of the legislation that *access to church service be public and free* (and that services must be held in the Danish language). The purpose of this legal security of common access was originally, most likely, to make state authorities able to ensure that nothing but Christianity was preached (and thus to prevent political uproar being prepared within the churches). During the 20th century, the newspapers (and now the internet) have made it possible for every single individual to identify the church he or she wants to access for church services on any given Sunday morning – and this facility is used. Currently, even some of the 98 deaneries have developed web-based information systems announcing access to church services (as well as for example concerts and public lectures) within the area. This open access system in itself supports churching alone, allowing access where and when it suits the individual.

The economic legislation developed in 1901 in order to ensure the change of the Folk Church from an economy based on tithes into an economy based on individual tax payment. Only church members pay church taxes. The economic support of the Folk Church is thus based on individual decisions of being a church member (Christoffersen 2017, see Chapter 4 for further details).

The change in the funding scheme from tithes to individual payment meant that it was no longer of interest to private people to be patrons of the church. Previously, such private patrons had received the tithes and taken it upon themselves to keep the church building in good order. Now, the church buildings were changed into legally independent foundations governed by the parish council. The parish councils were thus introduced in 1903 in order to have someone to 'take care of the heating of the churches during wintertime', as it was formulated when the bill was passed in parliament (Christoffersen, 1998, p. 144 f).

It is telling, however, that this 'someone' who is to take care of the buildings is meant to be representative of all church members of the parish. Several attempts from religious groups and positions within the church to formulate 'ecclesiastical guarantees' as conditions for becoming an elected member of these governing bodies, in order to ensure religious persuasion among the members, were blocked by the political parties in parliament. There was a joint understanding among the leading parties of the 20th century (the Social Democratic Party, the Liberal Party, the Socio-Liberal Party and the Conservative Party) that there should be free and equal access to church, including the ability to govern the church, for active as well as passive church members (Christoffersen 2017). The law emphasised[10] the idea that the only functions of parish councils were to maintain the buildings and ensure a good framework for the work of the parish priest. From their beginnings in 1903, the parish councils were (as was stressed with a change of the law in 1912) not allowed to involve themselves in the functions of the pastor. It was not until the 1970s that the parish councils could begin to support the pastor in his ecclesiastical work, and at the start, this was economic support only.

From the outset, the parish councils were representatives of the people of the parish, who needed to organize and maintain the church building, so they could access church. In this way, parish councils could be identified as representatives of churching together. On the other hand, their work supported the individual churchgoer and the individual's need for religious services as well as for the development of an increased churching alone.

As part of the economic reforms during the 20th century, the function of the parish priest was changed to fit the scheme of civil servants. This development finished with the reform of civil servant status, including the status of the parish priests, in 1969 (see Chapter 4). That time was at the peak of the welfare state, and the ideology behind it was, amongst others things, that parish priests should serve the people with ecclesiastical functions on an equal footing, without demanding anything from the church members (apart from their being church members). During the 1970s, a new generation of parish priests protested against this 'service-function', demanding church attendance from, amongst others, parents who wanted their children baptised. These parish priests were disciplined (Christoffersen 1977) and told that their obligation was to offer the parents education, not to set up conditions that would keep them from receiving religious services. It is thus compulsory for the parish priest to offer educational possibilities for the parents as well as for the children, and it is likewise compulsory for the parish council to ensure that it remain economically viable to run such possibilities.[11] These regulations have been the framework for the development of, for example, baby hymn singing in many parishes. It has also been possible since 1987 (and compulsory since 2014) for all parish councils to offer religious education for children at the age of 10 (introductory confirmation classes) as a (non-compulsory) preparatory class before the teaching hours in advance of their confirmation.[12]

The development of such offers of education instead of conditions for accessing religious services is an example of how the basic combination of a geographic parish structure with individual rights for church members further developed into greater individualisation.

In 2009, this development was taken further through a change of the law relating to membership of, and access to, religious services within the Folk Church.[13] The purpose was to increase the church members' access to baptism, confirmation, marriage and funeral so that it included many more parishes than before. The old laws gave access to a dissolution of the parish bonds (as per the 1855 legislation); and in the congregation of choice (as per the 1868 legislation), to which one was tied with family bonds.

The 2009 legislation now provides church members with access to ecclesiastical services in any parish to which the church member, as an individual person, has a special bond. Such special bonds are, according to the new legislation, established not only by family bonds, but also, for example, if the church member previously lived in the parish, or even by owning a summerhouse in the parish (combining that with using the church). In any of these situations, the local church pastor is obliged to serve the church member, and the church member has access to use of the church building on equal footing with those living in the parish (Christoffersen and Esdahl 2011).

The obligation to service the members of one's congregation, as the absolute general rule, is also emphasised in changed legislation from 2012 regarding gender-neutral marriages. This legislative package contained three elements: 1) A gender-neutral marriage law, upholding the previous right (but not obligation) to perform marriages for parish priests within the Folk Church and within other religious communities on equal footing. 2) The right for church members to obtain marriage rights under this legislation. At the same time, individual parish priests were given the right to reject to perform marriages if the couple was of same sex, or if one of the couple had previously divorced.[14] Finally, 3) a new marriage ritual was authorised for use in the church, not just for same sex marriages but for all marriages, that did not mention the 'created as man and woman' texts.[15]

As such, there is a small possibility that a parish priest may refuse to marry a couple. In this situation, however, the couple still have a right to marry in the church. A 'No' from the local parish priest is not a denial of a church marriage per se. The church members still have the right to church marriages. If a local parish priest does not want to perform this marriage, the dean is obliged to find a colleague who can perform the marriage in the same church and under the same conditions, as if it were the local priest who usually takes care of such services.

It is also possible, since 2013, for a couple to be married outdoors, for example in their own garden (instead of in the church building) with the local church pastor and the local organist acting 'out of space', that is, outside the church building.[16] It is the church member's right to get this service, but, again, there is no obligation put on the individual parish priest.

Even funeral practice is further individualised. A church service followed by cremation is now the most common format. It has even become common to have the ashes spread across the open sea.[17] One could argue that individualisation also paves the way for more marketisation in the way that the funerals are organized: the division of labour between church employees and the private undertakers is under constant pressure here.

Finally, the impact of the changed economic structures could be mentioned. Since the introduction of church tax, church services and the individual services for church members (baptism, confirmation, marriage and funeral) have both been financed through the payment of these taxes. Church taxes are used for keeping up the church buildings, paying salaries for some of the people working there and for part of the salaries of the church ministers (Christoffersen, 2015). Church taxes are, however, also meant to finance the local church life.

The increasing use of individual solutions has re-opened pressure from the congregation councils (and the deans) to demand individual payment from 'outsiders' (that is, people who have a right to obtain the service or use of the church, but who do not pay their church taxes within that specific congregation).

The law has always maintained the possibility for claiming individual payment for the use of individual church services, such as weddings.[18] Throughout the 20th century, the services were paid for through the church taxes and only the odd 'foreign use' for a wedding, or the like, was paid for by individuals. Such individuals were allowed to use the church, but without having the right to do so. There is also a market for romantic weddings in certain very popular church buildings, which can be performed if the parish priest is ready to do the services. Such a market already exists at certain town halls.

Recently, some churches also require payment for baby hymn singing, for literature clubs and other special offers. How much such individual payment is requested is unclear. The decision about whether the local church life is financed through the general church taxes or through individual payment is taken by the parish council, but the background for the distinction is unclear. This individualisation of the payment is upheld and still in use, even though individual payments were dissolved by law alongside with the dissolution of the tithes in 1903. This development of individual payments has appeared without any legal debate.

A more general debate might be sparked by another change from 2013. Since then, it has been compulsory for individual parish councils to decide on the financial structure regarding the use of the church cemetery separately from the budgeting for the church. Before 2013, cemetery and church buildings were budgeted under the same accounting system as were the other functions governed by the parish council. Since 2013, the economy of the cemetery must be not only independently accounted for, but it must also be economically self-contained. The salaries for the employees must be funded through the income of the cemetery. The income is the payment from individuals for their burial, the plot for their grave and for keeping the plots, if such upkeep is left with the employees (it is possible for an individual to perform the upkeep him or herself). All individuals living within the geographical area, regardless of whether they are church members or not, have the right to burial in the cemetery grounds. The church thus maintains the cemetery for the entire population.

The consequence of the separation of the accounting for cemeteries from the accounting for the church is that church members can be required to pay church taxes and to pay for the burial plot, too. There is still the possibility, however, that the deanery council can decide to use some of the income from the church taxes across the entire deanery to lower the price for using a cemetery plot for church members (meaning that church members would not pay twice). If a deanery council does not decide to do so, then church members will see the prices for using the cemeteries rise for them as well. One would imagine that church taxes would be lowered at the same time. That is not necessarily the case. The introduction of independently accounted budgets for the cemeteries is a central dimension in the introduction of NPM within the Folk Church and thus an example of state-driven marketisation of the church.

Nobody knows how often such individual payment is applied in practice. The decisions are made at a local level, based on local decisions, approved of by the deanery councils. There is no general overview of the mechanisms.

Recent legal changes at the parish council level

In the section above, we showed how changes in ecclesiastical law support marketisation and individualisation, both directly and indirectly. In this second part, we will discuss how recent legal changes of the function and competences of the parish councils, the division of labour amongst the parish priests, the budgeting procedures and the rules concerning church taxes further support the development towards churching alone.

These questions concerning competences, the use of church tax and the division of labour are historically intertwined. At first, the parish councils were introduced only as an experiment. When they were legally made a stable part of the church structure in 1912, it was a central requirement that there be a clear division of labour amongst the parish priests. Parish councils were only established in order to ensure the framework – the priest took responsibility for the content.

New legislation in 1922 was inspired from the areas that had been German during the period of 1864-1920. These areas had adopted the idea of councils at the deanery level with lay representation, having insight into the economy of the parish councils (Christoffersen, 1998). This representation made sure that parish councils only financed what was specified in the law. Until the early 1970s, that was still only the buildings, and so on. From that point on, the parish councils were allowed to use a small amount of money (so-called pocket money) for supporting the ecclesiastical life in the parish, which usually continued to be organized by the church pastor.

The secular structure of Danish society was changed in 2007 into 98 big municipalities. The then church minister, Bertel Haarder (*Venstre*) claimed that the church had to follow this secular structure, which meant that the structure of the deaneries changed in 2007, there now being 103. The Ministry of Ecclesiastical Affairs (in the official Report No. 1477/2006) proposed central changes in the tasks of the local parish councils as well as changes in the function for the deans and the councils at the deanery level in much the same vein, following the principles of the changes to the organizational structure of the secular society. The suggestion was that the congregation councils should concentrate more on ecclesiastical affairs in collaboration with the church minister, whereas the economic competences ought to be moved to the 103 deaneries.

The subsequent legislation[19] did not follow this route entirely. The budgeting and administrative competences remained in the parish councils. The responsibility of the parish councils was clarified, however. Now, the parish councils are responsible for not only the administrative function of the parish, but also the ecclesiastical function (§ 1). The parish priest is still independent of the church council in his or her way of professionally organizing activities as a pastor, but it is no longer possible to describe the ecclesiastical work as independent of the parish council. The formulations of the competences for the parish priest are now much more limited. The parish priest is, at the same time, also a member of the parish council, the idea being that the parish council decides the goals, including the ecclesiastical ones, and allocates the money to reach these goals (Iversen 2010, 146f). It is thus the parish council who decides, for example, whether there shall be a series of evening songs in the church during summer. The parish priest is still the one to organize the services.

The competences for the parish councils were further developed with legislation in 2009. Another official report (Report No. 1491/2007),[20] in line with the ideas in the previous report from 2006, had the underlying premise that more tasks and competences should be moved from the parish councils to the deanery councils and the deans. The government and parliament, however, opted for a middle solution. Previously, the law on the economy of the church listed which tasks the local councils could pay for using church taxes. Now, § 2 in the law was changed, giving the local councils the power to decide within broader frameworks. Since 2009[21], church taxes can be used to pay for:

1. The general ecclesiastical activities in the parish;
2. The activities in the parish regarding burial services;
3. Ecclesiastical activities in the deanery and the diocese;
4. Ecclesiastical activities within the Danish church abroad; and
5. Civil registration

This means that the only deciding factor is whether the local church council identifies a task as an ecclesiastical activity (within, of course, the limits of supervision from superior authorities). There is no longer a formal list of what the church council is allowed to pay for. It is possible, on this basis, for the parish council to reallocate church taxes in order to support more group-oriented work and diminish other ecclesiastical functions – and that is exactly what happens.

The same law, in § 4, No. 7 ff, clarifies the competences between the deanery council and the parish council in regard to budgeting in order to make it clear that the parish council is responsible for the budgeting and prioritisation, whereas the deanery council is responsible for how much church tax the individual parish can administer.

The parish councils thereby got the right to prioritise between different types of ecclesiastical tasks within the budget, approved of by the deanery, whereas the dean could invite all parish councils within the deanery to joint budgeting, and thus to shared joint responsibility for the entire church tax within a municipality.

Through this development, is it now possible for both parish councils and deanery councils to be much more active in identifying and prioritising the ecclesiastical tasks. They can now give priority to changed formats of services and to changed formats of clerical practices, and they can decide this locally, as long as there is agreement between the pastor and the lay members of the church council and they act within the legal framework of the rituals decided at national level. This ability to determine local priorities is supported by changed accounting systems, which ask for arguments to defend the way in which the economy is prioritised.

Churching alone refers to individual choices about how persons make use of church activities on the church market. The congregation councils further develop such a church market based on their new powers to allocate money to the locally identified needs, be they hymn singing, opt-in-baptism or similar. NPM methods are thus in use for locally decided changes that aim to meet the needs of churching alone.

Changes at the deanery level

The dean level implements many of the changes in legislation. Deans function as the day-today contact with the parish councils, and they are responsible for distributing the church tax to the parish councils. As a parallel to the changed legislation, this section will show how the roles of the deans changed during the same period.[22] At the dean level, the Folk Church was reformed by making deans the *change agents* of the Folk Church. The dean's office was changed with the 1922 legislation. From then, the office, along with the deanery councils, gained even more practical and administrative dimensions. Until the early 2000s, the dean's role had been administrative, and the dean had the authority of control (Brunés 2001). However, with Committee Reports 1427/2006 and 1527/2011 and the subsequent legislation, a new paradigm of the dean as a facilitator emerges. The dean goes from having qualifications to having competences (Andersen and Lindhardt 2014).

Thus, the dean's role was transformed from being an administrator into being a facilitator of change. The transformation took place through three influential changes.

First came the introduction of a new compulsory dean-training programme. A pilot project ran for a few years implemented by the Centre for Pastoral Education and Research, an institution under the Ministry of Ecclesiastical Affairs. In 2013, the institution launched a compulsory two-year training programme for all new deans, now with a focus on management (Leth-Nissen 2018, 109-111).

Second, parallel to the changes in the training, a new recruitment procedure of deans was implemented in 2012. Earlier, a dean was recruited solely from among the pastors within the deanery, but the change in 2012 opened up the possibility for all Danish pastors to apply for these positions (Leth-Nissen 2018, 109).

Third, the focus on management re-interprets the relationship of dean to bishop as a subordinate relationship set within a hierarchy descending from bishop to dean to parish pastor (Brunés 2014, 97; Report 1527/2011). Now, the dean's office is in many aspects equal to the office of any public manager (Report 1527/2011 in Lindhardt and Andersen 2014, 3). However, the Danish understanding of the Lutheran theology of the office has emphasised that there is only *one* office of pastor, which encompasses the roles of pastor, dean and bishop. The roles are part of one and the same office. The question of whether this opens up a subordination of the pastor under the bishop was discussed during the 1990s (Espersen 1999, 109). A court case in 1998 however emphasised that the bishop can administratively regulate the behaviour of the pastors to a certain degree (UfR 1998: 894H Villekjær, jf. Engberg 2011, 62). This has theological implications, as it opens up the risk of ignoring the spiritual dimension of the office (Nielsen 2011, 29).

Furthermore, the vertical relationship of management and the horizontal relationship of the theology of the office put a cross-pressure on the dean. This cross-pressure becomes evident in the qualitative interviews conducted by Leth-Nissen (2018) with ten deans, selected through purposive sampling after criteria of geography, urbanisation, age, professional experiences, gender, theology, participation in old or new dean training and covering all ten dioceses (2018, 114-115).

The deans tend to interpret the changes in the Folk Church as consequences of NPM. One of the deans in the study describes how he finds the level of NPM lower than in the rest of the public sector:

> We do not have as much reporting as in some of the other old institutions of society ... I do not have to report back which materials I used for teaching the confirmands as school teachers have to and gymnasium teachers have to. I am not obliged to report how many of the buried persons will go to hell and how many to heaven. I do not have to report why we maintain a parish council in three small parishes with less than 350 people. They are allowed to, because they want to. I need not report how many depressions there have been among my parish pastors and what I have done about it. I know exactly how many there have been, and I know what I have done about it with the bishop, but I have no reporting to do.[23]

This may be due to the aforementioned special Danish model of NPM (Ejersbo and Greve 2013, 16), which includes the people involved in any reform processes, and which may be linked to the local church tax collection.

Another dean feels that the greatest challenge for the Folk Church comes from the internal power struggle within it:

> We have a situation where you have at one end a traditional top-down management system, public governance, with rules of every kind. There you have the perception of a pyramid, with everything going from top and down and out into the pyramid. People have to follow the rules and all such things ... This is set in relation to a local reality where being a church is to a large extent dependent on the ability to put aside the formal roles: talking on equal terms and working on equal terms. This is what I mean. This is what you as a parish council have to understand, this whole formal system and what it takes. In addition, the knowledge of this is very poor.[24]

In the midst of this conflict, the pastors dominate the Folk Church and it should be the volunteers who were being empowered instead. The 'management thinking' creates dilemmas. Yet another dean sees two parallel tendencies opposing each other:

> I see a church more and more alive, and in which more people have an interest now than earlier. At the same time, I see a church with a falling member rate, and a dramatically declining baptism rate. A church, which in many ways seems rather vulnerable in the way it is structured right now.[25]

The interviews show that the deans generally employ the tools and procedures provided by the new paradigm of governance. Some even emphasise how they want more power of direction over the pastors of their deanery (Leth-Nissen 2018, 128). Both the older deans and the younger deans, who have been through the new dean training courses, work as facilitators of change with the parish councils (2018, 120-130). The deans mediate between the Ministry of Ecclesiastical Affairs, the parish councils and individual members, thus mediating between marketisation and local democracy.

Their explicit theologies according to the life-story interviews remain the same as earlier in their lives, and these theologies have developed through childhood background and education. The following quotes give examples of theologically based opinions on the Folk Church structure and New Public Management. One dean is afraid the Folk Church is becoming too service-oriented. He says:

> What matters in the Folk Church is that we have become so adaptable that everything has to be an event. It is my stance that as long as it works for the gospel it is OK with me, but sometimes it gets too silly. It needs to have some kind of solidity; otherwise, it is just hot air.[26]

Instead of worrying about the church and activities attendance, this dean thinks the Folk Church should give the volunteers better conditions. Continuing the present way, he thinks the volunteers will give up, which in his opinion would be a huge loss for the Folk Church. He sees this as a clear consequence of NPM. For him, the service and customer focus is wrong and cannot compensate for the widespread loss of tradition. Only an emphasis on the gospel will help the Folk Church thrive again. Another dean says:

> I think we now have a state church. I feel that the politicians see the Folk Church in the same way as they see universities and hospitals: 'The citizens have certain needs to be fulfilled'. They have begun intruding into the internal affairs of the church. The Ministry of Ecclesiastical Church Affairs, they are not theologians and their interest is not in theology, and they do not understand the fundamental essence of the church. We are not running a company.[27]

She finds that the politicians and the civil servants of the Ministry of Ecclesiastical Church Affairs are damaging the Folk Church. For yet another dean, the damage starts from within the Folk Church itself, in the parish councils, among the pastors and the deans:

> At this level there is a marketisation going on too, you exert yourself to please. This is something other than asking: 'Where are we going?' Because this is a question of dumping your luggage, I think. To please the individualising tendency of the postmodern loss of traditions in our population. You may do that to preserve the numbers of members. But then I must mention that the number of members is not so important.[28]

The deans are rather critical towards NPM in general. However, when it comes to their implicit theologies – what they do – they adapt to governance changes. The following quotes from deans show how they employ NPM tools (Hood 1991).

> In one deanery, the deanery council have just established a dedicated development fund. In another case, the deanery council did so too, and the dean explains how they want to facilitate the parish council's ability to do new things or to do things in a new way.

> ... We have agreed on some principles that we follow. We want to be a catalyst for development. We want to create a framework and space wherein development can take place. We want to support the individual parish council and the parish pastor in being the management of the parish, even when they move in different directions.[29]

> ... In order to apply for funds, two or more parishes have to apply for the projects together.

One dean uses project groups as tools. When she gets an idea for a new development, she puts together a project group of four or five people. In the project groups, they have been able to brainstorm and think in an 'anarchist' manner. After the process, the group presents its conclusions to the parish councils.

> Then we have presented it all to the large group who thinks in old fashioned ways, in terms of questions like: 'Do we dare?' and 'Is it legal?' and 'Will this work?' and 'What if she gets sick, the one we put here?' All the precautions. We may lose those ones, those with all the precautions, because it is very easy to sit in a small anarchist workgroup and plan something. Nevertheless, we have managed to sell it, to formulate the purpose in a short and easily understood form. 'What is the need and why do we do it?' We show that this is not just an idea of the anarchist group.[30]

The development processes, facilitated by the deans, are a typical example of NPM. Although the deans focus on maintaining a dialogue with the parish councils, they facilitate changes and development, just as the reforms prescribe. Talking about the activities of the parishes within the deanery, one dean talks of 'a market' for baby hymn singing. Asked why she talks of the Folk Church as being on 'a market', she laughs and says:

> ... it might be because I have been smitten with this language. A little, yes, maybe. We have begun thinking about showing the flag ... showing that we are here. Last year, we were some parishes in the deanery, no, this year, that put a joint advertisement in the newspaper talking about Easter. The bishop encouraged it ... But we are on the market because the world is on the market. That is how people think today. But from that to calling worshippers customers or users, that is a real hurdle to me. It adds something undefinable, when you enter a church. It is also a business, it is. When you must have a funeral or ... But I don't think I can find one parish council who will describe their own work as market-oriented. They are considering how they can provide good occasions for people to use the church. They do not see the church as a shop. And if they do, someone else will very quickly say 'hang on' ... We are not going to have bridal fashion shows here or ... no. It is still like this [gestures] the market is here and the church is here.[31]

Another dean and his deanery council have conducted a professional analysis of the use of the church magasine and found out how every church magasine was read by one or two readers per home. Half of all the non-members read it. One dean describes the current situation this way:

> I think the Folk Church has moved on, over the course of many years. The diversity is more present, and the understanding that there is no one size fits all. You can see that when you look at the many services in the Folk Church, right? A sense of the target groups for the services, with whom are you doing this service?[32]

She wants the church in her deanery to be a church for all segments, which most parish pastors agree, rather than being only for 'the elite'. She thinks it is the strength of the Folk Church that all segments are represented and, thus, all segments of her parish need to be addressed. She uses a theological argument for this:

> Everyone is created in the image of God. Diversity is an image of the Christian faith and part of my DNA. This is where I often get some slaps in the face. Since this is not always the self-perception of the Folk Church.[33]

The quotes here show how the deans tend to adopt a new view of human beings as customers (Leth-Nissen 2018, 120-150). Overall, the deans express a high degree of critique of NPM policies, but in practice, they implement most of the policies. The resistance exercised by the deans is mostly focused on protecting the parish councils' volunteer members. The deans perceive the Ministry of Ecclesiastical Affairs and the major stakeholder of the National Association of Parish Councils as a threat to the survival of the local parish councils, especially in the rural areas. When resisting NPM policies, the deans used theological arguments. Still, the analysis showed that the deans have adapted parts of NPM's view of the public as customers. The deans act, more or less, as if the users of the Folk Church were customers, offering target-oriented activities, using PR-strategies and user surveys, thinking in segments in order to reach out. Here, they support a change towards more 'churching alone'.

One dean emphasises how the introduction of NPM has had both good and bad consequences. He is positive about the way things can now change and how he has been able to be more active as a dean:

> It has given a sense of change being possible. There are not so many closed doors anymore. I think it has been doing good things. Change is possible. However, it has also stressed the administration. When tearing down the hierarchies, the very
>
> firm lines of command, you open things up for great confusion. Just look at the digital platform for the Folk Church, and all the committees now [in the deaneries]. Projects, these are very large part of my work now, taking energy away from the day-to-day operations, the house calls, for instance. If you can always take on exciting projects, instead of taking care of operations, this is a danger.[34]

With the changes in management focus, the deans have become more influential. They exercise a lot of power and they generally have no lack of financial resources. The high degree of compliance with the governance changes and the following marketisation may decline if there were to be a lack of resources. Things might look different if the deans had to choose between target group-oriented activities and the more classic diaconal work, say, if they had to choose between churching alone and churching together. In the current economically favourable situation, they can have both.

Implementing the reforms mainly through the dean level, the major stakeholders have ensured that the Folk Church parochial structure adapts to a more individualised practice of attending church activities across parish borders. As the deans have facilitated a higher degree of inter-parish cooperation regarding activities, both from the parish councils and the pastors, the Folk Church has adapted to the demands of the members. In this way, the Folk Church has moved towards churching alone.

Discussion

These examples at individual, parish and deanery levels show how legal changes have supported the individualisation and marketisation processes within the Folk Church. They also show, however, that the main rule has not been marketisation or individualisation until recently. The main rule in the

Folk Church is an organization that is structured in order to support churching together through its focus on parochial rights for the church members and parochial obligations for parish priests. Even though churching alone (including individually-based choices to church together with whichever people one wishes to) was originally the exemption, these rules and rights for individual church members have developed into a habit of being allowed to church alone – much more so than in other geographically organized national churches.

The question is, however, whether the development of marketisation and individualisation within the Folk Church is of relevance in a comparison to other cultural institutions, or, as one student recently asked, whether there is a system of freely chosen providers of welfare benefits within the church, as has been introduced as a central element in NPM in the health care system and other parallel organizations. As has hopefully become clear, the answer must be that there has always been a system of free choice with respect to organizing the provision of church benefits within the church. In that sense, the church has always (or at least since the constitution) been marketised. It is, however, a marketisation that has taken place (and still takes place) as an element within the otherwise geographically-ordered provision of church goods.

One could also compare the Folk Church to other cultural organizations, such as museums or libraries. In such a comparison, it becomes clear that museums (in contrast to the Folk Church) have never been organized according to a geographical, parochial structure. Such cultural organizations are thus much easier to re-organize according to NPM ideas. In contrast, things are the opposite with libraries. Local libraries were originally organized in order to provide the local people with access to literature. The organization and access for people was strictly kept within the local municipality, and it is only very recently that libraries have allowed access to people from other municipalities. In that sense, the Folk Church seems much more marketised and more welcoming of individualisation than were the libraries (see further Chapter 10).

To conclude, the legal structures and the leadership of the Folk Church increasingly support the development of marketisation and individualisation towards a tendency of *churching alone*. It is, however, still based on a parochial structure, offering to support all members with ecclesiastical goods on an equal footing, based on the traditional idea of *churching together*.

References

Andersen, Erling and Lindhardt, Mogens 2014. *Kompetenceprofil – Provsteembedet* (1-15). Copenhagen: Ministry of Ecclesiastical Affairs.

Brunés, Steffen 2001. 'Folkekirkens Ledelse – Provsten som Chef'. *Præsteforeningens Blad*, *2001* (21).

Brunés, Steffen 2014. *Folkekirkens Personale* (3. udgave). Copenhagen: Nyt Juridisk Forlag.

Christensen, Peter 2010: 'Omlægning af Statens Tilskud til Folkekirken. I Bekendelse og Kirkeordninger'. Zacharias Balslev-Clausen, Peter Christensen, Lisbet Christoffersen, Peter Garde, Anders Jørgensen and Kirsten Busch Nielsen (eds.) *Kirkeretsantologi 2010*, København: Anis, 159-174.

Christoffersen, Lisbet 1977: *Folkekirkens Dåbssager*. Unpublished MA thesis at the Faculty of Law, University of Copenhagen.

Christoffersen, Lisbet. 1998: *Kirkeret Mellem Stat, Marked og Civilsamfund*. Copenhagen: DJØF Forlag.

Christoffersen, Lisbet 2006. 'Intertwinement: a New Concept for Understanding Religion-Law Relations', *Nordic Journal of Religion and Society*, *19/2*, 107-126.

Christoffersen, Lisbet 2010: 'Delokaliserung der Dänischen Lutherischen Volkskirche? Die Neue Mitte der Kirche: Der Aufstieg der Intermediären Instanzen in den Europäischen Grosskirchen seit 1945'. Damberg, W. and Hellmans, S. (eds.). Stuttgart: Kohlhammer Verlag, Bind 42, 159-177 (Konfession und Gesellschaft, Bind 42).

Christoffersen, Lisbet 2015: 'A Long Historical Path towards Transparency, Accountability and Good Governance: on Financing Religions in Denmark'. Francis Messner (ed.) *Public Funding of Religions in Europe*, Farnham: Ashgate/Routledge, 125-149.

Christoffersen, Lisbet 2017: 'Fri og Lige Adgang til Vorherre. Kirken og Retten 1901 -2017', Niels Henrik Gregersen and Carsten Bach Nielsen (eds.) *Reformationen i dansk kirke og kultur: 1914-2017*. Odense: Syddansk Universitetsforlag, Bind 3, 195-228.

Christoffersen, Lisbet. 'By Law Established'. Woodhead, Linda and Hans Raun Iversen (eds.). *The Old National Churches of Northern Europe: The Persistence of Societal Religion* (in preparation).

Christoffersen, Lisbet and Pernille Esdahl. 2011: 'Offentligretlige Rammer for Præstens Arbejde. En Analyse af Begrebet "Særlig Tilknytning" som Grundlag for Kirkelig Betjening uden for Bopælssognet'. Kirsten Busch Nielsen, Lisbet Christoffersen, Peter Garde and Peter Lodberg (eds.) *Folkekirkens Embeder. Kirkeretsantologi 2011*, Copenhagen: Anis. 179-212.

Davie, Grace. 1994. *Religion in Britain since 1945: Believing Without Belonging*. West Sussex: Wiley.

Davie, Grace. 2006. 'Religion in Europe in the 21st Century: the Factors to Take into Account', *European Journal of Sociology*, 47/02, 271.

Davie, Grace. 2013. *The Sociology of Religion: A Critical Agenda*. SAGE.

Ejersbo, Niels, and Greve, Carsten 2013. 'Et Farvel Efter 30 år?', *Futuriblerne*, 41/3-4, 11-17.

Engberg, Morten 2011. 'Tilsyn og Delegation i Folkekirken'. *Folkekirkens Embeder. Kirkeretsantologi, 2011, 53-68*.

Esdahl, Pernille 2004: *Kirkeministerens økonomiske særkompetencer*. Kirkeministeriet.

Espersen, Preben 1999. *Kirkeret. Almindelig del. 2. udgave*. Copenhagen: Jurist- og Økonomforbundets Forlag.

Gauthier, François, Linda Woodhead and Tuomas Martikainen 2013. 'Introduction: Consumerism as the Ethos of Consumer Society'. François Gauthier and Tuomas Martikainen (eds.), *Religion in Consumer Society. Brands, Consumers and Markets*, Farnham: Ashgate.

Harbsmeier, Eberhard and Helle Christiansen (eds.) 2008: *Den Gratis Nåde og de Mange Penge. En Bog om Kirken og Pengene*. Løgumkloster: Teologisk Pædagogisk Center.

Hood, Christopher. 1991. 'A Public Management for All Seasons?', *Public Administration* 69/1: 3-19.

Hvidt, Jakob. 2004: 'Folkekirkens økonomi – Overvejelser og Fremtid', *Kirkeretsantologi 2004*, København: Anis, 495-504.

Iversen, Hans Raun 2010: 'Folkekirken som den Fremtræder og Definerer sig Selv. Betænkning 1477 og 1491 og Efterfølgende Lovgivning', *Bekendelse og kirkeordninger. Kirkeretsantologi 2010*, København: Anis, 127-149.

Leth-Nissen, Karen Marie. 2018. *'Churching Alone? A Study of the Danish Folk Church at Organisational, Individual, and Societal Level's*. PhD dissertation, Faculty of Theology, University of Copenhagen.

Nepper-Christensen, Henrik. 2010. 'Bloktilskud til Folkekirken?' *Kirkeretsantologi 2010*, København: Anis. 151-158.

Nielsen, Kirsten Busch 2011. 'Det Almene, det Særlige og det Helt Særlige Embede. Forholdet Mellem Folkekirkens Præsteembeder Teologisk Belyst'. Kirsten Busch Nielsen, Lisbet Christoffersen, Peter Lodberg and Peter Garde (eds.) *Folkekirkens Embeder. Kirkeretsantologi 2011*. København: Anis, 15-34.

Pedersen, Ove Kaj 2011. *Konkurrencestaten*. Copenhagen: Hans Reitzel.

Putnam, Robert D. 2000. *Bowling Alone: The Collapse and Revival of American Community*. New York: Simon and Schuster.

Notes

1. The work on this chapter has been divided so that Leth-Nissen is responsible for the theoretical conceptualisation, Christoffersen for the legal analysis and Leth-Nissen for the analysis of the deans. Leth-Nissen and Christoffersen are jointly responsible for the conclusion.
2. The *frihedslovgivning* is a legal framework of freedoms and rights for groups and individuals within the church, allowing for exemptions from the general parochial system. It is taken for granted in the Danish context. When compared to other Nordic countries and the UK, it does become clear, however, that such freedoms have led to the development of alternative church forms outside the national church. The *frihedslovgivning* is touched upon in Christoffersen (in preparation). The system has not previously been presented in any detail in an international context. The impact on the marketisation of the Folk Church is touched upon in Christoffersen (1998). The impact on individualisation has not previously been analysed.
3. PhD thesis by Karen Marie Sø Leth-Nissen, defended 9 May 2018.
4. Martikainen, 'Religion and the Welfare State under Neoliberal Hegemony', *What Money Can't Buy* opening conference, 4 December 2014.
5. The verb *churching* is in common use in English-speaking countries, alluding most often to 'going to church', or doing things related to church. 'Churching' as a word was used by the Emerging Church movement of the late 20th and early 21st centuries, which worked using a missional strategy on 'churching the people'. We were to be churched. It was a prescriptive. Churching was also used, for example, in the title of 'The Churching of America' (Finke and Stark 2005). The book is on how American religion became institutionalised.
6. For an overview (in the Danish language) of Danish Ecclesiastical Law from 1849 to the present, see Christoffersen, 1998, and Christoffersen, 2017. For more detailed analysis of the valid law at the turn of the millennium, see Espersen, 1999. No general introduction to the current Ecclesiastical law has yet been published in the 21st century.
7. Lov om sognebåndsløsning, 1855. The rules are still in force; the formal format has changed, however. The rules are now part of the law on membership of the Folk Church, Bekendtgørelse af lov om medlemskab af folkekirken, kirkelig betjening og sognebåndsløsning LBK nr 622 of 19/06/2012.
8. Lov om valgmenigheder, 1868. The rules are still in force, see Bekendtgørelse af lov om valgmenigheder (Valgmenighedsloven), LBK nr 797 af 24/06/2013.
9. Currently, these rules can be found in Lov om Bestyrelse og brug af folkekirkens kirker, LBK nr. 330 af 29/03/2014.
10. By a change of the law on parish councils in 1912, now § 37.
11. AND Nr. 1 af 2/1 om dåb i folkekirken, and in "Biskoppernes Vejledning om

Dåb i Folkekirken", which can be found on the homepages of each individual diocese, see e.g. www.haderslevstift.dk/vejledninger/vejledning-om-daab.
12 AND 301 af 20/5 1987 om forsøgsmæssig etablering af en frivillig indledende konfirmationsforberedelse, and AND nr 1027 af 24/09/2014 om børnekonfirmandundervisning og konfirmation.
13 Lov om medlemskab af folkekirken, kirkelig betjening og sognebåndsløsning, LBK Nr 622 af 19/6/2012, www.retsinformation.dk/forms/r0710.aspx?id=142350.
14 Medlemsskabsloven (see footnote 11), § 7a: En præst kan undlade at vie to personer af samme køn. The right to deny a new marriage to divorced people is based on a supreme court decision of 1908.
15 www.retsinformation.dk/Forms/R0710.aspx?id=142366.
16 www.fyensstift.dk/biskoppen/vejledninger/vielser-uden-for-kirkens-rum.
17 Prince Henrik, who died in 2018, had decided that half of his ashes should be spread over the open sea and the other half placed in an urn in a private place near Fredensborg Castle. See information regarding the spreading of ashes: www.km.dk/borgerinformation/doedsfald/askespredning/.
18 Betaling for brug af kirken ved særskilte kirkelige handlinger, kirkelige møder mv, fastsættes i en vedtægt, der udfærdiges af menighedsrådet og godkendes af provstiudvalget', LBK nr 330 af 20 marts 2014 om bestyrelse og brug af folkekirkens kirkebygninger mm, § 19.
19 Lov nr. 531 af 6. juni 2007 om ændring af lov om menighedsråd, lov om valg til menighedsråd, lov om folkekirkens økonomi og lov om udnævnelse af biskopper og om stiftsbåndsløsning (Menighedsrådets sammensætning, loyalitetskrav til valgte menighedsrådsmedlemmer og bindende stiftsbidrag m.v.).
20 Betænkning 1491/2007 Folkekirkens lokale økonomi.
21 Lov nr. 47 af 28/01/2009 om Lov om ændring af lov om medlemskab af folkekirken, kirkelig betjening og sognebåndsløsning, lov om folkekirkens økonomi og forskellige andre love (Effektivisering af folkekirkens økonomi og administration samt udvidet adgang til kirkelig betjening m.v.), § 4, nr. 4.
22 This paragraph builds on Leth-Nissen 2018, 73-150.
23 Interview with Peter, male, age 50-70. All interviews were conducted in Danish and translated by Leth-Nissen into English.
24 Interview with Svend, male, age 50-70.
25 Interview with Svend, male, age 50-70.
26 Interview with Lars, male, age 50-70.
27 Interview with Dorthe, female, age 50-70.
28 Interview with Finn, male, age 50-70.
29 Interview with Svend, male, age 50-70.
30 Interview with Lisa, female, age 50-70.
31 Interview with Ulla, female, age 30-50.
32 Interview with Dorthe, female, age 50-70.
33 Interview with Dorthe, female, age 50-70.
34 Interview with Leif, male, age 50-70.

8. The Level of Church Income: Different Explanations

Sidsel Kjems and Niels Kærgård

Introduction[1]

The five Nordic countries, as well as England and Scotland, all have old, established majority churches. Their theologies are very similar in many ways, but their financial systems are very different; and there are large differences between income levels of these churches. The established churches in Denmark, Sweden and Finland have a 'church tax' (a member fee collected together with ordinary taxes by the state) as their main source of income.[2] The churches of Norway and Iceland are both financed through the general taxes on the public. The Church of Scotland and the Church of England both have donations and fundraising as their main sources of income. The churches of Denmark, Sweden and Finland seem considerably richer than the other churches, of which the churches of England and Scotland seem the poorest, see Kjems (A) and Kjems and Bille (in press).

This chapter attempts to explain these empirical findings and will use, for the most part, traditional and behavioural economic theory. The reason why the incomes of the established churches in Iceland and Norway are higher than those of the Church of England and the Church of Scotland is probably because the former are embedded within the public structure. The Church of England and the Church of Scotland are dependent on the willingness of the population to donate to the churches. The budgets of the established churches in Iceland and Norway are also subject to budget control and political negotiation. Any increase in their budgets will have to be negotiated in competition with other areas of public welfare. This might be why church income is lower there than the income of the established churches in Sweden, Finland and Denmark, where the church itself decides the 'tax rate'.

The affiliation rate and the economy of the established churches

The situation of the seven churches will be summarised in this section. Table 1 shows the share of the population in the Nordic countries who were members of the established churches in 2014. The membership concept is quite different for the Church of England and the Church of Scotland, and the figures for these countries cover a self-reported affiliation with the churches.

Table 1: Membership rates and affiliation of the established church 2014

Country	Share of population %
Finland	74
Sweden	65
Denmark	78
Norway	74
Iceland	75
England	17
Scotland	21

Source: Kjems (A); The figures for Scotland and England represent self-reported affiliation (Hinchliffe et al. 2015; Clery, Curtice and Harding, 2017).

Regarding church economy, Sidsel Kjems has done a comparative analysis of the seven churches and found large differences in their respective levels of income (Kjems B, in press). In 2013, the level of income ranged from 0.10 to 0.61 percent of GDP, a six-fold difference between the highest and the lowest income. The distribution of high and low income seems to be related to the main source of income of the established churches, see Table 2.

This difference in the distribution of income is not caused by different side-activities. There are differences in the churches' activities with respect to religious schools, social activities, cemeteries, and so on. But, even if one considers income related only to core church activities, the differences remain, see Kjems B (in press).

The three wealthiest churches, the churches of Denmark, Sweden and Finland, get their main source of income from church tax. The two churches with the lowest income, the Church of England and the Church of Scotland, get their main income from private donations (which are tax deductible for the giver). The established churches of Norway and Iceland range somewhere in the middle and are financed by the general taxes from the public purse. In Iceland, half of the state support to the established churches is dependent on the number of members.

The figure for the churches' income (whether that be measured as income in euro per capita, or as proportion of the country's GDP) indicates that church tax is by far the best source of income and donations are by far the worst.

Table 2: Financing and main sources of financing for established churches

Country	Income per capita EUR	Income as part of GDP %	Sources of financing (%)					
			Church tax	General taxes	Donations and fund-raising	Income from capital	Sales and fees	Other
Finland	227	0.61	80	0	0	0	0	20
Sweden	242	0.53	80	2	2	5	0	11
Denmark	195	0.43	78	9	0	1	8	4
Norway	176	0.23	0	85	7	3	5	0
Iceland	96	0.27	0	78	0	2	19	1
Scotland	37	0.13	0	0	84	16	0	0
England	34	0.10	0	5	48	27	16	4

Source: Kjems and Bille (in press); Kjems B (in press)

The religious attitude as a rational explanation for income differences?

An explanation for the difference in income between the seven established churches, as shown in Table 2, could be non-economic differences between the countries, for example different degrees of religiosity. And, of course, there are indeed differences in the religious attitudes among the countries.

The hypothesis would then be that the people of Sweden, Denmark and Finland are more religious (and therefore more willing to pay money to the church) than people in the other four countries. However, this stands in contrast to Table 1, which shows that the number of members per 100 inhabitants in Sweden is by far the lowest among the Nordic countries. Some further indication of the religiosity levels is found in Table 3. There are differences, but these are far from being systematic differences which parallel the three groups in Table 2. Danes believe more in God than Norwegians do. But Norwegians believe far more in heaven than Danes. The proportion of persons baptised in Denmark and Norway is exactly the same. The respective religious landscapes in the countries do not seem to provide an explanation for the income differences in Table 2.

Table 3: Indicators of religiosity for different countries

Country	Belief in God %	Belief in Heaven %	Proportion baptised %
Finland	33	55	72
Sweden	18	31	46
Denmark	28	19	63
Norway	22	44	63
Iceland	31	57	-
UK/England	37	62	12*

*Scotland 7 percent
Source: 'Belief in God', Eurobarometer, 'Belief in heaven'; McCleary and Barro, 2006; 'Proportion baptised', Kjems (A).

An economic explanation for differences in church income

The central idea in mainstream economics, since its very beginning, has been that economic agents are rational and selfish; they maximise their own profit and utility. Such agents are consequently called *Homo Oeconomicus* or The *Economic Man*. The main laws of economic theory are developed from such assumptions: supply and demand functions Pareto optimality of a market equilibrium the benefit of foreign trade, and so on.

In such a theory, the utility of a unit of a good decreases when the consumer gets a bigger amount of that good. In economic terms this is called 'decreasing marginal utility'. The consumer will demand units until the utility of the last unit is equal to the utility of the spent money.

For reasons of simplicity, it could be assumed that church services can be considered as mainly a private good.[3] Agents will then pay as long as the marginal utility of ecclesiastical services is bigger than the disutility of the member fee. In other words, while the church services are worth more to a person than the member fee, that person will continue to pay the member fee. If the payment to the church is tax deductible, they will pay as long as the marginal utility of ecclesiastical services is bigger than the marginal disutility of the member fee minus taxes. Agents will be more willing to pay to the church because some of the fee is paid by tax deduction.

In such a neoclassical economic model, a rational agent will be a member of the church in Denmark, Sweden and Finland if the utility of the church services are bigger for him than the disutility of the church tax. In Norway and Iceland, the established churches are financed via public budgets and there is no direct payment from the members. In other words, members of the established churches in Iceland and Norway will remain members unless the utility of the church services are negative.

Naturally, for rational agents, it is important to them whether a fee is optional or mandatory; but, whether the fee is paid together with the taxes or collected separately by the established church makes no difference. Norwegian professor of economics Aamund Hylland (2006) followed this line of thought when he merged 'church tax' and 'member fee' into one category, calling it 'voluntary financing'[4] (Hylland 2006). Torkel Brekke follows the same line in a report written for the liberal think tank Civita, and makes 'mandatory' and 'voluntary' the key dichotomy for the evaluation of whether a payment type is judged liberal or nor (Brekke 2010).

It is worth mentioning that church tax is far from being a negligible amount. Danish church tax is on average 0.87 percent of the members' gross income.[5] Also, Danish church tax is decided locally by the church and varied from 0.41 to 1.30 percent in 2017.[6] In Finland, the church tax was 1.4 percent in 2012 on average and in Sweden the equivalent figure was 1.23 percent in 2013.[7] Danes, Swedes and Finns have a substantial economic incentive to unsubscribe from the established churches. Norwegians and Icelanders do not have that economic incentive.

These ideas would suggest that, all other things being equal, there would be a higher number of members in the Norwegian and Icelandic established church than in the Danish, Swedish and Finnish established churches. Moreover, these ideas suggest that it would be easier to collect money if the payments are tax deductible. Yet, none of this is borne out by the figures given above.

Choice environment: church tax as default

While the traditional economic theories do not explain why church tax yields the highest revenue for an established church, the behavioural economic theory of choice environment (Thaler, Sunstein and Balz 2012) helps provide an explanation. Choice environment theory informs us that people's choices and actions are greatly influenced by their environment by limited cognitive resources, bounded rationality (Simon 1955 and 1956) and bias (Kahneman 2011; Kahneman and Tversky 1984). It has been shown in other areas, such as organ donations and saving for pensions, that our default position wields great influence over our actions (Johnson and Goldstein 2004; Benartzi, Peleg and Thaler 2007).

Paying church tax is the default for most people in Denmark, Finland and Sweden, as they became members of the churches when baptised as infants. Church taxes are collected together with municipality taxes directly from the salary. The church tax payer does not have to take any action to pay the church tax, and the payment is not clearly visible. This stands in stark contrast to the choice environment of giving donations: the donor has to actively do something, and the donation is visible. Choice environment theory sees economic incentives as one element in the choice environment. Thaler et al. write:

> ... it is possible to elaborate and enrich the standard analysis by remembering that the agents in the economy are humans. To be sure, even mindless humans demand less when they notice that the price has gone up, but only if they are paying enough attention to notice the change in price. The most important modification that must be made to a standard analysis of incentives is salience. Are choosers aware of the incentives they face? (Thaler, Sunstein and Balz 2012, 437)

Economic incentives can be powerful, but they have to be salient, too. Thaler et al. give electricity consumption as an illustration. They argue that programming a thermostat to show how much money the consumer can save by lowering the temperature will probably have more effect on lowering electricity consumption than raising the price of electricity, which the consumer does not notice as easily.

Thus, choice environment theory does recognise that Danes, Finns and Swedes have an economic incentive to unsubscribe from the established churches. However, as the payment of church tax is not salient to the taxpayer, choice environment theory will predict that this incentive will not have much effect.

Choice environment: opting out to save money?

There is some discussion in the literature about whether church members opt out to save money. With respect to how much the size of church tax matters for membership rates, Lyytikäinen and Santavirta find that: 'a 1 standard deviation increase in church tax (143 euros) leads to a 0.5-1 percentage point decrease in the membership probability' (Lyytikäinen and Santavirta 2013, 1178).

Other scholars have found that members seem to opt out due to a lack of religious belief and there adherence to a politically secular position (Friis Jensen and Schønwandt Mortensen 2015; Niemelä 2007, 2015). Finnish sociologist of religion Kati Niemelä points to a number of reasons based on a qualitative study of persons who have left the church. Personal belief and the position of the church in political questions are the two most common reasons for leaving the church (Niemelä 2007, 202; Table 1).

In a recent study from Austria, investigators found two groups of unsubscribers: religious and non-religious. Church tax was the primary reason for the religious persons unsubscribing while ideology was the main reason for the non-religious (Berghammer, Zartler and Krivanek 2018).

In Norway and Iceland, people can unsubscribe from the established churches, but they cannot save money by doing so. In Norway, unsubscribing will not even affect the economy of the established churches, as the public grants are unrelated to the number of members (the number of members will, however, be important for maintaining support given to the other religious and ethical societies, because they get the same support per member as the established church). In Iceland, unsubscribing will partly affect the budget of the established church, but the individual will not save money.

As already mentioned, classical economic theory will predict that the church members will unsubscribe to a greater extent in Denmark, Sweden and Finland than in Norway and Iceland. The transaction cost of unsubscribing is about the same across the five countries. There is no fee for unsubscribing, but it requires some effort. Table 4 shows data related to unsubscribing from the five countries (more detailed figures, going as far back as it is possible to obtain data from each country, is found in Kjems C [in press]).

Table 4 shows that the rate of members unsubscribing is increasing. However, the data cannot be used to confirm the prediction of classical economic theory that the members will unsubscribe to a larger extent in the countries where the members pay a church tax. The picture is mixed. The five countries seem to place themselves into a group with relatively low rates of unsubscribing (Norway and Denmark), and a group with higher rates of unsubscribing (Sweden, Finland and Iceland).

Table 4: Members unsubscribing as percentage of the total population (average yearly)

Period	Sweden	Denmark	Norway	Finland	Iceland
1970-1979	0.15	0.17	0.16	0.33	
1980-1989	0.16	0.22	0.18	0.36	
1990-1999	0.19	0.17	0.12	0.36	0.36
2000-2009	0.62	0.20	0.13	0.57	0.43
2010-2017	0.65	0.26	0.26	1.05	0.96

Source: Kjems (C).

The rate of members unsubscribing from the established church in Sweden was similar to the rates in Norway and Denmark from the 1970s until around 2000. In Finland, the rate of unsubscribing was for decades at a higher level than in the other countries. For Finland, data relating to unsubscribing is available from 1924, and the opt-out rate was low between 1924-1947 (the yearly average was 0.1 percent). For the years 1948-59, the opt-out rate jumped to a yearly average of 0.39 percent. In 1958 and 1959, the rate reached 0.56 percent and 0.48 percent, respectively. In 1960, the rate dropped suddenly to 0.19 percent and through the 1960s it maintained this low level, stabilising at an average of 0.15 percent.

The explanation for the increasing opt-out rate in the 1950s and the sudden fall of the opt-out rate from 1960 could be the church tax collection system. Until 1959, church tax was collected directly by the church and it was not collected automatically from a member's salary. From 1960, church tax came to be collected with the municipality tax (Erä-Esko 2009, 54). This meant that the payment became more automatic and less visible. According to the standard economic theory mentioned above, rational agents should not be affected by the method of collecting church tax – it is the cost of the tax rather than the method of collecting it that should matter. However, in reality, the Finnish case shows that humans are highly affected by the method of collection, as there seem to be no differences regarding church tax and church membership in Finland between 1959 and 1960 other than the method of collection.

Triggers and drivers

In Finland, church members can unsubscribe any day of the year, but they have to pay the church tax for the rest of the year, until December 31st (Lyytikäinen and Santavirta, 2013). Writing from a classical rational economic perspective, Lyytikäinen and Santavirta conclude that:

> In our descriptive analysis using data on the timing of opting out from church, we find that individuals delay their opt-out decisions towards the end of the year, i.e., when no additional cost of membership is incurred, membership is on average prolonged. This supports the idea that opting out is, at least to some extent, affected by taxes. (Lyytikäinen and Santavirta 2013, 1178)

Choice environment theory would explain things slightly differently. The Finnish church tax system of having to pay for a whole year means that December 31st of each year functions as a deadline. Furthermore, mentions of this deadline by friends or in the media can function as a trigger for the person to take action. In this view, the person has not made a conscious decision to postpone their opting out. Rather, encountering a trigger (mention of church tax) combined with a deadline leads to action.

Media coverage, perhaps of controversial topics in particular, seems to cause members to unsubscribe. In 2014, the General Synod of the established church in Finland accepted same-sex marriages after years of debate (Niemelä, in preparation) and in 2014 the number of members unsubscribing jumped to 78,300. This jump could be due to the topic itself, or it could be that the media coverage just functions as a trigger.

Similarly, in Denmark, the number of unsubscribers was unusually high in 2012. Same-sex marriage in church became possible by Parliament legislation that year. The topic was covered by the media. It has not been investigated whether those who unsubscribed had negative or positive attitudes towards same-sex marriages. It is possible that some members unsubscribed because they opposed same-sex marriages in the church. Most Danes, however, are in favour of homosexual rights and equality, especially young people. And young people are unsubscribing to a greater extent.[8] Therefore another explanation could be that the new possibility of homosexual marriage in church was not the reason (the driver) for opting out, just the trigger. The media coverage made the person direct attention to his or her membership of the church.

Transaction costs or effort

In Finland, it became easier to opt out of the established church when a law was changed in 2003 making it possible to unsubscribe electronically. The opt-out rate went from 0.31 percent in 2002 to 0.52 percent in 2003, and the rate has stayed above 0.5 percent since 2003. Lyytikäinen and Santavirta interpret the data as a result of a lower transaction cost:

> In addition, we find that church membership dropped substantially when a law change made opting out significantly easier. This finding suggests that transaction costs play an important role in the membership decision. (Lyytikäinen and Santavirta 2013, 1175)

The Norwegian church made it possible to unsubscribe via the webpage using a digital signature in 2016. The technical solution was made very simple to use: sign in with the digital signature, click to check whether you are a member. If you are not already a member, with one click you are able to sign up. And, if you are already a member, it only takes one click to opt out. The member did not need to find information elsewhere to do this.[9] Strikingly, 10,854 members unsubscribed the very first day the solution was made available. 15,053 unsubscribed within the first four days.[10] The rate of unsubscribing for 2016 reached a historic high of 41,024 members opting out. However, by 2017, the rate of members unsubscribing was back to the 2015 level (15,621 and 15,486 respectively), which is still very high for Norway.

Transaction cost is equivalent to 'effort' in behavioural economics and choice environment theory. Empirical studies have shown that, most of the time, people stick with their defaults, even when very little effort is required to change the default (Thaler and Sunstein 2008). Effort can be physical (posting a letter) and mental (reflectively weighing the pros and cons of a choice) (Smith, Goldstein and Johnson 2013).

Both the Norwegian and Finnish cases suggest that the amount of effort it takes to unsubscribe has a great impact on the number of unsubscribers. Parallel to effort, media coverage probably also does play a part. In Norway, there was large media coverage of the new online way of unsubscribing, and coverage of the large numbers of members unsubscribing in the first days. This media coverage functions as a trigger, getting more people to pay attention to the option to unsubscribe.

Our conclusion that church membership and dropping out of the church are determined by factors other than rational economic decisions, where cost and benefits are evaluated, is well related to a number of sociological investigations, see Leth-Nissen (2016) and Lüchau (2014 and 2014a). Based on interviews (Leth-Nissen) and register statistics (Lüchau), these scholars found that traditional economic consideration only plays a very minor role in peoples' decision regarding membership and dropping out of the church.

Conclusion

If we look at the established churches in seven north-west European countries, their economic power separates them in three distinct different groups. The rich churches in Finland, Denmark and Sweden, the low income group of England and Scotland, with Norway and Iceland in the middle. This cannot be explained by differences in religion or religiosity. The source of these churches' income would seem to be the obvious explanation: the churches of Finland, Denmark and Sweden are mainly financed by a state-collected member fee, a church tax, the churches in Norway and Iceland are funded by the public budget and the Church of England and the Church of Scotland are funded by private donations. It seems as if the income differences can indeed be explained by looking at the respective church's main source of income. While these differences cannot be explained by a neoclassical economic model with rational agents, behavioural economics and choice environment do seem to give a credible and satisfying explanation. Choice environment theory recognises that the Danes, Finns and Swedes have an economic incentive to unsubscribe from the established churches. However, since the payment of church tax is not salient to the taxpayer, choice environment theory would predict that this incentive will not have much effect. In our investigations of the economy of the churches, behavioural economics seems to be more useful for capturing and explaining the data than traditional neoclassical economic theory.

References

Benartzi, Shlomo, Ehud Peleg and Richard H. Thaler 2007. 'Choice Architecture and Retirement Saving Plans'. https://papers.ssrn.com/sol3/papers.cfm?abstract_id=999420.

Berghammer, Caroline, Ulrike Zartler and Desiree Krivanek. 2018. 'Looking Beyond the Church Tax: Families and the Disaffiliation of Austrian Roman Catholics: Families and Disaffilliation', *Journal for the Scientific Study of Religion*, January. https://doi.org/10.1111/jssr.12361.

Brekke, Torkel 2010. 'Frihed og Religion'. Oslo: Civita, Akersgt. 20, 0158 Oslo.

Chaves, Mark and David E. Cann. 1992. 'Regulation, Pluralism, and Religious Market Structure: Explaining Religion's Vitality'. *Rationality and Society* 4/3, 272-90. https://doi.org/10.1177/1043463192004003003.

Clery, Elizabeth, John Curtice and Roger Harding. 2017. 'British Social Attitudes 34'. 34. NatCen Social Research.

Erä-Esko, Ensio. 2009. *Beskattningsrätt och Skattskyldighed för Kyrkan i Finland*. Helsinki: Hanken School of Economics.

Friis Jensen, Pernille and Bjarke Schønwandt Mortensen. 2015. *Uden Tro Og Praksis, et Religionssociologisk Studie af Irreligiøse i København, herunder Motiver for Medlemskab og Udmeldelse af Folkekirken*. University of Copenhagen.

Hinchliffe, Stephen, Anna Marcinkiewicz, John Curtice and Rachel Ormston 2015. 'Scottish Social Attitudes Survey 2014: Public Attitudes to Sectarianism in Scotland. Stephen Hinchliffe, Anna Marcinkiewicz, John Curtice and Rachel Ormston'. *ScotCen Social Reseach*.

Hylland, Aamund 2006. *Finansiering av Tros- og Livssynssamfunn 2006:1*. Oslo: Stiftelsen Frischsenteret for Samfunnsøkonomisk Forskning.

Johnson, Eric J. and Daniel G. Goldstein 2004. 'Defaults and Donation Decisions' *Transplantation* 78/12: 1713-16. https://doi.org/10.1097/01.TP.0000149788.10382.B2.

Kahneman, Daniel 2011. *Thinking, Fast and Slow*. London: Lane.

Kahneman, Daniel and Amos Tversky. 1984. 'Choices, Values, and Frames'. *American Psychologist* 39/4, 341.

Kjems, Sidsel (A). 'Decline and Stability. Membership and Rite de Passage'. Linda Woodhead and Hans Raun Iversen (ed.) *The Old National Churches of Northern Europe: The Persistence of Societal Religion* (in preparation)

Kjems, Sidsel (B). 'The Economy. Sources of Income and Annual Revenue'. In Linda Woodhead and Hans Raun Iversen (ed.) *The Old National Churches of Northern Europe: The Persistence of Societal Religion* (in preparation).

Kjems, Sidsel (C). 'The Significance of Church Tax: The Historical Background, the Concept and the Significance of Church Tax. The Case of the Established Church in Denmark' (in press).

Kjems, Sidsel and Trine Bille (In Press). 'Why Are the Level of Income of Established Churches so Different? A Comparative Study of the Financing of the Established Churches in the Nordic Countries, England and Scotland'. *Working Paper I*

Leth-Nissen, Karen Marie 2016. 'A Deliberate Action: Leaving the Danish National Church', U. Schmidt and H. Askeland (eds.), *Church Reform and Leadership of Change* Pickwick Publications. Church of Sweden Research Series, Bind 12, 135-151

Lüchau, P. 2014. 'Kirkestatistiske Kilder til Indsigt i Folkekirken og dens Medlemmer'. Marie Vejrup Nielsen, and Hans Raun Iversen (eds.), *Tal om Kirken: Undersøgelser af Folkekirkens Aktivitets- og Deltagerstatistik*. Copenhagen: Publikationer fra Det Teologiske Fakultet, Vol. 57, 7-27.

Lüchau, P. 2014a. 'Når Fårene Forlader Flokken: En Religionssociologisk Analyse af Udmeldelser fra Folkekirken'. *Religionsvidenskabeligt Tidsskrift*, 61, 89-106.

Lyytikäinen, Teemu and Torsten Santavirta 2013. 'The Effect of Church Tax on Church Membership'. *Journal of Population Economics* 26/3, 1175-93. https://doi.org/10.1007/s00148-012-0431-y.

McCleary, Rachel M. and Robert J. Barro 2006. 'Religion and Political Economy in an International Panel'. *Journal for the Scientific Study of Religion* 45/2, 149-75. https://doi.org/10.1111/j.1468-5906.2006.00299.x.

Minkenberg, Michael. 2012. 'Church-State Regimes and Democracy in the West: Convergence vs. Divergence'. *Geopolitics, History and International Relations* 4/1, 76-100.

Niemelä, Kati. 'Finland'. Linda Woodhead and Hans Raun Iversen (eds.) *The Old National Churches of Northern Europe: The Varied Fortunes and Unexpected Resilience of Societal Religion* (in preparation)

Niemelä, Kati. 2007. 'Alienated or Disappointed? Reasons for Leaving the Church in Finland'. *Nordic Journal of Religion and Society* 20/2, 195-216.

Niemelä, Kati 2015. '"No Longer Believing in Belonging": A Longitudinal Study of Finnish Generation Y from Confirmation Experience to Church-Leaving'. *Social Compass* 62/2, 172-86. https://doi.org/10.1177/0037768615571688.

Simon, Herbert 1955. 'A Behavioral Model of Rational Choice'. *The Quarterly Journal of Economics* 69/(January), 99-118.

Simon, Herbert 1956. 'Rational Choice and the Structure of the Environment'. *Psychological Review* 63/2, 129-38.

Smith, Craig, Daniel Goldstein and Eric Johnson 2013. 'Choice Without Awareness: Ethical and Policy Implications of Defaults'. *Journal of Public Policy & Marketing* 32/2, 159-172.

Stat-Kirke-Utvalget (ed.) 2006. *NOU 2006:2 Staten og Den Norske Kirke*. Norges Offentlige Utredninger, 2006,2. Oslo: Departementenes Servicesenter, Informasjonsforvaltning.

Thaler, Richard and Cass Sunstein 2008. *Nudge: The Gentle Power of Choice Architecture*. New Haven, Conn.: Yale.

Thaler, Richard, Cass Sunstein and John Balz 2012. 'Choice Architecture'. In Eldar Shafir (ed.) *The Behavioral Foundations of Public Policy*. Princeton: Princeton University Press. SSRN: https://ssrn.com/abstract=2536504 Chapter 25.

Notes

1. This chapter is based on Kjems A-C and Kjems and Bille.
2. We use the term 'established church' as it can comprise both the fully established 'state' churches in the Nordic countries and the partially established churches in Scotland and England (Minkenberg 2012; Chaves and Cann 1992).
3. Of course, churches do not just produce private goods. The aim here is to explain the high income for churches with church taxes, and this absolutely cannot be explained by a model which considers church services as public goods. On the contrary, such a consideration would lead to low income because of free-riding, see Kærgård Chapter 9.
4. Hylland's contribution is commissioned by the committee working with NOU 2006:2 (Stat-Kirke-Utvalget 2006).
5. Ministry of Ecclesiastical Affairs, http://www.km.dk/folkekirken/oekonomi/kirkeskat/ in 2017.
6. Ibid.
7. In Sweden, this 'tax' does include two different elements: a member fee of, on average, 1.01 percent of the gross income (in 2013), and a burial tax paid by all citizens of, on average, 0.22 percent. Both differ from place to place, Kjems A.
8. Unsubscriber data divided by age groups are accessible through *Statistics Denmark*.
9. In Denmark, members are required to find information about which parish they live in and which parish they were born in, https://www.folkekirken.dk/om-folkekirken/medlemskab
10. https://www.nettavisen.no/na24/15000-har-meldt-seg-ut-av-kirken-pa-fire-dager/3423253691.html

III. Cultural Institutions Facing Individualisation and Market Orientation

9. Economy in the Folk Church and Other Cultural Institutions

Niels Kærgård

Introduction

The structure of the Danish church's economy has deep historical roots, as does its recent organization with its 'church tax' (see Chapter 4). This chapter broaches relevant theories from economics and social science and presents an empirical comparison between the Folk Church and other cultural institutions.

First, a series of theoretical sections will be presented where the relevant theory is summarised: private and public goods are defined; then, the relation between market, profit and ethics will be discussed; the economic rationality in the public sector is then described; but, since economic rationality is insufficient for present theoretical purposes, the concept of public value will also be discussed. After these theoretical sections, the funding of a number of cultural institutions (the Folk Church, Danish Television, the Royal Theatre and the University of Copenhagen) is compared. However, since the Folk Church is not just a cultural institution but also a popular movement, the Folk Church is compared with other popular movements, too, especially the political parties. The final sections discuss the results of these comparisons and some conclusions are formulated.

Private or public goods

Throughout the history of economics there has always been an ongoing discussion of regulation and markets. The 'father' of economics Adam Smiths' seminal book *The Wealth of Nations* published in 1776 represented a showdown with the highly publically regulated society in which he lived. For this purpose, Smith developed a more sophisticated theory of the market. In an unregulated market, could the price mechanism – as an 'invisible hand' –

lead people to do what society needs, even though nobody has the needs of the society in mind?

If there is a lack of a product (e.g. clothes), the price will go up, consequently firms will observe that there is profit to be made in producing clothes, they will move to this industry and the lack will be remedied. Prices and profit get selfish people to do what is best for the society. To put it in Smith's own words:

> He intends only his own gain, and he is in this, as in many other cases, led by an invisible hand to promote an end which was no part of his intention. Nor is it always the worse for the society that it was no part of it. By pursing his own interest he frequently promotes that of the society more effectually than when he really intends to promote it. I have never known much good done by those who affected to trade for the public good. It is an affectation, indeed, not very common among merchants, and very few words need to be employed in dissuading them from it. (Smith 1776, reprinted 1937, 423)

And:

> It is not from the benevolence of the butcher, the brewer, or the baker that we expect our dinner, but from their regard to their own interest. We address ourselves, not to their humanity but to their self-love, and never talk to them of our own necessities, but of their advantages. (Smith 1776, reprinted 1937, 14, 14)

This regulation has since been a dominant part of economic theory and has always had strong supporters, for example the Nobel Laureate economist Friedrich A. von Hayek (1899-1992):

> I am convinced that if [the price mechanism] were the result of deliberate human design, and if people guided by the price changes understood that their decisions have significance far beyond their immediate aim, this mechanism would have been acclaimed as one of the greatest triumphs of the human mind. Its misfortune is the double one that it is not the product of human design and that the people guided by it usually do not know why they are made to do what they do. (Hayek 1945, 527)

This has also been summarised by the Economic History scholar Laurence S. Moss (1944-2009):

> The economics that I know and love had its origins in the work of that accused seventeenth century atheist Thomas Hobbes, who asked how a community of selfish and cheating individuals could ever get organized. Bernard de Mandeville, the Dutch cynic of the early eighteenth century, suggested it is the private vices of the masses that supply the social glue. Adam Smith argues that in a well-governed society, self-interest could promote the public interest, and in the twentieth century, economists such as Ludwig von Mises defined a 'well governed' society as one in which property rights were clearly defined and private contracts about the exchange of those rights enforced. The great insight of our discipline ... is that competition can serve to secure efficiency and meaningful organization. (Moss 1996, 493)

But, this has never been a theory which could stand alone. Even Adam Smith wrote about the necessity of national defence and a police force. Even in a society of 'economic men', the market is not in itself sufficient for the distribution of everything. In modern economic theory, this has resulted in the definition of private and public goods. *Private goods* are normal goods with *rivalisation* between the consumers; if one consumes a good (e.g. a meal) the same meal cannot be eaten by another. It is also *excludable*; if a good is a consumer's property, he can prevent others from consuming that good.

This is not the case for *public goods* such as the police, defence, television signals, and so on. Their use is neither rival nor excludable. It does not have any effect on my use of a television signal that my neighbour is watching the same television program. If the good, in this case a television program, is produced and broadcast, it is impossible to exclude anyone from watching the program.

The consequence is a market that does not work. There is a free rider problem. The selfish consumer will not pay but hopes that another will; and when the public good is produced, everybody can use it and no one can be excluded from its use. The production of and the payment for public goods must consequently be a matter for the community of all users, the state. That way, everybody is protected by the police and everyone pays.

But, even if the definition of private and public goods is clear, the distinction is difficult to maintain in practice. A theatre, a museum or a church gives its visitors an individual experience, which is a private good; but they can also contribute to the national cohesion and to society's ethics, which are public goods. A considerable number of the institutions related to culture, research and education are characterised by offering such a combination of private and public goods. This demands a more complicated funding structure than simply breaking things down into either market profit or common taxes. There is room for an open discussion of the division of labour between the market and the public sector. In fact, this is a main theme in political debate, and the balance has shifted considerably throughout history.

Profit and morals: The private sector

The boundary between the public sector and the private market is further blurred by other problems. A simple economic model with selfish agents does not give a realistic picture of the complicated real world. The aims of both private and public institutions are much more complicated than assumed in such models. Private firms are not simply aiming to maximise their profits, and public institutions are not simply producing services for the citizens.

Firms do not simply maximise their economic profit. There has been a considerable debate, for example, about shareholders and stakeholders. Hardcore liberalists argue that an optimal society will be created if as many things as possible are taken care of by the markets and that a rational market mechanism is a more effective regulator than more 'ethical' based systems. The words of the leading spokesman for the Chicago School of Economics, the Nobel Laureate Milton Friedman (1912-2006) are well known:

> There is one and only one social responsibility of business – to use its resources and engage in activities designed to increase its profits so long as it stays within the rules of the game, which is to say, engages in open free competition without deception or fraud. (Friedman 1970)

According to this point of view, an effective society does not need idealism and altruism. Rather, the optimal result is when everybody maximises his own interest:

> The deliberate striving for the common good would distract you from doing what you are most suited for – using your particular knowledge of time and space – and so decreases the overall effectiveness of the system. Furthermore, with the complex division of labour we have today you cannot have an overview of what the common good is. (Hayek 1988, 81)

Such points of view dominated the debate during the last decades of the 20th century. Before these times, there was a considerable number of local firms dominated by private owners with more mixed aims: a paternalistic attitude to their employees, stressing their reputation in their community and striving for a position on the city council or in politics.

In the 21st century, there has been a reaction against the simple profit maximising. Cooperate Social Responsibilities (CSR) and the triple bottom line with the 3 (or sometimes 4) 'Ps' (Profit, People and Planet, Purpose) has been a must for a modern firm. The stakeholders ('people') and the environment ('planet') play an important role for the firm running parallel to profit. This is also true of 'purpose', indicated by the discussion of 'market or cathedral' (Chapter 10). Part of what we have learned is that firms who treat their customers and their employees badly, or who do not take care of the environment, nor their use of resources, are often in trouble – this translates to trouble for their profits, too. Hardcore market supporters like Milton Friedman, unsurprisingly, do not like this new trend:

> What does it mean to say that the corporate executive has a 'social responsibility' in his capacity as businessman? If the statement is not pure rhetoric, it must mean that he is to act in some way that is not in interest of his employers. For example, that he is to refrain from increasing the price of the product in the best interest of the corporation. Or that he is to make expenditures on reducing pollution beyond the amount that is in the best interest of the corporation or that is required by law in order to contribute to the social objective of improving the environment. Or that, at the expense of corporate profit, he is to hire 'hardcore' unemployed instead of better qualified available workmen to contribute to the social object of reducing poverty. In each of these cases, the corporate executive would be spending someone else's money for a general social interest. Insofar as his actions in accord with his 'social responsibility' reduce returns to stockholders, he is spending their money. Insofar as his actions raise the price to customers, he is spending the customer's

> money. Insofar his actions lower the wages of some employees, he is spending their money. (Friedman 1970)

The intensive talk about responsibility can, as is pointed out by Friedman, sometimes have hidden motives and indicate some double standard (see Kærgård [2010]). But the debate indicates that a balance between profit and ethics, between market and community, between shareholders and stakeholders, between 'gesellschaft' and 'gemeinschaft' is necessary also in private business.

Rationality in the public sector

There has been a similar movement in relation to the public sector. In the 1950s and 1960s, there was a strong belief in a rational public sector and a strong scepticism in relation to the market mechanism. A number of statements from the leading Scandinavian economists of this period show a very different attitude to the market than those uttered a few decades later. For example, the first Nobel Laureate economist (perhaps the most prominent Nordic economist of any time) the Norwegian Ragnar Frisch (1895-1973) expresses strong scepticism about allocation via the market:

> It cannot be rational to let the big crowd of Norwegian housewives run from one shop to another to find out where, first one and then another item, is sold for a few pennies cheaper. This could be done much more rationally by being taken care of by experts. (Frisch 1958, [quoted in Munthe 1992] 114)

The most influential Danish economist since World War II, permanent secretary of economics for a couple of decades, Erik Ib Schmidt (1911-1998) stated that:

> The most important thing is, perhaps, that, generally speaking, understanding be created of the view that the economic wellbeing of society is not automatically attained, but needs permanent attention from the state, and that the administrative prerequisites for this role of the State have been gradually established. (Schmidt 1954, 42 [author's translation])

One could also mention Viggo Kampmann (1910-1976), prominent economist, minister of economic affairs and prime minister, as well as P. Nørregaard Rasmussen (1922-1998), professor of economics and head of the department of economics at the University of Copenhagen for many years: 'In a wide range of areas, the "free market" will not give a distribution of investments which is in accordance with the 'socially desired distribution' (Kampmann and Rasmussen 1954, 151 [author's translation]).

But this positive attitude to the public sector stopped in the early 1970s. The most remarkable showdown in Denmark with the 1950s and 1960s attitude to 'rational' public sectors involved Professor Jørgen Dich (1901-1975) with his book, *Den Herskende Klasse* (*The Ruling Class*) published in 1973, where he argued that the growth in the public sector was caused more by strong unions for the employees in the sector than by demand, and needs of the users of the sector. In 1973, the anti-tax movement 'Fremskridtspartiet' became the second biggest party in the Danish parliament. The market, not political control, came to be seen as the rational solution. An example of that view in relation to cultural institutions is found in a recent newspaper article about museums:

> And the world is – for better or worse – a market, which means that museums who avoid the concept of business must necessarily fail. … Because of that, new methods of business can strengthen a museum, not trivialize it. There are considerable fears associated with thinking of museums as businesses. It is as if the museum has a heart with a fine and delicate core which will be destroyed by the market. This is outmoded thinking. (Sandberg 2017 [author's translation]).

In Denmark, this process has been called 'djøfisering' (DJØF is the union for people with a university degree in social sciences). There has always been a conflict between the ethics and attitudes of different professions, and the ethics and attitudes of the economists seems to be dominating (see, for example, Hermann 2016). We have seen such conflicts regarding the hospitals, between professional administrators and the doctors, at the universities between administrators and researchers, and so on. New Public Management and 'djøfiscring' indicate that a simple version of the economic rationality, has won.

It is curious that this victory has been won at the same time that economic research has become increasingly sceptical in relation to simple models of incentives and selfish agents. 'Behavioural economics' reveals that agents' behaviour is much more complicated than profit and utility maximisation can capture, and 'experimental economics' reveals that real people are far less selfish than *homo economicus* (see Chapter 8).

There is no doubt, however, that there have been market failures, governmental failures and failures in the political decision-making process. One of the failures of New Public Management is the excessive emphasis placed on measurable indicators. It is, for example, much easier to measure the number of candidates within an education system than to measure their quality and it is easier to measure the number of research articles than the impact those articles have had, and so on. This is especially problematic for cultural institutions, where the measurement of the output is very hard to define in concrete ways. The utility of public goods is considerably more difficult to measure than market-driven and user paid private goods. Without doubt, there is a danger of a suboptimal supply of public goods.

Public value

Market orientation and New Public Management (NPM) have resulted in the concept 'public value'. This is a concept particularly discussed in the research of administrations in Australia and New Zealand. In these countries, the neoliberal market orientation has been stronger than in most other countries, consequently the drawbacks are also clearer to see. The new essential concept can be that 'a broader type of exchange than the restricted economic form of the customer transaction is needed' (Alford 2002, 337-338).

If the economic distinction between private and public goods is taken as the starting point, the public sector produces both public goods (police, defence, television, etc.) and private goods (hospital services, transportation, health care). Instead of 'customers', Alford (2002) talks about 'citizenry' using public goods produced by the community and 'clients' using private goods produced by the public sector. Furthermore, he separates the clients into 'beneficiaries' getting positive private goods (healthcare, education, etc.) from the public sector, and 'obligates' getting negative goods (prison, sanctions, etc.). His conclusion is that:

> ... a customer focus based on economic exchange is of doubtful usefulness in government. ... [public institutions] can offer not only economic goods and services, but also broader values such as fairness and normative values. ... They also raise awareness of collective purposes beyond material self-interest. ... a broadened conception of exchange may encourage citizens to engage more with the institutions and process of government. (Alford 2002, 344)

Such a broader consideration of the public sector's aims needs 'to develop a sense of a distinctive nonbusiness dimension to weigh in on which public services should be run. For the advocates of public value management, there is a strong sense that the public realm is different from that of the commercial sector' (Stoker 2006, 46). It is stressed that 'focusing on "public value" helps tell a useful new story. ... Public value is defined and redefined through social and political interaction. Such interaction involves politicians, officials and communities' (Smith 2004, 68). A short summary of this point of view is given by Jamine O'Flynn:

> The notion of public value is garnering considerable attention in practitioner and academic literature. This is especially the case in Australia where some of the most radical experiments with NPM took place through the 1980s and 1990s. The purpose of this article was to set out a new public value paradigm and compare and contrast it to NPM. It can be argued that under NPM, broader notions of public value were marginalized in the quest for efficiency and, consequently, the adoption of a public value perspective will represent a further paradigmatic change (O'Flynn 2007, 363).

It is worth mentioning how well this new school in administrative science fits with the new results in behavioural and experimental economics. Both can be seen as a critic, or a modifier, of at least a simple form of the neoclassical economic ideas.

The economic governance of cultural institutions in practice

The Lutheran church is, of course, unique in many ways and so are a number of other national institutions. It follows that it is not going to be possible to find other completely similar institutions. Therefore, a simple comparison (as would be possible for, say, the Danish universities) is not going to be possible. What can be done (and is done here) is a simple comparison of a number of prominent national institutions, the Folk Church, Danish television, the Royal Theatre and the University of Copenhagen.

These are institutions with budgets of approximately the same size as the Folk Church, but are different in the sense that their activities are more centralised around one location, while the Folk Church's activities are very decentralised. It is, however, very difficult to find decentralised institutions (Danish public libraries, the Danish Folk High schools, etc.) where the total national cost is accessible.

All the institutions that were analysed are governed in some sort of close relation to the state. The Folk Church is, in principle, managed by the Minister of Ecclesiastical Affairs, but it has considerable local autonomy (see Christoffersen 2010 and 2015; and Kirkeministeriet 2014). All the other institutions have autonomy and their own boards, but some of them have board members appointed by the government or the Parliament, and others have different sorts of monitoring by the government and its administration.

The production and the costs are very different for these institutions, so the investigation is concentrated on the funding. The funding for these institutions is shown in Table 1.

The different institutions have very different sorts of funding. The Royal Theatre and the University of Copenhagen get a significant part of their funding from the state (71 percent and 63 percent of their budget respectively), and the Folk Church has a smaller part funded by the state (9 percent). The funding for the church and the national broadcasting company DR are both mainly paid by the users. The 'church tax' is a member fee collected together with the ordinary taxes, but only paid by the members of the Folk Church. It is a locally-determined part of the taxable income (the rate varies in 2017 between 0.41 percent and 1.30 percent for the different municipalities). The families pay until now a media license of 2.527 kroner in 2017 per household (with a possible deduction for poor senior citizens).

Table 1: Funding for a number of Danish National Institutions 2016, per mill. DKK

	Folk Church	DR – the National Radio and Television Service	TV2	DR + TV	The Royal Theatre	The University of Copenhagen
State subsidies	750	0	0	0	569	5327
Church tax	6145	0	0	0	0	0
License	0	3697	0	3697	0	0
Advertisement	0	0	1264	1264	0	0
Ticket and subscription	0	0	1374	1374	125	0
Private funding	0	0	0	0	51	2806
Others	1426	436	49	485	56	308
Total income	8321	4133	2687	6820	802	8441

Source: The homepage of the Ministry of Ecclesiastical Affairs and the annual report for the other institutions. Note: The data for the Folk Church come from 2015-figures.

TV2 is mainly funded by advertisement and subscriptions and the Royal Theatre draws considerable income from selling tickets and subscriptions. Both the Royal Theatre and the University of Copenhagen have considerable private funding from different firms and foundations (16 percent and 33 percent of their total funding, respectively). The University of Copenhagen's main donors are foundations supporting specific research projects. It is extremely noteworthy that none of these institutions are funded only by the market.

The popular movements

Where all the cultural institutions are producers of specific cultural services – worship, television, theatre, education and research – the Folk Church is the only one of them that is also a popular movement with roots in the revivals of the 19th century. The cooperative movement in agriculture in the decades after 1880, the dominating political party 'Venstre', the Folk High Schools and the leading part of the Folk Church (inner mission and the Grundtvigians) are all children of the same movements in the 19th century.

All these movements are also important parts of Danish culture, but only the Folk Church is still a decentralised popular movement. The various local dairies and slaughterhouses have been consolidated into only one dominating big firm: 'Arla' in dairy and 'Danish Crown' in meat production. With 10 years compulsory school attendance, the Folk High School is no longer a natural part of the normal young person's education. And, in contrast to the church, the political parties have lost their deep roots in memberships, see Table 2. Where the Folk Church today has 92 percent of the membership it had in 1974, the political parties have only 38 percent (and only 23 percent of membership they had in 1960).

The figure for Folk Church membership remaining so high is, of course, partly a result of a growing population. But correcting for the growing population is complicated because part of the population growth is caused by immigration, and it is obvious that very few of the immigrants are joining the Danish Folk Church.

Table 2: Popular movements, the Folk Church and the political parties

Year	Members in 1000 members						
	The Folk Church	Venstre, the Liberal Party	Social Democrats	Social-liberals 'Radikale Venstre'	The Conservatives	SF Socialists	All political parties
1921	3200	-	-	-	-	-	-
1960	-	193	259	35	109	3	599
1974/75	4748	122	122	20	75	6	364
1990	4584	75	77	8	37	8	222
2000	4536	77	50	6	22	6	178
2015/17	4361	37	38	7	11	8	140

Source: Homepage of the Ministry of Ecclesiastical Affairs and the Danish Parliament and Kærgård (2006). There are no figures for the Folk Church between 1921 and 1974, and the figure for 1974 is taken from the tax statistics.

Figures relating to the decline of the proportion of the population that remain members of the Folk Church are shown in Table 3. This table confirms the impression that the Folk Church continues to do well among the Danes. Moreover, it is worth mentioning that the reason for this is not a cheap membership; the member fee for the church is considerable higher than for the political parties, see Table 4.

Table 3: Proportion of population remaining members of the Folk Church

Year	Proportion of total population	Proportion of Danes
1990	89.3 %	93.2 %
2000	85.1 %	91.7 %
2016	76.9 %	87.7 %

Source: Statistics Denmark, Rockwool Research Unit and Ministry of Ecclesiastical Affairs.
Note: 'Danes' are, in contrast to immigrants and their descendants defined by *Statistics Denmark* as persons having at least one parent who is a Danish citizen born in Denmark.

Table 4: Annual member fee per year for a number of organizations

Organization	Member fee per member, DKK
Folk Church tax (1)	4270
DR License (2)	1175
Venstre	300
Social democrats	400
Dansk Folkeparti	150
Social Liberals (3)	360-790
Conservative	365
Enhedslisten (4)	240-1460
SF (4)	75-250

Source: Homepages of DR and the Ministry of Ecclesiastical Affairs. The figures for the political parties are collected by DR, Midt and Vest.
Note 1: Calculated from an average tax rate of 0.87 percent and an average income of 490,800 DKK
Note 2: The license is per household, and an average size is assumed to be 2.15 persons (the average in 2011)
Note 3: The member fee is different depending on the local area.
Note 4: The member fee is income dependent.

Conclusion

All cultural and popular institutions need to balance market and economy on the one hand with aims and ideals on the other. This debate takes place both among social scientists and practitioners, and the arguments run parallel from institution to institution. The Minister of Ecclesiastical and Cultural Affairs, Mette Bock, said in 2017 about DR:

> One can choose two roads as a big public service institution. Either one can choose to lie as close as possible to the market to compete for the viewers in a media supply which becomes more and more variegated. Or one can choose to be a corrective and supply exactly what the huge media market neither can nor will supply, because it is part of an education, which we as a small language area want to hold on to. (Øhrstrøm 2017, author's translation).

Exactly the same debate takes place in the Folk Church and the Royal Theatre. Should the Folk Church stick to pure classical Lutheran Christianity, or should it follow a more open adjustment to the actual market and supply baby singing, spaghetti services, concerts and other less traditional arrangements? Should the theatre only supply high quality plays, ballets and operas, or should it follow the market and supply musicals?

A strategy going too far from the 'market' can create funding problems, even if such a supply produces public values. One can neither be sure that the politicians nor the public budget, nor even the market, are willing to pay for the production of long running public value which is difficult to measure. There are, obviously – as is documented both in economics and political science – market failures as well as governmental failures. Both market and government seem to take decisions biased in advantage of short run, measurable goods and services.[1]

Even if the 'church tax' is a strange combination of tax and member fee, it can have very rational properties. It seems to secure a cultural institution sufficient and stable long-term funding. This stands in contrast to what has been seen, for example, with the University of Copenhagen, where ups and downs caused by fluctuation in the political attitude to research and education and by shifts in the students' choice of education, has resulted in waves of firing and hiring.

Unlike license and member fees, the church tax is related to the size of a person's income. This seems to be an attractive property. Social balance has always been an important aim for the Danish society, and the marginal utility of money is also smaller for high income groups.

Finally, is the church tax growing parallel to the growth in income? This can be economically rational. Because the consumption of a necessity good (a good with an income elasticity smaller than one) will in an optimal situation grow more slowly than income. The consumption of a luxury good (a good with an income elasticity bigger than one) will grow more rapidly than income. It seems likely that most cultural goods are luxury goods and they should consequently, chosen freely, have a growing part of the Folk Church's income. But cultural goods are very often public goods, and as explained earlier, there are problems with funding a sufficient supply of public goods because of free riding. Perhaps the construction of the church tax is a way to secure a sufficient supply of a public good, and if the income elasticity is one, the optimal supply shall in fact develop approximately in parallel with the income.

References

Alford, John 2002. 'Defining the Client in the Public Sector: A Social-Exchange Perspective', *Public Administration Review*, 62/3, 337-346.

Christoffersen, Lisbet 2010. 'State, Church and Religion in Denmark', Lisbet Christoffersen, K.Å. Modéer and S. Andersen (eds.). *Law & Religion in the 21th Century – Nordic Perspectives*, Copenhagen: DJØF Publishing 145-161.

Christoffersen, Lisbet 2015. 'A long Historical Path towards Transparency, accountability and Good Governance: On Financing Religions in Denmark', Francis Messner (ed.), *Public Funding of Religions in Europe*, Surrey: Ashgate, 125-147.

Dam, Thea, Jørgen Dejgaard Jensen and Niels Kærgård 2008. 'Obesity, Social inequality and Economic Rationality', *Food Economics*, 5/3-4, 124-137.

Friedman, Milton 1970. 'The Social Responsibility of Business is to Increase its Profit', *The New York Times Magazine*, September 13.

Hayek, Friedrich A. von 1945. The Use of Knowledge in Society, *American Economic Review*, 35/ 4, 19-530.

Hayek, Friedrich A. von 1988. 'The Fatal Conceit – the Errors of Socialism', Vol. I, William Warren. Bartley III (ed.), *The Collected Works of F.A. Hayek,* London.

Hermann, Stefan 2016. *Hvor Står Kampen om Dannelsen,* Copenhagen: Informations Forlag.

Kampmann, Viggo and P. Nørregaard Rasmussen 1954. 'Beskæftigelse og Investeringer', Jens Otto Krag (ed.), *Tidehverv og Samfundsorden*, Copenhagen: Forlaget Fremad, 21-45.

Kirkeministeriet 2014. *Folkekirkens styre*, Copenhagen: Betænkning 1544.

Kærgård, Niels 2006. 'The Foundation for the Danish Welfare State: Ethnic, Religious and Linguistic Harmony', *Paper presented at the XIV International Economic History Congress*, 21-25 *August, University of Helsinki, Helsinki*.

Kærgård, Nils 2010. 'Corporate Social Responsibility, Economic Optimality and the Interest of the Poor', Jacob Dahl Rendtorff (ed*.), Power and Principles in the Market Place: On Ethics and Economics*, Surrey: Ashgate, 35-45.

Kærgård, Niels 2015. 'Religious Communities, Public Funding and Economics', Francis Messner (ed.), *Public Funding of Religions in Europe*, Surrey: Ashgate, 221-236.

Moss, Laurence S. 1996. 'Review of H.G. Brennan & A.M.C. Waterman (ed.) Economics and Religion: Are they Distinct?' *European Journal of History of Economic Thoughts*, 3, 490-494.

Munthe, Preben 1992. *Norske økonomier – Sveip og Portretter*, Oslo: Universitetsforlaget.

O'Flynn, Jamine 2007. 'From New Public Management to Public Value: Paradigmatic Change and Managerial Implications', *Australian Journal of Public Administration*, 66/3, 353-366.

Sandberg, Jane 2017. 'Museer må ikke være bange for markedskræfterne', *Politiken feature article*, 14 June.

Smith, Adam 1776 [1937]. *An Inquiry into the Nature and Causes of the Wealth of Nations*, The Modern Library of the World's Best Books, New York: Random House.

Schmidt, Erik Ib 1954. 'Den økonomiske og sociale forvaltning'. Jens Otto Krog (ed.) *Tidehverv og Samfundsorden*. Copenhagen: Forlaget Fremad, 21-45.

Smith, R.F.J 2004. 'Focusing on public value: Something New and Something Old', *Australian Journal of Public Administration,* 63/4, 68-79.

Stoker, Gerry 2006. 'Public Value Management – A New Narrative for Networked Governance', *American Review of Public Administration,* 36/1, 41-57.

Øhrstrøm, Daniel 2017. 'Der er altid lys foran en', *Kristeligt Dagblad*, 22 July.

Notes

1   For a parallel discussion about irrational short horizon and time inconsistency problems in relation to health, see Dam, Jensen and Kærgård (2008, 132-133).

10. The Quest for Public Value. The Folk Church and the Other Cultural Institutions between Market and Cathedral

Hans Raun Iversen

Who is afraid of the market?

'Museums should not be afraid of the forces of the market. When rethinking the concept of the museum, it is decisive to focus on the importance of museums for society'. These were the headlines of a feature article in *Politiken,* June 14th 2017, by Jane Sandberg, director of *Enigma*, the Copenhagen-based museum of post, TV and communication. A society without access to the material expressions of its own culture from its past and into the present will suffer from a lack of cultural formation and will have a lowered capacity for democratic debate. As Sandberg puts it: 'Our times are at risk of being existentially impoverished. Museums have a unique possibility to stand up as safeguards against fake news, blindness and acceleration sickness'. So far, museums have not really succeeded in convincing the rest of society that culture is 'not only the cream on the top of the cake, but on the contrary, the whole cake would implode without the cultural glue binding the layers of society together'. Thus, the task of museums is to make people benefit from the experience of the truth of this statement.

If museums are to face their task and challenges today, they must invent new models for business, according to the situation of their local surroundings. Being as independent of public financing as possible, cultural institutions today must emphasise what they give back to society. As the Enigma director emphasises:

> Our core product is supporting communication between people. We do this in our research, working to develop a third road between research and communication, calling this 'Researching Exhibitions', a continuing dialogue between researchers and citizens with a format of exhibitions building on questions and hypotheses. We

also do this in our program from the stage where we are in offline dialogue with what is going on online – with a program designed to blow up the filter bubbles that our smartphones tend to create around us. We also do this in our restaurant where long tables make room for living conversation between people who are strangers to one another ... This is our way of making money. (Sandberg 2017)

Cultural institutions must 'take their own medicine' by practising what they believe in, inviting people in, not for a one-way sermon, but for a process of co-creation and dialogue where different people meet and interact. If you only count so-called visitors when calculating criteria for subsidies, as the government does, you miss the point. What counts is much more the content and quality of the dialogue and cultural formation among people, including those who are only digitally present. At its best, a cultural institution must believe in its own message, practise it and be able to survive without public subsidies, says the director (presenting here a rather radical stance, that, if introduced, would threaten the survival of most Danish cultural institutions).

2001 was the year of the first major step the liberalisation of the Danish book market. And 2003 was the first year for the decentralisation of all power handled at the local level of church tax and budgets (plus the content and level of activities in the parishes) to parish and deanery boards.[1] As such, the book market and the church both had a signal to move from rather strong state regulations to a more or less free activity at the 'market'. Marketisation and the development of IT, including the new possibilities offered by the internet, changed the conditions of work for the book branch rather radically, and to some extent for other cultural institutions, too, including the Folk Church. As we shall see in this chapter, such changes are visible in:

1. the increased orientation towards the customers by means of surveys and studies of sale and participation;
2. a new emphasis on purpose and profile;
3. changes in forms of organisation and activities;
4. new types of personal employment; and,
5. at the book market in particular, the introduction of splendid new forms of Greenfield work alongside the Brownfield innovations of the old activities[2].

To sum up, a basic condition for the continued existence of cultural institutions like Enigma is that they deliver what this chapter will call *Public Value*. Cultural institutions have to survive on the conditions of the present market situation for culture, and at the same time sticking to and utilising their core competences and heritage, which this chapter calls *cathedral*.

On the one hand, the Folk Church has followed the patterns of development displayed by other cultural institutions. On the other hand, institutionalised conservatism combined with critical attitudes to marketisation and procedures known from *New Public Management* mean that the Folk Church – for better or for worse – is far from the level of development shown in the book branch, but closer to the level of development found in museums and libraries. For both of these sorts of institutions, modernisation has the form of an intensified focus on *Public Value* more than the introduction of the whole packet of New Public Management. This chapter argues that the Folk Church generally follows the same track as other cultural institutions. The challenge for all cultural institutions is to combine the care for their tradition and quality-based 'cathedral' function while at the same time coping with the conditions of the 'market'.

Firstly, I shall take a broader look at the development of Danish cultural institutions during the last ten years. My sources for studying the current way of thinking in Danish cultural institutions are statements from leading directors in five feature articles and three major interviews from *Politiken* and *Kristeligt Dagblad* from 2017 (one from 2018)[3], which I read against the background of available, though somewhat scattered, statistics and research in the development of Danish cultural institutions. Only when we come to the book market is there fully up-to-date research to build on. We shall therefore use the development of the book market to estimate the level of development in selected cultural institutions and the Folk Church.

Cultural institutions facing the market

Political rhetoric and a number of recent reforms in Denmark are, to a great extent, based on figures and calculations from economists, especially from the Ministry of Finance. It is evident that the Danish state has accepted that the central political struggle is no longer about East against West. It is about everybody competing with everybody, at all levels. At present, we have a

Competition State where, to take one example, the public-school system has been reformed with the intention of producing workers for the competition market (Pedersen 2013). However, competition on economic terms is not what policy in Denmark is all about. The former (strongly absolutist) Danish state has a specific constitution, a special tradition for administration and a tradition for interacting with civil society institutions. That means that New Public Management has been introduced in limited ways in Denmark (Rhodes 1999). This also reflects the political tradition for negotiating consensus democracy at work in Denmark. The implementation of New Public Management in Denmark has thus focused more on rationalisations and economic efficiency than on letting the institutions be exposed to full-scale market conditions (Greve 2006). In fact, some researchers in the field have posed the question of whether Denmark represents a case of New Public Management without marketisation (Pedersen and Löfgren 2012).

Cultural institutions in Denmark tend to think of and promote themselves as 'basic' to Danish culture, in line with the program from the *Enigma* director quoted above. In this chapter, I deal with the following cultural institutions that are, it can be argued, also 'basic' to Danish society:

1. Arts, history and nature museums, each with their messages and material to be shared with people whom they can attract to visit them or use their digital services;
2. Libraries, which traditionally specialised in lending out books and are today fighting to find new ways of working in a digitalised society; and
3. The book market with its 500 years of tradition for production and distribution of books.

Enigma is not alone among cultural institutions in striving to find the right new direction for its operations and self-understanding. We shall try to outline some of the features in recent challenges and subsequent development in cultural institutions, using material from the three above-mentioned types of cultural institutions.

'Culture has become the Human Relations Department of the competition state'. This is the headline of an interview in *Kristeligt Dagblad,* July 15th 2017, with the director of the Danish Museum for Industry, David Holst Olsen. He opens with the following statement:

> ... [Culture] is what all municipalities want. Industry is what we have down there, in the past – they say, that we cannot live from that. Then they transform old buildings for industrial production into creative workings places for innovation and cultural centres. It is a Phoenix story where cities raise themselves from their own ashes and resurrect themselves as something new, creative and innovative, pointing forward ... (Schjørring 2017)

Out of the 98 municipalities in Denmark today, 38 promote themselves as cities of culture and experiences (even if this is not the full truth when looking at the economy and the number of employees in the cultural sector). Danish museums have tried to follow that track for a long time, shifting from being centres for exhibitions to centres for experience in accordance with the concepts of 'experience economy' (Skot-Hansen 2008; Christensen 2016). Olsen continues by commenting on the tendency for cultural institutions to be eager to make themselves useful and relevant to the users and visitors, and thus to society at large:

> When self-development of the individual is put at the centre in cultural institutions, the content – the historical artefacts and the artworks – become secondary. Then culture loses its own value, becoming ornaments that aim at making the rationality from the work market nice to live in. (Schjørring 2017)

Olsen is critical about the enthusiasm by which, for example, the *Enigma* director quoted above wants to serve society. Olsen is indicating that her way of thinking is too influenced by the conditions at work when cultural institutions apply for the attractive and often badly needed subsidies from municipalities and other public sponsors. A bench in a park in such applications must be renamed 'an urban space for community, uploading of energy and contemplation'. Olsen is sure that his museum has a purpose, preserving the artefacts of the past, as to him this is what culture is about. He does not like turning his museum into a theatre for experience and self-development. Olsen seems to be alone in making these points in the debate among museum directors. Christian Gether, director of *Arken*, a museum of modern art in the south of Copenhagen, is certainly more in agreement with the *Enigma* director. Gether, wanting to contribute to societal development by developing the museums, writes in his feature article in *Politiken* July 26th 2017:

> In the future, Danish museums must be seen as one big learning organisation. That means an organisation that all the time attends to major societal and cultural changes which we have been witnessing these past years (digitalisation, movement from mono- to multi-culture, globalisation, inclusion of customers in co-creation etc.), enabling us to rethink our workplace and at the same time keep on running the old ways of creating value, where they function well. (Gether 2017)

The book market is a cultural institution rather different from the museums, which attempt to appeal to people for visits. It produces a special sort of goods, books for sale. Introducing development in the book market, I start with research by Stig Hjarvard, professor of Media Studies, who is also the chair of the Book and Literature panel of the Danish Ministry of Culture. Hjarvard uses the terms *cathedral* for the clarity of the purpose and quality of the product that most cultural institutions aim at, and *market* for the conditions of work that cultural institutions, including museums and books, live with as part of our increasingly neo-liberal market- and competition-oriented society (Hjarvard and Helles 2015). It is not an option for Danish book companies to be afraid of market forces. The book companies have no option other than to make money on the market as it is.

Until recently, old book publishing companies would, officially at least, stick to the sole purpose of publishing quality books according to their standards of quality and literary profile. In a similar way, the specialised bookshops, with literary-qualified personnel, would aim at only one purpose: selling the same sort of books. Since 2001, when the book market was gradually liberalised and, for example, supermarkets started developing their own strategies for buying and selling books, new business models have been penetrating into the old book publishing companies. They have, as their managers put it, to look at publishing and selling books 'with fresh eyes', with the help of new types of employees who know how to use new IT technologies and not least who know how to act in the market. This is especially clear when it comes to the distribution of books where the new internet-based book companies in Denmark may somehow coexist peacefully with the old Danish bookstores while both of them lose the competition against the major international companies like Amazon, Apple and Google.[4] In Denmark, big data about readers' preferences, as they can be generated from the digital internet market, have quickly become a key factor in the competition. As the international companies depend heavily on their knowledge about customers, this is becoming true of the local book branch in Denmark, too.

For the book branch, the conditions of the liberalised market have become clear: *compete or perish*. This also applies to the public libraries whose traditional function, the lending out of books, records and CDs, are about to be outdated by cheap books sold in supermarkets, and digitalised media (Münster 2017). The lending out of books and CDs has been reduced by 50 percent in 15 years. As it is with the museums, so it is with the book market as well: if you want to stay in business and not only make a profit over the short term, you must give priority to the content and quality of your products as well as strengthening your position on the market. Above all, you must know your people, your customers.

In the media, and thus the book market as well, current technological development leads to convergence of media as new devices, for example smartphones, have many functions previously spread over several media. This, taken together with market competition, tends to lead to convergence and fusion of organisational forms and business models – and not least to the employment of IT professionals who can cope with the newest technology combined with market strategy. The centre of power of the book branch thus tends to move from the literary-educated personnel to market and IT personnel (Hjarvard and Helles 2015). Digital communication, well-known from the news media, is also becoming increasingly important in museums and libraries. There is no doubt that cultural institutions can promote better and wider dissemination to their potential customers, not least the younger generation, via the internet and other digital media. If the physical institutions are modernised at the same time, the number of physical visits can also increase significantly (Rudloff 2013; Kobbelmagel et al. 2015).

To the tension between the traditional criteria of the 'cathedral' and the modern ways of the 'market', Hjarvard and Helles add the tension between inventing a splendid new business model at the book market and transforming the old model. New companies reliant on fully internet-based production and distribution of books are rising. Old companies have their traditional production and distribution of books supplemented with digital editing as well. Hjarvard and Helles (2015) call these two new forms of organisation 'Greenfields' and 'Brownfields' respectively. These labels are used in the business market, where investors can opt for an entirely new organisation of production and marketing (Greenfield) or investors can go for radical innovations in an old business organisation by taking control over the old firm (Brownfield). In the business world, Brownfield is a sort of hybrid that investors can opt for instead of taking over (full acquisition of) an existing company and setting up fully new business organization (Meyer and Estrin 2001). Among the cultural institutions studied here, the models of Brownfield and Greenfield are only fully practised in the book market; the other cultural institutions dealt with all seem to have a rather high degree of continuity in their development, in spite of fusions and reorganisations.

Recent appointments of directors for major cultural institutions in Denmark seem to indicate that the boards go for new directors who are good at public performance, successful in business and, if possible, have knowledge of the field in each particular case. The director of the Royal Theatre, Morten Hesseldahl, who has formerly made his way into the book branch, has been appointed director of Denmark's biggest book company, Gyldendal, after the number of visitors in the nationwide activities of the Royal Theatre went up by 60,000 to 806,465 in 2017.[5] University professor of anthropology, Rane Willerslev, who is famous for his public appearances, was appointed director of the National Museum in 2017. In one of his many presentations in the media of his vision for the museum, he says:

> Like it or not, the National Museum must operate in the economy of experiences. It is only a question of how to do so. I do not think that we shall be a new edition of Tivoli. We are based on knowledge, but we have to be a place where you gain knowledge through something exiting. Contrary to the newspapers, the museums are on an upward movement worldwide today. The museums having success are, however, those who understand the need of combining great knowledge with a popular approach ... What makes people learn is when they are presented with knowledge in an engaging way. That was how it was with my father. The reason that I cared about doing my homework with him was that he made himself engaged and took an interest in me. In the same way, we shall take on an interest in our users. (Øhrstrøm 2018)

Finally, let us have a look at the libraries. Recent developments indicate that libraries have managed to transform themselves with popular activities and events, such as singing together, public lectures, discussions and social services including teaching IT for free to customers. The number of public events at Danish libraries has increased from 13,500 in 2011 to 20,000 in 2015. This has resulted in the total number of visitors rising from 34 million a year in the late zeroes to 38 million visitors in 2015. 'Previously, we provided access to material, now we provide access to activities with the same material', the chief librarian at the main library in Copenhagen, Jakob Heide Petersen, has said (Benner 2017). What attracts people is not primarily the material found in the libraries, but the common rooms for common activities. Easy access to your 'culture' for all sorts of people is decisive. If the libraries can save us from being victims of fake information by securing access to correct information in digital forms, the libraries may have found their safe road to survival (Nielsen 2017; Oksholt and Ørding 2017). In the face of much scepticism (Münster 2017), libraries may be able to prove that they deliver so much 'Public Value' that society (e.g. the municipalities) will continue paying the bill (2.5 billion DKK annually) – or ask the users to pay a major part of the services they get.

Like other publicly-funded institutions (e.g. the universities), cultural institutions are making claims about their contributions to Public Value.[6] Jamine O'Flynn from The Australian National University uses the term to describe what cultural institutions aim at when they offer something to the benefit of individual customers and society as well. O'Flynn outlines the following criteria for management according to Public Value, which seem to come pretty close to the aspirations of Danish Cultural institutions:

1. You must move beyond simple criteria for competition, such as counting the number of customers;
2. You must be responsive to your users' needs and preferences, having various sub-goals for your work;
3. You must be aware of the full scale of results: service outputs, satisfaction, trust and legitimacy, measured by multiple accountability systems, including customers; and
4. You must select new directions in pragmatic ways (O'Flynn 2007, 361).

Summing up in general terms, we find five clear elements in the present transformation of cultural institutions in Denmark. Herein, these institutions, to some extent and in different ways, adapt to the conditions of market competition as they are known from business, or to their quest to prove that they offer Public Value:

1. *Turn to the user*. It is no longer enough that cultural institutions invent fancy products and tell people that they will become happy by using them. They have to come closer to their customers, let them be participants, maybe even co-creating the product. They have to study the patterns of users' behaviour in the statistics of visitors and try to understand the lives and challenges of their users.
2. *Turn to the purpose*. It is not enough that cultural institutions stick to traditional products or core goods, which used to render them stable in business. They must make clear to themselves and their users that their work has a higher purpose or calling, helping individuals to a better life for all of society, creating stability and growth in ways that potential users think of as needed. When striving to live up to the purpose in a way so that the users get the point, cultural institutions may have to change their products or at least reshape them radically.
3. *Make your organisation flexible*. Competing in their parts of the market, cultural institutions must be ready to kill several old darlings, not least in terms of the structures and internal culture of the organisation. Fusion, mergers and new forms of cooperation and business alliances are the rule of the day in private production and business, and often in cultural institutions as well where such strategies are possible. Not least, modern technology such as media and digitalisation may demand this.
4. *Employ the new kinds of experts needed*. To meet the demands of the business principles mentioned above, cultural institutions are likely to need new forms of employees, not only smart bureaucrats who can run a flexible organisation, but more importantly, people who understand the users (the market) and the new IT-based technological possibilities. Often such people with modern education and experience will end up being even more influential in the work of cultural institutions than the old-school workers who know the classical culture from which the cultural institution emerged.
5. *Be ready to produce radically new goods*. Strategies for modern cultural institutions may mean that cultural institutions must cultivate new fields, transforming the old forms of operating into new ones that would

not even have been dreamt of a few years ago (Brownfield). Alternatively, they leave the old organisation to set up a very new organisation to produce and sell radically new forms of product, for example establishing a new internet company selling only digital books (Greenfield).

The Folk Church facing the market

Recent research in the sociology of religion suggests that religion in Europe, which used to be an instrument for state politics, is now among the goods for sale on the market (Gauthier et al. 2013). Marcus Moberg sums the state of affairs and its implications for the Nordic Folk Churches up as follows:

> There are now ample empirical grounds for arguing that marketisation discourse ... has indeed had an impact on contemporary social and cultural life that extends far beyond the commercial and business world proper ... a growing emphasis in civil service, customer orientation, and advertising have developed intro recurring tropes in official Nordic church discourse. ... the Nordic Churches have both adopted and implemented a range of market-related organisational and managerial values. (Moberg 2016, 242f.)

At the level of language used in documents on church management and so on, Moberg is right. Since the 1990s, the language of vision, mission, strategy, etc. has been increasingly used in Danish church organisations, parishes, deaneries, dioceses. And since 2003, such language has been used by Ministry of Ecclesiastical Affairs (see Chapter 6). This development in the Folk Church, which has taken place since the 1990s, amazingly parallels the development in cultural institutions such as museums (Flemming 2015). The most frequently used slogan in the Folk Church over the last 10 years has undoubtedly been 'More Church for the Money' (Kirkeministeriet 2007). The question is, however, what this and similar new forms of language indicate?

Dividing the five points from the conclusion on the development of the cultural institutions into three, we will now explore them further to see how far the Folk Church adapts to marketisation by use of New Public Management, or to deliver Public Value, in the same way as other Danish cultural institutions. The material and data that we might refer to here is endless and generally quite disconnected, too. An overview is found in Iversen 2018, and this chapter refers to that overview with respect to general documentation. Extant research directed specifically towards our questions is limited, particularly when turning to the Danish church (see Nielsen 2009 and 2015, and Chapter 11).

The turn to the users

Until the last decades of the 20th century, the dominating paradigm in the theology and communication strategy of the Folk Church was 'preaching' (see Chapter 5). As such, the core activities were Sunday morning services plus church rituals (baptism, confirmation, weddings and funerals), confirmation classes, a few public lectures and, occasionally, pastoral care. During the first two decades after the Second World War, church attendance as well as conformity to the basic teaching of the church went down dramatically (Iversen 1986; Lüchau 2005). Since 1970, Sunday morning service participation has decreased slowly whereas alternative forms of services, and the development of a range of new forms of activities, means that the total number of visitors to the church on an annual basis has been and still is growing.[7]

Making calculations based on public church statistics in 2016, the 2,354 local churches in the Folk Church arranged approximately 500,000 events with approximately 20 million visitors a year – compared to 15 million visitors to all Danish museums and 38 million to Danish libraries combined (Iversen 2018). The Folk Church has been increasingly intent on being 'close to the people', as it is often expressed on homepages and statements of purpose. Due to the tradition-based resistance to 'counting' and to its decentralised (somewhat anarchistic) organisation, the Folk Church has, however, no comprehensive statistics regarding participation in its activities (Nielsen and Iversen 2014).

The Ministry of Ecclesiastical Affairs does offer all parishes, deaneries or dioceses the opportunity to have all data for annual participation in church activity collected, if the leaders in charge at the various levels want to use it. The system is simple: if a parish announces its activities on the national digital church calendar, the person in charge will receive a text asking to report the number of participants when the activity has finished.[8]

The official knowledge centre of the Folk Church offers a model for analyses and presentation of church statistics on participation in all sort of church activities primarily at diocesan and deanery levels. So far, such analyses have been carried out (in 2016) for the Diocese of Haderslev and for the Diocese of Viborg (2014-16), including a comparison with figures from 2001.[9] When looking at all figures available at the national level, including those from 2001, the patterns of development in terms of participation become quite clear: the number of activities has been growing quickly, whereas the participation in the various sorts of activities is growing slowly.

At the parish level, the Danish church consultant organisation *Kirkefondet* introduced in 2017 a full report and discussion of data on activities and participation for the church boards in parishes where these data have been collected systematically. The opportunities that are part of this presentation live up, to a great extent, to what professional marketing people might do to promote the activities of, say, a cultural institution. The parish boards can have full information on what sort of activities are attended, at which week days and major feasts during the church year (see Fusager 2017). Thus, it will soon be possible to know how many attendees you get if your give priority to arranging a given activity, in a given way, at a given time or other. Church attendance is not just dependent on the will of God, but also upon the smartness of the parish boards!

Church statistics – scattered and rarely fully accurate – represent only a modest beginning of the use of statistics for planning in the Folk Church. The movement towards this development of church statistics, or to be precise, the opportunities to have church statistics at this level, has been introduced slowly and never full scale (Nielsen and Iversen 2014). As long as the data are not comprehensive, or at least somehow representative for all sorts of parishes, it is difficult to use the figures constructively in a comparative and analytical way. To this, it must be added that figures for activity and participation do not tell the full truth about the relations of church and people in a parish. As pointed out above by museum director Jane Sandberg, what should be studied is rather the content and quality of the dialogue and cultural formation that takes place among people when participating in this or that activity. Relating to this, only one preliminary survey on the behaviour and expectations of people regarding the church has been carried out so far (Felter with Bjerrum 2015). Here, the general figures from church participation are mirrored at the level of persons, when asking, for example, about individual participation in various activities. Statistics and research on the book market are more advanced here, as they deal with such questions as sources of inspiration for and individual motives behind buying books as well as dealing with the parameters readers use when talking about quality in literature (Hjarvard 2016a). So far, a few local surveys have been carried out focusing on valuing of varies elements in, say, church services among ordinary people from the parish compared to regular church attenders (Schröder 2006 and 2008). In general, people give priority to the music, the choirs and hymn singing, even though the official idea in the Folk Church and among regular attendees is that the core priority is the sermon and the Lord's Supper.

In an article from September 2017, two young pastors argue that it is theologically legitimate and practically necessary to work with 'orientation towards the users', which they distinguish sharply from 'being governed by the users'. Orientation towards the users has a missional purpose; it is not business, but gospel:

> It must be clear that the Sunday service, like various church activities, can reach some, but not all, which in the final instance is part of the liberation of the gospel … There must be a living connection to the life situation or family situation, or a concretely felt physical or spiritual need to motivate participation. (Rønkilde and Phil 2017)

From a theological point of view, all efforts to understand why and how people like to participate in given church activities are meaningless if there is no clear understanding of how those given activities contribute to the purpose of the church. Until a few decades ago, the wish to have vision and a mission statement for the Folk Church was often turned down with the argument that the church and the pastor can only work according to the state regulations of the church – the rest must be left to God. As I argued in Chapter 5 on the theological accommodation to individualisation in the Folk Church, the church is working with a new understanding of what conditions Christian faith: it is not preaching but participation that is most important. Following this, a new understanding of the mission of the church is also developing, more fit to guide the activities of the church in times of individualisation and demands for authenticity.

Flexible organisation and new employees

In 2003, as mentioned previously, all power to make decisions about the local level of church tax and budgets, plus the content and level of activities in the parishes, was decentralised to the parish and deanery boards. At the same time, the parish boards were challenged to move from the old system of ruling by regulations to new ways of governing by goals – and thus also towards undertaking some kind of evaluation of their activities. In addition, the boards were encouraged to streamline the organisation to work efficiently, in order to get 'More Church for the Money'. This development has, however, been rather slow, caught up in the tension between modern-thinking people, often at the top levels (e.g. at the Economy and IT offices at the Ministry of Ecclesiastical Affairs, and at diocesan and deanery levels), and more conservative people at local parish levels who want to preserve their church and its traditions. In spite of generally sceptical attitudes when it comes to new forms of organisation, such as mergers of activities and even fusion of parishes, the structures in the Folk Church have been developing significantly since 2003.

The number of full mergers of parishes in the Folk Church is still low. The pattern of 'fusion' in the Folk Church is primarily one of joining parish boards. In 2004, the number of parishes with joint boards was 54 (with 25 such boards). In 2017, the number was 734 parishes with joint boards (altogether 311 boards had two or more parishes). As one of the consequences from this jump between 2004 and 2008, the number of lay members of the parish boards decreased from approximately 17,000 to approximately 13,300, following the regulations by the Ministry of Ecclesiastical Affairs and as a consequence of the mergers of boards and parishes. In 2017, the Folk Church has 2,169 parishes with 2,354 church buildings governed by 1,689 parish boards. More than 200 parishes have less than 100 inhabitants, and only 100 parishes have more than 10,000 inhabitants.[10] This organisational structure has been decisive so far, as experience shows that no church board with only one parish and one church building will suggest closure of its one and only church, and only rarely do they want to merge with neighbouring parishes. The possibility for rationalisations only opens up if a board has more than one church (Iversen 2015). In the meantime, many arrangements common for several churches are being organised and – for better or worse – churches in medium-sizes cities in the province are successfully arranging new forms of services and events that attract people from the surrounding rural parishes. Thus, 'regional congregations' are being established around specific activities across the parish boarders (Rasmussen 2014 and 2015).

Has the Folk Church gone digital like major parts of the book market and other cultural institutions? The short answer is '*no*'. However, the Danish people, including the members of the Folk Church, have turned to the internet when seeking information on religion and Christianity as well as when considering spiritual and existential questions. The Ministry of Ecclesiastical Affairs has set up a homepage with basic information on all parishes. Most parishes, deaneries and dioceses have their own homepages and the dioceses have set up a semi-official homepage for the Folk Church in general found at www.folkekirken.dk. The two most important homepages on religion on the net, run by the private newspaper, *Kristeligt Dagblad* (Christian Daily), have had a significant growth in terms of unique visitors during recent years: at www.religion.dk the number of unique monthly visitors has risen from 5,000 in 2008 to 200,000 in 2017. The figures for www.kristendom.dk were 3,000 in 2008 and 150,000 in 2017 per month. In surveys since 2005 (e.g. Hjarvard 2005 and 2008), Stig Hjarvard has documented how such media have become the primary option when people seek information on religion or spiritual, existential and moral orientation, and even for structuring the day, as the church bells did 100 years ago. In a mediatised environment, religious legitimacy is not only produced by means of the old Weberian sources of authority, tradition and charisma, but it rests more upon individual acceptance and references in terms of popular media culture:

> Media [thus] may not only destabilize existing religious communication practices but also enable other practices to emerge, both inside and outside of established religious organizations and movements. ... the presence of religion across various media reflects a much more multi-faceted development in which religion is evoked, contested, and subject to transformation. (Hjarvard 2016b)

A huge amount of church money has been invested in digital equipment in the Folk Church, largely for bureaucratic reasons, (i.e. the need for the Folk Church to be a collector of the basic data for the Danish Civil Personal Registration, to cope with the digital development in public Denmark). Where pastors often did not even have computers in their offices in the 1990s, since

2003 it has become compulsory for church personnel to handle all church matters at the safe church net – just as the internal channel of communication in the Folk Church is the church intranet (Højsgaard 2003). A few years into our current millennium, a small voluntary group attempted to develop a virtual church in cyberspace – with no lasting results (Sørensen 2007). In 2010, a survey revealed that the Folk Church still only used its IT-capacities for the most part as a blackboard for announcements (Fisher-Nielsen 2010). In 2017, 8.3 million DKK was spent on a new service of pastoral care on the internet, with five pastors working part-time on that project (*Kristeligt Dagblad* February 2 2017). During the first year, the services were used by 3,954 people with 2,568 of them being responded to. The great majority had an anonymous chat with a pastor, some were referred to a local pastor (*Kristeligt Dagblad* February 1st 2018).

During the last ten years, a number of dioceses, deaneries and parishes have employed journalists and other media-trained people for communication work – and the Folk Church has invested in a common logo and a nationwide internet design. Due to its lack of central leadership, exact figures are lacking. One estimate may be that, in 2018, the Folk Church has 50-100 professional people working full-time with communication, in particular with the internet. An interesting development in terms of 'personnel' in the Folk Church is the group of now 20 'church consultants', who offer their services to the Folk Church on questions of organisation, communication, leadership, and so on. The majority – 12 out of the 20 consultants – did not study theology but business-related topics. Notably, all of the consultants focus on the ways in which the church operates, not on the content of church work.[11] Unfortunately, we have no study of the work and impact of these new church consultants so far to draw upon.

One way of interpreting the position of the Folk Church, as caught between traditional cathedral attitudes and modern market behaviour, is to suggest that the modern methods are used strategically to defend the Folk Church from more marketisation and rationalisation and, even worse, central interference in local activities. This is indicated by 10 interviews carried out by Karen Marie Leth-Nissen for her PhD thesis. The deans can thus be seen as functioning as mediators between the Ministry of Ecclesiastical Affairs, local democracy (parish boards) and members of the Folk Church. The ability to document a high degree of activity in church buildings and many rites of passage contribute to legitimising the deans, proving that they are in control. This increases their ability to resist the introduction of more centralised management (Leth-Nissen 2018, Chapter 7).

Brownfields and Greenfields

The tension between the traditional criteria of the 'cathedral' and the modern ways of the 'market' is not the only one. Hjarvard and Helles have observed the tension existing between inventing a splendid new business model with new money in an old business (greenfield) and transforming the work in an established model for production and distribution of books, supplemented with digital editing as well (brownfield, Hjarvard and Helles 2015). Again, the Folk Church – especially since 2003 – has to some extent followed a similar, but much modified, pattern of development. The bulk of the work in the Folk Church adheres to the established traditions, whereas a minor but still rather visible part goes into more or less untested ways of working with new formats. The three most significant and visible examples are night churches, baby hymn singing and school service.[12]

The first night church was established in the cathedral of Copenhagen in 1999. It was initiated by a young theologian who was employed only part-time as a parish worker. Today, she is a full-time night church pastor leading the night church together with a full-time colleague, a parish worker and a big, fluctuating group of volunteers. The parish board has given priority to the night church due to the simple fact that it attracts 6,000-7,000 visitors per month and thus 2-3 times as many people as the ordinary services in the day church.[13] The night church movement has spread from Copenhagen to all Nordic countries. In Denmark in 2017, 33-night churches were at work in 25 cities.[14]

The school service of the Folk Church began in Copenhagen in 1992. It is organised locally, often at deanery level, and at work in almost all parts of the country.[15] The fact that perhaps up to 100 teachers and pastors devote a major part of their time to creating educational (non-preaching) programs offered for free to the public schools is due to the simple fact that these activities reach out to the majority of Danish school children. The resources available, and the creativity invested in the programs, means that they are popular with children and teachers in schools, as the teachers of religion in schools themselves would not have the opportunity to create teaching activities of the same quality (Larsen and Sørensen 2015).

Weekly sessions with baby hymn singing for babies and mothers (sometimes fathers, too) during maternity leave was initiated in 2001, and it is now offered across almost all of the country. Again, participation is usually free, and the quality of music and instruction for dancing with the babies is professional. Notably, the money for the salaries is made available rather quickly in the parishes and deaneries as soon as it becomes clear that this service is popular with the mothers, and maybe even impacting the babies, too (Marstal 2014; Nielsen et al. 2015).

These three forms of church activities are rather 'green' in their organisation and in their participatory nature, involving groups of children and adults as well. To a great extent, they reuse resources available in the church framework, such as buildings, art, music, hymns and ritual traditions, but the local entrepreneurs have a high degree of freedom to work with local people in the ways they feel most appropriate. As an extra asset, the programs invented are – slowly and rather carefully – also often reformulated and used to some extent in established church work and services, too. Comparing these new activities with the traditional activities, one factor seems very clear: *all participants are happy with their participation*. The activities are continuously evaluated and adapted in relation to how they are received by the participants. This was not always the case with the old activities, e.g. when confirmands found their [compulsory!] church attendance extremely boring (Hansen 2017) – and guests at baptism services find the whole situation and performance of the ritual in the church extremely odd (Enggaard 2016). On the other hand, critical studies, such as the ones by Hansen and Enggaard, are being noticed. It is obvious to most responsible people in the church that youngsters and parents easily end up leaving church practices if these are not found to be enjoyable (see Chapter 11).

Internationally, for example in the Anglican Church in England, something like 'Greenfield' activities are seen as mission work, called 'fresh expressions of church', organised in a para-structure with a special budget ('double economy') and leadership, even with its own bishop. In England in 2012, an investigation in 10 dioceses counted 518 examples of 'fresh expressions' within 'emerging churches' outside the established churches, amounting to 15 percent of church activities in the area covered (*An Analysis* 2013, *Mission-shaped* 2005). In the Folk Church, the Diocese of Roskilde has a program directly inspired by these 'fresh expressions'. It is working with local projects such as church services at local cafes, professional education of 12 'apostles' to become (Christian) story-tellers, and discussions of new forms of Church during courses at a public school for people's education, leading to the formation of new Christian fellowships.[16]

Where fresh expressions in England are organised outside the established church, even though they are sponsored by the church, new activities are generally found inside the Folk Church in Denmark, as there is enough room, flexibility and resources for this to happen. Thus, the new forms of operation in the Folk Church cannot be described as Greenfields because they emerge inside the old organisation. Nor can they be labelled Brownfield, as there are no investors from outside who attempt to transform the old organisation and its production in a radical way. Employees and volunteers inside the old organization carry out the activities. This is a strong witness to the high degree of flexibility in the Folk Church's old organisation.

All cultural institutions must find time and space for their 'big traditions' (Redfield 1973), focusing on their purpose and traditions. They cannot survive only by inventing new 'small traditions' in the form of events and new activities. In the case of the Folk Church, the big tradition, the Christian story, is most explicitly unfolded in the Sunday services and core rites of passage. This is where 'the cathedral' is more or less automatically visible. Here, 'the cathedral', if not setting the criteria for the church's activities, is at least setting some sort of horizons for all the other, often newer activities, where new 'small traditions' are created with the help of forms of activity that are flourishing among people today. This, however, does not detract from the reality that the new activities, generally speaking, tend to be more popular than the old ones.

Conclusion

We have seen how language and management methods known from the market, taken together with the development of IT and the internet, influence all cultural institutions. All over, this is made visible in the orientation towards the customers (the people) by means of surveys and studies of sale and participation, changes in the forms of organisation and activities. new types of personnel and the introduction of new forms of work supplementing or innovating older activities. Producing and selling books is today an activity strongly regulated by the market, even if the Ministry of Cultural Affairs is for political reasons eager to know what happens on the book market. The Folk Church is only moderately influenced by the methods of marketisation and business management. The Folk Church, however, cannot escape proving that is up-to-date in its management. The most important criterion for the survival of the Folk Church remains, however, making its members stay on and continue paying their church tax (c.f. Chapters 4 and 8). Somewhere in between, in terms of having been influenced by market forces, we have cultural institutions like museums and libraries. Like many other public institutions (e.g. universities) they are supported economically by public purses. However, this support, and their overall budget, depends heavily on their 'success' with the users.

Money-making businesses in the market often have a hard time legitimising themselves in the same way as cultural institutions and central public institutions, such as hospitals and the police. One of the decisive factors here seems to be the degree of 'inappropriability' (i.e. the security that the institution and its users have when the institution cannot be taken over by foreign companies or investors). It is hard to trust an institution or a business which may have a new owner, boss and target tomorrow! In this respect, the Folk Church is in a good position, as it is near unthinkable that it can be taken over by foreign investors. As indicated in Part II of this book, there are many factors influencing the destiny of a cultural institution such as the Folk Church. Money matters, but what money can't buy does, too.

References

An analysis of fresh expressions of Church and church plants begun in the period 1992-2012, 2013. Church Army and Church of England.
Andersen, Steen Bording 2017. 'Biblioteket er meget, meget mere end bøger'. *Politiken* November 29, 2017.
Benner, Torben 2017. 'Her samler bøger støv' and 'Vi går oftere på biblioteket, men ikke for at låne bøger og musik'. *Politiken*. July 14, 2017.
Bjerring-Nielsen, Bent et al. (eds.) 2013. *Den Mangfoldige kirke: Menighedsformer i Danmark. Ny Mission 24*. Copenhagen: Dansk Missionsråd.

Christensen, Hans Dam 2016. 'Museumssociologi: En slags genlæsning af især Dorte Skot-Hansens 'Museerne i den danske oplevelsesøkonomi (2008)'. *Nordisk Tidsskrift for Informationsvidenskab og Kulturformidling*, 5/2, 73-78.

Enggaard, Nete Helene 2016. *Højmessen set fra kirkebænken. En sammenlignende undersøgelse af gudstjenestedeltagernes oplevelse af højmesse med dåb i fire kirker med forskellig liturgisk profil og praksis i Frederiksberg Provsti*. Rapport, Det Teologiske Fakultet, Centre for Kirkeforskning.

Felter, Kirsten Donskov with Ruth Sønderskov Bjerrum 2015. *Hvad forventer folket af kirken? Rapport*, Det Teologiske Fakultet, Centre for Kirkeforskning.

Fischer-Nielsen, Peter 2010. *Mellem sogne- og cyberkirke: En analyse af folkekirkens kommunikation på internettet*. PhD thesis, University of Aarhus

Flemming, David 2015. 'The Essence of the Museum. Mission, Values, Vision'. *Museum Practice. The International Handbooks of Museum Studies*. West Sussex: Wiley Blackwell.

Fusager, Sille 2017. *Kirketællinger i Ballerup*. Copenhagen: Kirkefondet.

Gether, Christian 2017. 'Nytænk museerne og styrk lokalforankringen'. *Politiken*. July 26, 2017.

Gauthier, François, Linda Woodhead and Tuomas Martikainen 2013. 'Introduction: Consumerism as the Ethos of Consumer Society', in François Gauthier and Tuomas Martikainen (eds.), *Religion in Consumer Society. Brands, Consumers and Markets*, Farnham: Ashgate, 1-24

Greve, Carsten 2006. 'Public management reform in Denmark'. *Public Management Review* 8/1, 161-169.

Gundelach, Peter, Hans Raun Iversen and Margit Warburg 2008. *I hjertet af Danmark. Institutioner og mentaliteter*. Copenhagen: Hans Reitzels Forlag.

Hansen, Karen Toksverd 2017. *Konfirmandernes oplevelse af gudstjenesten*. Master Thesis. University of Copenhagen.

Hjarvard, Stig 2005. 'Medialisering af religiøse forestillinger', Morten Thomsen Højsgaard and Hans Raun Iversen (eds.), *Gudstro i Danmark*. København: Anis, 163-192.

Hjarvard, Stig 2008. *En verden af medier*. Roskilde: Samfundslitteratur.

Hjarvard, Stig 2016a. 'Danskernes smag for litteratur'. *Passage. Tidsskrift for litteratur og kritik* 76, 145-167.

Hjarvard, Stig 2016b. 'Mediatization and the changing authority of religion'. *Media Culture and society,* 38, 8-17.

Hjarvard, Stig and Rasmus Helles 2015. 'Going digital: Changing the game of Danish Publishing. *Northern Ligths* 13, 49-64.

Højsgaard, Morten Thomsen (ed.) 2003. *Den digitale kirke. Syv artikler om internet og kristendom*. København: Anis

Iversen, Hans Raun 1986. 'Mødet mellem kirke og folk i Danmark', Iversen, Hans Raun and Thyssen, Anders Pontoppidan (eds.). *Kirke og folk i Danmark. Kirkesociologisk dokumentation*. Århus: Anis, 318-347.

Iversen, Hans Raun 2015. 'Kirkebygninger i religionsmodellens grænseflader. Mellem fælles kulturarv og folkekirkeligt magtmonopol'. *Religionsvidenskabeligt Tidsskrift 62*, 29-44.

Iversen, Hans Raun 2017. 'Kommunikationsformer og medier', 'Kirken og demokratiseringen: Teologisk og kulturelt belyst', Kirkelivet og dets forgreninger', Niels Henrik Gregersen and Carsten Bach-Nielsen (eds.), *Reformationen i dansk kultur og kirkeliv 1914-2017*. Odense: Syddansk Universitetsforlag, 125-154, 195-228 and 331-358.

Iversen, Hans Raun 2018. *Ny praktisk teologi. Kristendommen, den enkelte og kirken i det danske samfund*. Copenhagen: Eksistensen.

Jensen, Elisabeth Krarup 2008. 'Den pastorale børnehave'. *Tidehverv*, September.

Jensen, Elisabeth Krarup 2015. 'Kan det betale sig?' *Tidehverv*, November.

Kirkeministeriet August 2007. *Betænkning 1491. Folkekirkens lokale økonomi. Betænkning fra udvalget om den lokale økonomi i folkekirken*.

Kobbelnagel, Kristian, Kim Schrøder and Kirsten Drotmer 2015. *Danske unges museums- og medieforbrug*. Odense: DREAM.

Larsen, Irene and Peter Green Sørensen 2015. *Selvom man tror på noget andet kan man godt være et sødt menneske. En undersøgelse af samarbejde mellem folkeskolen og folkekirken med særligt henblik på en vurdering af de folkekirkelige skoletjenesters anvendelse og betydning*. Aarhus: Folkekirkens Uddannelses- og Videnscenter.

Leth-Nissen, Karen Marie 2018. *Churching Alone*. PhD thesis, University of Copenhagen.

Lüchau, Peter 2005. 'Danskernes Gudstro siden 1940'erne', in Morten Thomsen Højsgaard and Hans Raun Iversen (eds.), *Gudstro i Danmark*. København: Anis, 31-58.

Marstal, Inge 2014. 'Babysalmesang', Balslev-Clausen, Peter and Hans Raun Iversen (eds.). *Salmesang. Grundbog i hymnologi*. Det Kgl. Vajsenshus's Forlag.

Meyer, Klaus E. and Saul Estrin 2001. 'Brownfield Entry to Emerging Markets'. *Journal of International Business Studies*. Third Quarter 32, 3, 575-584.

Mission-shaped Church. Church Planting and fresh Expressions of Church in a Changing Context. 2005 London: Church Publishing House.

Moberg, Marcus 2016. 'Exploring the Spread of Marketization Discourse in Nordic Folk Church Context', Frans Wijsen and Kocku von Stuckrad (eds.). *Making Religion. Theory and Practice of the Discursive Study of Religion*. Leiden: Brill.

Münster, Ole 2017. *Bibliotekernes krise – vejen til en ny lokal kulturpolitik*. www.biblioteksvennen.dk.

Nielsen, Henrik 2017. 'Skal museerne kun være for middelklassen'. *Politiken* December 1, 2017.

Nielsen, Marie Vejrup 2009. 'Transformationer i folkekirkekristendommen i Danmark i dag'. *Religionsvidenskabeligt Tidsskrift* 53, 63-79.

Nielsen, Marie Vejrup 2015. 'Changing Patterns? Occasional Customers of New Activities in Old Churches'. *Nordic Journal of Religion and Society*, 28/2, 137-153.

Nielsen, Marie Vejrup and Hans Raun Iversen (eds.) 2014. *Tal om kirken. Undersøgelser af aktivitets- og deltagerstatistik*. Publikationer fra Det Teologiske Fakultet 57.

Nielsen, Marie Vejrup et al. 2015. *'Tager man barnet ved hånden, tager man moderen ved hjertet'. En undersøgelse af babysalmesang*. Centre for Samtidsreligion, Aarhus Universitet.

O'Flynn, Janine 2007. 'From New Public Management to Public Value: Paradigmatic Change and Managerial Implications'. *The Australian Journal of Public Administration*, 66/3, 353-366.

Oksholt, Emilie and Arendse Ørding 2017. 'Digitaliseringen er bibliotekernes store chance'. *Politiken* December 16.

Pedersen, John Storm and Karl Löfgren 2012. 'Public Sector Reforms: New Public Management without Marketization? The Danish Case'. *International Journal of Public Administration,* 35/7, 435-447.

Pedersen, Ove Kaj 2013. *Konkurrencestaten*. Copenhagen: Hans Reitzels Forlag.

Rasmussen, Steen M. 2014. *Den relevante folkekirke – et sociologisk grundlag for målsætningsarbejde, aktivitetsstatistik og brugerundersøgelser*. Det Teologiske Fakultet, Københavns Universitet.

Rasmussen, Steen M. med bidrag af Marie H. Thomsen 2015. *Forskellige vilkår for folkekirken på landet*. Sabro: Landsforeningen af Menighedsråd.

Redfield, Robert 1973. 'Peasant Society and Culture', Robert Redfield. *The Little Community and Peasant Society and Culture*. Chicago: The University of Chicago Press.

Rhodes, R.A.W 1999. 'Traditions and Public Sector Reform: Comparing Britain and Denmark'. *Scandinavian Political Studies*, 22/4, 341-370.

Rudloff, Maja 2013. 'Det medialiserede museum: digitale teknologiers transformation af museernes formidling'. *MedieKultur* 54, 65-86.

Rønkilde, Martin Bendixen and Ole Phil 2017. 'Hvorfor skal kirken henvende sig til særlige målgrupper?'. *Kirken i dag*, Nr. 3. September 2017.

Sandberg, Jane 2017. 'Museer må ikke være bange for markedskræfterne'. *Politiken* June 14, 2017.

Schjørring, Esben 2017. 'Kultur er blevet konkurrencestatens HR-afdeling'. *Kristeligt Dagblad*. July 15, 2017.

Schröder, Linda Bak 2006*: Brugerundersøgelse i Helligåndskirken,* Aarhus. http://helligandskirken.dk/page/5268/sociologisk-unders%C3%B8gelse-2006

Schröder, Linda Bak 2008. *Rapport til Silkeborg kirke.*

Skot-Hansen, Dorte 2008. *Museerne i den danske oplevelsesøkonomi: Når oplysning bliver til oplevelse*. Copenhagen: Samfundslitteratur.

Sørensen, Poul Bo 2007. 'Cyberkirken er mere end en fiasko', *Kristeligt Dagblad May 3.*

Thomsen, Marie Hedegaard 2012. *Et åbent hus med mange indgange – empiriske studier i folkekirkeligt menighedsliv med valg, fri- og sognemenigheder som eksempler.* PhD-Thesis, Faculty of Arts, University of Aarhus.

Washuus, Dorte 2018. 'Museer har godt tag i publikum'. *Kristeligt Dagblad* May 2018.

Øhrstrøm, Daniel 2018. 'Det skaber rygrad og rummelighed at lade sig ryste'. *Kristeligt Dagblad* March 3.

Notes

1. The idea for this comparative chapter came from Margit Warburg, emerging from a conversation with Stig Hjarvard on his research on the book market. After Hjarvard's presentation of his research for the 'What' group it was agreed that the three of us should work on a comparative analysis of the development at the book market and in the Folk Church. As these two institutions were too different for at fruitful comparative study, other cultural institutions were included in a more general survey. I thank Stig Hjarvard and Margit Warburg for their generous contributions to this chapter in terms of ideas, references, critical comments and suggestions for the analysis.
2. These terms are being introduced later, see p. 214f.
3. See Andersen, Benner, Gether, Nielsen, Sandberg, Schjørring, Oksholt and Ørding, all 2017 and Øhrstrøm 2018. It is remarkable that so many directors of cultural institutions published elaborate policies for their institutions within one year. I use these statements as sources, as the directors deal with most of the questions used in interviews by Stig Hjarvard and colleagues when researching the book market.
4. Amazon does not dominate the market for books in Danish. A digital Danish company, saxo.com, has taken major parts of that market.
5. Appointments of strongly business minded bosses at old cultural institutions are rarely without strong reactions. When Hesseldahl made it understood that he is now the boss for all sorts of decisions at Gyldendal (*Politiken* October 1, 2018), leading writer Jes Smærup Sørensen left the book company because the boss can now overrule the professionals in the field of literature (*Kristeligt Dagblad* October 5 2018).
6. In Danish, the term *offentlige goder* (public goods) is used for the services that state and municipalities provide to be used freely by several citizens at the same time, such as street lights, public parks, law and order, and the prevention of diseases. For further discussion of the concept, see Kærgård in Chapter 9.
7. A few pastors still work according to the old regulations in the same way that their grandparents did 50 or 100 years ago. All sorts of modern activities they label e.g. 'church as kindergarten' which to them is a very bad notion since they themselves would not send their own children to real kindergartens (see, for example, Jensen 2008 and 2015). The great majority of parishes today are, however, activity churches emphasising new ways of communicating Christianity (Thomsen 2012). The formerly very homogeneous Folk Church is finding its place in a pluralistic and still more ecumenically-influenced church picture (Bjerring-Nielsen et al. 2013).
8. See http://www.the Folk Church.dk/aktuelt/kirkekalenderen.
9. See http://www.fkuv.dk/videnscenter/kirkestatistik/deltagerstatistik.

10   Information from www.km.dk, supplemented and corrected with help from Steen Marquard Rasmussen, (cand. scient. soc.) FUV by June 23rd 2017.
11   http://kirkekonsulenter.dk/
12   Other significant examples might be the introduction of classes for mini confirmands (in their 3rd year of schooling), slowly beginning in 1987, and more recently, the rather quick growth in the number of grief groups, philosophical salons and existential conversations for pregnant women and church work with immigrants. The latter has led to an official suggestion in 2017 that church legislation be changed so that non-Lutheran migrant churches can be invited to become members of the Folk Church.
13   http://www.natkirken.dk/
14   https://kirkenikbh.dk/nyheder/ny-opgoerelse-natkirker-har-nu-bredt-sig-til-hele-danmark
15   http://www.folkekirkensskoletjeneste.dk/
16   http://www.kirkvej.dk/

11. Occasional Consumers in the Folk Church

Marie Vejrup Nielsen

The Folk Church has started to direct its marketing efforts at specific user groups as part of a shift away from power exerted from above to power exerted from below, concepts presented by Linda Woodhead as central elements of the transformation of religion in a contemporary context (Woodhead 2004; Nielsen 2009). In this way, the Folk Church now increasingly positions itself as a cultural institution located somewhere between market and state (Chapter 10).

This chapter will further explore this aspect by focusing on the consumer profiles of the users of the Folk Church using the concept of 'occasional consumers', taken from marketing research (Pino et al. 2012). The material analysed consists of recent empirical research into the relationship between the Evangelical Lutheran Church of Denmark and its users, primarily in the form of extant research carried out by a range of different researchers, and to a lesser extent in the form of new material. The aim of the chapter is to present an analysis of the consumer profiles of the users of the Folk Church.

Theoretical perspectives – consumer profiles in the lived religion of institutions

Researchers into contemporary religion often see the traditional majority churches of Europe as being severely affected by a shift towards individualism in society and culture, to the point of these institutions' extinction, or, alternatively, their relegation to the status of institutions of cultural memory or vicarious religion (McGuire 2002; Davie 2002; Heelas et al. 2005; Hervieu-Léger 2006). In a world of fluid, individualised religion, these churches are not viewed as potentially vital centres of religious innovation. In the discussion concerning the secularisation and/or spiritualisation of religion in a Western context, both sides seem to agree that the traditional churches of Europe will suffer from decline in all respects: membership, belief among members and participation. They also agree that these churches are likely to suffer a general decline in terms of their cultural and societal power and influence (Bruce 2002; Woodhead 2004).

In recent years, there has been an increased focus on how the pattern of the Scandinavian, Lutheran majority churches fit into this general picture. They continue to have relatively high membership levels as well as high levels of participation in traditional rituals, such as baptism, confirmation, weddings and funerals. They also continue to play a role in society and culture (Furseth 2018; Pettersson 2013; Christoffersen et al. 2012; Nielsen 2009; Iversen 2005).

This means that there is a need for researchers to study the transformation of religious institutions such as the Folk Church. For purposes of this chapter, analysis will be conducted from within a perspective of the lived religion of institutions. In recent years, there has been a call to study 'lived religion' within religious institutions (Ammerman 2016; Orsi 2003; Nielsen 2015). Initially, the main aim of focusing on the perspectives of lived religion, everyday religion and the religion of the streets was to draw the attention of researchers away from official, dogmatic, institutional religion – a shift in focus that is part of the necessary development of the study of contemporary religion (Hall 1997; McGuire 2002; Ammerman 2007; Orsi 2010).

The call to include traditional church institutions in the lived religion perspective resonates with several studies of the Folk Church, which have focused on how to describe the majority pattern of religion in Denmark today. Hans Raun Iversen developed the concept of 'cultural Christians' to describe the pattern identified in his work, underlining the dialectical relationship between these cultural Christians and the more traditional church Christians, with both groups contributing to a dynamic which upholds the pattern despite the different ways in which they use and understand the church (Iversen 2005). Moreover, following her analysis of four YouGov surveys in 2013-2015, Astrid Krabbe Trolle has identified the profile of Danes in relation to the Folk Church as being: 'secularists in principle' and 'conservators of the concrete'. These concepts were developed in order to describe how Danes hold secular attitudes, while – at the very same time – they support church rituals and the role of the Folk Church in society. The study found a strong, overall pattern of individualisation in the relations between Danes and the church (Krabbe Trolle 2015, 5 and 19ff).

Others have examined typologies of membership and user profiles through sociological perspectives (Lüchau 2012). Research on the Folk Church has stated that a shift towards a user perspective has taken place within the church as an institution (Nielsen 2009 and 2015). Here, the argument was that the Folk Church is an example of how non-official religion is constantly incorporated into the official religion of the church, both in the form of a large degree of freedom for the members, and in the form of a constant negotiation and adaption to general cultural shifts and trends. Using Woodhead's terminology of a shift away from power from above to power from below, the Folk Church is presented as a church which has very much incorporated this shift by adapting to power from below, both structurally and in relation to its practices (Nielsen 2009).

With a view to examining more than just the transformation of the official levels of the church, theories of consumer profiles have been applied in relation to the majority patterns within the Folk Church using the concept of 'occasional consumers' (Nielsen 2015). Similar perspectives have also been explored in other Scandinavian contexts, for instance the point that membership of the Church of Sweden is 'made up in the main of occasional users of the Church, who attend at the times in their lives when they have personal need, while the Church organization primarily aims at promoting regular attendance at a specific activity, Sunday Service' (Pettersson 2013, 48). The aim of using consumer profiles here is to understand the motivation behind this behaviour in more detail, based on studies of consumer profiles in market studies. In these studies, occasional consumers are juxtaposed with habitual or ethical consumers. The primary difference between them is that habitual or ethical consumers motivate their consumption using a strongly defined identity, which they link to an ideological standpoint, whereas occasional consumers have more direct, situational motivations relating to safety and family wellbeing (Pino et al. 2012).

This typology will provide a link between previous studies of majority patterns of religion in Denmark related to the Folk Church as the background for examining what users consume in relation to the Folk Church. This chapter examines some of the results of recent empirical studies within a Danish context, thereby contributing to a discussion of the flexibility of traditional religious institutions and how this relates to the questions raised by the market or consumer perspectives on religion.

Consuming the church from cradle to grave

Recent studies have focused on the core activities of the majority of members, such as baptism (Leth-Nissen and Trolle 2015), confirmation (Schweitzer et al. 2015), weddings (Johansen 2015, Johansen and Nielsen 2017) and burials/funerary culture (Kjærsgaard 2017). At the same time, researchers have also provided initial studies of new activity patterns by focusing on baby hymn singing (Nielsen 2015). Other recent studies provide insights into the relationship between the church and its members through other lenses, for instance studies of church closures (Chapter 12) and studies of the social capital of the church (Chapters 13 and 14).

These studies comprise both qualitative and quantitative approaches as well as different theoretical perspectives. As such, it is necessary to be cautious when attempting to present a combined image. Nevertheless, this article will extrapolate some of the conclusions from these studies in order to discuss the pattern of occasional consumers and the lived religion of the Folk Church.

The studies mentioned above make it possible to construct an imagined route of life stages, from early childhood to old age and death, as a framework for examining what it is that users choose in relation to the Folk Church. In other words, the focus is placed on rituals which are still a stable part of the religious practices of the Danish population. In 2015, 61.5 percent of all new-borns were baptised, there were church funerals for 83.7 percent of the deceased, 71 percent of the relevant generation were confirmed and approximately 33 percent of the weddings were church weddings (www.km.dk). Although these numbers are declining slowly but steadily, the majority of Danes are still in contact with the church in relation to these life events, including participation in such events for family and friends.

Families with young children – baptism and baby hymn singing
The choice to baptise or not has been studied in a quantitative and qualitative study by Leth-Nissen and Trolle (2015). This research project focused directly on the reasons why people chose to have their children baptised (or not). It was a national survey with 1,042 participants, and three primary reasons for choosing baptism were identified: maintaining family tradition (45 percent), naming the child (45 percent) and being part of Danish culture

(32 percent) (Leth-Nissen and Trolle 2015, 17). The choice to baptise a child was therefore rooted in the cultural traditions of family and country, and it was not formulated as a personal, religious choice in relation to salvation or a personal relationship to the church.

Those who decided not to baptise their child were primarily motivated by the idea of giving their child a choice later in life (51 percent), their unwillingness to say 'yes' to the creed (32 percent) or the fact that they belonged to another religion (17 percent). This led the researchers to the conclusion that individualism very much affects the choice to baptise or not. The positive value of letting children decide for themselves is the primary motivation for most of the respondents who decline to have their children baptised, not a direct critical stance against the church or religion (Leth-Nissen and Trolle 2015, 19). At the same time, the non-religious position of the parents also plays a role in a significant number of cases as does increased religious diversity, which is the third largest motivation for declining.

These patterns are also discussed in relation to the important question of contact between church and members. In this respect, the study found that the parents who choose baptism are more in contact with the church than those who opt out of baptism. Those who participate in church events, for example baptism, confirmation, weddings and funerals of family and friends as well as children's services etc., are more likely to have all their children baptised (Leth-Nissen and Trolle 2015, 23). The people who choose not to baptise their children also opt out of the other activities of the church, including Sunday services and the many other activities. The special case of baby hymn singing will be discussed further below. But, in short, the study found less of a difference between those who choose baptism and those who do not, specifically in relation to attendance of baby hymn singing (Leth-Nissen and Trolle 2015, 24). Concluding the analysis of the survey, the researchers point to both individualisation and secularisation as key factors, and emphasise that their survey also indicates that younger generations born after 1970 increasingly choose not to baptise their children, have lower levels of faith and regard baptism as a cultural event without religious meaning (Leth-Nissen and Trolle 2015, 32).

The research project also included a qualitative study of parents in a specific parish in the Copenhagen area, allowing for a more in-depth study of the processes behind the choice of baptism in the context of the family. In this chapter, the focus is on the findings garnered from the parents interviewed (25 parents, representing 17 households, 2015; Ibid. 48), which were supplemented by interviews with other relevant groups, such as staff in the care sector. The qualitative interviews further underscored the aspect of individualism found in the national survey. In the interviews, the free choice of the child was important not just for those choosing not to baptise their children, but also for those who chose to baptise them. In this connection, the argument presented by parents who chose to baptise their children was that they were giving their children something to base their later choices on (Leth-Nissen and Trolle 2015, 50). The researchers link this position to Ida Marie Høeg's concept of baptism as 'preliminary' (Høeg 2009), articulated in her study of the choices made by Norwegian parents. The implication is that baptism is preliminary because children can decide for themselves whether they wish to be confirmed or not at a later stage of their lives.

Infant baptism is still the primary pattern of behaviour for the majority, but changes are occurring within this majority pattern, thereby transforming the lived religion of the Folk Church so that baptism becomes a choice based on the values of individualism. The Folk Church offers an increasing number of activities designed for families with young children (Nielsen 2009, Nielsen 2015). In relation to the understanding and choice of baptism, the activity of baby hymn singing is of special interest, as it is framed officially by the church as catechetic, that is, as a form of preparation for baptism ('dåbsoplæring') (Kilpeläinen and Nielsen 2018, 26).

The research project on baby hymn singing included a national survey of both participants and providers of the activity as well as interviews and participant observation at nine selected locations across the country. The initial mapping showed that approximately 55-60 percent of all Folk Church parishes ('pastorater') offered this activity. The primary motivation for providing the activity was 'to reach a different audience than those attending Sunday service' (97 percent agree/partially agree), and to familiarise parents and children with the church and the church space (98 percent). 'Preparation for baptism' also figured in heavily (84 percent totally agree/partially agree). Another key motivation was to 'market the church in a new way' (63 totally agree) (Report 2014).

Both the survey and the interviews showed that the participants were similar to the majority pattern of Danes and they could therefore be characterised as cultural Christians. The participants responded in a variety of ways when asked why they chose to attend this particular activity.

The option of 'I want the church to be part of my life and my child's life' had 23 percent answering 'totally agree' and 41 percent 'partially agree', with a slight increase in the category 'I want to familiarise my child with the hymns' (30 percent totally agree and 39 percent partially agree). The church space is also important: 51 percent totally agree and 21 percent partially agree that it is important that the activity takes place in the church. When asked directly if they use baby hymn singing as a preparation for baptism, only 3 percent totally agree and 13 percent partially agree, whereas 55 percent totally disagree and 22 percent partially disagree (Report 2014).

There is common ground between providers and users in relation to the idea of becoming more familiar with the church, and there is a discrepancy between them regarding the idea that this activity can be used as a preparation for baptism. This can be related to the findings of the study of the choice of baptism where, interestingly, participation in baby hymn singing did not have any correlation with the choice to baptise or not. This pattern of discrepancy was confirmed by a word count performed on the material, with the main words used being 'child' (220 times), 'a cosy atmosphere' (115 times), 'church' (98 times) and 'music' (96 times). The word religion was only present once (Report 2014). Elements of tradition and official religion such as the church and the music are important. At the same time, the participants also emphasised that they valued the fact that the activity was open to all and that it was not a form of indoctrination (Nielsen 2015).

The research project concluded that the users of this activity fitted the consumer profile of occasional consumers. The conclusion based on the material of the research project was that the parents (mothers) participating in this activity were very satisfied, occasional consumers and that the positive evaluation of the activity did not translate into new patterns of belief or practices, or new commitment. They participated enthusiastically and evaluated this activity very positively, focusing in particular on the fact that it was open to all and free from indoctrination. The focus was primarily on the activity being a positive context for interaction between mothers and children, with the church providing a unique space, music and the special atmosphere and time needed to create a special emotional space for both mothers and children (Nielsen 2015).

These two research projects indicate that at the life stage of the cradle, for example the life of families with infants, many choose the church. The projects make it very clear that the motivation of the users is focused on free choice and family. These conclusions provide further perspectives in the examination of the preliminary and occasional consumer patterns of the users of the church.

Choosing tradition – confirmation classes in the Folk Church

Two projects focusing on the ritual of confirmation will be examined here: a local Danish study of confirmation in the diocese of Roskilde performed by a private research institute (Østergaard and Munksgaard 2008) and a large international study which also included the Folk Church in Denmark (Schweitzer et al. 2015). The project in Roskilde resulted in a report primarily designed for use in the church in relation to the development of its confirmation work (Østergaard and Munksgaard 2008, 12). This report examines aspects of the life of young people in late modernity as well as focusing on the specific reasons why young people choose to be confirmed. The primary reason given was: 'It was my own choice' (86 percent), with the other options being 'belief in God' (52 percent), 'tradition' (48 percent) and 'because of the party' (42 percent) (Østergaard and Munksgaard 2008, 70). The researchers behind the report use the term 'collectively oriented individualists' to explain the motivation behind choosing tradition as 'my own choice' (Østergaard and Munksgaard 2008, 71). Tradition is combined with choice, which is also found as a motive in the interviews presented in the report (Østergaard and Munksgaard 2008, 72). With regard to the reasons why young people took part in the preparation for confirmation, there was a strong focus on various ideas, such as gaining a better knowledge of Christianity and obtaining a better foundation for one's own choice (Østergaard and Munksgaard 2008, 77).

The international research study had many aspects, especially in relation to comparisons between Lutheran churches in very different contexts across Europe, and it provides an analysis of change over time by surveying the same individuals at the beginning and end of the confirmation preparation class. Following a very short presentation of one of the general conclusions of the research, the primary focus here will be the results in Denmark with respect to the reasons why young people chose to participate in confirmation classes in the Folk Church. When looking at some of the conclusions based on the entire dataset from all participating countries, the researchers remark:

> From this point of view, confirmation work is not only the teaching of basics of the Christian faith and tradition, but gives space for personal reflection of their spiritual quest. [...] The extent to which confirmands perceived how much they "have been enabled to come to their own decisions about faith" and how much "their questions concerning faith were addressed" presents a relatively strong predictor of their commitment to the church membership in several countries (Schweitzer et al. 2015, 91).

Commitment and freedom of individual choice were not mutually exclusive, quite the reverse. The quote also seems to indicate a call for a change in the official view of confirmation preparation from traditional teaching to becoming a space for individual choice.

What about Denmark? Firstly, it is noteworthy that, when asked about their religious identity, 16 percent of the Danish confirmands answered that they were not Christians and 30 percent answered that they were Christians 'only occasionally' (Schweitzer et al. 2015, 217). The top four motivations for taking part in confirmation classes given by the respondents in the survey were as follows: 1) I wanted to take part; 2) I wanted to have a beautiful celebration; 3) I wanted to receive a blessing on my confirmation; and 4) I was baptised when I was a child. In contrast, the bottom four motivations were: 1) my friends were taking part as well; 2) because confirmation training is fun; 3) because I felt obliged to take part; and 4) because my family wanted me to take part (Schweitzer et al. 2015, 217).

The researchers' first conclusion regarding this pattern is that: 'the motives illustrate a strong individualistic tendency. The most important motive is their own free choice, and among the least important is pressure from friends and family'; and they also note that the high ranking of the blessing is unique for the Danish confirmands in the material (Ibid.).

In the examination of change over time, these scholars conclude that: 'Only the importance of belonging to the church and the notion that the Church does a lot of good things changed significantly. [...] Overall it seems that the Church affirms itself during confirmation time' (Schweitzer et al. 2015, 218).

When examining the topics that were perceived as the most and least relevant in confirmation preparation, researchers found that there was, to some degree, 'a discrepancy between the interests of the confirmands and the ministers' (Schweitzer et al. 2015, 219-220). For instance, friendship and love/sexuality were at the top of the list for confirmands, but at the bottom of the list for ministers. But, when surveying the level of satisfaction, the researchers find that 'the discrepancy does not have a huge impact' and 'the perceived lack of relevance, and the discrepancy between prioritised topics do not seem to influence satisfaction' (Schweitzer et al. 2015, 220).

From the theoretical viewpoint of this chapter, the confirmands display an occasional consumer profile. They can be very satisfied with their participation in the overall concept (after all, it was entirely their own choice) and identify themselves as occasional Christians at the same time. They have a certain degree of consumer flexibility within the tradition. The discrepancy between users and providers, which is also found in the baby hymn singing-project, does not dampen the satisfaction of these occasional consumers, but is part of their preliminary, tentative consumer profile, leaving them free to choose tradition in their own way.

Wedding couples and the Folk Church

Recent research also sheds light on the dynamics of the choices connected to the ritual of church weddings. In her study of the wedding ritual in the Folk Church, Kirstine Helboe Johansen focused on various aspects of the meaning of the ritual (Johansen 2015, 2017; Johansen and Nielsen 2015). These researchers examined the motivations behind the choice of pastor for weddings, using data derived from a qualitative study among wedding couples. The material consisted of interviews with 13 wedding couples who fitted the profile of cultural Christians. Two patterns could be detected in the motivations behind the choice of pastor: the personal qualities of the pastor, and the pastor as a representative of the church as an institution. In both these patterns, personal relations were important. Having a personal connection to the pastor performing the ritual was the ideal situation for wedding couples (Johansen and Nielsen 2015, 232). They focused on choosing the right pastor to fit their ideals, and a relationship with the pastor was key here. The interviewees did not see the pastor as authoritative in a traditional sense, and they evaluated the pastor based on their own experience. One couple expressed it as follows:

> We did not know much about the pastor when we chose him, but we took that baptism and we planned to get married, but I have no doubt that if we had had just a little bit of a negative experience with the baptism then we would not be here today (Couple 12, Johansen and Nielsen 2015, 233)

Others focus more on the pastor as a representative of the church as an official institution, commenting that the pastor 'handles the religious service for us', or 'she is the one who manages the church' (Johansen and Nielsen 2015, 234). The pastor is in charge of the wedding in the church, and wedding couples will, to some degree, accept this contextual, occasional authority. But this is not connected to their personal beliefs: 'My religious belief doesn't go through the pastor ... you know, I have a direct connection to God in my mind ... but the priest is like the one who promotes and handles the religious service to us, well he is the priest' (Ibid.). When examining the words used directly in relation to the choice of pastor, the researchers found a recurring theme of 'niceness' and said there was a focus on 'a personal positive emotional response' among some of the couples, whereas others focused on having a good guide through the process of planning the ritual (Ibid.).

In general, the study of wedding couples and their motivations indicated that the pastor has authority over the ritual, and the users choose to engage with this authority because it corresponds with their view of how to achieve a good wedding. Across the material, the choice aspect is clear and the motivations behind these choices are connected to the values of the individual and their perspective of what the church and the pastor are and what they do. The overall trends of individualisation and power from below transform the ritual within the institutional setting through the shaping of the space and the ritual as well as the choice of pastor (Johansen 2017). The couples exercise ideals of free choice and creative influence, but they do so in a negotiation that has a framework, which also develops in relation to a user perspective. Continuing with the terminology used in the chapter, the wedding couples can be presented as occasional consumers of a traditional ritual, and this occasional aspect is also visible in the title of the Helboe-Johansen and Nielsen's 2015 article 'Choosing a pastor for the day' (239).

Incorporating change – Folk Church, cemeteries and funerary culture

The Folk Church holds a near monopoly on the rituals performed in relation to burials (82.9 percent of all burial services took place in a church in 2016) as well as controlling where the remains are buried, for instance in Folk Church cemeteries. In other words, a large majority of the Danish population use the church to bury their dead.

Anne Kjærsgaard conducted a study of aspects of Danish funerary culture in her recent PhD dissertation (Kjærsgaard 2017). Kjærsgaard states that it is necessary to pay attention to what goes on in Folk Church cemeteries because: 'Graveyards seem to be locations of lived religion' (Kjærsgaard 2017, 79). Kjærsgaard focuses on what she calls the limits of secularisation in Denmark and discusses her findings in relation to the concepts of belonging and believing. She argues that the lived religion of the Danes, as expressed through funerary culture, shows a dynamic of constant modernisation of the church and an adaptation to new practices. One example of this is the rapid shift from casket burials to cremations and urn burials in Denmark (82.3 percent cremation rate in 2015, Kjærsgaard 2017, 97). According to Kjærsgaard, this adaptation indicates something significant about the Danish context:

> … with overlapping views on materiality as adiaphora, church and cremation society could join forces. In Denmark, it was henceforth possible to feel both modern-cum-rational and Christian, while these stances became opposites in many other countries. Today, the Lutheran Church thus owns two thirds of Danish crematoria, whereas crematoria are seen as features of secularization elsewhere. The Danish development therewith exemplifies that modernization did not always exclude the church. (Kjærsgaard, 2017, 97)

This adaption did not only take the form of accepting the choices of the users, but also occurred on a very fundamental, institutional level, through the incorporation of crematoria as part of the institutional framework of the Folk Church, with two thirds of the crematoria now being run by the church (Kjærsgaard 2017, 97). This history, which Kjærsgaard presents in detail in her work, is an often-overlooked aspect of transformation through adaption and inclusion in the Folk Church. The initial opposition between cremation societies and church, and a negative stance towards cremation in some theological circles, has developed into a full incorporation of the practices of cremation as part of the church. That is, when the consumers wanted cremation, the Folk Church responded with a full incorporation into its institutional structures and practices.

Funerary culture is a central aspect of the relationship between church members and the church itself, and Kjærsgaard points out that 'Continued membership is strongest in places where church and graveyard still form a unity' (Kjærsgaard 2017, 80). Kjærsgaard points out that the official religion has been transformed in this area: '… the situation would be one of "belonging but believing in something else," or, of doing rather than believing. The institutional framework of institutional religion, in other words, would have allowed people to be religious in a different way' (Kjærsgaard, 2017, 81). As such, Kjærsgaard is arguing along the same lines as other recent studies of the Folk Church as a church, which through its official religion incorporates aspects of non-official religion in the form of new practices, thereby making them part of the church in a process of adaption to the lived religion of the members. This does not happen without conflict, in the form of confrontations over cemetery practices, some of which have been widely discussed in the Danish media, as well as the more day-to-day negotiation and regulation of what is allowed and accepted (Kjærsgaard 2017, 102). Using the theoretical perspective of this article, it could be argued that, while the church maintains a strong hold on funerary culture and a near monopoly as the primary space for the laying to rest of the dead in Denmark, in recent decades it has constantly developed new choices for its users as can be seen in the manner in which it has incorporated cremation as an option within the church. In other countries, such conflicts became motivations for 'opting-out' of the church domain.

A recent research project at Aarhus University further confirms this development of choice within a church framework – in particular, the development of new sections in Folk Church cemeteries.[1] New sections, such as woodland areas and open spaces, are constantly being developed, as are new sites for casket burials and urn placements. The churches that provide these options emphasise the importance of giving a choice to those who are making the decision of a final resting place for the deceased (Holst Thomsen 2017). At the same time, this choice is negotiated within the frameworks of already established contexts, wherein the providers (e.g. the church council and the cemetery staff) construct new choices for the users. Special options and regulations apply to each section, coming into force once a choice is made (Holst Thomsen 2017). Although it is too early to draw overall conclusions based on the research material collected so far, in terms of church cemeteries, the preliminary analysis of the material seems to indicate a pattern of transformation in favour of a consumer focus and a high degree of focus on individual choices. The needs of the users constitute a key value for the cemetery staff. There are strong indications that grave sites are being transformed through new practices (e.g. the objects placed at the grave site when visiting, headstone design and new rituals for urn placement), which are sometimes performed by cemetery staff.

Discussion

This chapter has focused on some of the most recent studies, which offer empirical reference points for a discussion of the pattern of religion in Denmark in relation to the consumer profile of the users of the church as well as the shift to a user perspective in the Folk Church. Some of the results of these studies indicate that individualism and choice have become a key part of the lived religion of the Folk Church. The transformation of tradition is taking place both in relation to the key rituals and in the form of new activities. The various recent research projects presented here show that the dynamics of individual choice are central in terms of the motivations of the users, and that the theme of choice figures clearly in their use of the church. They choose to engage with the church as well as choosing the values and experiences they regard as most attractive.

Parents who choose to have their babies baptised feel that they are giving their children a choice by giving them a connection to a tradition, and this tradition is also connected to family and national culture. Mothers who choose to take part in baby hymn singing do so because they want to give their babies the best possible setting for development and happiness, and the church provides this for them in this phase of their lives. Confirmands choose confirmation training because they want to attend, not because it is fun or because other people think they should. They present themselves as individual consumers with a free choice, and they engage in the tradition from this standpoint. Wedding couples choose pastors for the day based on their view of what a pastor should be, emphasising the importance of either their personal relations, or the fact that the pastor represents the institution of the church. And finally, the bereaved choose locations in cemeteries to reflect their life values. This all happens as part of a constant adaption, with the church negotiating these choices and, in general, moving in the direction of incorporation rather than demarcation. The consumer profile of the occasional consumer is reflected in the other concepts used by the researchers in the various projects mentioned here: preliminary baptism, occasional Christian confirmands and choosing a pastor for the day. In the case of cemetery practices, the patterns already examined point to occasional consumption of the cemetery, although further studies are needed here.

Danes are choosing tradition and choosing to transform tradition into a form, which fits the occasional consumer profile. They do not express a personal, Christian identity; instead, they opt in and out of church activities and rituals based on their situational needs. This article argues that they do not reveal a pattern of a deep-set Christian, personal identity linked to the traditional, official religion of the church. However, they do reveal a different form of sporadic enthusiasm, which is connected to elements of official religion and tradition: many of the users of the activities analysed in this article express a high degree of consumer satisfaction. They are enthusiastic about their involvement in occasional consumption based on their individual choice, and their enthusiasm includes aspects of the official, institutional religion: church room, hymns, pastors and rituals. The argument in this chapter therefore is that there is more than mere nostalgia at play in this consumer pattern – it is not simply a leftover relic from the past, but a pattern shaped by the choices of contemporary individuals in relation to the various options available to them.

It has been argued here that, when studying the dynamics of lived religion within the Folk Church (not just in the form of the motivations and practices of church members, but also looking at the actions of the church), a stable pattern of adaption becomes visible. The choices made by occasional, individualised consumers are integrated into the lived religion of the official religion of the Folk Church. This is by no means painless, or without conflict and debate, perhaps especially among the religious elite, both lay and clergy. However, when looking at the overall trends, the adaption is remarkable. Cremation, first seen as utterly opposed to the church, was transformed into a new official church practice. And, the dynamics between the life rituals of baptism, confirmation and weddings have been deeply transformed in relation to traditional official religion. This transformation has been substantial, for example when the choice of a pastor for a wedding is made on the basis of the previous baptism of a child, or when baptism leads to confirmation, which becomes the primary context for commitment. These are substantial challenges to the official, theological understanding of these rituals, but in the majority of cases, this seems to lead to a development of the theological understanding of these events. For example, the researchers focusing on confirmation training concluded that, instead of teaching official faith, the classes should become a space for individual choice.

These occasional consumer patterns indicate that the majority of members opt in and out of the church, and feel they have a large degree of freedom to do this. In relation to the study of confirmands, the researchers concluded that the church confirms itself. When surveying recent studies, it seems that the church also confirms the pattern, in that it provides more and more platforms for occasional confirmation of the relationship to the church. Naturally, this does not in itself indicate that this pattern will continue, nor does it safeguard against rapid collapse, as the whole model is firmly based on the free choice of individuals who can opt out of both participation and membership very quickly.

Conclusion

This chapter has presented a number of empirical cases revealing why people choose to use the Folk Church for various rituals and activities. Their motivations all centre on individual freedom of choice in the form of the freedom to opt in and out of church rituals and activities as part of an occasional consumer pattern. The conclusion is that there has been a shift in favour of power from below, visible in the 21st century as a shift towards a user perspective within the church. From cradle to grave, new and traditional frameworks of religion are now offered by the church. And, all these frameworks (new activities developed locally and spreading, like hymn singing for babies, or core rituals such as baptism, confirmation or weddings) are contexts which offer a range of choices within the institutional context. This gives the late-modern consumer options within the church structure instead of having to opt out in order to consume the goods.

References

Ammerman, Nancy (ed.) 2007. *Everyday Religion: Observing Modern Religious Lives*. Oxford, New York: Oxford University Press.

Ammerman, Nancy 2016. 'Lived Religion as an Emerging Field: An Assessment of its Contours and Frontiers' *Nordic Journal for Sociology of Religion*. 29/2, 83-97

Bruce, Steve 2002. *God is Dead – Secularization in the West*. Oxford: Blackwell.

Christoffersen, Lisbet, Margit Warburg, Hans Raun Iversen and Niels Kærgaard (eds.). 2012. *Fremtidens Danske Religionsmodel*. Frederiksberg: Anis.

Davie, Grace 2000. *Religion in Modern Europe*. Oxford: Oxford University Press.

Davie, Grace 2002. *Europe: the Exceptional Case*. London: Darton, Longman and Todd.

Furseth, Inger (ed.) 2018. *Religious Complexity in the Public Sphere – Comparing Nordic Countries*. Palgrave Studies in Religion, Politics and Policy. London: Palgrave Macmillan.

Gauthier, Francois and Tuomas Martikainen (eds.) 2013. *Religion in Consumer Society: Brands, Consumers, and Markets*. Burlington: Ashgate

Hall, David D. (ed.) 1997. *Lived Religion in America – Toward a History of Practice*. Princeton: Princeton University Press.

Heelas, Paul, Linda Woodhead, Benjamin Seel, Bronislaw Szerszynski, and Karin Tusting 2005. *The Spiritual Revolution: Why Religion is Giving Way to Spirituality*. Malden, MA: Blackwell.

Heelas, Paul, Scott Lash and Paul Morris (eds.). 1996. *Detraditionalization: Critical Reflections on Authority and Identity*. Cambridge: Blackwell.

Hervieu-Léger, Danièle 2006. *Religion as a Chain of Memory*. Cambridge: Polity Press.

Holst Thomsen, Rikke 2017. *De Dødes Fællesskaber – et Kvalitativt Studie af Jyske Kirkegårde*. Master's Thesis, Aarhus University.

Høeg, Ida Marie 2009. *'Velkommen till oss'. Ritualisering av livets begynnelse*. PhD Dissertation, University of Bergen.

Iversen, Hans Raun 2005. 'Gudstro i den Danske Religionspark', Hans Raun Iversen and Morten Thomsen Højsgaard (eds.) *Gudstro i Danmark*. Frederiksberg: Anis, 101-123.

Johansen, Kirstine Helboe and Marie Vejrup Nielsen 2015. 'Choosing a Pastor for the Day: Representations of the Pastor in a Contemporary Context'. *Journal of Empirical Theology*. 28/2, 226 – 241.

Johansen, Kirstine Helboe 2017. 'Weddings in the Church of Denmark: Traditional and Modern Expectations to an Efficacious Ritual', in Hans Gerald Hödl, Johann Pock and Teresa Schweighofer (eds.). *Christliche Rituale im Wandel: Schlaglichter aus*

Theologischer und Religionswissenschaftlicher Sicht. Göttingen, Wien: Vandenhoeck & Ruprecht, 65-86.

Johansen, Kirstine Helboe 2015. 'When Religion and Spirituality Converge in Ritual: Weddings within the Church of Denmark'. Pamela Couture, Robert Mager, Pamela McCarroll, Natalie Wigg-Stevenson (eds.). *Complex Identities in a Shifting World: Practical Theological Perspectives*. Zürich: LIT Verlag, 53-63.

Kilpeläinen, Aino Elina and Marie Vejrup Nielsen 2018. 'Teaching Rituals: New Church Activities and Religious Education.' *International Journal of Practical Theology*. 22/1, 23-39.

Kjærsgaard, Anne 2017. *Funerary Culture and the Limits of Secularization in Denmark. Death Studies – Nijmegen Studies in Thanatology* 4: Zürich: Lit Verlag.

Krabbe Trolle, Astrid 2015. *Blandt Principielle Sekularister og Konkrete Konservatorer – Danskernes Holdninger til Religion og Folkekirke i Fire YouGov-Undersøgelser*. Center for Kirkeforskning, Københavns Universitet.

Leth-Nissen, Karen and Astrid Krabbe Trolle. 2015. *Dåb eller ej? Rapport om småbørnsforældres til- og fravalg af dåb*. Det Teologiske Fakultet, Københavns Universitet.

Lüchau, Peter 2012. 'Seks Teser om Danskernes Medlemskab af Folkekirken', Lisbet Christoffersen, Hans Raun Iversen, Niels Kærgård and Margit Warburg (eds.). *Fremtidens Danske Religionsmodel*, Frederiksberg: Anis, 311-328.

McGuire, Meredith 2002. *Religion: the Social Context*. Belmont CA: Wadsworth Thomson Learning.

Nielsen, Marie Vejrup 2009. 'Transformationer i Folkekirkekristendommen i Danmark i dDg'. *Religionsvidenskabeligt Tidsskrift*. 53, 63-79.

Nielsen, Marie Vejrup 2015. 'Changing patterns? Occasional Consumers of New Activities in Old Churches'. *Nordic Journal of Religion and Society*. 28/2, 137-153.

Orsi, Robert 2003. 'Is the Study of Lived Religion Irrelevant to the World We Live in? Special Presidential Plenary Address, Society for the Scientific Study of Religion, Salt Lake City, November 2, 2002. *Journal for the Scientific Study of Religion*. 42/2, 169-174.

Orsi, Robert 2010. (3rd ed.). *The Madonna of 115th Street: Faith and Community in Italian Harlem, 1880-1950*. New Haven, CN, London: Yale University Press.

Pettersson, Per 2013. 'From Standardised Offer to Consumer Adaptation', *Religion in consumer society: Brands, consumers, and markets*. Francois Gauthier and Tuomas Martikainen (eds.): 43-57. Burlington: Ashgate Pub. Company.

Pino, Giovanni, Allessandro M. Peluso and Gianluigi Guido 2012. 'Determinants of Regular and Occasional Consumers' intentions to Buy Organic Food. *The Journal of Consumer Affairs* 46/1, 157-169.

Reintoft Christensen, Henrik 2017. 'Denmark: The Still Prominent Role of the National Church and Religious Traditions', Nelis, Sagesser and Schreiber (eds.), *Religion and Secularism in the European Union: State of Affairs and Current Debates*. Peter Lang, Dynamiques citoyennes en Europe. 51-57.

Report 2014. *Når du Tager Barnet ved Hånden, Tager du Moderen om Hjertet – Rapport om Babysalmesang.* 2014. Center for SamtidsReligion: (last viewed January 23rd 2017): http://samtidsreligion.au.dk/oevrige-projekter/babysalmesang/.

Schweitzer, Friedrich, Kati Niemelä, Thomas Schlag and Henrik Simojoki (eds.) (2015). *Youth, Religion and Confirmation Work in Europe*. Gütersloher Verlagshaus.

Stark, Rodney and Laurence R. Iannaccone 1994. 'A Supply-Side Reinterpretation of the "Secularization" of Europe'. *Journal for the Scientific Study of Religion*. 33,. 230-252.

Thompson, John B. 1996. 'Tradition and Self in a Mediated World', Paul Heelas, Scott Lash and Paul Morris (eds.) *Detraditionalization: critical reflections on authority and identity*. Cambridge: Blackwell, 89-108.

Woodhead, Linda. 2004. *An Introduction to Christianity*. New York: Cambridge.

Østergaard Søren and Suzette Munksgaard. 2008. *Mere end Blot Forberedelsen til en Fest – Konfirmandprojekt Roskilde*. Center for Ungdomsforskning.

Notes

1   The results of the research project have not been published yet. The analysis here is based on the preliminary findings of the project.

12. The Significance of Cultural Buildings: Inventing a Ritual for Church Closures

Jes Heise Rasmussen

The research project *What Money Can't Buy* adheres to the notion that the Danish Folk Church is a cultural institution comparable to other cultural institutions such as schools, libraries, theatres, and so on. Even though each of these institutions has distinct qualities, they are experiencing many of the same challenges (for example what to do with their significant buildings when they are closed). The closing of churches evokes strong feelings, both among the former congregation and among the wider public, and often results in a collision between cost-benefit rationality and the emotions attributed to the religious activities that have taken place within the churches. In this chapter, I explore one of the consequences of the closing of churches and the invention of a ritual for church closures. This has not been done before in Denmark, but in a Scandinavian context both Olaf Aagedal and Jörgen Straarup, among others, have examined the relationship between religious communities and the building used for their religious activities (Aagedal 2003; Straarup 1985). Aagedal has argued, convincingly, that buildings reserved for religious purposes have become more important to the religious communities that use them, as those very same cultures have experienced a general decline in the public. The buildings become a safe haven which signifies that, even though the religious communities might experience hardship, they are still alive and relevant (Aagedal 2003, 529). This might explain why the need for a closing ritual was expressed in the cases presented in this chapter. In his extensive research of the Swedish Church, Straarup has studied the views and attitudes towards the building of new churches in residential areas (Straarup 1985). This chapter is also focused on the relationship and attitudes towards church buildings, but where Straarup applied a quantitative approach to explore the impact of new churches, this article makes use of a qualitative approach focusing on the impact of church closures.

The Danish Folk Church has no official ritual for the closing and deconsecration of churches. This is in itself interesting, since it suggests that such a ritual has not been in high demand, or that the powers that be within the Church have not felt the need for supplying such a ritual. However, the lack of an official ritual has led to ritual innovation on a local level as and when the need arose. In this chapter, I present two examples of rituals constructed in connection with the closing of two parish churches in the Diocese of Copenhagen. The article revolves around the issue of ritual necessity and the reasons given by the priests involved in the rituals. A common theme for the two cases was the issue of remembrance and coping. The priests insisted on constructing a ritual because they felt that the former use of the building was worth noting. However, there are also instances to the contrary. In the instance of Absalon Kirke, the former parish council refused to create or participate in any kind of ritual to mark the closure of that church. Their refusal was an act of defiance against the dean and the bishop whom they felt had acted unfairly towards them. The participation in any form of ritual, with the dean or bishop being present, would be the same as publicly accepting the fate of their church, something they were unwilling to do.[1] Interviewing priests and laypersons involved in the rituals marking the end of a parish church is an opportunity to gain insight into the religious practice of closing and, in some cases, deconsecrating the building. It is also an opportunity to understand the role of the church building itself. It became apparent while conducting the interviews that a twist on the theoretical perspective of *lived religion* (Hall 1997) would be useful in analysing the situation. The priests had no official guidebook to consult when constructing the rituals and each congregation dealt with the situation in their own way. Traditionally, the focus of *lived religion* has been the context and content of the practices of religious laity and their 'everyday thinking' (Hall 1997, vii). This perspective has been criticised because it neglects the everyday life of professionals in religious institutions. Instead, it creates a false contrast between the religiosity of the masses and that of the professionals (Ammerman 2016, 87). By examining the arguments behind the construction of closing rituals it becomes clear that, in many cases, the choices that were made were not grounded in official religious discourse, but in everyday feelings and the need to make the rituals matter on a personal level.

Rituals and iconic religion

To understand the interplay between religious discourse and material constructs, such as buildings, I apply the theoretical concept of *iconic religion*, recently introduced into the study of religion (Knott, Krech and Meyer 2016). I expand upon this approach by introducing the concept of 'affordance' into the discussion (Gibson 1986; Norman 2000). From a sociological perspective, all rituals can be perceived as symbolic actions representing religious discourse (McGuire 1997, 16). The great diversity of rituals makes any overall categorisation difficult. However, Catherine Bell, the late professor of Religious Studies at Santa Clara University, has provided a more general, accessible overview of religious rituals (albeit with a comprise of putting aside detailed, extensive classification). Bell's list of genres includes life-cycle rites (rites of passage), calendrical and commemorative rites, rites of exchange and communion, rites of affliction, rites of feasting, fasting and festivals and political rituals (Bell 1997, 94).

The rituals described by Bell could be categorised as distinct forms of rites of passage, in accordance with the pattern put forth by the French ethnographer Arnold van Gennep (Gennep 1965). Concerned with ritual transformation, Gennep proposed a three-stage analytical model of separation, liminality and reintegration. Gennep's analytical attention was on the transformation of people participating in a rite of passage. The rituals constructed for the closing of churches have another object of interest, namely the building itself. The ritual has some resemblance to a funeral where the participants must realise that a living member of the community has died. In both examples of church closure in this chapter, the buildings start out as parish churches, located within the religious sphere, but through the different rituals they undergo a substantial change. In the case of Gethsemane Kirke, the building remains a place of Christian religious practice, though it is no longer a parish church. In the second case, concerning Samuels Kirke, the ritual involves moving the building from the religious to the secular sphere.

Centring the ritual on a material construction (a building instead of a living person) requires a new way of thinking about religion. I am not just interested in the religious discourse and practices of a Christian community, but also in the interaction between people and inanimate objects. In an effort to gain greater understanding of the religious change in urban spaces, Kim

Knott, Volkhard Krech and Birgit Meyer proposed the analytical concept of *iconic religion*:

> [W]e suggest treating 'iconic religion' as a heuristic and analytic concept in the study of religion … helps us grasp the emergence of a sense of a sacred surplus. Religious icons are not essentially given … but develop as socio-cultural constructs. Once established, they foster religion in all its dimensions of experience, materiality, cognition and action. We suggest that artificial and natural objects (or sets of objects) such as buildings … can be referred to as religious icons if they trigger religious communication, including action and experience that is attributed with religious meaning. (Knott et al. 2016, 132)

Applying that to the topic of this chapter, churches can be seen as examples of religious icons that may become secular icons: 'religious iconicity can change into a nostalgic iconicity after a church has been secularised, or in general, if sacred objects become part of cultural heritage' (Ibid. 133). By describing and analysing closing rituals it is possible to grasp the fluidity of iconic change as it happens.

All of the priests interviewed were attentive to the fact that they constructed the rituals based on their own conceptions of what would be fitting and appropriate. They had no higher authority telling them what to do or how to do it. While they could have asked the dean or bishop for help, these figures remained in the background, going along with the drafts presented by the local priests. None of the priests expressed annoyance at this division of labour, but gave the impression that this was what they expected. Indeed, one of the deans interviewed remarked that he 'expected to be left standing alone at the altar, if he began preaching a different tune than what the priests wanted'.[2] Both of the rituals draw upon known religious elements, showing that, while the rituals are innovative, the priests reuse well-known traditional ritual expressions.[3]

Case 1: The rite of passage of Gethsemane Kirke

Gethsemane Kirke was closed as a parish church on October 10th 2010. Vesterbro parish had decided that the building should be used for religious and secular activities targeted at the youth in the city. The closure ritual combined elements from traditional church services: the ritual used for consecrating a new church, and elements signifying the future use of the building. To mark the transition Thomas Nedergaard, who would continue his work in the soon-to-be former church, was of the opinion that the ritual had to begin firmly rooted in tradition, only then gradually incorporating more experimental, innovative elements. Opening the service with traditional elements was intended to create a sense of familiarity. Furthermore, this approach was also intended as a way of showing respect, both to the parish members who had come to say goodbye and to the building itself. Retrospectively, Nedergaard argued that the incorporation of elements from the consecration ritual was a way of creating a ritual link between the opening and closing of the Church.[4]

The ritual began, following the directions established in the liturgy of the Folk Church for the Sunday service. First, an organ prelude announced the beginning of the ritual. This was followed by an introductory prayer given by the chairman of the parish council. Normally, this prayer would be read by the parish clerk or a choir singer, but appointing the chairman, Frode Benedikt Nielsen, to this task was a symbolic way of emphasising the importance of the parish council (both in the institution of the Folk Church as such, but also in the specific case of Gethsemane Kirke). Nedergaard wanted to include members from the parish council because they had been a driving force in creating a new future for Gethsemane Kirke. The ritual then continued, still adhering to the structure set down for the Sunday service, with an opening hymn accompanied by organ.[5] Traditionally, this would be followed by the reading of a small text from the Old Testament. In this case, the Bishop of Copenhagen, Peter Skov-Jakobsen, took the role normally reserved for the priest and read 1 Kings 8:22-23 and 27-30. The bishop had not chosen the text himself, but followed the passages recommended by Nedergaard, who presented the bishop with a draft for the ritual. The passages from the Book of Kings were chosen for two main reasons. The first reason was the content of the passages (especially verses 27-30), which Nedergaard felt fitted the occasion:

> But will God indeed dwell on the earth? Behold, heaven and the highest heaven cannot contain you; how much less this house that I have built! Yet have regard to the prayer of your servant and to his plea, O Lord my God, listening to the cry and to the prayer that your servant prays before you this day, that your eyes

> may be open night and day toward this house, the place of which you have said, 'My name shall be there', that you may listen to the prayer that your servant offers toward this place. And listen to the plea of your servant and of your people Israel, when they pray toward this place. And listen in heaven your dwelling place, and when you hear, forgive.

The scriptural passage was meant to console the congregation by clearly stating that the God they worshipped was greater than any building. It was also a reminder that, while the building was no longer a parish church, it would still be a place of Christian worship. The second reason for choosing verses from the 1 Kings did not surface until after the interview with Nedergaard. The passages, 8:22-23 and 27-30, are used in the first readings from the Old Testament in the ritual used when consecrating a new church (Ritualbogen 1992, 189). Nedergaard had no recollection of this during the interview, but later reasoned that this was due to the fact that seven years had gone by since the ritual. Retrospectively, Nedergaard argued that it would make sense 'to connect the opening with the closure'.[6] This indicates, that the inclusion of elements from the ritual in the past with the ritual in the present emphasises the fact that this church building has come full circle.

After the reading from 1 Kings, the Vesterbro Parish Youth Choir performed the hymn 'Herre ræk ud din almægtige hånd' accompanied by organ and keeping to the usual structure of readings followed by hymns.[7] Then another traditional element followed, a reading from the New Testament, where the bishop once again took the place normally reserved for the priest and read Colossians 3:16-17:

> Let the word of Christ dwell in you richly, teaching and admonishing one another in all wisdom, singing psalms and hymns and spiritual songs, with thankfulness in your hearts to God. And whatever you do, in word or deed, do everything in the name of the Lord Jesus, giving thanks to God the Father through him.

This text was also chosen by Nedergaard, but once again, he could not recollect why. During the interview he suggested that it was due to the passage highlighting that humans, not places of worship, are what defines Christianity. This off the cuff explanation from Nedergaard adds to the interpretation that the ritual was meant as a coping mechanism for the congregation. As with the passage from 1 Kings, the verses from Colossians are also used in the ritual of consecration.

According to the official liturgy for a Sunday service, it would then be time for the Apostles' Creed, followed by the sermon. However, in this case the bishop, Peter Skov-Jakobsen, delivered the sermon after which the ritual diverged significantly from any known rituals within the Church. The sermon was composed without any input from Nedergaard and began with the reading of Colossians 3:12-15. The main theme of the text is how Christians should behave towards one another, preferably with love and forgiveness. The bishop then continued his sermon, making an analogy between the changes that were demanded of the first generation of Christians and the changes that were needed in Copenhagen today if the Church were to avoid being bogged down by tradition:

> As a church, we cannot just stick to tradition and pretend nothing is happening! We live in a time that demands a new course of action! But the departure, this new course of action, is not foreign to us. It has always been the case …. Our everyday lives are filled with people who have no sense of tradition. It is important that we show that tradition appreciates the Gospel as something that should not be locked away in old buildings in accordance with old regulations. … We are now depositing the baptismal dish, chalice and the holy books of the church in moving boxes, which we will carry into a new and different church that has yet to arise! If anyone wants to be mournful over what has ended, then by all means, be so. It was good in its day!

Analytically, the bishop normalises the anomalous by using religious discourse. By quoting Colossians he creates a link between the first Christian communities and the congregation at Gethsemane Kirke. He is assuring them that they, as Christians, are well-equipped to handle this unusual situation. In doing so, the bishop uses a defining characteristic of ritual action, as proposed by Catherine Bell regarding rites of passage and calendrical rites. These rituals work because they 'impose cultural schemes on nature' (Bell 1997, 103). Nature, in this context, is not 'coming of age' or 'the return of the seasons', but the way of the world as defined by the bishop. He makes it clear to the congregation that change is inevitable in our world. What is happening to Gethsemane Kirke might be sad, but it is natural. By introducing the cultural

Deconsecration ritual in Gethsemane Kirke. Photo: Malene Lauritsen.

scheme (the quote from Colossians), he reminds them that this is nothing new. He thereby reestablishes normality. The sermon concluded with the bishop reading a transitional prayer, describing the good work that has been done in Gethsemane Kirke, and articulated hopes for a fruitful future, both for the congregation and the church building.[8]

After the bishop had left the altar, the lights were switched off. A contemporary dancer, Tore Peters-Munch, then entered the aisle from the antechamber dancing his way up towards the altar. He was partly naked, wearing only shorts, and his arms were adorned with shapes in green paint. The shapes were not Christian, but were made up of circles and wiggly lines. Once he reached the steps in front of the altar, the performance took a different turn with the introduction of fire. In the subdued light, the dancer began juggling with burning torches while moving in front of the pews and up towards the alter. This went on for a couple of minutes before the dancer turned his attention to a flight case on wheels. Members of the choir had positioned it

Deconsecration ritual in Gethsemane Kirke with a view of the flight case in the lower left-hand corner. Photo: Malene Lauritsen.

on the aisle near the front pews. The burning torches were extinguished and a green spotlight was switched on following the movements of the dancer. The performance culminated in the dancer removing the holy objects one by one and placing them in the flight case. When the last item was safely stored away, he closed the lid and positioned himself in a handstand on top of the flight case. At that moment, Vesterbro Parish Youth Choir took up position near the altar and, accompanied by band, performed 'My life is in my hands'. Four members of the choir approached the flight case and pushed it down along the aisle into the antechamber while the dancer was still maintaining his handstand on top of the case. The song was followed by another hymn performed only by the band. The transition from the choir to the band was meant to signify that Gethsemane Kirke had now become a place reserved for the Christian youth, no longer confined to doing anything according to tradition.[9] Nedergaard led the final prayer of the evening as a sign that he was the new priest in charge of the activities in Gethsemane Kirke.

Case 2: The two closures of Samuels Kirke

Samuels Kirke on Nørrebro was closed on two separate occasions. The first time was on June 2nd 2013 and the second time was on October 2nd 2013. Unlike Gethsemane Kirke, Samuels Kirke did not have a future within the religious sphere, but was sold to the housing association VIBO and rebuilt into youth apartments. The deconsecration ritual was the result of a collaborative effort by three priests from the parish of Kingo-Samuel and the dean from Nørrebro Deanery. The parish of Kingo and the parish of Samuel merged into one in 2008, and in 2013, Samuels Kirke was approved for closure by the Ministry of Ecclesiastical Affairs. After the merger, the last priest to hold a full-time position in Samuels Kirke left the church when it became clear that the church would no longer have its own parish register or a regular Sunday service. The last three years leading up to the closure were, in the words of the parish clerk, 'A downward spiral'.[10] From 2009, the church became home to a variety of different congregations, and each Wednesday afternoon the church would serve a hot meal for the needy and hold a short church service. Otherwise, the church was used by a Faroese, a Serbian Orthodox and a Coptic congregation. When the time came to close Samuels Kirke in 2013, the parish council discussed whether or not a ritual was needed since Kingos Kirke had already taken over all of the regular churchly functions in the parish. However, a parish clerk, who originally held a position at Samuels Kirke, argued that the closure should not be ignored and the priests from Kingos Kirke felt that a deconsecration ritual was needed. An outline of the final ritual can be seen below.

> Prelude
> Hymn: Kirken den er et gammelt hus[11]
> Salutation: Priest A
> Collect: Priest A
> Brief sermon: Priest B
> Hymn: Guds ord det er vort arvegods[12]
> Blessing: Priest C
> Deconsecration: Dean
> Hymn: Må din vej gå dig i møde
> Postlude: Procession to office.

The ritual outlined was not the first choice. Initially, the date for the deconsecration ritual was June 2nd 2013. The parish had organized a full-day event celebrating the history of Samuels Kirke with a budget of 40,000 DKK. The day was scheduled to start at ten a clock with a deconsecration service beginning with a procession of all the priests and the dean of the parish. The ritual would follow the structure of a regular church service, but, in addition, a band and a children's choir would take part in the service, and a number of former parish council members would address the attending crowd. The sermon was supposed to be held by the dean and the ritual would conclude in a procession where the holy objects would be moved out of the church, thus symbolising the closure and deconsecration of the building. When everyone was gathered in the street, hundreds of coloured balloons would be released, each with a little note saying: 'A loving greeting from Samuel's Church in Thorsgade, which now lives on in Kingos Kirke'. The rest of the day would be centred on speeches and events commemorating the history of Samuels Kirke.

Shortly before June 2nd the parish council was informed that the holy objects could not be removed from the church because the administrative paperwork in the Ministry of Ecclesiastical Affairs was not in order.[13] This news created turmoil and consternation in the parish. It was decided to go ahead with the arrangement since the invitations had already been sent out. However, the last part of the ritual was changed. They would go through with the procession, but the holy objects would remain in the church. This decision was hard to cope with for a number of former parish council members, who then decided to stay away since the day would not mark the final day of the church anyway. After this event, the church was closed to the public.

By the end of September, the parish was informed that the paperwork had gone through and the holy objects could now be removed from the church. On the evening of October 2nd the three priests, the dean and seven members of the old congregation of Samuels Kirke went through with the ritual. The dismantling of the church had already begun, the baptismal font and dish were gone, both having been sold to Ulse Kirke near Haslev. This encouraged the priest, Arne Kappelgaard, who outlined the ritual (seen in Box 1), to add 'a bit of gallows humor to the ritual'.[14] He selected the first hymn 'Kirken den er et gammelt hus' (The Church is an old house), because he was quite unhappy about the situation. The first verse in the hymn begins with the lines 'The Church is an old house, standing, though towers fall'. The main theme of the hymn is the belief that the true church is the congregation and not

The releasing of balloons from the first closing of Samuels Kirke.

the structures of wood and stone, emphasising that any given building is of little consequence when compared to Christian belief. Kappelgaard felt that the deconsecration ritual showed that this idea was not the case. The church building of Samuels Kirke was closed as a consequence of a dwindling congregation, and he was concerned for the future of the Folk Church in general.[15]

Deciding on the actual words used for the deconsecration itself was a collaborative effort between the priest, Jens Christian Raabjerg Larsen, and the dean, Gert Blak Mogensen. Larsen shared a draft with the dean who wrote the final version.[16] When interviewed, the dean no longer had his final version of the ritual, but he believed that it was true to the draft presented by Larsen. The length of the draft was ten lines, opening with an expression of gratitude for the years where Samuels Kirke had been a place reserved for Christian religious discourse and practices. The deconsecration culminated with these words:

> We ask you: remove the blessing that you once placed over this house and open it to the world. Hereafter, let people gather in Kingos Kirke, or other places, that have been consecrated in your name. Let this house be like all other houses and

let it be a place of good use and happiness. This is what we ask of you Lord, Jesus Christ, your Son, who lives and reigns with you in the unity of the Holy Ghost, One true God from eternity to eternity. Amen.[17]

To Jens Christian Raabjerg Larsen, the ritual was necessary in order to uphold the respect for the religious discourse; he stated:

I am not of the opinion that a church stops being a church just because it's not in use. You have to do something, you have to short-circuit or dispel it ... Something changes with your theology if you think that what happens to the building and the objects are of no importance. When does it cease to be religious? That is why you need to make a ritual, to make it stand out and to maintain.[18]

What Larsen is expressing here is that there is a difference between the church's condition before and after the ritual has been performed, that this occurs by going through the ritual. Indeed, the quote gives a tantalising insight into the interplay between religious discourse and practice. Larsen felt troubled by the lack of an official ritual. From a legislative point of view, everything was in order once the Queen of Denmark had put her signature on the ministerial papers confirming the closure of Samuels Kirke. This meant, in effect, that the deal was done, the building was no longer a part of the Folk Church. To Larsen, this was problematic since a ritual transition was needed in order to uphold the respect for the Christian religious discourse. To him the closure was about Samuels Kirke, but it was also about so much more, it was about upholding the integrity of his profession.

The ritual ended with a procession where the holy objects were removed from the altar and taken to what used to be the old clerk's office. The dean led the procession that consisted of eleven persons, with the three priests bringing up the end. When the procession reached the office, the ritual ended and afterwards the holy objects were put back in their usual place of storage until they could be removed for good.

Changing icons and affordances

The two rituals were very different from one another, but they are an account of the same ritually enforced transition. The building starts out as

Former members from the congregation of Samuels Kirke visiting their old baptismal font now residing in Ulse Kirke, Haslev.

a church and transforms into a structure resembling a church, but with a different purpose. This gives weight to Kim Knott, Volkhard Krech and Birgit Meyer's argument that icons – in this case buildings – are developed as socio-cultural constructs. This entails that once a building is designated as religious it remains so for those who contribute to the religious practices within, either active or passively. However, the agency of religious icons is somewhat vaguely described by Knott et al. as something that: '... trigger[s] religious communication, including action and experience that is attributed with religious meaning' (Knott et al. 2016, 132). They fail to accurately describe *why* it triggers religious communication and action in the first place. I propose that by using the concept of affordance, this vague point within the framework of *iconic religion* becomes quite clear. Affordance was first introduced by James Gibson in an attempt to describe how animals perceive their natural surroundings. An example of this is a river that offers water for drinking, swimming or drowning, depending on the state and nature of the animal. Gibson describes this as the affordance of the environment (Gibson 1986, 127). Donald A. Norman has since moved the concept of affordance into the world of human design. Affordance becomes a quality through which we can judge the effectiveness of everyday tools, objects and other man-made devices:

> When used in this sense, the term affordance refers to the perceived and actual properties of the thing, primarily those fundamental properties that determine just how the thing could possibly be used ... A chair affords ('is for') support and, therefore, affords sitting. (Norman 2000, 9)

Affordance explains why it is necessary to create a ritual for church closures. A church has an abundance of religious affordance for the faithful believers. The architecture and all the artifacts, symbols and paintings invoke religious practice and discourse. This adds a new layer of interpretation on the comment by Larsen, one of the priests from Samuels Kirke. He stated that an unused church is still a church, and that 'you have to short-circuit or dispel it'.[19] Furthermore, he reflected that this 'dispelling' was needed in order to uphold respect for the religious discourse. The ritual is a way of changing the affordance of the building by physically removing artifacts that exact religious affordance. In Gethsemane Kirke, Nedergaard reflected upon his redecoration of the building and said that it was important to him to show that the building had changed status. It was still used for religious purposes, but it was not supposed to remind people of a normal parish church. The closing rituals were a symbolic way of changing the affordance of the religious structure for those participating in, or observing, the ritual.

As shown in this chapter, cultural practices become linked with the building in which they are located. This is not unique to the Folk Church but a common feature of cultural institutions. The building becomes part of the institution's message and is viewed as an extension of the cultural practice itself. A threat to the building therefore becomes a threat to the culture. In addition, buildings that stand out are known by the locals, whether or not they participate in the cultural practices associated with the building. They signify 'home' and the buildings thereby gain a significance that transcends the specific activities practised in the building. Although church buildings are rather unique when compared with other cultural institutions, because they are used for religious activities, a thorough study would likely reveal that other significant cultural buildings also need to be handled with care if they are taken out of their specific cultural use. Failing to do so will result in alienating the wider public who make use of these buildings.

References

Aagedal, Olaf 2003. *Bedehusfolket. Ein Studie av Bedehuskultur i tre Bygder på 1980- og 1990-Talet.* Trondheim: Tapir Akademisk Forlag.

Ammerman, Nancy T. 2016. 'Lived Religion as an Emerging Field: An Assessment of its Contours and Frontiers'. *Nordic Journal of Religion and Society,* Volume 29, no. 2, 83-99.

Bell, Catherine 1997. *Ritual Perspectives and Dimensions.* Oxford: Oxford University Press.

Folkekirken 1992. *Ritualbog, Gudstjenesteordning for den Danske Folkekirke.* København: Det Kongelige Vajsenhus' Forlag.

Gennep, Arnold van 1965. *The Rites of Passage.* London: Routledge & Kegan Paul.

Gibson, James 1986. *The Ecological Approach to Visual Perception.* London: Lawrence Erlbaum Associates.

Hall, David 1997. *Lived Religion in America: Toward A History of Practice.* Princeton: Princeton University Press.

Johansen, Kirstine. H. and Marie V. Nielsen 2017. 'Nye Processioner som Udtryk for Gamle Religionsmønstre'. *Religionsvidenskabeligt tidsskrift* 66, 166-181.

Knott, Kim, Krech, Volkhard and Meyer, Birgit 2016. 'Iconic Religion in Urban Space'. *Material Religion: The Journal of Objects, Art and Belief.* 12/2, 123-136.

McGuire, Meredith 1997 [1981]. *Religion: the Social Context (4th ed).* London: Wadsworth Publishing Company.

Norman, Donald. A. 2000 [1988]. *The Design of Everyday Things.* London: The MIT Press.

Straarup, Jörgen 1985. *Kyrkan i Förorten: Folklig Religiositet och åsikter om Nybyggda Kyrkor.* Uppsala: Förlaget Förortskyrkan.

Notes

1. Interview with the former parish council of Absalon Kirke, March 13th 2015.
2. Interview with Gert Blak Mogensen, 5th September 2017.
3. The use of traditional religious elements has recently been noted and explored with regard to the use of processions in new rituals within the Danish Folk Church (Johansen and Nielsen 2017).
4. Interview with Thomas Nedergaard, 30th August 2017.
5. The priest, Thomas Nedergaard, and the former Parish Council Chairman, Frode Benedikt Nielsen, no longer had any recollection of the exact hymn, and it is not recorded in any of their documents.
6. Interview with Thomas Nedergaard, 30th August 2017.
7. The title translates as 'Lord, stretch out your almighty hand'. The hymn was composed in 1993 by Knut Nystedt, a Norwegian orchestral and choral composer.
8. Unfortunately, neither Thomas Nedergaard nor Peter Skov-Jakobsen were in possession of a written version of the prayer.
9. Interview with Thomas Nedergaard, 30th August 2017.
10. Interview with Dorte Krogh Eriksen, 31st August 2017.
11. Translation: 'The Church is an old house'. The hymn was composed by N.F.S. Grundtvig in 1836.
12. Translation: 'The Word of God is our inheritance'. The hymn was composed by N.F.S. Grundtvig in 1814.
13. It was not possible to establish the exact date of the rejection from the Ministry on the basis of the interviews conducted with Dorte Krogh Eriksen, Jens Christian Raabjerg Larsen, Arne Kappelgaard and Gert Blak Mogensen. Inquiries to the Diocese of Copenhagen and the Ministry of Ecclesiastical Affairs were also in vain.
14. Interview with Arne Kappelgaard, September 4th 2017.
15. Interview with Arne Kappelgaard, September 4th 2017.
16. Email from Jens Christian Raabjerg Larsen on September 26th 2013 to Gert Blak Mogensen.
17. Email from Jens Christian Raabjerg Larsen on September 26th 2013 to Gert Blak Mogensen.
18. Interview with Jens Christian Raabjerg Larsen, August 30th 2017.
19. Interview with Jens Christian Raabjerg Larsen, August 30th 2017.

IV. Social Capital, Majority Religion and Discrimination

13. Interrelations between Social Capital and Religion

Ingrid Storm

There is agreement across the social science literature that there exists a relationship between religion and social capital, but not about precisely what this relationship is or what the mechanism is. One possibility is that religious activity could increase social networks and skills which, in turn, could increase participation in other social and civic arenas and contribute to increased trust and belonging to society. Another possibility is that, as a moral community, religion increases trust in other members of the same religion, which in turn is translated into more generalised trust, social activity and civic participation.

I would like to address two main questions in this chapter. Firstly, how do we best understand the relationship between religion and social capital? And secondly, how do we apply this understanding to the particular context of the Danish Folk Church? Denmark has remarkably high levels of social trust and civic participation and similarly high levels of religious membership, but without corresponding levels of belief or religious service attendance. These factors make the Folk Church a particularly interesting case study in which to explore the relationship between religion and social capital.

The main argument of this chapter is that religion often generates particularised trust more than generalised trust, and bonding social capital more than bridging social capital. Analysing data from two population surveys, we find that the Folk Church appears to facilitate social trust, volunteering and bonding social capital, but not bridging social capital or political engagement. Further, the relationship between religion and social trust in Denmark appears to be based on an underlying assumption of cultural homogeneity. Religious diversity may present a challenge to the relationship and make us ask whether the Folk Church is the most relevant institution for securing the future high levels of social capital in Denmark.

The relationship between religion and social capital

The concept of social capital is central to studies of civic engagement and trust and commonly refers to beneficial non-economic relationships between people. As a concept with multiple origins, social capital has been defined in several ways. The most important difference in perspective concerns whether the social relations are profitable for the group or for the individuals (Lin 1999, 31). Such relations may, on the one hand, be seen as instrumental (Coleman, 1988, S98; Bourdieu 1986) by increasing an individual's opportunities to acquire other forms of capital such as human, cultural and economic capital. Robert Putnam's (1993; 2000) focus, however, is on the possible social benefits of increased social capital such as increased social trust and community cohesion, which may lead to better functioning democracies. In the seminal book, *Bowling Alone*, Putnam (2000) argues that the growth of individualism in the US has led to a drop in community activity. The decline of participation in religion, sports clubs and voluntary organizations, he argues, leads to a loss of 'social capital', furthering the individualisation and privatisation of social lives. In *American Grace*, Putnam and Campbell (2010) further detail how civic engagement in America is strongly associated with the relatively high levels of belonging to, and participation in, religious congregations.

The communal orientation and shared moral values of religious groups would appear to make them especially conducive to social capital. Smidt (1999) identified three possible associations between the two. First of all, religious groups, like all organized communities, may facilitate the creation of friendships and network ties, or what Putnam (2007, 143) calls 'bonding social capital'. Secondly, an altruistic ethos and traditions of volunteering may connect people from different social backgrounds (Wuthnow 2003, 436), thus creating 'bridging social capital' (Putnam 2007, 143). Thirdly, religious organizations may increase civic participation by providing people with informal skills training and opportunities to vote in congregational elections, speak in public settings or organize events and campaigns. Smidt (1999) found that, even when controlling for socioeconomic and demographic variables, religion had an independent effect on civic participation in both the US and Canada. His results were not uniform, however, and the relationship between civic participation was found to vary by country as well as by religious tradition (Smidt 1999, 190-191).

The social networks provided by religious communities seem to account for much of the relationship between religion, social capital, trust and civic engagement, and works the same way irrespective of individual beliefs or behaviours (Putnam and Campbell 2010). On a small scale, this includes friendship ties and links between religious groups and voluntary organizations and charities (Becker and Dinghra 2001; Wuthnow 1991). On a larger scale, people in countries with high levels of religiosity are more likely to volunteer, independently of individual levels of religiosity (Ruiter and De Graaf 2006).

Trust and moral communities

According to Putnam (1993, 89), trust is fundamental to social capital. Trust provides the benefits of reduced transaction costs in social relations and enables networks of reciprocity and cooperation, without constant monitoring or systems of punishment for defection.

One reason why religious communities may facilitate trust is the homogeneity of religion as a 'moral community'. When interacting with people of the same faith, it is reasonable to assume that they share the same moral values, or will answer to the same moral authorities (whether supernatural or clerical), and are subject to the same sanctions of social exclusion or divine punishment if they take advantage of a fellow believer. This is particularly the case for people who regularly interact with others in their congregation. Coleman (1988) uses the example of New York Jewish diamond traders who lend other traders valuable samples on the basis of trust – they belong to the same closed network of mutual trust and reciprocity. Their shared religious, ethnic and professional identity facilitates smooth running of the business, as does living in the same neighbourhood, having children in the same schools and attending the same synagogue. Coleman's example illustrates a somewhat unusual situation in modern life, however, in that all the transaction partners are in regular contact. According to evolutionary anthropologist Robin Dunbar (1993), between 100 and 200 (or 150, known as 'Dunbar's number') is the approximate cognitive limit to the number of people with whom one can maintain stable social relationships. Based on the size of the neocortex and studies of human tribes and non-human primates, he suggests that when a group grows larger than this it either splinters or grows into a completely different form of social community where members do not have direct contact with all the others.

Uslaner (1999, 34) makes a distinction between trusting close acquaintances whom there is good reason to rely on for reasons of personal experience or reciprocal relations, and generalised trust, which he describes as a 'moral value'. The latter is a general cognitive heuristic to trust people in most situations even if there is no previous experience of their trustworthiness, nor any expectation of future reciprocity. Generalised trust allows for the phenomenon that Granovetter (1973) refers to as the 'strength of weak ties'. The main advantage of social networks, from this perspective, is that they make it easier to connect and reconnect with distant acquaintances. Because people are generally regarded as trustworthy, beneficial social networks can grow beyond the roughly 150 people one regularly meets. Consequently, social relations that do not require resources to be maintained could potentially have substantial influence on people's lives. Francis Fukuyama (1995) argues that such general social trust is the basis for the capitalist economy, and describes it as the source of spontaneous sociability that allows enterprises to grow beyond family into professionally managed organizations.

According to Uslaner and Brown (2005), there is very little evidence that social connections lead to greater generalised trust. Using data from several European panel surveys where the same individuals were surveyed a number of times, Bekkers (2012) and van Ingen and Bekkers (2015) found that the relationship between volunteering and trust could be entirely accounted for by selection effects, with low trusters being less likely to join and stay on as members of voluntary organizations. Uslaner and Brown (2005) suggest that generalised trust should be seen as a stable value orientation, which leads to greater social connectivity in civic life, but which is not affected by civic engagement.

Despite the 'bridging social capital' that can potentially be generated through religious volunteering and outreach work (Wuthnow 2003), religion may not always be suited for promoting generalised trust and weak ties. Paciotti et al. (2011, 300) found that 'religious institutions, and the effect these have on individual dimensions of religiosity, are not a strong force to explain generosity, trust and cooperation among individuals paired within unknown social networks'.

Diversity and inequality

An important question in research on social capital is what effects cultural differences and economic inequality have on the levels and types of trust. Generalised trust is associated with bridging social capital, namely social relations, with people who differ regarding important socio-demographic indicators such as social class and ethnicity. Particularised trust, in contrast, depends on bonding social capital. Particularised trusters only place confidence in people whom they know or consider to be like themselves. Putnam (2000) argues that bonding and bridging social capital often occur together and that both contribute to the civic life of society as a whole.

Uslaner contends, instead, that different types of social networks and participation lead to different forms of civic engagement, pointing out that particularised trusters are 'more likely to get involved in civic life, but only with "people similar to themselves"' (Uslaner and Brown 2005, 873). Examining data from ethnic minorities in Britain, Storm (2015) found that religious people were more likely to participate in organizations where their religion or ethnicity represented the majority. However, they were less likely to participate in organizations where their religion or ethnicity were in a minority. In other words, while religion may increase bonding social capital with people of the same background or social network, it is not clear that it would also increase bridging social capital.

Immigrants who only join ethnic organizations, Uslaner and Conley (2003) argue, do not increase their civic engagement in a way that contributes to public social capital, and might even reduce their participation in the larger community. A counterargument would be that the choice is often not between which organization to join, it is between joining or not joining. Particularised trusters, such as recently arrived immigrants wary of people outside their ethnic community, would not be likely to join a mainstream organization in any event. Ethnic organizations could provide them with the skills and knowledge to navigate the wider civil society once they have settled in. That said, the point that not every kind of civic engagement is likely to lead to greater generalised trust is well taken and highlights a need to differentiate between bonding and bridging social capital, generalised trust and parochialism.

Putnam's (2007) essay *E Pluribus Unum* looks at the effects of ethnic and cultural diversity on trust in the community as a whole and finds that diversity tends to affect both bonding and bridging social capital in a negative way. From a perspective of social identity theory (Tajfel and Turner 1986), one could easily imagine that people faced with visible ethnic differences and cultural value disagreements with their fellow citizens would become more distrustful of outsiders, while strengthening their in-group loyalties. Putnam (2007) found that in-group trust in such societies was weaker, too, with people 'hunkering down' and becoming more socially isolated in general. Other studies have found more complex relationships between diversity, social capital and trust (see, for example, Fieldhouse and Cutts 2010; Dinesen and Sønderskov 2012), but there is general agreement that cultural diversity could reduce generalised trust, at least under some conditions.

Inequality is also strongly negatively associated with both trust and civic participation at aggregate levels (Kawachi et al. 1997; Putnam 2000). Uslaner and Brown (2005) found that generalised trust is an important mediating factor between economic equality and civic engagement. The reason for the relationship between equality and trust, they suggest, is twofold. Firstly, high levels of inequality lead to less optimism about the future, or to use Inglehart's term, less 'existential security'. Secondly, large class and income differences lead to a reduced sense of solidarity and shared fate (Uslaner and Brown 2005, 869). With the absence of generalised trust, people are less likely to take part in civic society outside of close-knit ethnic and political interest groups, and the result is a less vibrant civil society.

Civil religion

The apparent lack of a consistent relationship between religion and bridging social capital could be an effect of the same tendency for group identification, loyalty and 'ingroup bias' (Galen 2012, 887) that makes religion a promoter of bonding social capital and in-group trust. However, there may be exceptions to this in situations where a national or cultural ethos is associated with religion, wherein society and the religious community are perceived as being one and the same.

In his seminal essay, *Civil Religion in America*, Robert Bellah (1967, 8) argues that there has been 'an implicit but quite clear division between the civil religion and Christianity' where the former is centred on a unitarian God with a special concern for the United States. This makes the American civil religion compatible with other religions (especially monotheistic Judeo-Christian ones) without being specifically equated with any of them. In this way, the national holiday, Thanksgiving Day, can be celebrated by people of all faiths even if it makes reference to 'God' (Bellah 1967, 11). This may explain the strong normative stereotype of religious people as good and happy, which is not replicated in less religious societies (Galen 2012, 892). It could also mean that Americans presume that other Americans are part of the same moral community, even if they do not know what their specific religious affiliations are, creating the conditions for generalised trust. The same mechanism may of course operate in other countries where the majority of people are highly religious, as Ruiter and de Graaf's (2006) results indicate.

Galen (2012) argues that most Americans would assume that their compatriots are Christians unless informed otherwise, and that this might account for why religion is associated with prosociality in psychological studies, most of which have been conducted using American sample sets. Saroglou (2012) points out the same assumption would not work in the largely secular context of Belgium, and thus Galen's critique would not undermine his own research which shows similar results. However, this argument assumes that people require knowledge of others' degree of religiosity in order to feel cultural kinship, whereas we know from qualitative studies that it could just as well be affiliation to the religious or cultural collective that is most important (Storm 2011; Day 2011). It is possible that participants in psychology experiments make an assumption about sharing other people's moral values and religious belonging on the basis that they live in the same country or area or attend the same university. This does not make the research any less relevant, since there is little reason to believe that they would not make similar assumptions in real world situations. However, it makes it all the more important to conduct such studies in different contexts with varying degrees of religiosity and diversity (Galen 2012, 892).

There is good reason to believe that the national context matters a great deal for social capital. Hall's (1999) analysis of social capital in Britain and Torpe's (2003) analysis of social capital in Denmark found no evidence of a decline similar to that described by Putnam in the US. Hall suggests three main reasons for this: the expansion in higher education, the growth of the middle class and government policies encouraging civic participation, and volunteering (Hall 1999, 434). Similarly, Torpe mentions the welfare state, facilitating a civil society infrastructure as well as participation in public institutions. Although it can be seen as a central part of Putnam's argument, religious communities do not feature strongly in either of these accounts. However, in both the UK and Denmark, the national churches are closely associated with the state, and state involvement (in the form of increasing equality and facilitating civil society) could be seen as an alternative to religious sources of social capital (Gill and Lundsgaarde 2004).

The Danish Folk Church

The Folk Church makes an interesting case study for the relationship between religion and social capital. It can be described as a form of civil religion (Repstad 2009), but one that is more firmly anchored in Christianity (and a particular form of Lutheran Christianity) than the more pan-religiously accommodating American version (Bellah 1967). That said, specific moral values and religious beliefs vary greatly among members, and it may be that the Folk Church's welcoming openness and lack of stance on controversial issues are what allows it to thrive (Jørgensen 2012). Although membership has declined from more than 90 percent in most of the 1990s, 76 percent of the Danish population were still members of the Folk Church in 2017 (Statistics Denmark 2017). The church is considered important as an institutional provider of rituals, both for the nation state in the form of Royal or governmental ceremonies and private rites of passage, such as baptism, weddings and funerals. A similar arrangement can be found in the other Scandinavian countries. The homogeneous population of cultural Christians and the high rates of membership make this form of civil religion possible. However, this raises important questions as to what extent Danish civil religion promotes social capital, trust and civic engagement to its members, and just how important Christianity is for Danish national identity. With religious decline and increasing religious and ethnic diversity in Denmark, it is also important to ask how inclusive the folk church form of social capital is to non-Christians and ethnic minorities.

It is very difficult to know precisely what contribution the Folk Church makes to social capital and civil society on a macro-scale. Comparing Denmark with other countries in Europe, it does have a high level of religious belonging and also high levels of trust and civil society (Pichler and Wallace 2007). However, these variables are not necessarily causally connected, and there are countless other factors that could account for the high levels of trust such as high economic development, economic equality, education, welfare and so forth. An indication that religion plays a limited role is the fact that, while membership in the Folk Church has declined and non-affiliation and religious diversity has increased since the 1970s, Denmark is one of the few countries in the world that we know of where generalised trust has increased over the same period (Dinesen and Sønderskov 2012).

In order to get some sense of what contribution church membership and church attendance in the Folk Church makes to social capital in Denmark we can compare active and passive church members with non-members on various indicators of social capital. This does not necessarily tell us very much about the effect on society as a whole. However, the assumed mechanism in much of the literature on social capital and religion is that religious belonging and church attendance increase the social resources of individuals, which in turn facilitate the improvement of civic engagement and generalised trust on a larger scale (Putnam and Campbell 2010; Smidt 1999). An examination of individual level attitudinal data will at least give us insight into the first of these two assumptions.

We use two representative surveys, both from 2014: The European Social Survey (ESS 2014) which had 1,500 respondents, and the International Social Survey Programme – Citizenship (ISSP 2004) which had 1,700 respondents in Denmark. Both datasets ask about the respondent's religious affiliation and attendance as well as setting out a number of questions about social networks, political participation, trust and social attitudes. Data from both surveys are archived and available free of charge from www.europeansocialsurvey.org (ESS) and www.gesis.org (ISSP), respectively.

We distinguish between four groups: 1) Attenders: those who say they belong to the Folk Church (ISSP) or Protestant Church (ESS) and attend at least once a month, 2) Members: those who belong to a church, but attend less frequently than once a month, 3) Other religion: those who belong to a different religious denomination and 4) No religion: those who do not belong to or participate in any religion.

Note that the categories are not identical in the two surveys: the ESS asks respondents what religious denomination they belong to, with 'Protestant' being the most chosen option, whereas in the ISSP the question is: 'Are you a member of the Folk Church or another religious community?' with 'The Folk Church' as one listed option. In practice, this does not necessarily mean that there are many members of other churches in the ESS's Protestant groups, as by far the majority of Protestants in Denmark are Folk Church members. If anything, more people count themselves as Folk Church members than think of themselves as Protestant, as can be seen from the numbers of each survey sample who belong to each category (bottom of Table 1). Where the same or similar questions were asked in both surveys, 'Protestants' (ESS) and 'Folk Church members' (ISSP) respond in very similar ways, but it is worth being aware of the discrepancy in wording.

Logistic regression analyses were conducted on a number of binary variables (some of them recoded from more detailed response categories [ESS 2014; ISSP2014]). Each model controlled for age, gender and a 5-category variable of highest level of completed education as these are demographic variables that may be associated with both religion and social capital. For example, on average, women and older people are more religious than men and younger people (Voas, McAndrew and Storm 2013), and there may be age and gender differences in civic engagement due to norms and integration in the labour market (Musick and Wilson 2008, 184-191).

Table 1: Predicted probabilities of social capital and national identity indicators

	No religion	Member	Attender	Other religion	Data source
Social networks					
One to one contact with at least 10 people in a typical day	54%	57%	51%	57%	ISSP
Meet socially with friends, relatives or colleagues at least once a week	70%	72%	75%	69%	ESS
Know at least three people who can talk about personal matters with	72%	73%	73%	64%	ESS
Have any close friends from different race or ethnic group	58%	51%	53%	77%	ESS
Civic and political membership					
Belong to political party	10%	6%	14%	9%	ISSP
Belong to trade union	54%	68%	67%	58%	ISSP
Belong to sports club or similar	43%	57%	68%	47%	ISSP
Belong to other voluntary organization	36%	43%	71%	45%	ISSP
Political engagement					
Voted last election	92%	96%	95%	80%	ESS
Voted last election	93%	96%	100%	81%	ISSP
Signed petition in the past year	29%	28%	32%	32%	ISSP
Boycotted certain products the past year	41%	32%	35%	39%	ISSP
Attended a political meeting or rally in the past year	12%	7%	13%	9%	ISSP
Contacted a politician in the past year	14%	6%	7%	13%	ISSP
Took part in a demonstration in the past year	8%	3%	5%	6%	ISSP
Taken part in lawful demonstration last 12 months	7%	4%	3%	9%	ESS
Interpersonal trust					
Most people can be trusted	75%	80%	84%	48%	ESS
Most people can be trusted	77%	84%	83%	60%	ISSP
Most people try to be fair	82%	85%	85%	70%	ISSP
Most people try to be fair	82%	87%	84%	66%	ESS

People mostly try to be helpful	62%	62%	61%	60%	ESS
Trust in institutions					
Trust in parliament	56%	65%	65%	58%	ESS
Trust in the legal system	81%	84%	89%	75%	ESS
Trust in police	83%	91%	92%	79%	ESS
Trust in politicians	39%	48%	46%	33%	ESS
Most of the time we can trust people in government	39%	46%	54%	36%	ISSP
National identity					
Feel very close to country	61%	78%	76%	51%	ESS
Better for a country if almost everyone shares customs and traditions	25%	34%	30%	26%	ESS
Religious beliefs and practices undermined by immigrants	66%	73%	66%	60%	ESS
Christian background should be qualification for immigration	13%	22%	28%	13%	ESS
Being committed to country's way of life should be qualification for immigration	54%	64%	70%	54%	ESS
Being white should be qualification for immigration	6%	8%	8%	10%	ESS
N ESS	634	615	137	87	1,473
N ISSP	275	1,308	76	41	1,700

Predicted probabilities based on logistic regression models controlling for age, sex and education. Figures in red and green signify that the difference from the 'no religion' category is statistically significant at P<0.05

Table 1 shows predicted probabilities, that is the percentages of each category that would respond 'yes' to each of the questions, if they all have the same (average) age, sex and level of education. Each of the three 'religious' groups are compared with the reference category, those who say they have no religion and do not attend services once a month or more often. When the difference is statistically significant, the number is shown in bold, with green indicating a higher probability and red a lower probability than the non-religious. The data source is indicated in the righthand column, and where the same or similar questions were asked in both surveys, both results are shown in the table.

As can be seen from Table 1, Folk Church members are no more likely to have frequent social interactions with friends, relatives and colleagues (bonding social capital) and even less likely to have friends from different ethnic or racial background (bridging social capital) than those with no religion, even after controlling for age and education. In other words, if church members have more social capital, this cannot be attributed to a higher frequency of social interactions or to more diverse social contacts.

Where Folk Church members do differ from non-members is in their other memberships. Church members are considerably more likely to belong to trade unions, sports clubs and other voluntary organizations. This is particularly the case for those who attend church regularly. We know that people who participate in one organization are more likely to also join another (Musick and Wilson 2008). This could either be because they are more interested in joining groups in general (for example because they have high levels of trust) or because, through membership in one organization, they get more information about opportunities for volunteering and social activities in other organizations. Since most members of the Folk Church in Denmark start their membership at birth, belonging to a church is more likely to lead to belonging to a sports club than vice versa. Membership in primarily religious organizations was asked about separately and not included under 'other voluntary organizations'. It is possible that some voluntary organizations have a religious ethos or are funded through the church even if their primary function is not religious, e.g. youth groups, poverty relief, choirs etc., however, this is unlikely to account for the whole relationship.

The one notable exception to the increased tendency for church members to also be members of other organizations is political parties, where there is no significant difference between members and non-members. In general, there is mixed evidence for the political engagement of church members. While they are slightly more likely to vote in general elections, on most other measures passive church members are *less* likely than non-members to actively participate in politics.

Church members have higher generalised trust than non-members and tend to believe most people try to be fair rather than act out of self-interest. The differences are small, however, and not uniformly significant, as interpersonal trust is generally very high in Denmark. That said, it is possible that the slightly higher generalised trust accounts for some of the religious differences in organizational membership, as high-trusters are more likely to join and remain members of voluntary organizations (Bekkers 2012; van Ingen and Bekkers 2015). A previous study by Lüchau (2013) found that religiosity in Denmark was associated with social trust only through its association with higher membership in voluntary associations. However, Christians in Denmark who did not belong to voluntary associations were *less* trusting than non-Christians with the same level of civic participation. If one sees trust as being an outcome of social capital, religious and other associational involvement, this result appears puzzling. However, if trust is seen as a stable value (Bekkers 2012; Uslaner and Brown 2005) that predicts civic engagement the result makes more sense. If being religious is associated with more opportunities for volunteering, Christians who do not take these opportunities may be those who are less trusting than average.

A more striking difference is the very high levels of trust in state institutions among church members, with more than 90 percent thinking the police can be trusted, compared to just over 80 percent of the non-religious. Attenders and passive members give similar answers to most of these questions, although attending members are significantly more likely to trust people in government[1]. As a state institution, it is perhaps unsurprising that membership of and participation in the Folk Church should be associated with confidence in the state more generally. It is also possible that church members feel themselves to be part of a cultural majority that is protected by the state to a greater extent than religious minorities and non-religious people.

Finally, we examine the relationship between membership in the Folk Church and attitudes to civil religion and national identity. Church members are considerably more likely to feel 'very close to' the country. Passive members are also more likely to think that cultural homogeneity is an important quality for a country to have. The Folk Church could be seen as an institutional anchor for customs and traditions, whose function is to ensure some homogeneity and continuity of norms and rituals even when beliefs and attitudes are diverse. Much of the continued support for, and membership of, the church despite declining belief and practice may stem from an appreciation of this role of the church as an upholder of a set of common values in the population through the use of symbols and rituals (Lüchau 2009; Warburg 2005). Repstad (2009, 8) points out that one of the purposes of a national church (often used as an argument in debates about de-establishment) is to provide a tolerant inclusive church which can act as a barrier against sectarian manifestations of religiosity. The Danish civil religion accommodates the majority, in part, by not being overtly 'religious', and this may be alienating for those who prefer to express their religion publicly (Jensen 2008, 390).

Ideally, the Folk Church civil religion represents an inclusive national identity, which accepts diversity of individual views as well as a pragmatic conformity in cultural expression to promote belonging and generalised trust (Bellah 1967; Warburg 2005). However, we also see that, when it comes to the question of immigration, religious people seem to have less faith in the ability of the Danish model to overcome cultural differences and especially religious differences. 73 percent of passive members think religion is undermined by immigrants to some extent, and 22 percent think a Christian background should be a qualification for immigration. While it is unsurprising that Christians would be more likely to think Christianity is important, what is worth noting is that the differences are just as stark on the more general question of whether being committed to a Danish way of life should be required for immigration. If this is a form of racism, it is not an overtly biological one. Protestants are not significantly more likely than the non-religious to think being white should be a qualification for immigration. This nevertheless raises the question of how inclusive the Folk Church actually is, or perhaps how inclusive its members would want it to be. It could seem as if the high levels of generalised trust among church members are in part based on an idea of a homogeneous population of other Christians (Galen 2012; Storm 2011; Day 2012). As religious decline and religious diversification continue in Denmark, it is important to consider what happens once this is no longer the case.

Summary

Religion could increase social capital for a number of reasons, but in the literature we can identify two main pathways. On the one hand, religious participation can increase participation more generally, which contributes to increased social networks and a more vibrant civil society. On the other hand, religions can be seen as moral communities of like-minded individuals who have reason to trust one another. This trust, if generalised beyond the religious group, can further encourage social activity and engagements in other arenas. From much of the research on social capital, the latter mechanism seems to be the predominant one: religion appears to generate particularised trust more than generalised trust and bonding more than bridging social capital. Only in cases of 'civil religion', when the religious group is considered to be interchangeable with the nation or society as a whole, does religion have the power to increase social capital on a general scale.

Examining the relationship between religion and social capital in Denmark, where both social capital and church membership are very high, provides empirical support for this theory. Membership of the Folk Church is associated with a high level of membership of voluntary associations and high levels of interpersonal trust and trust in state institutions. However, it is not associated with more social networks or social interactions, and is also not associated with higher levels of political participation with the exception of voting in general elections. Members of the church are also less likely to have diverse social networks, are more likely to value cultural homogeneity and to view Christianity as an essential part of Danish national identity.

To understand the relationship between religion and social capital, it is essential that we understand the causal relationship between social trust and associational membership. If the Folk Church is responsible for only part of the high levels of social capital and social trust found in Danish society, then what happens to that church really matters for the rest of society, and other forms of organizational involvement will be needed to compensate for its likely decline. If, however, the high level of trust the Danish place in their state institutions as well as in each other, is instead a *predictor* of their high levels of civic organizational membership – including church membership – then we can be confident that social capital will remain high as long as there are high levels of economic equality and state support for civil society (Dinesen and Sønderskov 2012; Torpe 2003).

References

Becker, Penny E., and Pawan H. Dhingra 2001. 'Religious Involvement and Volunteering: Implications for Civil Society', *Sociology of Religion*, 62/3, 315-335.
Bekkers, René 2012 'Trust and Volunteering: Selection or Causation? Evidence From a 4 Year Panel Study', *Political Behavior*, 34/2, 225-247.
Bellah, Robert N. 1967. 'Civil Religion in America', *Daedalus*, 96/1, 1-21.

Bourdieu, Pierre 1986. 'The Forms of Capital', in J. E. Richardson (ed.), *Handbook of Theory of Research for the Sociology of Education*. New York: Greenwood Press, 241-258.

Coleman, James S. 1988. 'Social Capital in the Creation of Human Capital', *The American Journal of Sociology* 94/Supplement: Organisations and Institutions, 95-S120.

Day, Abby 2011. *Believing in Belonging*. Oxford: Oxford University Press.

Dinesen, Peter T., and Kim M. Sønderskov 2012. 'Trust in a Time of Increasing Diversity: On the Relationship between Ethnic Heterogeneity and Social Trust in Denmark from 1979 until Today', *Scandinavian Political Studies*, 35/4, 273-294.

Dunbar, Robin I. M. 1993. 'Coevolution of Neocortical Size, Group Size and Language in Humans', *Behavioral and Brain Sciences*, 16/4, 681-694.

ESS 2014. *European Social Survey wave 7* (accessed 03 August 2017). Retrieved from http://www.europeansocialsurvey.org

Fieldhouse, Edward, and David Cutts 2010. 'Does Diversity Damage Social Capital? A Comparative Study of Neighbourhood Diversity and Social Capital in the US and Britain', *Canadian Journal of Political Science*, 43/2, 289-318.

Fukuyama, Francis 1995. *Trust: The Social Virtues and the Creation of Prosperity*. New York: The Free Press.

Galen, Luke W. 2012. 'Does Religious Belief Promote Prosociality? A Critical Examination', *Psychological Bulletin*, 138/5, 876-906.

Gill, Anthony, and Erik Lundsgaarde 2004. 'State Welfare Spending and Religiosity: A Cross-National Analysis', *Rationality and Society*, 16/4, 399-436.

Granovetter, Mark S. 1973. 'The Strength of Weak Ties', *American Journal of Sociology*, 78/6, 1360-1380.

Hall, Peter A. 1999. 'Social Capital in Britain', *British Journal of Political Science*, 29/3, 417-461.

ISSP 2014. *International Social Survey Programme. Citizenship II Module* (accessed 03 August 2017). Retrieved from http://www.gesis.org

Jensen, Tina G. 2008. 'To be "Danish", Becoming "Muslim": Contestations of National Identity?', *Journal of Ethnic and Migration Studies*, 34/3, 389-409.

Jørgensen, Jonas A. 2012. 'Danskerne Sætter Pris på en Ikke-Autoritær Kirke', *Kristeligt Dagblad* (accessed 09 January 2018). Retrieved from www.religion.dk/religionsanalysen/danskerne-sætter-pris-på-en-ikke-autoritær-kirke

Kawachi, Ichiro, Bruce P. Kennedy, Kimberly Lochner and Deborah Prothrow-Stith 1997. 'Social Capital, Income Inequality, and Mortality', *American Journal of Public Health*, 87/9, 1491-1498.

Lin, Nan 1999. 'Building a Network Theory of Social Capital', *Connections*, 22/1: 28-51.

Lüchau, Peter. 2009. 'Toward a Contextualized Concept of Civil Religion', *Social Compass*, 56/3: 371-386.

Lüchau, Peter 2013. 'The Spiritual Revolution and Social Capital in Denmark', in Joop de Hart, Paul Dekker and Loek Halman (eds.), *Religion and Civil Society in Europe*. Dortrecht: Springer, 189-202.

Musick, Marc A., and John Wilson 2008. *Volunteers: A Social Profile*. Bloomington: Indiana University Press.

Paciotti, Brian, Peter Richerson, Billy Baum, Mark Lubell, Tim Waring, Richard McElreath, Charles Efferson and Ed Edsten 2011. 'Are Religious Individuals More Generous, Trusting, and Cooperative? An Experimental Test of the Effect of Religion on Prosociality', Lionel Obadia and Donald C. Wood (eds.), *The Economics of Religion: Anthropological Approaches*. Bingley: Emerald Group Publishing, 267-305.

Pichler, Florian, and Claire Wallace 2007. 'Patterns of Formal and Informal Social Capital in Europe', *European Sociological Review*, 23/4, 423-435.

Putnam, Robert D. 1993. *Making Democracy Work*. Princeton, N.J: Princeton University Press.

Putnam, Robert D. 2000. *Bowling Alone: The Collapse and Revival of American Community*. New York; London: Simon & Schuster.

Putnam, Robert D. 2007. 'E Pluribus Unum: Diversity and Community in the Twenty-first Century', *Scandinavian Political Studies*, 30/2, 137-174.

Putnam, Robert D., and David E.Campbell, D. 2010. *American Grace: How Religion Divides and Unites Us*. New York: Simon and Schuster.

Repstad, Pål 2009. 'Civil Religion in an Age of Changing Churches and Societies: A look at the Nordic Situation', in Annika Hvithamar, Margit Warburg and Brian A. Jacobsen (eds.), *Holy Nations and Global Identities: Civil Religion, Nationalism, and Globalisation*. Leiden; Boston: Brill, 199-214.

Ruiter, Stijn, and Nan Dirk de Graaf 2006. 'National Context, Religiosity, and Volunteering: Results from 53 Countries', *American Sociological Review*, 71/2, 191-210.

Saroglou, Vassilis 2012. 'Is Religion not Prosocial at All? Comment on Galen (2012)', *Psychological Bulletin*, 138/5, 907-912.

Smidt, Christian 1999. 'Religion and Civic Engagement: A Comparative Analysis', *The ANNALS of the American Academy of Political and Social Science*, 565/1: 176-192.

Statistics Denmark 2017. 'Members of the National Church' (accessed 03.08.3017) Retrieved from http://www.dst.dk/en/Statistik/emner/kultur-og-kirke/folkekirken/medlemmer-af-folkekirken.

Storm, Ingrid 2011. '"Christian Nations"? Ethnic Christianity And Anti-Immigration Attitudes in Four Western European Countries', *Nordic Journal of Religion and Society*, 24/1, 75-96.

Storm, Ingrid 2015. 'Civic Engagement in Britain: The Role of Religion and Inclusive Values', *European Sociological Review*, 31/1, 14-29.

Tajfel, Henri, and John C. Turner 1986. 'The Social Identity Theory of Intergroup Behavior', in Stephen Worchel and William G. Austin (eds.) *Psychology of intergroup relations* (2nd ed.). Chicago: Nelson Hall, 7-24.

Torpe, Lars 2003. 'Social Capital in Denmark: A Deviant Case?', *Scandinavian Political Studies*, 26/1, 27-48.

Uslaner, Eric M. 1999. 'Trust but Verify: Social Capital and Moral Behavior', *Social Science Information* 38/1, 29-55.

Uslaner, Eric M., and Mitchell Brown 2005. 'Inequality, Trust, and Civic Engagement', *American Politics Research,* 33/6, 868-894.

Uslaner, Eric M., and Richard S. Conley 2003. 'Civic Engagement and Particularized Trust: The Ties that Bind People to their Ethnic Communities', *American Politics Research*, 31/4, 331-360.

van Ingen, Erik, and René Bekkers 2015. 'Generalized Trust Through Civic Engagement? Evidence from Five National Panel Studies', *Political Psychology*, 36/3, 277-294.

Voas, David, Siobhan McAndrew and Ingrid Storm 2013. 'Modernization and the Gender Gap in Religiosity: Evidence from Cross-National European Surveys', *KZfSS Kölner Zeitschrift Für Soziologie Und Sozialpsychologie*, 65/S1, 259-283.

Warburg, Margit 2005. 'Dansk Civilreligion i Krise og Vækst', *Chaos. Dansk-Norsk Tidsskrift for Religionshistoriske Studier,* 43, 89-108.

Wuthnow, Robert 1991. *Acts of Compassion: Caring for Others and Helping Ourselves*. Princeton, NJ: Princeton University Press.

Wuthnow, Robert 2003. 'Overcoming Status Distinctions? Religious Involvement, Social Class, Race and Ethnicity in Friendship Patterns', *Sociology of Religion,* 64/4, 423-442.

Notes

1   This difference cannot be accounted for by political sympathies. At the time of the survey, the left-leaning Danish coalition government was led by the Social Democrats. Passive members were slightly more likely to vote on the right, and attending church members were equally likely to vote on the left and the right of the political spectrum in the last election.

14. Rites of Passage and Creation of Social Capital in the Folk Church

Karen Marie Leth-Nissen

Introduction

The relationships between social capital and religion are complicated in real life, and this is also reflected in the empirical studies. I am privileged because the topic and its challenges have been so well introduced in the previous chapter, Chapter 13, by Ingrid Storm. As such, this chapter can go almost directly to my examination of the relationships between participation in rites of passage and social capital in the Folk Church. Rites of passage offer themselves as the best choice for a quantitative study into the Folk Church as more than half of the people coming to the Folk Church on an annual basis come for baptisms, confirmations, weddings or funerals. As indicated in the introduction to this book – and as supported in the chapter by Storm – one risk of reflecting society, as the Folk Church does to a great extent, is the tendency to further entrench the social inequality found in neo-liberal societies (Piketty 2014). This is also reflected in the Folk Church.

This chapter builds on studies and findings from my PhD dissertation 'Churching Alone' (Leth-Nissen 2018). The main theories used here are Robert Putnam's concept of *collective social capital* as the sum of networks, norms and trust (Putnam 2000) and, to expand those ideas, I am also drawing on Coleman's concept of *social structures* (Coleman 1990) as well as the notion of *institutional structures* (Stolle 2003 in Lüchau 2013; Rothstein and Stolle 2008). As Christian Bjørnskov and Kim Mannemar Sønderskov (2013) pointed out, when working with the concept of social capital, it is crucial to use a strong definition and operationalisation of the term. In terms of the empirical analysis, I build on the two main social cohesion approaches from social and political science (see Jenson 1998; and Berger-Schmitt and Noll 2000). Regina Berger-Schmitt and Heinz-Herbert Noll built their European System of Social Indicators (ESSI) on the work of Jane Jenson (1998). Their overall framework had two overarching dimensions. The first dimension measured the things a nation does to 'reduce isolation, exclusion, non-involvement, rejection and illegitimacy within the population' (Berger-Schmitt 2000, 4). The second dimension measured what a nation does to 'strengthen the sense of belonging, inclusion, participation, recognition and legitimacy within the population' (2000, 4). Because it measures 'social relations and ties established, maintained and experienced by individuals' (Berger-Schmitt 2000, 7), Berger-Schmitt and Noll's operationalisation can be said to measure collective social capital.

My objective was to investigate how the Folk Church adds to the social capital of Danish society. So, I designed a survey that focused on Berger-Schmitt's second dimension of strengthening belonging, inclusion, participation and more.[1] I searched for correlations between how respondents build *social capital in social networks and trust* and their participation in *rites of passage*, both religious and non-religious.[2] I measured social capital as the frequency of all the variables measuring networks and trust. These included close contact with family and friends, participation in associations, volunteering, the individual's level of trust in social networks level of general trust; and trust in institutions. The other element measured was the individual respondents' level of use of the Folk Church, both in terms of taking part in *bonding* and in *bridging* social activities. My concept of 'use of Folk Church' for the survey was rather broad. I included being a member, using rites of passage, taking part in target-oriented activities, attending church on Sundays and being active in church associations for diaconal, volunteer work. I also included variables relating to other uses of the church, such as church attendance and visits to church buildings and variables relating to belief to get some wider sense of perspective. I conducted my survey through the analysis institute YouGov for the Centre for Church Research, University of Copenhagen.[3] The 1048 respondents were representative of the Danish population in terms of their distribution across age groups, gender, education and geographical spread.

Findings

For the findings on social capital and participation in rituals, I asked respondents whether they had taken part in any religious or non-religious rites of passage during the last year. Their answers revealed that rituals such as funerals, confirmations and baptisms attracted a large share of the population. Funerals were top of the list with 45 percent of the respondents answering in the affirmative.[4] Only 24 percent of the respondents did not take part in any ritual, religious or non-religious (Leth-Nissen 2018, 221).

I combined the participation patterns of the respondents with their answers relating to contact with family, close friends, associational activity and their levels of general and institutional trust. I tested for background variables such as age groups, gender, geography and broader use of the Folk Church. Statistical tests gave the overview presented in Table 2.

The findings reveal that gender had no impact on participation in rituals. For age groups, being older had an impact on funeral participation and being younger had an impact on baptism participation. This should be little surprise, as older persons generally have more family members, friends and acquaintances in their own age group, and thus a higher likelihood of experiencing deaths and funerals in their social network. Likewise, younger persons have more young people in their network and are thus more likely to be invited to a baptism. Living in a rural area (low urbanisation) made it more likely that the respondents had participated in a confirmation. This may point to social networks being structured differently in rural contexts, as one may rely more on neighbours and thus invite them for celebrations.

The variable of 'church practice and belief' covers church attendance, visits to the respondent's church building and churchyard outside of services or activities, prayer, belief in God, church association engagement and membership of the Folk Church. Having a higher level of this combined variable made the respondents more likely to participate in baptism, weddings and funerals, but had no impact on their likelihood of participating in non-religious rituals. This finding was expected, as it is reasonable to expect that use of the Folk Church makes one more prone to attend rituals in the Folk Church. However, one might have expected that a higher level of 'church practice and belief' lowered the likelihood of participation in a non-religious ritual. As this was not the case, it seems that participation in non-religious rituals is not dependent on church use, but only dependent on one's friends.

Table 1: Total overview of the significant variables and their prediction of participation in rites of passage (binomial logistic regressions)

Independent variables	Dependent variables								
	Baptism	Confirmation	Church wedding	Funeral	Naming ceremony	Non-firmation	Civil wedding	Memorial service	No participation
Age groups	↓				↑				
Gender									
'Geography'		↓							
'Church practice and belief score'	↑		↑	↑					↓
'Near contact to close friends'	↑	↑		↑	↑	↑	↑	↑	↓
'Trust'									
Family									

↑ = positive effect on use of rite of passage; ↓ = negative effect. The ' ' on names of variables indicates an aggregated variable

Source: Leth-Nissen 2018, 222.

The main finding of the study is that rites of passage are connected to bonding social capital when associated with friends. This is bonding social capital because it relates to strengthening the internal ties of a group (Putnam 2000). In the survey, respondents having a close and frequent contact with friends were more likely to participate in both religious (Folk Church) and non-religious rites of passage, except for church weddings.

For participation in Folk Church rituals, as mentioned above, other background variables had an impact, too. For non-religious rituals, only close contact with friends had an impact on the likelihood of participation in a ritual.

Close contact with family had no impact on participation in rites of passage. The missing impact of 'near contact to family' was a surprising finding, as I had expected all social network variables to have some impact on participation in rites of passage. Checking if participants in the rituals were mostly participating as family or friends did not explain the missing impact of family, as parents and close relatives (54 percent) of the child were the most frequent attendees at an infant baptism. Friends of the child's family made up only 27 percent of the participants. A pattern of 'more friends than family' revealed itself again when analysing the participation in funerals.

Trust had no impact on participation in rites of passage, either. The missing impact of 'trust' was also a surprising finding. As Danish society is in general associated with a high level of trust, it may have been more difficult to discern any difference that trust might make in the survey's findings. In the research literature (Pettersson 2011), the widespread use of rites of passage is often linked to Folk Church membership. In the previous chapter, Storm showed that church membership is connected to a high level of trust. In light of all this, this missing impact of trust on participation was all the more surprising.

For the correlations between associational activity and use of Folk Church, I performed bivariate analyses (Table 2). Respondents answered whether they were members of and engaged in various types of associations. Besides church rituals, I tested for church membership, church attendance, prayer, and belief. The non-religious rituals showed no significant correlations with associational engagement and I left them out of the table.

Table 2: Bivariate analyses. Associational engagement and church practice and belief

Associational engagement	Infant baptism	Confirmation	Wedding	Funeral	Church membership	Church attendance	Prayer	Belief
A political party, club or association				X		X	X	
A trade union or professional association			X			(X)		X
A church or other religious organization	X		X	X	X	X	X	X
A sports group, hobby or leisure club		X	X	X		X		
A charitable organization or group						X	X	
A neighbourhood association or group			X	X		X		
Other associations or groups			X	X	X	X	X	X

Source: Leth-Nissen 2018, 225.

A higher level of engagement in associations indicated that participants were more likely to participate in a rite of passage in the Folk Church. However, this related more to weddings and funerals than to baptisms and confirmations. Baptism was only related to church or 'other religious organization'. Confirmations were only related to participation in sports and leisure clubs.

Associational engagement was weakly associated with membership of the Folk Church. Folk Church membership only had a significant relationship to 'church or other religious organization' and 'other organizations or groups'.

For all associations, engagement was associated with church attendance. The pattern confirms the findings of Jaak Billiet et al. (2010, 251) who found that church attendance was associated with being engaged in other associations, and in this way, church attendance was connected to building social capital. A higher level of prayer was associated with being engaged in a political party, a church organization, a charitable organization or other organization. A higher level of belief was connected to engagement in trade unions, church organizations and other organizations.

Discussion: bonding or bridging social capital?

Some groups gather people of the same kind, whilst other groups cross age gaps and ethnic and other differences. When a group strengthens its internal bonds, making the network closer between members who know each other, the group is building *bonding social capital*. When another group strengthens the external ties, reaching out to connect with people not in the same group, this group is building *bridging social capital*. Some associations build both bonding and bridging social capital. Putnam emphasises that both kinds of groups are important for society, that a society needs both bonding and bridging social capital (2000, 22-23).

Why did the variable of 'close contact to near friends' make up the strongest indicator for the likelihood of participating in a church ritual? This finding may point to a change in the status of friends. That is, *that friends have become closer than family*. On the other hand, it may tell us that friends make up the difference between individuals more than family. Everybody has a family, and although one may not have close contact with them, for most people they are part of one's social network one way or another. Friends are more unevenly distributed, as the survey revealed. Some people have many friends whom they see all the time. Other people have no friends. Thus, friends make a greater difference in building up social capital than family does. As being with friends is a way of strengthening internal ties in a group, the connection between rites of passage and friends indicates that participation in rites of passage is connected to building bonding social capital.

The analyses showed that other uses of the Folk Church were connected to building up social capital. Connections of associational engagement and church attendance, prayer, belief, and, to some smaller extent, Folk Church membership showed that these aspects of Folk Church use are also connected with building up social capital. These sorts of Folk Church uses build both bonding and bridging social capital.

The analyses of associational engagement point to the building of bridging social capital, as one often meets new people when engaging in an association. Moreover, associations are open to new members. The connection between being connected to an association and taking part in a funeral or wedding indicates that participation in rites of passage can also be connected to building bridging social capital.

Summing up, all the rites of passage were connected to bonding social capital. This result was strong, as I tested for all background variables. For bridging social capital, associational engagement was connected to funerals and weddings more than baptisms and confirmations. Admittedly, this result was less clear, as I did not test for background variables. Even so, I argue that rites of passage are connected more to bonding than to bridging social capital. Participation in a rite of passage is the most widespread use of church. As mentioned, 45 percent of respondents had attended a funeral during the last year, most of them in the Folk Church.

The Matthew effect

In a research context, sociologist Robert K. Merton spoke of the Matthew effect (Merton 1968). Merton studied the effects of first or second authorship on academic recognition and termed the differences he found a kind of 'Matthew effect'.[5] Another sociologist, Christian von Scheve used the concept when doing a meta-analysis on the research in collective emotions in rituals (Scheve 2012). Scheve reported that the existing literature in the field showed that groups that were already close-knit and linked through a shared horizon prosper most from collective participation in a ritual. They profited at both individual and group levels. Scheve's use of the concept described how strong groups become even stronger through their members' participation in rituals, while participation does not strengthen more loosely-knit groups in the same way.

In the present context, which is the use of Folk Church rituals, my studies point to a similar effect. The Folk Church contributes more bonding than bridging social capital to Danish society. We may ask if there is a so-called 'Matthew effect' present here, giving more capital to those who already have it. I suppose that those with close contact to many near friends are part of a close-knit, interconnected group, and as such are also more likely to take part in baptisms, confirmations and funerals. Using Scheve's insights, it seems these groups are even strengthened more than other, more loosely-knit groups through taking part in such rituals together. Already being strongly connected, the strong group becomes stronger through the participation in a ritual. This is the Matthew effect in a Folk Church context.

There may be nothing wrong with strengthening strong groups. Bonding social capital is important for a society, as Putnam argued. However, is this the highest purpose of the Folk Church, supporting the stronger groups at the cost of more weakly-connected groups? When looking at rites of passage in the Folk Church, we have one more indication that the Folk Church is following the general tendency in neo-liberal society, wherein the many free choices individuals have contribute to social inequality.

References

Berger-Schmitt, Regina 2000. *Social cohesion as an aspect of the quality of societies: concept and measurement.* Paper 14. Mannheim: Social Indicators Department, ZUMA.

Berger-Schmitt, Regina and Heinz-Herbert Noll 2000. *Conceptual Framework and Structure of a European System of Social Indicators.* ZUMA, Social Indicators Department, EUReporting Working Paper No. 9, 1-73.

Billiet, Jaak, Karel Dobbelaere and Bart Cambré 2010. 'Christian Churches as Social Capital'. *Transformation of the Christian Churches in Western Europe, 1945-2000*, 2010. Leuven: Leuven University Press, 236-252.

Bjørnskov, Christian and Kim Mannemar Sønderskov 2013. 'Is Social Capital a Good Concept?' *Social Indicators Research,* 114/3, 1225-42.

Coleman, James 1990. *Foundations of social theory.* Cambridge, MA: Belknap Press of Harvard University Press.

Jenson, Jane 1998. *Mapping Social Cohesion: The State of Canadian Research.* CPRN Study No. F03. Ottawa.

Leth-Nissen, Karen Marie 2018. *Churching Alone: A Study of the Danish Folk Church at Organisational, Individual, and Societal Levels.* PhD dissertation. Publikationer fra Det Teologiske Fakultet, No. 79, Copenhagen: Faculty of Theology, University of Copenhagen.

Lüchau, Peter 2013. 'The Spiritual Revolution and Social Capital in Denmark'. In Joep de Hart et al. (eds.) *Religion and Civil Society in Europe*, Dordrecht: Springer, 189-202.

Merton, R.K. 1968. 'The Matthew effect in science: The reward and communication systems of science are considered'. *Science* 159, 56-63.

Pettersson, Per 2011. 'Majority Churches as Agents of European Welfare'. In Grace Davie et al. (eds.) *Welfare and Religion in 21st Century Europe*, Farnham: Ashgate, 15-60.

Piketty, Thomas 2014. *Capital in the 21st Century*. Cambridge, Mass: Harvard University Press.

Putnam, Robert D. 2000. *Bowling Alone: The Collapse and Revival of American Community*. New York: Simon and Schuster.

Rothstein, Bo and Dietlind Stolle 2008. 'The State and Social Capital: An Institutional Theory of Generalized Trust'. *Comparative Politics* 40/4, 441-59.

Scheve, Christian von. 2012. 'Collective Emotions in Rituals: Elicitation, Transmission, and a "Matthew effect"' Michaels, Axel, Wulf, Christoph. (eds.) *Emotions in Rituals and Performances*. London: Routledge, 55-77.

Notes

1. I should emphasise that my survey had no data on how the Folk Church may be reducing social capital in society (dimension 1).
2. As the Folk Church is most likely to be represented in the life domain of social and political activities and engagement, I focus on the 24 indicators found in Berger-Schmitt's operationalisation of this domain (Berger-Schmitt 2000, 7).
3. 1048 CAWI-interviews (computer assisted web interviews) were conducted, with Danes in the age group 18+ in the period 16 to 23 November 2016.
4. From the questionnaire, it cannot be determined whether the respondents took part in a Folk Church funeral or other funeral. 82.9 percent (2016) took place in the Folk Church, 1 percent in other churches, 14 percent with no clergy present.
5. This is a reference to Matthew 13:12, which states: 'Whoever has will be given more, and they will have an abundance. Whoever does not have, even what they have will be taken from them' (NIV).

15. Legal Re-Organisation of the Danish Religious Market

Lisbet Christoffersen[1]

Introduction

The Danish constitution, with its religion clauses, comes unmistakably from the mid-19th century. The constitution establishes the idea of maintaining the Evangelical-Lutheran Church as the national church, the state church, the Folk Church, through four elements. The first element is the obligation of the state to support this church as long as it remains the majority church (the Folk Church).[2] The second element is that the Monarch is obligated to belong to the Evangelical-Lutheran church.[3] The third is that the common legislative, administrative and judiciary rules (both procedural and institutional) also apply to the church.[4] The fourth element, however, fully grounds this special system of an established Folk Church on a concept of *full freedom of religion*, based directly on the constitutional articles.[5] The legislative powers are thus expected to legislate for the internal structure of the Folk Church and to organize the conditions for other religious communities, but not to legislate on their internal affairs.[6] Moreover, no discrimination based on religion is allowed in Danish society.[7] Until recently, these points have been the common way of describing the Danish religion-law-system (see Christoffersen 2015a).

In this book, the Folk Church is discussed as a cultural institution. In Chapter 7, it was shown how current individualisation and marketisation internal to the Folk Church is based on, and further supported by, old (albeit recently renewed) legislative traditions in Danish ecclesiastical law.[8] This chapter focus on the general development of regulations of what could be seen as the religious market in Denmark, that is: regulation of other religious communities compared to legislative practice regarding the Folk Church. The need for changed regulation of this market is, among other things, based on a rapid change in the societal situation of Denmark over the last generation.

It is obviously the right of legislative powers to regulate such a market. One question is, however, to what extent the market can be regulated in a way that is economically fair. I shall not discuss that question here.[9] My focus is on how old legislative practice regarding the Folk Church influences upcoming legislative ideas in the new regulation of the religious market as such, and especially to what extent there are constitutional limitations to legislative practice.

In the 21st century, a new, state governed marketisation is one of the elements, that brings into question how far special links between the state and the Folk Church are necessary and fair. Also, it is being asked whether the national cultural institutions, including the Folk Church, should be put onto the competitive market. At the same time, state governed marketisation wants to govern not only the old national institutions, but also other organizations in the same market in order to ensure fair competition (and perhaps in order to ensure support from state and from non-state-organizations). While this is a general social development, it also appears in what I name here: *the religious market*. The possible constitutional limits to such developments in the religious market are analysed in this chapter.

This question has been raised recently in the Danish parliament when dealing with conflicts cases regarding proposed new legislation. Instead of the previous understanding of the religion-law relationship as being an untouchable sphere, religion-law is now becoming part of a new politic regarding not only national identity, but also national coherence and social capital – as it was in the years around the constitution in the mid-19th century, albeit now based on new conditions.

This chapter first presents the most recent legislation of relevance to the religious communities in Denmark (from the *imam-package*[10] and onwards).[11] Second, there will be a discussion of the most recent concrete example in more detail, namely the proposal of prohibiting religious male circumcision. Third, the chapter looks at the interpretation of the constitutional clauses and the role of legislative practice regarding the Folk Church in this context. Fourth, a theoretical approach is presented through the idea of a previous, also legal, *Konfessions-kultur,* which now seems to be replaced by a *post-confessional-culture* as the background of the new constitutional and legislative practise in the Danish parliament. Finally, the chapter discusses whether these changed constitutional and legislative approaches will affect the understanding of religion, and especially the Folk Church, as part of (and as contributing to) social capital in society. That is: whether the current re-organization of the religious dimension of the Danish national identity will lead to a re-creation or perhaps a rejection of the religious dimension in that identity altogether.

The question is relevant, not only in and for the Danish context. And, one might say that it is not just out of a purely neighbourly interest in Danish society that major German newspapers, such as *die Zeit*, have been following these developments in Denmark.[12] The fear is that more countries, in addition to Poland and Hungary, will include the religious majority culture in a national development towards what is now named an 'illiberal democracy'.

Recent Danish Religion-Law-Developments

The latest development in the Danish system of religion-law was first sparked by a change in the law on marriages in 2012.[13] The purpose of the changed law was to make the legal concept of 'marriage' gender-neutral, meaning that marriage can include a couple of two different genders or a same-sex couple. In Denmark, one can be married in three venues: within the Folk Church, within one of the acknowledged religious communities or at the town hall, before the mayor. Each of these marriages have the same level of civil recognition (Christoffersen, 2015). The change of the marriage law into a gender-neutral form, however, opened up discussion of whether the Folk Church would also want to perform marriages for same-sex couples (see Vinding and Saggau 2016 for further details). The discussion had been taking place for more than 20 years when the government (also in 2012) proposed a change in the legislation concerning the Folk Church. According to these changes, members of the church have the right to be married within the church (also as same-sex couples), however, the law also allows priests to refuse to perform such a marriage. In that situation, the dean has the obligation to find another priest who is willing to perform the marriage for the couple.[14] Consequently, the rituals for marriage performance within the Folk Church also had to be changed. Based on a proposal from the majority of the bishops, the government Minister of Ecclesiastical Affairs proposed that the Queen (who, according to a historical construction, has the right to legislate in the narrow area of rituals within the church) set her signature under a new ritual for use under these circumstances.[15]

Whether the legislative authorities had the right to conclude this legislation was challenged in a very rare case in the Danish courts, which was finally heard in the Supreme Court in March 2017.[16] The argument from the claimants was that the new ritual and the new, legally acknowledged, practice for performing same-sex marriage was against the Evangelical-Lutheran identity of the Folk Church. The Supreme Court in its verdict acknowledged that the Folk Church is an Evangelical-Lutheran church. However, it also stated that the legislative authorities have a wide scope for estimating how this precondition limits the legislation. In the course of this case, the legislative authorities asked the bishop of Copenhagen to advise them regarding the impact of this condition concerning the Evangelical-Lutheran character of the church (even though, according to the Supreme Court, they were not obliged to do so). Thus, the legislative authorities had not just gone ahead and legislated unilaterally, but to the contrary, they had done so on basis of the advice of the bishop (who had the majority of bishops, members and priests behind him). On that basis, they had estimated the legislation to be within the framework of Evangelical-Lutheran Christianity. The Supreme Court also stated that, according to Article 66 of the constitution, there are no further limits to the legislative powers conferred with the parliament regarding the Folk Church. The legislation was therefore found to be constitutional.

With this verdict, the Supreme Court followed the majority position in a previous official report concerning the future structure of the Folk Church, arguing that the legislative authorities are not obliged to ask anybody before they legislate regarding the Folk Church.[17] On the other hand, the court did also check that the legislative authorities had actually paid attention to the 'Evangelical-Lutheran' condition, and had done so by asking church authorities. A total blank check had not been issued by the court.

This question of whether there are limits to the legislative regulation of religion in Denmark is the general, underlying question in the changes of Danish religion-law these days, and I shall come back to that question and how this relates to coherence in society as such towards the end of the chapter.

The second round of legislation appeared in December 2016, when five laws[18] were passed that, taken together, formed what was called: 'The Imam-Package'. The background was a TV broadcast at the beginning of February 2016, showing that one or more Imams from a specific mosque in West Aarhus had given recommendations that were either directly against Danish law, or at least suggested that Muslim authorities were to be preferred in the solution of family problems instead of Danish law, police and other public support institutions. This was perceived as encouraging the development of a legal parallel society. At the same time, this mosque appeared to be economically supported both directly and indirectly through Danish public funding (cf. Christoffersen, 2012). The argument behind the legislation was that 'we' – the Danes, the politicians, the majority population – do not want to be ridiculed with our own money.[19] The purpose of the legislation concerning free schools and concerning public funding for cultural organizations was, therefore, to force all (including religious) organizations to adhere to democracy in their bylaws as well as in their concrete cultural and educational practices.

The purpose of the change of the law on marriages was to ensure that religious leaders, who are authorised to perform marriages, also know and understand that they do so on the basis of Danish law, not on the basis of any religious law, even though most religious leaders tend to think otherwise. Thereby, it was also highlighted that religious law is not acknowledged as part of Danish marriage law. And, at the same time, it was highlighted that the right to perform marriages could be withdrawn from the individual, if he or she did not follow the broader and more general Danish norms (*decorum*). The change of migration laws was an attempt to close the doors for religious leaders who try to incite their followers against the democratic state and against society, including equal rights for men and women. Finally, there was also a change of the criminal law, criminalising the approbation of certain criminal actions as an element of religious teaching. This last law has been criticised the most in the public debate. Not because it is regarded as acceptable to approve of criminal actions as part of religious teaching, but because the same approbation is not criminalised if it is based on, say, political conviction. Thereby, religious teaching and religious leaders are criminalised beyond the level of other actors in Danish society. Such a criminalisation was seen by some (including myself in a public answer in the hearing process, Christoffersen, 2016) as singling out religious people and religiosity as more dangerous than other movements, and even – possibly – as being against the Danish constitution. This argument was, however, rejected in the political process. The counterargument was that the constitution, Article 70, prohibits discrimination against individual religions ('sin religion' in Danish), whereas it does not prohibit discrimination against all religions and all religious people, compared to secular people in the same situation. I think this is a very dangerous argument!

Prohibition of religious discrimination has, since 1849, been a central element in the Danish constitutional protection of freedom of religion and belief. This protection may now, as can be seen, have found its limits: as long as all religions, all religious practices and all religious leaders are discriminated against equally (compared to secular people, practices and organizations in the same situation), this is seen as acceptable. I will also return to this change of Danish religion-law at the end of the chapter.

The third general change in Danish religion-law came in December 2017 with the law on religious communities outside the Folk Church.[20] The law does not change the general right to individual and collective freedom of religion and belief in society, since it only regulates the access to public recognition and thereby (indirectly) to the right to perform marriages and (indirect) public economic support (see Christoffersen 2016b for the question of economic support). The law is also generally seen as an attempt to live up to the constitution by establishing clear rule-of-law conditions for receiving state recognition as a religious community. The law is seen as an attempt to give religious communities some of the same official status as that of the Folk Church (Lassen 2019, forthcoming). Some anxious murmurs were raised during the UN Special Rapporteur on freedom of religion and belief's visit to Denmark (see report 2016). The law does not open up any discrimination against religious communities. On the contrary, actually: the law accepts that religious communities be allowed to discriminate on the basis of gender, not only within clerical orders, but also in general (for example in regard to voting rights), without losing access to public support.[21]

Worth highlighting in this context are the regulations in §§ 2-3. Here, the law states that a religious community can freely be organized within the framework of the law, and that a religious community can freely practise its rituals and so on, as long as nothing is proposed or done against law and order.[22] The formulation is a modernisation of the public order requirement in the constitution's Article 67. The semantic question, however, is whether the term *public order* means the same thing as the term *nothing done against law and order*. Or, in other words: the formulation in the law raises the question of whether there are in Denmark any constitutional limits to what the legislative authorities can impose on religious communities through this term 'law and order'. Could *any* change made into law make an ordinary religious practice illegal? The question is whether Danish constitutional freedom of religion and belief is a material right with an untouchable core, or whether it is a formal right only, solely establishing who (namely the legislative powers, not the executive powers) can delimit this freedom. If we have a material freedom of religion and belief, then there are also limits to the legislative powers' wish to delimit (such as the conditions from the European Convention of Human Rights, Article 9: necessity, proportionality and based on the protection of other freedoms and rights). It must be stressed that the bylaws, explaining the effects of Articles 2-3 in the law on religious communities, refer to exactly this necessity-clause as the condition for their regulation. This question will be discussed in more detail in section two of this article, concerning the example of the prohibition of ritual circumcision in Denmark, and against that background in the general discussion at the end of the chapter.

Further minor changes are also worth mentioning here; they do not formally change much in the Danish religion-law model, but they do tell us a lot about the general strategy behind the model. First, the century-old prohibition against blasphemy was repealed from the criminal law in 2017.[23] The suggestion had been discussed several times in the parliament. Previous proposals from the right-wing parties were formulated as a kind of aggression against Islam, arguing that Christianity can accept blasphemy, Islam cannot. Next, the left-wing parties argued that laws against blasphemy are a hindrance to the free critique of all religions. That has not been the case in Denmark since 1849, but the argument still goes around. Other parties were in favour and pointed to international pressure to repeal (as did the UN Rapporteur, mentioned above). Only the Social Democratic party voted against the proposal, arguing that there must be a final limitation of how much we can criticise each other's religious acts and books.

Second, the criminal law was changed in 2018 in order to prohibit religious clothing, specifically covering the face, in the public sphere.[24] A more fundamentalist understanding of the public sphere as secular now repealed the former pragmatic approach (Christoffersen 2013). And, finally – which will not appear to be 'final' – the latest political negotiations regarding the budget of the country also include an attempt to prohibit international donations to religious communities in Denmark 'if the purpose of the donation is to counteract or undermine democracy and fundamental freedoms and rights', as it is formulated.²⁵ How such a prohibition will fit with state support via the budget to Danish churches abroad will be a central element to be discussed in that context.

Possible Prohibition of Male Circumcision on Children

The central question of whether the Danish rule-of-law understanding can be open to *any* legislative decision regarding religious communities and their rituals has come to a critical point. This is due to a new factor in the Danish legislative system. It is now possible for a group of 50,000 persons to require that a piece of legislation be discussed in parliament as a citizen-proposal (albeit with the condition that the proposal not be obviously unconstitutional). During the spring of 2017, a proposal was formulated in order to prohibit underage male circumcision.²⁶ The proposal reached 50,000 signatures during summer 2017, and the parliamentary secretariat decided in a note from 7th September 2018 that the proposal was constitutional and could be discussed in parliament.²⁷

The argument from the secretariat was, first, that the reasons behind the proposal are not an animosity against any religious community, but a wish to protect the physical integrity of the child. Second, it was suggested that the parliament have a free right to interpret the limitations to freedom of religion and belief, as formulated in the constitution (Article 67).

The parliamentary committee for religious and ecclesiastical affairs had by March 2018 already received a similar answer from the Ministry of Justice, arguing that a limitation of a religious practice is possible, if the argument behind is based on the protection of, say, the child, and if there is proportionality between the protected purpose and the limitation of the religious practice.²⁸ Both the Ministry of Justice and the secretariat of the parliament assumed that the Jewish ritual practice of circumcision was protected by the Danish freedom of religion clause (even though the ministry was not totally convinced). They did, however, refer to the possibility for the legislative powers to delimit such practices under the purpose of protecting other values. The committee regarding health affairs had also asked the Minister of Ecclesiastical Affairs whether it is a membership condition for any religious community, including Jewish communities in the country, to be circumcised.

To this the Minister just responded that the membership rules are set by the communities themselves[29] – implying that such rules can also be changed by the communities themselves.

The proposal to prohibit ritual circumcision of children was first publicly formulated in 2014 by three organizations fighting for children's rights. Even though that was not part of the negotiations, these organizations find that the Children's Convention protects the physical body of the child, even – or perhaps especially – against thousands of years of religious ritual practice.[30] On the other hand, it is not just the Jewish communities in Denmark, but also the Council of Danish Churches that are against such a prohibition.[31] The argument from the side of the churches is that parents have a right to decide the cultural and religious ways in which their child should be fostered. They fear that, say, baptism practices will be the next to be problematised. The Council of Danish Churches is presided upon by one of the bishops from the Folk Church. All the bishops were informed of the position from the Council during a regular bishop's meeting in April 2018.

The question of prohibiting ritual circumcision was being discussed in the parliament by spring 2018 (before the citizens' proposal had attained 50,000 signatures) in order to reach some general understanding.[32] Five ministers participated in a non-public hearing, 20th April 2018, before the public discussion in the parliament: the Minister of Defence, the Minister of Foreign Affairs, the Minister of Justice, the Minister of Health Affairs and the Minister of Ecclesiastical Affairs. Their recommendations were sent to the parliament, but all papers are confidential. The public discussion in parliament ended with a decision, supported by the Social Democrats, the old liberal parties and the centre-right parties, whereas the socialist parties and the new liberal parties[33] voted against. The decision was that the debate is complex and that a dialogue with the respective religious communities is necessary in order to sharpen registration for, control and regulation of male underage ritual circumcision. The public health authorities must sharpen their regulations, but no prohibition was envisaged. The role of the Minister of Defence seems to have been to recommend caution against producing a new 'cartoons crisis', whereas the Minister of Ecclesiastical Affairs referred to the recently adopted law on religious communities. A prohibition of circumcision would, according to that law, also imply that religious communities that practice circumcision could no longer be recognised in Denmark.

Two other discussions regarding prohibition of male underage circumcision shall be referred to here, because the question of the role of the majority church appears in those discussions. Since 1987, Denmark has had an ethical council whose task it is to advise public authorities in difficult ethical questions, not least within the health care system. The members are appointed by the government. In June 2018, the ethical council published a statement concerning male underage circumcision.[34]

The council was divided into different groups, and this was reflected in its statement. 9 out of 17 members found circumcision practice unethical (the remaining eight members found it ethical on the basis of it being a traditional cultural practice). Two members supported a prohibition by law, whereas 15 members argued that a prohibition of such an old and established practice would lead to severe problems for children who would still be circumcised only without any medical assistance (these are similar arguments from debates concerning abortion: that the practice would simply be driven underground, where safety standards could not be checked and regulated). It is interesting to register that a rather young female member of the council, an economist who works as an advisor concerning welfare systems within the super liberal think tank CEPOS, is one of the two members who clearly supports a legislative prohibition. This position fits well with the group of liberals in parliament, who – even though they are super-liberal – do not want to allow space for this religious practice in society anymore. It is also interesting to note that a priest from the Folk Church, previously a political advisor for a former Minister of Ecclesiastical Affairs, is one of the nine who finds the practice unethical.

Two arguments are central in the report. One is the argument concerning cultural autonomy. Here, one position is that anyone, including any child, has a right to autonomy in decisions relating to itself. This means a right not only to decide for him- or herself regarding body and culture, but also a right to an 'open future', meaning that no one (including the parents) is allowed to close that future by, for example, setting cultural markers on the body. The opposite argument is that, in reality, everyone is embraced by a cultural rooting set by the parents, school and other conditions, and that no one can escape this cultural rooting. In this argument, religious cultural rooting is no worse than any other cultural rooting.

The other central argument in the report is this: in Denmark, we have (and are used to having) a tradition for demanding that the Folk Church adapts to social developments. Legislation concerning rituals for same-sex marriages within the church and concerning female priesthood are examples of that. It must be possible to require other religious communities to likewise adapt to Danish values and the general social developments, if their rituals and practices are to be performed in Denmark.[35] One of the questions in this chapter is how regulatory strategies for the Folk Church spill over and become regulatory strategies on the entire religious market. From what has just been argued here, such a position becomes quite clear.

The citizens' proposal regarding circumcision was, as mentioned above, debated in the parliament in the autumn of 2018.[36] In this debate, the representative from the Prime Minister's party, MP Jane Heitmann (V), argued along much the same lines. Seen through the Christian glasses that most of us Danes use to look at the world, she said, it is natural to disassociate from the idea of circumcision. She continued that, to most of us, it is unthinkable to let anyone cut our children without any medically valid reason.[37] Again, the tradition of regulating the Folk Church tightly through legislation is also used here with an eye towards other religious communities.

Thus, even though the bishops and the Danish Church Council have argued in favour of protecting an old, Jewish (and Muslim) tradition, central to Jewish identity, it is other arguments from the Christian side, that come through in the public debate. One argument is that this practice is against what Christian people find acceptable (as per MP Heitmann [V]). Another argument is that the 'other' religious communities should have to accept what the Folk Church has long suffered: regulation from parliament (without any reflection of the difference in being majority and minority).

Freedom of Religion as a Protection against Legislation Regarding Rituals – is there a Material Protection of Freedom of Religion and Belief?

Denmark does not have a constitutional court, nor does it have an administrative court. The general understanding in constitutional law is that the parliament has the legitimate remit to interpret the constitution, and that – only in very rare cases – do the courts have a right to overrule the legislative powers (particularly if the question is 'political'). In the constitution, this is formulated as the idea that the court only controls whether the administration/executive powers have transgressed their powers. The constitution does not mention the possibility that the courts should control the powers of the legislative institutions.

The Supreme Court has, however, made use of that power in very few cases. The first case (in 1919) regarded basic freedoms and rights for individual citizens versus the common good of society as such, by questioning legislation concerning the expropriation of real estate (and church land) to be used for small hold farms. The Supreme Court decided to support the legislation. Another case from the 1990s concerned a legislative attempt to prevent citizens from bringing their cases to the court – which was seen as unconstitutional![38] There has also been a series of cases regarding the constitutionality of the conferral of powers from Danish legislative authorities to the EU institutions as well as one case where the court actually rejected a statutory law as unconstitutional. In all such cases, the Supreme Court will normally focus on procedural matters: have the right procedures been followed? Are the relevant arguments in place? Have the most relevant persons been involved (as in the case regarding the ritual for same-sex marriages within the Folk Church, previously mentioned). If such procedural guarantees are maintained, the Supreme Court will usually not go into the substance of the matter, especially not if the case concerns the protection of different values or groups against each other. Such an evaluation is seen as matters for the political authorities, not the court.

The question is where that leaves the core of freedom of religion and belief, and whether that leaves us with no constitutionally protected core of freedom of religion and belief (and thus only a procedural protection), meaning that only the legislative powers can delimit the right, for whatever reason, apart from the prosecution of a specific religion.

In regard to the more than 160 year old Danish constitution, there is no doubt that freedom of religion and belief can be delimited, if necessary, in order to prohibit practice or teaching against good morals and public order.

The question just is: what are 'good morals and public order'? And who decides what that is? Is it possible that a religious ritual, which has been accepted in Denmark since the first Jewish community was recognised as foreign believers in 1683, can suddenly become a practice 'against good morals and public order'? It was, after all, re-recognised when the Jewish community was given citizenship in 1814, not problematised in relation to the constitutional clauses in 1849 and also not questioned when the convention on the protection of children's rights was first signed and ratified in 1991. That is the question Danish politics is currently facing.

The notes given to the politicians from the secretariat in parliament and from the Ministry of Justice (presented above) are not exactly helpful. They just state that the parliament decides what is against good morals and public order, as long as the purpose of the legislation is not to prosecute one specific religion.

In order not to end up in a circular argument or with a merely formal protection, or in a situation where legislation is suddenly above the constitution, one has to try to find other formats for the concept of 'good morals and public order'.

One way forward could be to turn to the European Convention of Human Rights. Here, limitations to free practice of religion and belief must meet a series of requirements. A limitation must be necessary in a democratic society: it must be proportionate in order to reach other legitimate aims, and these other legitimate aims must have to do with the protection of others' freedoms and rights.

If such an understanding is used to analyse the question of male underage circumcision, one argument in favour of a prohibition would be, of course, the aim of protecting others' freedoms and rights (even though we must bear the discussion from the council on ethical matters in mind). Against a prohibition the following arguments can be presented, namely that it is not necessary to prohibit the practice in a democratic society, since no health problems from the procedure have been proven. On the contrary: in a democratic society, it could be necessary to uphold the legitimacy of the practice in order to be able to regulate it. Also, there is no clear proportionality. A prohibition hits a very small Jewish population in the heart of its ritual practice (it also hits some Muslim groups, but not as severely). The protection concerns the same group, even though it goes against the will of that group.

It is a central element in the argument above that the proposed legislation hits the heart of the relevant ritual practice for the traditional and transnational definition of Jewishness. In order for legislative powers to legitimately prohibit such a practice, the consequences for those who are taken through the ritual must be very severe in order to meet the proportionality test.

A relevant parallel is to ask whether, according to constitutional and international human rights norms, it could be legitimate to prohibit Christian baptism of children. That ritual also sets a cultural marker on the child, a marker which cannot be taken away again. That ritual also 'makes' the child a member of specific religion and thus closes the autonomous free choice of a cultural future for the child. Voices in the Danish debate have also proposed such a prohibition. Again, the question is about proportionality.[39]

The standard, used under the European Convention of Human Rights, would thus enable the legal advisors to the Danish parliament to determine where the limits for constraining freedom of religion and belief are, as well as clarifying that the Parliament is *not* the final authority concerning the limits of freedom of religion.

The question in relation to the Folk Church is different, even though the ethical council, as mentioned above, seems to understand it as a parallel. In this regard, the Folk Church is understood as a state church, and leading legal scholars have so far interpreted this legal position as one in which the legislative powers – as long as they keep the Evangelical-Lutheran identity of the church – can re-interpret the rituals according to their understanding of what Evangelical-Lutheran identity means. This reference to the Evangelical-Lutheran identity of the Folk Church is, as mentioned previously, already a constitutional limit for how far the legislative powers can change the church. However, this is also a constitutional limit to what legislative ideas are possible. This delimitation would most likely mean that, not only is it not possible to prohibit baptism as being un-proportionate, but that prohibiting baptism would also be against the Evangelical-Lutheran identity of the Folk Church.

One could ask if there should not be the same protection of other religious communities. One way of formulating such a constitutional framework could be as follows: that it should not be possible by law to prohibit the basic identity, or any religious community's rituals, unless they are obviously against criminal law, as that is developed alongside the old religious communities.

Post-*Konfessions-Kultur*-Legislation?

The understanding that religion can be regulated in a more or less unlimited way by law and legislators is not only linked to the Scandinavian concept of a state church. It is most likely also linked to the (West-)Scandinavian version of Lutheranism[40] as this has developed not only through the times of Reformation and absolutism, but also after the constitutional changes in the 19th century. This link to a version of Lutheranism can be referred to as a sort of *Konfessions-Kultur*, in the Scandinavian (and especially the Danish) context, which is a further development that followed on from the Reformation, at least until the constitutional change in the middle of the 19th century (Holm and Koefoed 2018, 9-25).

Within law, it can be argued that such a *Konfessions-Kultur* was also upheld with the constitutional changes in the 19th century. It was thus central to all the Scandinavian constitutions of the 19th century that the new democratic legislators regulated church affairs through laws on the state churches. It was, however, also a central dimension in all Scandinavian constitutions of the 19th century that the new democratic legislators should *not* regulate the other religious communities in as detailed a manner as the Folk Churches. That established a principal, material, constitutionally-based limitation of legislative power.

The pluralistic situation, with acknowledgement of foreign religious believers (from 1683 in Denmark, including the Jewish community amongst others) and later with religious pluralism among Danish citizens (from 1814 the possibility of being a Danish citizen with a Jewish identity), only changed the regulation of church affairs through laws aimed at the state churches to some extent. It was a central dimension in the acknowledgement of the Jewish community in 1814 that the members of the community should abide by state law in all matters outside the core of the religious rituals. The rituals, however, in other religious communities remained untouchable to legislators, both in the late absolutist period and during democracy from 1849 until now (Christoffersen, 2015a).

The idea that law is above religion and that legislators can regulate religion without limits builds, to some extent, on a common (though hidden) understanding of religion and the requirements within religion. This common understanding of what could be understood as a Judeo-Christian legal culture was based on common school education and an introduction to Judeo-Christian culture through confirmation for an absolute majority of the population. This common introduction has functioned as a *social imaginary* (Holm and Koefoed 2018, 17ff), also within the legal culture, for all generations of Danes since the Reformation and until the generation which frequented the Folk School until circa 1980. The generation of politicians and members of parliament, who are now representing their political parties in discussions regarding conflicts between the most central Jewish ritual versus calls for body-protection, is the generation of Danes who were not taught this common Judeo-Christian normative culture in school. And, if they are confirmed in church, they have understood this culture as specifically Christian (as we saw above in relation to the proposed prohibition of religious male underage circumcision). They have thus kept the understanding that law prevails, even over religion, albeit without understanding that a society, based on law, must respect the core of religious rituals. As the title of this section suggests, we are moving towards a *Post-Confessional culture* within religion-law.

The European (and Western) concept of 'the Rule of Law' does build on a distinction between democracy and law (see, for a recent discussion of that, the head of the German Constitutional Court, Andreas Vosskuhle, in *die Zeit,* September 26th 2018). Parliamentary democracy decides new legislation. But new legislation and a majority within a political institution can be constrained by basic principles, such as fundamental rights for individuals and groups (amongst which the respect for freedom of religion is one of the most fundamental). In a democracy building on the Rule *of* Law, a democratic majority can only delimit the freedom of religion if it is necessary and proportionate with respect of other freedoms and rights, as per above.

The Scandinavian democracies tend to build, not on the Rule of Law, but the Rule *by* Law. The ideology tends to be 'none above the parliament', including an understanding that constitutional guarantees are also mostly ideological norms to be interpreted by the actual majority in parliament. It is this tendency, which – supported by a legislative tradition concerning the Folk Churches – can lead the Scandinavian democracies to think that no constitutional limitation exists regarding the core of other religious communities, either.

There is no doubt that the legislative leadership in the Scandinavian majority churches, as well as the legislative borders for other religions in a society such as the Danish, tend to include religion and religious life in society as normal and balanced with other normal functions in society. The risk is, however (especially in a value-based ideological fight against what is seen as non-Danish values), that such an understanding tends to be the basis for excluding groups instead of including groups. Petersen and Kristiansen (2019) suggest that the new approach to religion-law, described above, can be understood as moral panic, based on fear and leading to what they identify as a populist focus on old, national-religious identities. And, of course, fear is a central component, not least regarding any acceptance of religious norms identified as law. Another component is the new, nearly religious protection of the body, as well as the idea of an open, cultural future for anyone in the new, individualised markets. There, it seems, old religious traditions are not allowed to hold anyone to a confessional past.

Instead of basing religious law on fear, one ought to reflect on ideas of combining, as Hanne Petersen puts it (Petersen 2019, 11), 'progressive conservatism and/or subversive traditionalism into pragmatic paradoxes significant for contemporary Europe, producing sites for developments of trans-religious solidarity'. It seems that a legislative politics, regulating both the Folk Church and other religions under the general values of society, whilst leaving room for internal self-regulation of the core of the religious rituals, would support such a development. Even though the European landscape is in flux and gives rise to anxiety, as Petersen formulates it, in such a developing solidarity there are 'glimpses of hope for a peaceful coexistence and solidarity between secular and religious values as well as across religions' (Petersen 2019, 16). At least, that seems to be a more hopeful path to follow than the new, Eastern-European concert between church and state in excluding liberal democratic institutions as well as religious pluralism (see, for example, Kjærum 2018).

Folk Church and Religious Communities versus Social Capital

The legislative practices concerning the Folk Church throughout the 20th century have contributed to the acculturalisation of the Folk Church as an institution, being managed in the same way as other cultural (state) institutions. The recent legislative framing of the other existing religious communities in the country can contribute to the same 'normalising' of religion as part of the pluralistic cultural landscape in society.[41] Thus, a state governed marketisation of, and attempt to govern, all religious communities as much as possible on a more and more equal footing with the Folk Church can, in itself, contribute to the acculturalisation of all religious communities, and thereby to their contributions to the general social capital.

Until now, this legislatively-driven state governance of religious communities has had as its precondition that religions have a certain sacrosanct core, so to speak, that the legislation cannot transgress (as we saw with the example regarding the Folk Church as an Evangelical-Lutheran church, which can bear and include a ritual for same-sex marriages). If this precondition is clearly upheld and reformulated, the current legislative practice contributes to a re-creation of the Danish national identity as including not only the Folk Church, but also other, legislatively-governed and regulated religions, such as the old acknowledged religions (the Jewish community, the Catholic Church, and so on).

Such a re-creation also requires, of course, that the religious communities *want* to contribute to the Danish national identity, not by reforming society in their own ideological mirror, but by opting in and out of their own religious identities, and at the same time being part of society at large. Also, the role of the Folk Church will, over the coming years, need to be re-formulated towards being an institution alongside other religious communities in the collective Danish identity. This simply follows from the change in numbers of the population affiliated with the Folk Church.

If, instead, the core respect for what is untouchable in the various religions is transgressed by the legislators, or if the respect for legislative approaches is transgressed by religious leaders, a legislative approach wherein the law is always above religious traditions, and thus (for example a prohibition of Jewish male underage ritual circumcision) could well lead to a rejection of all religious dimensions in Danish national identity.

References

Christoffersen, Lisbet 2012. 'Religion and State', Jørgen S. Nissen (ed.) *Islam in Denmark. The Challenge of Diversity*. Lanham, Maryland: Lexington Books, 57-80.
Christoffersen, Lisbet 2013. 'A Quest for Open Helmets: On the Danish Burqa Affair'. Alessandro Ferrari and Sabrina Pastorelli (eds.) *The Burqa Affair Across Europe: Between Public and Private Space,* London: Ashgate/Routledge, 171-188.

Christoffersen, Lisbet 2015a. 'On Law and Religion in Denmark', *Encyclopedia of Law and Religion*, BrillOnline Reference Works: referenceworks.brillonline.com/browse/encyclopedia-of-law-and-religion/alpha/v

Christoffersen, Lisbet 2015b. 'A Long Historical Path towards Transparency, Accountability and Good Governance: on Financing Religions in Denmark'. Francis Messner (ed.) *Public Funding of Religions in Europe.* London: Ashgate/Routledge, 125-149 (Cultural Diversity and Law in Association with RELIGARE).

Christoffersen, Lisbet 2016. *Høringssvar til religionsretlig lovpakke sommeren 2016: Fire høringssvar til lovudkast fra Justitsministeriet, Kulturministeriet, Undervisningsministeriet og Kirkeministeriet;* https://rucforsk.ruc.dk/admin/editor/dk/atira/pure/api/shared/model/activity/editor/otheractivityeditor.xhtml?id=57274874

Christoffersen, Lisbet 2017. 'Fri og lige adgang til Vorherre. Kirken og retten 1901 – 2017'. Niels Henrik Gregersen and Carsten Bach-Nielsen (eds.) *Reformationen i dansk kirke og kultur: 1914-2017.* Odense: Syddansk Universitetsforlag, Bind 3, 195-228.

Christoffersen, Lisbet 2019 (forthcoming) 'Towards Re-Sacralisation of Nordic Law?' Marius Mjaaland (eds.) *Formatting Religion,* chapter 11. London: Routledge.

Christoffersen, Lisbet 'By Law Established'. Woodhead, Linda and Hans Raun Iversen (eds.). *The Old National Churches of Northern Europe: The Persistence of Societal* Religion. (in preparation).

Christoffersen, Lisbet, Anders Jørgensen, Svend Andersen (eds.) 2019 (forthcoming), *Trossamfundsloven mv. Kirkeretsantologi 2019.* Frederiksberg: Eksistensen.

Christoffersen, Lisbet, Kjell A. Modéer and Svend Andersen (eds.) 2010. *Law & Religion in the 21st Century – Nordic Perspectives*, Copenhagen: DJØF Pbl.

Holm, Bo Kristian and Nina Javette Koefoed 2018. 'Studying the Impact of Lutheranism on Societal Development. An Introduction'. Bo Kristian Holm and Nina Javette Koefoed. *Lutheran Theology and the Shaping of Society: The Danish Monarchy as Example.* Göttingen: Vandenhoeck & Ruprecht, 9-24.

Kjærum, Morten 2018. 'Orbáns drejebog: Vejen til det udhulede demokrati'. *Kronik. Politiken* 15. September 2018.

Lassen, Eva Maria 2019. 'Bekymring, lettelse og lidt mere bekymring: Internationale menneskerettighedsstandarder og de danske regler'. Lisbet Christoffersen, Anders Jørgensen and Svend Andersen (eds.) *Kirkeretsantologi 2019*, Frederiksberg: Eksistensen (forthcoming).

Petersen, Hanne 2019. 'Changing Normativity and solidarity: European Legal and Trans-religious Perspectives'. Helle Krunke, Hanne Petersen and Ian Manners (eds.) *Transnational Solidarity – Concept, Challenges and Opportunities*, Oxford: Oxford University Press (forthcoming).

Petersen, Hanne and Bettina Lemann Kristiansen 2019. 'Pluralisme og populisme i lovgivningsarbejdet. Om tilblivelsen af loven om trosamfund uden for folkekirken i Danmark'. Reza Banakar, Kurt Dahlstrand and Lotte Rydberg Welander (eds.) *Festskrift til Håkan Hydén*, Lund, Juristförlaget (forthcoming).

Vinding, Niels V., and Emil B.H. Saggau 2016. 'Challenges of the Institutionalization of Same Sex Marriage for Religious Pluralism'. Ednan Aslan, Ranja Ebrahim, Marcia Hermansen (eds.) *Islam, Religions, and Pluralism in Europe*, Springer VS Fachmedien, Wiesbaden, 173-192.

Vosskuhle, Andreas. 2018. Justiz und Demokratie. Rechtsstaat unter Druck. *Die Zeit online,* 26th September 2018 (ed. 29th September 2018). https://www.zeit.de/2018/40/justiz-demokratie-asylverfahren-dieselskandal-rechtsstaat-deutschland (attached 29th Dec. 2018).

Øhrgaard, Per 2018. Demokrati og retsstat. *Kristeligt Dagblad*, 7th December 2018.

Notes

1. I thank the external peer reviewer for the helpful comments on the first draft of this chapter, and I would like to thank the co-editors for the very clear and stringent comments on the final versions. Outside our own group, I want to thank Professor Hanne Petersen, the Faculty of Law, University of Copenhagen, for visionary conversations that helped me over a stumbling block, and Professor Bettina Lemann Kristiansen, Sociology of Law, Aarhus University, both for general and very concrete comments on a final draft. They both, together with Professor Margit Warburg (member of the editorial group), were members of the committee, which proposed the 2017 law on religious communities in Denmark outside the Folk Church.
2. The Danish constitution, Article 4, says in a direct translation from Danish that the Evangelical-Lutheran Church is the Danish Folk Church and is, as such, to be supported by the state (Den evangelisk-lutherske kirke er den danske folkekirke, og understøttes som sådan af staten). The semi-official translation instead has it that this church is the established church – which, however, is the consequence, not the rule. Legally speaking, the state does not have any obligations to support this church if it is not the majority church.
3. Constitutional Article 6 (Kongen skal høre til den evangelisk-lutherske kirke) means that the monarch could, in principle, belong to any Evangelical-Lutheran church. Until now, the clause has been interpreted, not only as a condition of belonging to the state church, but even as legally normative, such that the monarch is understood as being the head of that church.
4. Article 66 (Folkekirkens forfatning ordnes ved lov) implies that the legislative powers are obliged to, or ought to, establish the church with an internal structure with competences in legislative, executive and judiciary matters. Instead, the article is interpreted as the state's right for its legislative, executive and judiciary institutions to take responsibility for all matters regarding and within the church, including, of course, a change of rituals.
5. Constitutional Article 67.
6. Constitutional Article 69.
7. Constitutional Article 70.
8. In Chapter 7, on legislative support to individualisation and marketisation, written in collaboration with Karen Marie Sø Leth-Nissen. I have also, in Christoffersen in preparation, written on how Nordic churches, being 'By Law Established' also ensure the acculturalisation of these churches.
9. I here refer to articles by Sidsel Kjems and Niels Kærgaard in this volume, as well as to Christoffersen (2017).
10. The Imam-Package, which contains a negotiated agreement between the then government (Venstre, the Liberal party) and three other parties in the parliament

(the Danish People's Party, the Conservative Party and the Social Democratic Party) on initiatives aimed at limiting the activities from 'religious preachers, who try to undermine Danish laws and values and support parallel legal understandings', as the paper is titled (my translation).

11 It is, to the best of my knowledge, the first entire overview over this legislation published.

12 Professor emer. Per Øhrgaard, in an article in *Kristeligt Dagblad* (7 December 2018), titled: *Demokrati og retsstat*, refers to major German newspapers for anxious observation of the Danish development. The concern is whether Denmark is currently following the path now trodden by Hungary and Poland. His reference is to discussions of the Burqa-prohibition in *Die Zeit* (2 August 2018. For the German understanding of *Rectsstaat*, see Andreas Vosskuhle (27 September 2018). Vosskuhle is the president of the German *Bundesvervassungsgericht*. I thank Per Øhrgaard for these references.

13 Lov nr. 532 af 12. juni 2012 om ændring af lov om ægteskabs indgåelse og opløsning, lov om ægteskabets retsvirkninger og retsplejeloven og om ophævelse af lov om registreret partnerskab (Ægteskab mellem to personer af samme køn).

14 Lov nr 532 af 12. juni 2012 om ændring af lov om ændring af lov om medlemskab af folkekirken, kirkelig betjening og sognebåndsløsning (Præsters ret til at undlade at vie to personer af samme køn m.v.)

15 Vielse af par af samme køn Vejledende ritual Autoriseret ved kgl. resolution af 12. juni 2012

16 Højesterets dom af 23. marts 2017 om ritual for vielse af par af samme køn

17 Betænkning 1544/2014 om Folkekirkens styrelse. It behooves me to mention that I, as a minority member of the commission behind the official report, found that not only the concept 'Evangelical-Lutheran' but also the concept 'church' and the concept 'Folk Church' are constitutional limits for the legislation regarding the Folk Church. I therefore found that the legislative authorities would be obliged to hear different groups within the church before a legislation was brought forward – which they actually also did in this case, and on the basis of which the Court actually also made its decision.

18 Lov nr 1533 af 13/12/2016 om ændring af Folkeoplysningsloven og Ligningsloven (Indsats mod foreninger, som modarbejder eller underminerer demokrati eller grundlæggende friheds- og menneskerettigheder)
Lov nr 1563 af 13/12/2016 om ændring af friskoleloven (Styrkelse af kvaliteten på de frie grundskoler m.v.)
Lov nr 1723 af 27/12/2016 om ændring af Straffeloven (Kriminalisering af udtrykkelig billigelse af visse strafbare handlinger som led i religiøs oplæring)
Lov nr 1 ½ ½2729 af 27/12/2016 om ændring af Ægteskabsloven (Decorumkrav og obligatorisk kursus i dansk familieret, frihed og folkestyre).

Lov nr. 1743 af 27/12/2016 om ændring af udlændingeloven (Indførelse af en offentlig sanktionsliste over udenlandske religiøse forkyndere m.fl., som kan udelukkes fra at indrejse)
19   The then Minister of Ecclesiastical Affairs and of cultural affairs, Bertel Haarder (Venstre).
20   Lov nr 1533 af 19/12/2017 om trossamfund uden for folkekirken
21   This part of the law was of course criticised. The discussion, however, falls outside the framework of this chapter. For details, see articles by Gammeltoft-Hansen, Lodberg, Ryberg, Warburg and Lemann Kristiansen in Christoffersen, Jørgensen and Andersen (2019, forthcoming).
22   Trossamfundslovens § 2. Trossamfund kan frit dannes med ethvert lovligt formål. § 3. Et trossamfund har ret til at udøve sin religion, herunder ved overholdelse af religiøse ritualer og skikke samt religiøs undervisning, såfremt der ikke herved opfordres til eller foretages noget, der strid er mod bestemmelser fastsat ved lov eller i medfør af lov.
23   Lov nr 675 af 08/06/2017 om ændring af straffeloven (ophævelse af blasfemi-bestemmelsen)
24   LOV nr 717 af 08/06/2018 om ændring af straffeloven (tildækningsforbud). The law criminalises public wearing of clothes that hide the face of a person, unless the purpose of the clothing is done for a 'credible' reason (anerkendelsesværdig in Danish). For example, being dressed as Santa Claus at Yuletide is credible, whereas the wearing of a burqa is not.
25   Aftale mellem regeringen og Dansk Folkeparti: Finansloven for 2019 (30. november 2018), s. 39-40.
26   B 9 2018-19 Forslag til folketingsbeslutning om indførelse af 18-årsmindstealder for omskæring af raske børn (borgerforslag).
27   Notat fra Folketingets Lovsekretariat om lovsekretariatets indstilling om fremsættelse af borgerforslag nr. FT-00124 om 'indførelse af 18 års mindstealder for omskæring af raske børn', Sundheds- og Ældreudvalget 2018-19, B 9, bilag 3.
28   Kirkeudvalget 2017-18, KIU Alm.del, JM endeligt svar på spørgsmål 24 om, hvorvidt det jødiske ritual med omskæring af drenge er beskyttet af grl. § 67. – Kirkeministerens svar på spm nr 15 Kirkeudvalget Alm. Del. 2017-18 om omskæring af drenge
29   Sundheds- og Ældreudvalget 2017-18 SUU Alm.del Kirkeministerens svar (endeligt svar) på spørgsmål 893 om drengeomskæring er en afgørende forudsætning for, at den pågældende kan være medlem af et bestemt trossamfund.
30   Børnerådet, Børns Vilkår og Red Barnet går sammen i fælles erklæring mod omskæring: Lad drengene bestemme selv. 10. februar 2014. The UN Convention on the Rights of the Child (1989) was ratified by Denmark in 1991, see BKI nr 6 af 16/1/1992, and is thus a relevant legal argument in Danish cases. The convention is, however, not implemented in Danish law and there is no doubt that the constitution prevails over obligations regarding the convention.

31 Danske Kirkers Råd Omskæringsdebatten og frygten for det anderledes. Pressemeddelelse forretningsudvalget, 20. April 2018 (bragt som artikel i KD samme dato).
32 F 24 2017-18 Forespørgsel i Folketinget om omskæring.
33 Alternativet and Liberal Alliance.
34 Det Etiske Råds udtalelse om ritual omskæring af drenge. 25. juni 2018. Til folketingets sundheds- og ældreudvalg.
35 "I dansk sammenhæng er der tradition for, at man udmærket kan stille krav til folkekirken om at forny sig og tilpasse sig til tidens nye krav. Dette vidner lovgivningen angående homovielser og kvindelige præster om. Det forekommer derfor nærliggende at der også bør være mulighed for at stille krav til andre religioner, for så vidt som de udøves i Danmark." (Det etiske råds udtalelse af 25. juni 2018, s. 120 – The translation in the text of the chapter is my translation).
36 B9 2018-19 borgerforslaget. Fremsat af DF, EL, LA, ALT, RV, SF, K
37 The representative from the party Venstre in the parliamentary debate, Jane Heitmann: "en helt naturlig reaktion at tage afstand fra det set gennem de kristne briller, som et flertal af os danskere anskuer verden igennem, for de allerfleste danskere er det utænkeligt, at vi skulle lade nogen skære i vores børn uden en medicinsk begrundelse" (ordfører, B 9 2018-19, 1. behdl. 6-12-2018, the translation in the text of the chapter is my translation). Also, the representative from the Danish People's Party was against the cutting in healthy children.
38 In the Tvind-case, U 1999.841 H, the supreme court for the first – and until now last – time rejected a statutory law as unconstitutional. The central argument was that the organizations in case according to the law was not allowed to bring the case to court. That was too much, even for Danish courts.
39 It should be mentioned that the Ministry of Justice, in its notes to the parliament, regarding the possible prohibition of male underage ritual circumcision mentions that the question must also be probed in relation to the European Convention of Human Rights. The Ministry of Justice, however, did not check this relation in the papers sent to the parliament.
40 There is a clear distinction here between the development of state-church-relations in East Scandinavia (Sweden and Finland) and West Scandinavia (Denmark and Norway). In Sweden and Finland, the church has always kept some national identity and some legislative power, whereas this totally disappeared in Denmark and Norway (see Christoffersen, Modéer and Andersen, 2010). In Norway, this is about to change with the legal independence of the Church of Norway from 2017, (see Christoffersen 2019, forthcoming).
41 Not to be mistaken with the concept of multiculturalism, which I deliberately am not dealing with here, since it, as I see it, is irrelevant in a description of the Danish society

16. The Folk Church and the Public Debate Before and After Individualisation and Marketisation

Niels Kærgård

Introduction

In 1960, the then incoming Danish prime minister, Viggo Kampmann, and some of the leading politicians had a three day meeting with leading members of the cultural life, fiction writers, philosophers and, amongst others, a professor of theology. This meeting was held at Krogerup folk high school and its neighbour institution, the Louisiana museum of modern art. Kampmann was an economist through and through, former permanent secretary of the Ministry of Economic Affairs and Minster of Financial Affairs and the leading pioneer in the construction of the Danish National Account in the 1940s. His overall aim was to get the cultural elite engaged in the public societal debate. His message to the cultural life was that 'governing is going to happen anyway' (in Danish regeret bliver der alligevel), see Smidt (2016) and Kærgård, Thage and Topp (2019). Cultural institutions have a right, and a challenge, to participate in the public debate even concerning economic and political matters. If the public debate is to be unbiased, it is important that the cultural institutions do not leave the debate only to political scientists, economists and professional politicians.

It seems uncontroversial to observe that modern society is more differentiated in relation to jobs and education than before (for example in 1960). The research and education sector are very specialised in terms of their disciplines. A couple of years ago at the Danish Agricultural University there was an interdisciplinary research project about health and obesity. Characteristically enough, the economists presented the main reasons for the problems as being that fat and sugar are too cheap, the sociologists concentrated on social relations and meal structure, and the historians focused on pork and butter, whilst the medics focused on genes and appetite stimulants.

This specialisation is part of the modern scientific method as formulated by economist Ragnar Frisch who later received the Nobel prize in economy:

> In our mind we create a microcosm for our use. A model of the world that is not more complicated than we can encompass within our field of view. And then we proceed to study this microcosm instead of studying the real world. This little trick contributes the rational approach to research. (Translated from Norwegian: Frisch 1928-29 reprinted in Bergh and Hanicsh 1984, 156)

But if the different researchers do view the society from an angle that simplifies it, this means that a full and realistic picture of the real world is only found if all the relevant disciplines contribute to the picture. This is even more pressing now than in 1960. In a society where social scientists and economists have dominating roles (even among the politicians, a majority are educated in economics and political science), competition, economic incentives, utility and profit, and maximising behaviour have become the dominant keywords in the public debate. Sayings like 'maximum usefulness for the money', 'it must pay economically to work', 'the economic incentives are insufficient' and so on have become common coin. Economic incentives are seen as the main motivation for citizens and firms, and as the most effective political management tool. Such profit maximising as the rational allocation mechanism of society was formulated long ago by the father of economics, Adam Smith in 1776:

> He (the businessman) intends only his own gain, and he is in this, as in many other cases, led by an invisible hand to promote an end which was no part of his intention. Nor is it always the worse for society that it was not part of it. By pursuing his own interest he frequently promotes that of the society more effectively than when he really intends to promote it. I have never known much good to be done by those who affected to trade for the public good. It is an affectation, indeed, not very common among merchants, and very few words need be employed in dissuading them from it (Smith 1937 [1776], 423).

In fact, the price mechanism is a very powerful mechanism and so is the theory about it. But it is blind to a number of aims and motives (for example distributive justice). Most people (at least in Denmark) are of the opinion, often more or less founded in a Christian social ethics, that this 'invisible hand' economic view cannot stand alone. A rather equal society where 'few have too much and fewer too little' (a famous quotation from the poet, priest and politician N. F. S. Grundtvig) is seen as needing to be a main aim, along with a political system willing to enforce such an equal society by law and taxes, as has been formulated by K. E. Løgstrup:

> A realignment of society towards a more equitable distribution of income will force people to share out consumer goods amongst a greater number of recipients, as if the strong had come to love the weak, and ignores the fact that the strong will gnash their teeth over having a lower income in order to give a higher income to the weak. If we expect to invoke the principal of "Love thy neighbour", we will find that no-one actually does, but that some people will be forced to behave as if they actually do. (Translated from Løgstrup 1971, 254)[1]

Such a redistribution is also supported by recent philosophy and ethics, see amongst others Rawls (1971) and the Nobel laureate economist Amatya Sen's *The Idea of Justice* from 2009. This demand for protection of the poor and weak is not only about economic redistribution. A basic attitude, formulated in, for example, a declaration of human rights aims for the protection of all sorts of minorities, religious, racial and sexual.

Greater respect for nature and the environment than is demanded by traditional economics with its profit and utility maximisation is another dominant point of view in the public debate. It might even be said that the dominating view is a kind of contemptible anthropocentrism. Or, as K.E. Løgstrup put it:

> Take the case of pollution. It is not enough just to ask whether pollution has already become too heavy and too threatening, seen as a social cost of production. Neither will it suffice just to discuss whether the cost of stopping pollution should be borne by the firm causing it or covered by public funds. The whole analysis needs to be turned around. The preservation of nature is a valid goal in itself, and one of the goals behind the need to have an economic system at all. ... The goal of the economic system must be something other than an economic goal. The purpose of the economic system must be something non-economic. Otherwise economics will lose its meaning. (Translated from Løgstrup 1997, 169-170)

These attitudes towards the protection of nature, the weak and the poor have often been supported by people from cultural institutions, who stress goals other than economic growth, profit and utility maximisation and rational incentives more than mainstream economists do.

In Denmark, members from the Folk Church have often been a voice for such non-economic aims[2]. But there has always been disagreement in the Folk Church about the attitude to the welfare state, to environmental policy, and so on. And many people outside the church, atheists and those from other religious communities have also been important spokesmen for such views. Nevertheless, a social attitude to the weak and poor and a respect for nature and environment, seen as 'our Lord's creation', have always been a main pillar of the Christian belief.

The Folk Church and the public debate

What exactly constitutes the optimal role of the church in public debate will, of course, depend on one's general political and religious attitude. There has always been, within and outside the Folk Church, disagreement about the right attitude towards the welfare state and to environmental policy. Similarly, a condemnation of abortion and divorce will be considered as a natural and relevant position for a church by some, whilst others will consider that a harmful barrier for people's happiness. For all the (more than) thousand years we have had Christianity in Denmark, the church and the clergy have always participated in public debate.

Before the Reformation in 1536, the Roman Catholic Church was an important power in society, and often in conflict with the king. A number of conflicts between the Danish king and the Danish archbishop make up a remarkable part of our history during the Middle Ages.

With the Reformation, the king became the head of the church, and conflicts between state and church were consequently impossible. But a number of the leading members of the public church nevertheless played important roles in the public debate in the following centuries. We can mention a few examples.

Erik Pontoppidan (1698-1764), bishop of Bergen in the Norwegian part of the kingdom 1748-54, was one of the founding fathers of the Danish Academy of Science and Letters in 1742 and editor (1757-1764) of the journal *Danmark og Norges Oeconomiske Magasin*. This journal was central to the political debate in Denmark-Norway during this period (Sæther, 1989).

With the change from absolute monarchy to a free constitution 1849, freedom of speech was introduced and a number of the leading persons in the church participated in this free debate. In fact, the free constitution was mainly written by the theologian D.G. Monrad (1811-1887), bishop (1849-54 and 1871-87), member of the government (1848-49 and 1859-64) and member of parliament (1849-1865 and 1882-1886).

Many others from the church have had leading positions in public debate, often in conflict with the ruling classes. We can mention H.L. Martensen (1808-1884), bishop (1854-1884), who wrote a pamphlet about Christianity and Socialism in 1874 and a big volume about social ethics (the third volume of his Christian ethics) in 1878. At that time, the ruling classes were afraid of socialism – the very first socialist leaders were in prison and contact with Socialist International was forbidden. Even so, Denmark's leading bishop H.L. Martensen wrote very positively about socialism and against liberalism (Venstre, the liberal party, had absolute majority in the 1st chamber of parliament at that time). 'Social egoism has in our time, behind the shield of liberalism, grown strong', wrote Martensen, who summarised the debate in a letter:

> It must not be said, at the end of the day, that the church has remained silent and neglected to speak out on what Christianity ought to say: for in spite of all contradictions, the Christian truth is that industry must serve mankind, rather than mankind serve industry (Kærgård 2018, 171).

During World War II, when Denmark was occupied by the Germans, the theological professor Hal Koch (1904-1963) was a leading figure in a national revival. After the war, he and his colleague K.E. Løgstrup demanded justice for the supporters of the German occupation and were very critical towards the dominating wish for revenge.

When the Nazis started their persecution of the Danish Jews in 1943, the Danish bishops wrote a letter to all local congregations which opened[3]: everywhere persecution of Jews as such, for racial or religious reasons, are taking place, it is a Christian church's duty to protest against it', and finished:

> There is a clear understanding of our obligation to be law-abiding citizens, who do not oppose those who exercise authority over us, but at the same time we in our

conscience are bound to enact justice and protest against any violation; therefore we will in any case unequivocally acknowledge the word that we should obey God more than men.

This should be sufficient to show that, on a considerable number of historical occasions, part of the Folk Church has served as society's conscience in opposition to the ruling classes. For a more general discussion of the relation between the church and the political system, see Kærgård (2016) and Kærgård and Jensen (in preparation).

The formal possibilities for the Folk Church in the Danish debate

If it is intended that the voice of cultural institutions, and of the Folk Church, shall be part of public debate in Denmark today, the institutional framework of the Folk Church can be seen to have both advantages and disadvantages.

Where most other churches have an archbishop or a governing assembly, there are no such things in the Folk Church. This is partly for theological reasons and partly for political reasons. Theologically, the church is strongly based on the Lutheran attitude that all who are 'crawled out of baptism are pastor, bishop and archbishop', there are no hierarchical structures and nobody between the single Christian and God.

But there are more than theological reasons. With the Reformation in 1536, the king became the head of the Folk Church, and when the democratic constitution was formulated in the hectic year of 1849, there was no time to find solutions for all constitutional problems. One of the unsolved problems was the governing of the church. So, the constitution of 1849 has only a paragraph saying that the governing of the Folk Church shall be determined by law. But despite a considerable number of attempts, the latest in 2014 (see Kirkeministeriet 2014, and Christoffersen, 2017), it has never been possible to get a majority in parliament for a proposal. So, while the king (at present, the queen) is still the formal head of the Folk Church, in practice (in a modern society with restricted monarchy) this means that the secular government's church minister is the head of the church in any practical matters. And this person need not even be a member of the church. The minister is only in charge of practical matters and is not at all a spokesman for the church.

The ecclesiastical structure is consequently very flat. There are no archbishops, and the bishops do not form a council, which can express an 'official' or definitive point of view, nor can any other form of common council. This means that, contrary to most other countries, there are no persons or no formal body to express the views of the church.

But the single members of the church, the pastors and the bishops can, and do, express their views on theological and political matters. Except for the declaration about the Jews in 1943, all the examples of statements in the section above are individual contributions to the debate.

The possibilities for the bishops and the pastors are attractive. All bishops, and most of the pastors, are civil servants ('tjenestemænd') with high job security (according to Danish tradition), and no chiefs nor church boards can restrict what they are saying – neither within nor outside the church. This stands in contrast to most other jobs in Denmark. Almost all other jobs are now part of the Danish *flexicurity* system with very few restrictions on discharge. This system has gradually spread to almost all parts of the labour market (for example university professors had the same conditions as civil servants until the mid-1990s, but can now be fired without extended notice). The same is the case for most academics in the public administration. This is important, because job security is a necessary foundation for expressing controversial statements.

The use of the possibilities

A number of pastors have used the possibility of participating in the public debate as an opportunity to become politically active. A total number of 26 pastors, in the period 1960-2012, have been members of the Danish parliament. But none of them are seen as representing the Folk Church, and they are split rather equally between the different political parties, see Table 1.

Table 1: Christian theologians in the Danish Parliament 1960-2012 and their political affiliation

Political party	Theologians among parliament members
Socialist party – SF	3
Social democrats – Socialdemokratiet	6
Social liberals – Radikale Venstre	1
Christian democrats – Kristeligt Folkeparti	3
Liberals – Venstre	7
Conservative – Det konservative folkeparti	3
Danish People's Party – Dansk Folkeparti	3

Source: Kærgård 2016, 259.

Few of these pastors used their Christianity as arguments in the political debate. Only members of the Christian Democrats and the Danish People's Party have allowed their Christianity to be used as a main component of their arguments. The Christian Democrats started in 1970 and were in parliament 1973-1994. It was started mainly as a traditional Christianity's protest against the law concerning free pornography in 1969 and free abortion in 1973. Danish People's Party's pastors were mainly protesting against the use of Christianity for social attitudes in the political debate. They are very nationalistic and stress that the Christian duty of charity only refers to your personal neighbour (and not, say, international refugees). They argue, consequently, for a very restrictive immigration policy and talk about a fundamental difference existing between Christianity and Islam.

The leaders of the Folk Church are, however, very careful to be neutral in relation to political matters. This tendency seems to have got stronger and stronger during the last half century. An indication of this is seen in the sermons at the opening of every new year in the parliament. Such an opening worship has been a tradition since the first elected parliament met in 1850. The whole collection of sermons has been analysed by ecclesiastical historian Professor Martin Schwarz-Lausten. Highlighting the differences between previous sermons and recent ones, he concludes:

> Some urged politicians to show themselves to be men of faith striving to accomplish the will of God. Others wanted religion and politics to be separated, despite maintaining that the Gospel must have implications for political life. Still others, however, declared that preachers ought to express social and political opinions and, in effect, give advice to the politicians about certain questions. They made their opinion clear on foreign affairs, military rearmament, patriotism and other national values. Some also deal with political matters directly concerning the church, such as church and state, female ministers of religion, etc. Many preachers gave the politicians direct moral admonitions and expressed their opinion on, for instance drunkenness, unemployment, housing problems, famine in the world. In general, the preachers in recent times have avoided controversial issues of this nature and have instead delivered classic Evangelical-Lutheran sermons (Lausten 2014, 426).

Another indication of the same tendencies can be seen in the bishops' and pastors' participation in political life. In 1966, there were five actual and former priests of the Folk Church who were members of parliament; in 2015, there was only one.[4]

These are but two of a number of indications of a more careful handling of political matters among the leading persons of the Folk Church. Even if, as argued above, there is a need for ethical and religious statements in the recent political debate, dominated by political science and economic arguments, the major portion of the Folk Church do not participate in the debate.

Christianity and Danishness

The conclusion of the section above could seem to be in contrast to the fact that a number of seemingly religious questions have been a central part of the public debate during the last decades: religion's role in the public space, religious scarves, burkas and niqabs, circumcision of Jewish and Muslim boys, praying rooms in public institutions, holidays other than the Christian Christmas and Easter (for example Ramadan), integration of Muslim refugees and so on (see Chapter 15). A number of political declarations about Denmark as a Christian society are seen (for example in the program of the recent government). The Folk Church has, however, not been a major part of these debates.

A main theme for many of the participants in these debates is a critical attitude towards Muslims, and the main spokesmen for this attitude is the Danish People's Party (though gradually followed by many others). The Danish People's Party is related to part of the Folk Church, but the very specific part of the church called 'Tidehverv'. Tidehverv started in the 1920s as a Barthian and existentialistic theological movement stressing Christianity as a personal belief without implications for political and social attitudes. In the 1980s, this led the movement to a strong opposition against social-Christian attitudes, especially against positive attitudes to refugees, and against religions such as Islam, with its specific rules for eating, family life and so on. This opposition led to a political engagement in the national-conservative Danish People's Party, with its very critical attitude to Islam and great favouring of a restrictive immigration policy, see Kærgård (2006). Such attitudes have also been supported by a number of pastors who are very active in the public debate. But Tidehverv, and these pastors, are not seen as any coalition between the Folk Church and a political party, but perhaps more as a opposition against both mainstream church Christianity and mainstream political parties. Many of the most active pastors are regarded more as politicians (e.g. Søren Krarup, Jesper Langballe and Christian Langballe), or columnists and activists (e.g. Sørine Gotfredsen and Kathrine Winkel Holm) than as pastors.

The Danish newspaper *Kristeligt Dagblad* had conducted surveys among priests (2006 and 2011) about how they would vote politically. The results are shown in Table 2 and compared with the results for the whole population. Two interesting observations seem clear. The Danish People's Party's position among the priests is very weak, whereas the most refugee-friendly parties, the socialists and the social liberals, have a very strong position. Even if Christianity in the political debate is often described as part of Danishness, this is a point of view not found in the Folk Church outside of Tidehverv and other rather narrow, related circles, but mainly found in political circles around or inspired by the Danish People's Party.

It should be noted that the Danish People's Party is (except for the small fraction of Tidehverv, which is very active and visible in the public debate) far from being a party with Christianity in its foundation. In fact, the party's voters are, next to the left-wing socialists, the most negative of the Danish political parties in relation to the church, see Table 3.

Table 2: Survey among pastors in the Danish Folk Church and among all voters 2005-06 and 2011

Party	Number of voters among priests, per cent		Number of voters, among all, per cent	
	2006	2011	2005	2011
Socialists	25.7	22.1	9.4	16.8
Social Democrats	15.5	17.8	25.9	26.1
Social Liberals	18.9	23.9	9.2	10.0
Christian People's Party	6.3	6.1	1.7	0.8
Liberals	16.0	11.7	29.0	28.1
Conservative	13.4	9.5	10.3	5.2
Danish People's Party	2.5	6.1	13.3	13.0
Total	100	100	100	100

Note: Socialists include both SF and Enhedslisten. The per cent indicates the proportion of voters of the parties included here, not from the whole sample, because new parties are introduced between the two samples and the 'don't knows' are reported differently. Source: Thomsen (2006) taken from Kristeligt Dagblad August 10, 2006 and the election 2005 and Johansen (2011). The survey in 2011 was sent to 2170 priest and 597 answered.

In fact, many of the 'religious' topics in the debate (religious scarves, burka and niqab, circumcision of Jewish and Muslim boys and praying rooms in public institutions) are not religious at all, but part of a political debate about Danishness (a traditional Danish society versus a multicultural society with immigrant minorities, cf. chapter 15). Here, Christianity is seen in the eyes of many politicians as an indication of Danishness and the acceptance of Islam as an indication of multiculturalism.

Table 3: The political parties and church activities

Political party	Proportion of the party's voters never visiting a church
Left wing socialists – Enhedslisten	64 %
Danish People's Party – Dansk Folkeparti	50 %
Social liberals – Radikale Venstre	50 %
Social demokrats – Socialdemokratiet	48 %
Socialists – Socialistisk Folkeparti	42 %
Conservative – Det konservative Folkeparti	37 %
Liberals – Venstre	37 %
Christian Democrats – Kristeligt Folkeparti	7 %

Source: Kærgård (2006) and Hoffmann-Hansen (2006)

In this debate, the main portion of the Folk Church has often formed an alliance with the minority religions. It has done so in a common acceptance of religion and religious ceremonies as an important part of life, and in opposition to political attempts to ban circumcision, praying rooms and so on.

The Folk Church's relation to the minority religions can perhaps be illustrated in the Luther-anniversary, 2017, where the Roman Catholic, the Jews and even the Muslims were invited to a number of arrangements in the church. This contrasts starkly with the period before the 'Danishness debate' (as illustrated by the Pope's visit to Denmark in 1989, where a considerable part of the Folk Church refused the Pope's invitation to meet).

However, this does not mean that the spokespersons from the Folk Church play an important role as defenders of religious minorities in the debate about religious scarves, burka and niqab, circumcision of Jewish and Muslim boys and praying rooms in public institutions. They have been very careful *not* to play too dominating a role. This seems primarily to be caused by a fear of becoming involved in a harsh political debate beset with many controversial statements.

Why is the Folk Church so cautious?

There can be many reasons for this cautiousness. Many segments of the surrounding society seem to be less tolerant towards views different from their own. An indication is the opening sermons for the meetings in the parliament and the debate about them. In 2018, a considerable proportion of members of parliament boycotted the ceremony because the chosen pastor (though a supporter of same-sex marriage) had said ten years ago that the permissibility of same-sex marriage does not imply that such couples necessarily have a right to adopt children. Decades ago, political attitudes amongst the church's spokesmen were fully accepted. Leading members of the church have political opinions. Henrik Dons Christensen was bishop of Ribe (1957-1980) and at the same time vice-president in the liberal political party Venstre (1962-65). Ole Bertelsen was bishop of Copenhagen (1975-1992) and was called 'the red bishop' (known for the saying 'a good sermon is always political, but political sermons are always bad'), and he was commonly regarded as supporter of the socialist political party. Both of them were, at that time, accepted within and outside the church.

This shift may have been caused in part by individualisation and functional differentiation, following Niklas Luhmann, see Ziemann (2007) and Warburg (2015). Functional differentiation has separated society into more or less autonomous systems. The religious section and the political section are now seen as two separate divisions which should not be mixed. A legitimisation of this view is found in an interpretation of Luther's two regimes, the religious and the material. In its most extreme form, it has been argued (for example by former Prime Minister Anders Fogh Rasmussen) that religion should be completely separate from policy and the public debate – 'religion should not be seen in the public space in a secular society'. If this is the point of view, the space for the church in the public debate is very narrow, and practically the opposite of Viggo Kampmann's invitation to the cultural institutions to take part in public debate.

This political neutrality stands in contrast to the earlier dominating part of the Folk Church: the Grundtvigian movement included the church, the folk high schools, the political party Venstre as well as the cooperative movement, as formulated by the famous ecclesiastical historian P.G. Lindhardt:

> The cooperative dairy's chimney, the castles of the folk high schools and the church steeple of the "free" congregations are equal symbols of the movement; whether you take economic, cultural or religious perspectives, these are the same people. The Grundtvigianism was and remained the farmer's religion; it was a mighty force with roots in a class conscious state, strengthened by economic recovery and social community (translated from Lindhardt 1976, 126).

The general trend towards individualisation can be seen to have been supported by the fact that a leading school in Danish theology in the middle of the 20th century was existentialistic theology – a movement of which Tidehverv was a part. These theologians were mainly interested in the human individuals' life, responsibility and belief, and were in opposition to social-Christian theology's engagement in society. If the focus is on the individuals, it is less obvious why one should participate in debating the problems in society.

The ecclesiastical passivity in the public debate can also be caused by the marketisation. If the church is seen as a business and the members as customers, it is important not to bother any of the actual and potential customers by making controversial statements with which they perhaps do not agree, or which might actually antagonise them. Blaming somebody for their unethical behaviour while stressing moral restrictions as well as the obligation to take care of others is not necessarily a message one wants to highlight when trying to attract one's customers.

Conclusion

Society is often described as a body with individual limbs, and there is a need for a voice in society which stresses the interdependency between the limbs. Therein, the strong limbs sometimes have to support the weak. A voice which stresses the single limb's responsibility in relation to the other limbs and the total system is needed. This point of view was basically that of the first Danish sociologist, Professor Claudius Wilkens, see Wilkens (1874-76) and Kærgård (2008). It is also central for Hans Lassen Martensen's monumental *Christian Ethics* from 1878, see Kærgård (2018).

A well-known opposite point of view is that of Margaret Thatcher from *Women's Own* (1987): 'There's no such thing as society. There are individual men and women and there are families. And no government can do anything except through people, and people must look after themselves first.'

The debate between these two opposite points of view is part of the discussion in many disciplines, especially economics. The main effort in economics in the 1970s was to develop a micro-foundation for macroeconomic theory based on representative individuals. The hope was to derive a macroeconomic theory from a summation of rational utility and profit maximising individuals. The basic theory must be founded in individual acting. But some, for example the post-Keynesian school, considered this approach to be fundamentally mistaken. They called it 'the atomistic fallacy' or 'the fallacy of composition', see Jespersen (2009). The community has its own life, which cannot be derived from individual acting. 'That which is right for one person is not necessarily correct for the entire society, when the action is conducted by a large number of people at the same time' (Jespersen 2009, 14).

Certainly, one can stress the individual limbs and the interaction between them differently, but there seems to be no doubt that a realistic description and management of a society needs to include considerations of both individualism and the society as a whole. Social capital and cohesion are important concepts, which cannot be derived simply from individuals acting.

In a time that has individualisation and marketisation as dominating trends, there is more need for a voice which stresses respect for the community and social cohesion above the contrary voices. If individual utility and profit maximisation represent the dominating attitude, and atomistic market regulation is the main mechanism for resource allocation, there is definitely a need for a voice which points out the importance of goods external to the market, such as: the environment and nature, cohesion in society, support for the weak as a protection against social conflicts and so on. But if the Folk Church considers itself to be an institution working totally under market conditions, and considers individuals as customers (and potential customers) for whom the church should be as attractive and uncontroversial as possible, then the church cannot serve as this voice. But the church, with its long tradition for being the society's conscience, having a staff with job security and with more than three quarters of the population as its members, has a very attractive position for being such a voice. And in a society with a flexecurity labour market model without job security for almost all others, it is difficult to see any other group that has the conditions for being such a voice.

References

Bergh, T. and Tore J. Hanisch 1984. *Vitenskap og Politik – Linjer i norsk sosialøkonomi gjennom 150 år*, Oslo: Aschehoug.

Christoffersen, Lisbet 2017. 'Kirken i samfundet – Fri og lige adgang til Vorherre: Kirken og retten 1901-2017' in Niels Henrik Gregersen and Carsten Bach-Nielsen (eds.), *Reformationen i dansk kirke og kultur III 1914-2017*, Odense: Syddansk Universitetsforlag.

Hoffmann-Hansen, Henrik 2006. DF's vælgere holder sig væk fra kirken, *Kristeligt Dagblad*, January 12.

Jespersen, Jesper 2009. *Macroeconomic Methodology – A Post-Keynesian Perspective*, Cheltenham: Edward Elgar.

Johansen, T.S. 2011. Præster vil have radikal statsminister, *Kristeligt Dagblad*, August 31.

Kirkeministeriet 2014. *Folkekirkens styre*, Betænkning 1544, Copenhagen: Kirkeministeriet.

Kærgård, Niels 2001. 'Løgstrups etik og økonomiens morale', Carsten Fenger-Grøn and Jens Erik Kristensen (eds.), *Kritik af den økonomiske fornuft*, Copenhagen: Hans Reitzels Forlag, 69-87.

Kærgård, Niels 2006. 'Det tidehvervske i dansk politik: Liberalt Centrum og Dansk Folkeparti', in J. H. Schjørring and T. Bak (eds.), *Udfordringer til Folkekirken: Kirke – staten – folket*, Copenhagen: Anis, 169-220.

Kærgård, Niels 2008. 'En ubrugt inspirationskilde: Økonomi, psykologi og Claudius Wilkens', *Filosofiske Studier 14 – Festskrift tilegnet docent, dr. phil.Carl Henrik Koch*, pp.207-224.

Kærgård, Niels 2015. 'Religious Communities, Public Funding and Economics', in Francis Messner (ed.), *Public Funding of Religions in Europe*, Farnham, UK: Ashgate, 221-236.

Kærgård, Niels 2015a. 'Law, Religion and Economics', in Silvio Ferrari (ed.), *Routledge Handbook of Law and Religion*, London & New York: Routledge, 285-299.

Kærgård, Niels 2016. 'The Entanglement Between Religion and Politics in Denmark', in Michael Böss (ed.) *Bringing Culture Back In*, Aarhus: Aarhus University Press, 254-271.

Kærgård, Niels 2018. H. L. 'Martensen og D. G. Monrad: to biskoppers økonomi', *Kirkehistoriske Samlinger* 2018, 132-178.

Kærgård, Niels, Bent Thage and Niels-Henrik Topp 2019. 'Finansminister og statsminister Viggo Kampmann – Det moderne Danmarks idemand, men ikke driftssikker', Niels Kærgård, Jørgen Hansen and Jens Thomsen (eds.) *Med hånden på statskassen – Økonomer i regeringen,* Copenhagen: DJØF's Forlag.

Kærgaard, Niels and Pernille Friis Jensen. 'Patterns of Politics and Religion in Four Countries'. Linda Woodhead and Hans Raun Iversen (eds.) *The Old National Churches of Northern Europe: the Persistence of Societal Religion* (in preparation).

Lausten, Martin Schwarz 2014. *Politikere og prædikanter*, Copenhagen, Anis.

Lindhardt, P. G. 1976. *Vækkelser og Kirkelige Retninger*, Aarhus: Aros.

Løgstrup, K.E. 1971. 'Etiske begreber og problemer', in Gustaf Wingren (ed.), *Etik og Kristen tro*, Copenhagen: Gyldendal, 205-286.

Løgstrup, K.E. 1997. *System og symbol*, Copenhagen: Gyldendal.

Rawls, John 1971. *A Theory of Justice*, Cambridge, USA: Harvard University Press.

Sen, Amartya 2009. *The Idea of Justice*, Cambridge, USA: Harvard University Press.

Smidt, Poul 2016. *Viggo Kampmann – modig modstandsmand, klog finansminister, ustyrlig statsminister,* Copenhagen: Gyldendal.

Smith, Adam 1776 [1937]. *An Inquiry into the Nature and Causes of the Wealth of Nations*, The Modern Library of the World's Best Books, New York: Random House.

Sæther, Arild 1989. 'Danmarks og Norges Oeconomiske Magazin – et fristed for den økonomiske tenkning på 1700-tallet', *Norsk Økonomisk Tidsskrift*, bind 103, 99-114.

Thomsen, Jens Peter Frølund 2006. *Konflikten om de nye danskere*, Copenhagen: Akademisk forlag,.

Warburg, Margit 2015. Den danske religionsmodels grænseflade, *RVT – Religionsvidenskabeligt Tidsskrift,* bind 6.2, 5-14.

Wilkens, Claudius 1874-76. *Liv – Nydelse – Arbejde: Et samfundsfilosofisk Skrift I-III*, Otto B. Copenhagen: Wroblewskys Forlag.

Ziemann, Benjamin 2007. 'The Theory of Functional Differentiation and the History of Recent Historiography', *Sociale Systems*, vol. 13, 220-229.

Notes

1. For more on the conflict between K. E. Løgstrup and mainstream economics, see e.g. Kærgård (2001).
2. For more about the church generally, such attitudes and the effect of them, see Kærgård (2015, 2015a and 2018).
3. How this letter was created is a complicated story but the fact is that it actually was sent.
4. In 1966 Børge Diderichsen, Niels Gottschalck-Hansen, Poul Hartling, Orla Møller and Johan Nielsen and in 2015 Christian Langballe.

Summary of Main Points

17. The Danish Folk Church in the Age of Marketisation and Individualisation. A Challenged Cultural Institution

Hans Raun Iversen, Lisbet Christoffersen,
Niels Kærgård and Margit Warburg

The research results published in this book aim at contributing to the national and international debate on the consequences and limits of market orientation in cultural institutions. The Danish Folk Church has been the central example in this book. The purpose is to analyse and discuss consequences and limits to market orientation in cultural institutions. The primary questions relate to how individualisation and marketisation change old cultural institutions, how institutions maintain but also change their cultural core, and how they continue to contribute social capital. The aim, therefore, is to understand the extent to which changes in societal factors surrounding cultural institutions also change the way they contribute to the social capital in their society.

Based on Woodhead and Iversen (in preparation), it is to be expected that a 'societal church,' such as the Folk Church is, would be marked by societal trends like marketisation and individualisation. It is to be expected that the Folk Church would likewise be marked by the consequences attached to these forms of societal development. In this book, we have then analysed the extent to which this is the case.

The working hypothesis applied in this book is, as mentioned in Chapter 1, that the Danish Folk Church's ability to accept individualisation as a pre-condition for its work has given it a position of strength – one that has enabled it to contribute to society's social capital while simultaneously setting limits to market orientation.

At first glance, labelling religion in general (and Danish Folk Church Christianity in particular) as part of culture may seem self-evident. If these are a part of culture, it would be reasonable to envisage the Folk Church as a cultural institution on a par with other cultural institutions. On closer inspection, however, this is not at all self-evident. Viewing religion and Danish

Folk Church Christianity as parts of culture is certainly not a commonly held perception in, for example, public administration, politics and academic studies. There is a long theoretical (and not least theologically-theoretical) discussion on this labelling (Chapter 1). And the very first product of this book is a detailed discussion about the history by which the following conclusion is reached: that it is possible to understand the Folk Church as a cultural institution *in its own right* (Chapter 1), which now fits into the modern category of cultural institutions (Chapters 2-4, and generally throughout the book).

Our study of the case of the Danish Folk Church is, as mentioned, an *example* of the consequences and limits of marketisation and individualisation in relation to cultural institutions in general. As such, it contributes to the international debate on modern societal conditions for cultural institutions. Cultural institutions in Denmark, and most probably in other parts of the world, especially in Western Europe, work under the same basic conditions and keep on learning from one another's development in complicated ways. Against the background of the studies presented in this book, we can point to the following general observations:

First, it is a general observation in this book that the way of gaining money, and the amount of money gained, are decisive for the future of cultural institutions. However, money alone is not enough for a cultural institution to survive. In addition to money, the degree of relations to larger cultural traditions in society matters significantly for cultural institutions' stability. Cultural institutions have been coming closer to their users during recent years. But, at the same time, they must be sharp in defining their purpose when they modernise their work and organization. Obviously, modernisation of organization and administration must take place and, therefore, will inevitably influence cultural institutions. In our studies, it has been illustrated how a built-in condition in modernisation must be that it takes place in a way which allows for controlling the influence of modernisation (e.g. the introduction of NPM). Finally, our results also point to the concern that even old cultural institutions, such as national churches, must be aware of the risk they face in potentially ending up contributing to social inequality and discrimination when working in and adapting to an increasingly neoliberal society.

The dynamics between market orientation, individualisation and social capital

Before we go into the more detailed analysis of the studies, it is worthwhile underlining another central result of this study, namely the overall dynamics that we see between market orientation, individualisation and social capital.

Against the background of our studies, it is possible to argue for a renewed focus on *public value* concerning old cultural institutions (O'Flynn 2007). Such institutions, including the Folk Church, must all defend their economy in a state-governed market, but they must also defend their relevance in relation to individuals as well as relating to social cohesion across society.

When it comes to the Danish Folk Church, our central example, we find that it has not yet been as strongly marked by marketisation as, for example, the book market and, to some degree, the museum sector, too (Chapter 10). Even so, we have found clear imprints of the dynamic interplay between market orientation, individualisation and social capital in the Folk Church. For a church with 75 percent of the population as members, it is not very surprising to find that it accommodates itself to society in general.

These imprints are mainly visible in the subtle interactions between the individualistic tendency towards 'churching alone', the liberalising free-choice-legislation in church laws and a new management culture centred around the deans of the Folk Church (Chapter 7).

The same tendency is also very clear when it comes to the Folk Church's accommodation to the individualisation found among members and users of the church, in the practices of the congregation and in the theological self-understanding among pastors in the Folk Church (Chapters 5 and 11).

Even though we are still lacking longitudinal studies, Chapters 13 and 14 indicate how more individualised and market-driven activities in the Folk Church may lead to a strengthening of bonding (but not bridging) social capital. As with the rest of the neo-liberal market society (Piketty 2014), we end up finding 'the Matthew effect': those who have, come to enjoy more benefits; whereas those who do not have (for example a lot of friends and resources), are more easily marginalised by such societal developments.

Significant societal consequences are also highlighted when studying the more indirect societal impact of the state organized Folk Church, as well as the role of the Folk Church within the political debate (Chapter 15 and 16).

What is said above indicates that we have also found significant connections between the development of the social structure in the Folk Church and the development of the (individualised) mentality and aspirations of the members and users of the Folk Church as a cultural institution (Chapters 5, 6 and 7). The Folk Church, like other cultural institutions, is literally forced to prove that it offers public value to society and not least to its individual citizens in the midst of their lives today. In order to do so, it must come close to its users while at the same time sticking to its purpose and adjusting its organization, staff and products to the situation (Chapters 9 and 10).

Other main findings

In the following section, we present the main findings relating to the project's three basic questions: (1) how do individualisation and marketisation change old cultural institutions? (2) How do such institutions maintain but also adapt their own self-understanding regarding their cultural core? And (3) to what extent do changes in societal factors surrounding those cultural institutions also change the way in which they contribute to the social capital in society?

Market or Meaning? Being a Church member in the Age of Individualisation
At the level of the individual church members and users of the Folk Church, the following findings have emerged: decisions regarding membership and baptism mostly depend on members' relation to tradition and their individual existential orientation. They are only related to the payment of church taxes that follows membership of the church to a rather limited extent (Leth-Nissen and Trolle 2015, Leth-Nissen 2016 and Nielsen 2017). The users of the Folk Church consider its services, for example rites of passage, not so much as commodities that one can buy, but rather as access to a tradition, a common narrative and as an identity-marker. The use of rites of passage by individuals contributes to their social capital by strengthening group coherence between family members and bonds of friendship around the individual (Leth-Nissen 2018). The main tendency that was found, however, is that people tend to use the church by 'churching alone,' that is, according to personal decisions made by individuals in their individual situation, much more than by 'churching together,' following family and neighbourhood traditions (Chapter 7, and Leth-Nissen 2018).

Administration and New Public Management (NPM)

For better or for worse, surviving as a cultural institution in the market takes considerable adjustment of the organization, its ways of operating and even of the products offered by cultural institutions. One common criticism of NPM is that, when rationalising the work of an institution, it can easily harm values that cannot be bought for money (Sandel 2012).

The introduction of NPM in the Folk Church is studied in Chapters 6 and 7. Chapter 6 points out that NPM manifests mostly in the form of performance management at the national and regional level, which are the directly state-controlled parts of the Folk Church. In Chapter 7, it appears that the deans have also been challenged to introduce tools from NPM into the management at deanery and parish levels, even though they only reluctantly do so. The fact that a lot of modernisation and rationalisation goes on in the Folk Church is confirmed in Chapter 10, whereas Chapter 11 focuses on how the Folk Church's current accommodation to the market seems to fit rather well with the needs and habits of the users of the Folk Church.

The Folk Church has a number of strengths that help it maintain qualities that cannot be bought for money, even though the conditions that help these strengths to survive in the Folk Church require a lot of money and (modernised) organization: The Folk Church is rather professional in its work, combining several professions, which requires a high educational standard (including post-education for which finances are available). To this is added a rather strongly decentralised local leadership within a visible but slimly demarcated state framework. This system depends on the historical tradition for church-state relations in Denmark (and a general tradition for governance in the Danish State). When the system is allowed to survive in the Folk Church, it is very much due to the simple fact that the money is available to uphold this (economically and administratively seen) hardly rational system. It is also important that the Folk Church adheres to a strong basic Christian narrative that can integrate individualism and set limits for orientation towards the market (Chapter 5). The continuing renewal and communication of this (Christian and Biblical) narrative takes a lot of money, which is also available. Finally, the Folk Church represents a societal rather than an ecclesial type of church, focusing to a great extent on society outside the core congregation. Many externally-oriented or societal activities (for example the Church School Service, open night churches and baby hymn singing) can only be upheld and offered for free by a wealthy church. These points are to various extents documented and discussed in Chapters 7 and 10, and in Woodhead and Iversen (in preparation). For a comprehensive introduction and documentation about the way the Folk Church works, see Iversen 2018.

Public economy in the Folk Church as a counterforce to marketisation
'Money makes the world go round!' Or so it was put in the musical *Cabaret*. To a great extent, it is also money that makes the Folk Church go round. The Folk Church, with its comparatively strong and safe economy, is able to finance the activities desired by the congregations with the help of the money from the church tax that, so far, keeps coming in every year. The church tax is a key to understanding the comparatively strong economy of the Folk Church. Chapter 4 outlines the historical background of the economic strength of the Folk Church. Some of the consequences of this strength compared to other churches and other cultural institutions are reflected upon in Chapters 8 and 9, respectively (see also Kjems in preparation).

Needless to say, all cultural institutions can benefit from safe sources of financial income, for example grants from the state, municipalities or funds, participants' payments, membership fees or income from various market shares. Next to taxation, state funding or state regulated licenses from users (as for the national broadcasting company) also seem to be beneficial. However, both of these sources can be cut down or changed to something else, as is presently happening with licenses for the national broadcasting company in Denmark. Money matters a lot – but cultural institutions are at the same time dependent on sticking to their purpose, message and core values in order to be trustworthy in what they do. Regarding the Folk Church specifically, we conclude here as follows:

Even though the Folk Church lives with marketisation and individualisation on a par with other cultural institutions, the impact of these factors is felt less in the Folk Church, mainly because of the beneficial economic system: the locally decided amount of church tax is collected automatically by tax authorities from all church members. The importance of this point has been supported by the following findings:

Church tax, as a way of securing income for churches, is also decisive for the high level of financing in the Swedish and Finish majority churches which have an economy income system similar to the Folk Church (Chapter 8). Despite continuing secularisation and the gradual weakening of the former unity between state, church and people, the budget of the Folk Church still maintains a stable share of the Danish Gross National Product (Kjems 2018). The income of the Folk Church is highly decisive for its ability to perform and deliver professional quality services in its activities. A Lutheran parish in Denmark has 10 times as much money for its work than a similar Anglican parish in England (Leth-Nissen and Gould in preparation). In the Folk Church – as in the welfare state – the solidarity among the members is built into the tax system as long as the handling of the economy appears trustworthy to the members.

An illuminating perspective on the economy of the Folk Church comes from the Danish churches outside Denmark. They represent proper examples of marketisation of the Folk Church, as each individual church must mobilise the majority of the resources necessary for covering the running costs of that church. This is done, to a great extent, according to commercial conditions and in ways wherein the bonds between the members are strengthened at the same time. This is demonstrated in the annual Christmas fairs, which play a very important role in the life of most Danish churches abroad. Using Tönnies' concepts of *Gesellschaft* and *Gemeinschaft*, the Christmas fairs serve *Gesellschaft* purposes through the provision of money, and *Gemeinschaft* purposes through creating a space where Danish expatriates nurture their Danish belonging. The latter cannot be bought for money (Warburg 2018a).

Changes in cultural traditions in an old cultural institution

The next question we have been dealing with in this book relates to how a cultural institution stays true to its cultural tradition, while also adapting it alongside the individualisation and marketisation trends. It appears to be of importance that there is a match between the mentality and appearance of the Folk Church as a cultural institution and that of its users. That the Folk Church may have a historical advantage in this respect is indicated in Chapter 3. However, it is just as important that a cultural institution remain close to and have a deep understanding of its users. This is so that it can be sharp in presenting and sticking to its purpose to people, and thereby demonstrate its value for individuals and society. This is reflected upon in Chapter 5 and in comparative perspectives in Chapters 10, 11 and 12. We can sum up our related findings as follows:

The Folk Churches represent a societal 'Christianity' in its own right – as distinct and different from other 'Christianities,' in a way similar to, for example, Orthodox or African Christianities (Woodhead and Iversen in preparation). During the last 20 years, a number of researchers have convincingly argued for the connection between the Scandinavian welfare state model and Lutheranism. Both institutionally and in terms of their conscious public perception; Chapter 3 presents the case that this connection can be seen to be even deeper when we look at the structural similarities between the program of the Lutheran Reformation and society and church in Denmark today.

Danish Folk Church Christianity is to a considerable degree historically intertwined with nationality. This is seen in particular when studying Danish churches abroad. Comparing the Danish church in London with the Anglican St. Alban's Church in Copenhagen, the two congregations differ considerably with respect to the nation-religion balance in everyday church life. In the Danish churches abroad, people gather primarily to nurture their Danish culture, whereas the congregation in St. Alban's Church, people primarily gather for confessional reasons. These differences are illustrated in a new model depicting the overlap of religion, nation and ethnicity in the two churches (Warburg in preparation).

The Danish celebration of the 500th anniversary of the Lutheran Reformation was remarkable for its emphasis on the *national* perspectives of the Reformation, in comparison with the celebrations in other countries. The different events, even the official Pentecost church service, were often used as fora for expressing Danish civil religion as much as expressing Lutheranism in its confessional sense (Chapter 2; Warburg 2018b). The Folk Church acts as a cultural institution on a par with other cultural institutions, and, the fact that the Folk Church is a community with a certain faith and confession is actually often played down. Probably this, together with the way the Folk Church is connected to the state in Denmark (Christoffersen in preparation), also means that the Folk Church has no or only few possibilities to voice criticism of the state. One of the few exceptions was during World War II in connection with the persecution of the Danish Jews. Because the Folk Church is anchored in a long cultural tradition, it can easily be used politically when politicians want to strengthen the framework around religion outside the Folk Church (Chapter 15).

An important part of the strength of the Folk Church in Denmark is found in its buildings, the status of which (symbolic capital) is placed in a position above the political and market forces of the day (Iversen 2015 and Rasmussen in preparation). The buildings of the Danish Folk Church, which, legally speaking, own themselves, for historical, legal and economic reasons make the Folk Church visible and somehow untouchable in every single parish. They are identity markers that cannot be appropriated easily by people with money – as may happen in other cultural institutions, not to mention banks and businesses (Chapter 12).

The Folk Church's contribution to social capital
The third question this book has been concerned with is how contributions from a cultural institution to the social capital in society might change when individualisation and marketisation take over.

One important strength belonging to the Folk Church as a cultural institution is its ability to accept individualisation among people as a precondition for its work (Chapters 5, 10 and 12). One example might be when a widow asks to have a sailor's song played at the funeral of her husband, who loved the sea so much. In this situation, the pastor has a good position and can take the time to encourage the widow agree to replace the (sad) sailor's song with a Christian hymn which reflects the significance of the ocean. The pastor, if capable of handling the situation, can easily be serious about the wish for a funeral 'in the spirit of the deceased' in ways where both the widow and the pastor feel that this is an authentic (church) funeral (Chapter 5).

We have also found that the Folk Church, at the organizational level, is able to contribute to social capital whilst simultaneously setting limits to market orientation (Chapter 7). When it comes to the contribution to bridging social capital and the support for minorities, the role of the Folk Church is, however, at best ambivalent (Chapters 13, 14 and 15). Our positive findings on the Folk Church's contribution to social capital can be summed up as follows:

Historically, the Folk Church has been a founding cultural institution in Danish society, contributing to the co-creation of, for example, social capital, coherence and a work ethic (Kærgård 2017 and Warburg 2018b). The contribution to social capital by a church depends on the model of the church. An inward-looking ecclesial church will influence society less than a broad, open societal church, as is found in most parishes and branches of the Folk Church (Kærgård 2016). Since the beginning of the 20th century, the Folk Church has contributed to democratisation in Danish society by accommodating itself to democracy. At the same time, it represents a model for economic equality through its church tax that is paid according to personal income (Christoffersen 2017).

The Folk Church's special positions of strengths compared to other cultural institutions

This book's working hypothesis has been that it is in the ability to accept individualisation as a pre-condition for its operations that the Danish National Church has remained strong enough to contribute to Danish social capital whilst simultaneously setting limits to market orientation. In the following, we bring together the points where the Danish Folk Church can be seen to occupy a special position, having considerable quantities of five sorts of capital:

The Folk Church has a unique way of securing its finances, namely through the church tax, calculated according to the income of the church members (economic capital). The Folk Church is strongly linked to a long Lutheran societal tradition within Danish society – even though, today, this tradition is somewhat weakened (cultural capital). As with the majority of other cultural institutions, the Folk Church is strongly identified with its buildings. They – like the cross in the Danish flag – have a unique and untouchable place in the Danish cultural landscape all over the country (symbolic capital). The Folk Church's mode of governance, using a decentralised day-to-day leadership combined with a rather slim but strong state administration system, contributes to the experience that people can trust that their church cannot be sold and taken over by anybody else (social capital). The basic Christian story not only offers a strong narrative for the Folk Church, but in being continuously retold and performed by church members, the story may also be intertwined with and thus contribute to individual life stories, for example amongst people attending the rites of passage in the Folk Church (narrative capital, cf. Goodson 2013).

***

In Woodhead and Iversen (in preparation), we highlight the strengths of the Folk Church as compared to six other old, national churches in Northern Europe. In this book, we have pointed out that the Folk Church also seems to have a rather strong position compared to other cultural institutions in Denmark. That being so, in adjusting to a neo-liberal society, the Folk Church may run the risk of contributing to social inequality and politics that are in disagreement with its own Christianity's demand for the love of one's neighbour. These are risks the Folk Church should pay continual attention to. Needless to say, these tendencies need further attention in future research as they are probably found in other cultural institutions as well. Finally, yet importantly, cultural institutions must ask themselves what happens to *What Money Can't Buy* in their response to marketisation and individualisation.

References

Christoffersen, Lisbet 2015. 'From Previous Intertwinement to a Future Split in Governance Structures, Cultural and Religious Use of Buildings: On Danish Funding of Religious Heritage'. Anne Fornerod (ed.) *Funding Religious Heritage*. Farnham Surrey: Ashgate/Routledge, 75-102.

Christoffersen, Lisbet 2017. 'Fri og Lige Adgang til Vorherre: Kirken og Retten 1901-2017'. Niels Henrik Gregersen and Carsten Bach-Nielsen (eds.). *Reformationen i dansk kultur og kirkeliv 1914-2017*. Odense: Syddansk Universitetsforlag, 195-228.

Christoffersen, Lisbet. 'By Law Established. The Reformation Churches in the Nordic Countries'. Linda Woodhead and Hans Raun Iversen (eds.) *The Old National Churches of Northern Europe: The Persistence of Societal Religion* (in preparation).

Goodson, Ivor (ed.) 2013. *Developing Narrative Theory: Life Histories and Personal Representation*. Abingdon: Routledge.

Iversen, Hans Raun 2015. 'Kirkebygninger i Religionsmodellens Grænseflader. Mellem Fælles Kulturarv og Folkekirkeligt Magtmonopol'. *Religionsvidenskabeligt Tidsskrift 62/2015*, 29-44.

Iversen, Hans Raun 2018. *Ny Praktisk Teologi. Kristendommen, den Enkelte og Kirken*. Copenhagen: Eksistensen.

Kjems, Sidsel 2018. *The Significance of Church Tax. The Historical Background, the Concept and the Significance of Church Tax. The Case of the Established Church in Denmark*. PhD thesis. Faculty of Science, University of Copenhagen.

Kjems, Sidsel. 'Church Economy. Sources of Income and Annual Revenue.' Linda Woodhead and Hans Raun Iversen (eds.) *The Old National Churches of Northern Europe: The Persistence of Societal Religion.* (in preparation).

Kærgård, Niels 2017. 'Det Danske Samfund, økonomien og Reformationen'. Ole Høiris and Per Ingesman (eds.). *Reformationen: 1500-tallets Kulturrevolution.* Vol. 2. Aarhus: Aarhus Universitetsforlag, 453-465.

Kærgård, Niels 2016. 'Kirken på Landet: et Dilemma Uden Simple Løsninger'. *Kritisk Forum for Praktisk Teologi.* 143, 34-46.

Leth-Nissen, Karen Marie 2016. 'A Deliberate Action'. Harald Askeland and Ulla Schmidt (eds.). *Church Reform and Leadership of Change.* Church of Sweden Research Series. Eugene: Pickwick, 135-157.

Leth-Nissen, Karen Marie. 2018. *Churching Alone? A Study of the Danish Folk Church at Organisational, Individual, and Societal Levels.* PhD-thesis, Faculty of Theology, University of Copenhagen.

Leth-Nissen, Karen Marie and David Gould. 'Comparing Parishes. Longbridge in England and Sydhavn in Denmark'. Linda Woodhead and Hans Raun Iversen (eds.) 2019. *The Old National Churches of Northern Europe: The Persistence of Societal Religion* (in preparation).

Leth-Nissen, Karen Marie and Astrid Krabbe Trolle 2015. *Dåb Eller ej. Rapport om Småbørnsforældres til- og Fravalg af Dåb.* Det Teologiske Fakultet, Center for Kirkeforskning, Københavns Universitet.

Nielsen, Christina Øager 2017. *Når Danskerne Forlader Folkekirken.* MA-thesis in sociology of religion. University of Copenhagen.

O'Flynn, Janine 2007. 'From New Public Management to Public Value: Paradigmatic Change and Managerial Implications'. *The Australian Journal of Public Administration,* 66/3, 353-366.

Piketty, Thomas 2014. *Capital in the 21st Century.* Harvard: Harvard University Press.

Rasmussen, Jes Heise. 'Church Buildings and Closure in England and Denmark' Linda Woodhead and Hans Raun Iversen (eds.). *The Old National Churches of Northern Europe: The Persistence of Societal Religion.* (in preparation).

Rasmussen, Jes Heise 2018. *Lukketid? En Religionssociologisk Analyse af Kirkelukninger og Markedsgørelse.* PhD-thesis. University of Copenhagen.

Sandel, Michael J. 2012. *What Money Can't Buy. The Moral Limits of Markets.* New York: Farrar, Straus and Giroux.

Warburg Margit 2018a. 'Christmas Fairs in Danish Churches Abroad: a Resource Mobilisation Perspective'. *Religion.* 48, 367-371.

Warburg Margit 2018b. 'The Danish Reformation Celebrations as Civil Religion' *Journal of Church and State.* Accessible at DOI: 10.1093/jcs/csy030.

Warburg, Margit. 'National Churches Going Abroad. Balancing Nation and Religion'. Linda Woodhead and Hans Raun Iversen (eds.) 2019. *The Old National Churches of Northern Europe: The Persistence of Societal Religion.* (in preparation).

Woodhead, Linda and Hans Raun Iversen (eds.). *The Old National Churches of Northern Europe: The Persistence of Societal Religion.* (in preparation).

About the Authors

LISBET CHRISTOFFERSEN, PhD, is Professor of Law & Religion, at Roskilde University, Professor of Ecclesiastical Law, at the University of Copenhagen, and Director of the HERA-funded project *Protestant Legacies in the Nordic Countries*. She is the author of *Kirkeret Mellem Stat, Marked og Civilsamfund (1998)* and co-author of *Law and Religion in the 21st Century – Nordic Perspectives (2010)*. She has contributed to the book series *Cultural Diversity and Law in Association with RELIGARE,* and her articles have appeared in leading international and Danish legal journals. Her scientific foci are state-church-religion relations and domestic religious law, especially in the Nordic countries, as well as transnational and international law, public law and law and society studies.

HANS RAUN IVERSEN, MA in Theology, 1976, dr. theol. h. c. 2012. Iversen was Associate Professor of Practical Theology at the University of Copenhagen (1982-2018) and director of a range of cross-disciplinary projects on religion and society, including: the Interfaculty Priority Area in Research; *Religion in the 21st Century,* 2003-2007; *Center for Church Research,* 2011-2018; and *What Money Can't Buy,* 2014-2018. His publications are focused mainly on Denmark, and he has produced several edited volumes in Danish, including the second edition of his textbook *Ny praktisk teologi. Kristendommen, den enkelte og kirken* (2018). He has twenty articles in English that have been published in as many edited books and periodicals.

SIDSEL KJEMS is a PhD Fellow at the University of Copenhagen, in the Department of Food and Resource Economics. Her research is centred on the economic conditions of established churches in Northern Europe, with a particular interest in the state churches in the Nordic countries. Her work compares finance methods, such as church tax, public grants and private donations, drawing on behavioural economics as theoretical background and using choice environment as an analytical tool. She has also undertaken research into the concept of church tax, and into the historical development of the economy of the Nordic state churches. Her most detailed work in this regard relates to the Danish Folk Church.

NIELS KÆRGÅRD, dr. polit., is Professor Emeritus at the University of Copenhagen's Department of Food and Resource Economics. He was Professor of Agricultural Economics 1993-2017, a member of the Presidency of the Danish Board of Economic advisors 1992-2001 and chairman 1995-2001. Between 2002-2012, he was on the board of the Carlsberg Foundation and Carlsberg Brewery between 2007-2013 he was on the board of the University of Copenhagen and between 2008-2013 he was Vice-President of the Danish Academy of Science. He has been published in Danish as well as in various international journals and books about economic policy, ethics, Christianity and economic history. Recently, he has also produced a number of publications about economics and the Danish Reformation.

ANNETTE MARIE KRUHØFFER, MTh, MA, MPA, is currently a parish pastor at Glumsø, Sjælland. She has extensive management and communication experience, in particular as principal of a high school, a member of the board at the University of Aarhus, chairperson at the parish council in *Davids sogn*, Copenhagen and as a journalist. Her scientific publications are primarily conference contributions focusing on history, in particular the Viking Age and Medieval times.

KAREN MARIE LETH-NISSEN, PhD, is a postdoc at the Center for Church Research, in the Faculty of Theology, at the University of Copenhagen. Her 2018 dissertation, *Churching Alone?*, explores how the Danish Folk Church changes with societal trends relating to individualisation and the dominant management strategies. She co-authored the 2015 report on changes in the use of baptism amongst Danish parents (with Astrid Krabbe Trolle) titled *Baptism or not?* Karen has written comparative studies on the Danish Folk Church and the Church of England. Her special interests include churches and social capital, and churches and power. She worked as a minister in the Danish Folk Church for ten years before going into academic research.

MARIE VEJRUP NIELSEN, PhD, is Director of the Centre for Contemporary Religion and Associate Professor in the Study of Religion, at the School of Culture and Society, Arts, at Aarhus University. Her primary research area is contemporary Christianity in the Scandinavian and European context. She is the editor of *Religion in Denmark*, a yearly online publication of data and analysis of approved religious groups in Denmark. She was part of the research team of 'The Aarhus Project' 2012-2013 and editor and co-author of *Religion in Aarhus* (2013). Her publications also include articles in the *Nordic Journal of Religion and Society* and the *Journal of Empirical Theology*.

JES HEISE RASMUSSEN, PhD is Associate Professor in the Sociology of Religion, at University College, Copenhagen. His special interests include the impact of New Public Management on religious institutions, the closure of Danish churches, radicalisation and religion and secular religious education in public schools.

INGRID STORM, PhD, is a Fellow at the University of Birmingham's Department for Social Policy, Sociology and Criminology. She was previously a British Academy Postdoctoral Research Fellow at the University of Manchester's Cathie Marsh Institute for Social Research. Her work concerns the relationship between economic insecurity and religion, religious and ethnic identities in Europe, attitudes to immigration and minorities, moral values and civic engagement and inter-generational religious change. Her primary research method is quantitative survey analysis, and her work is published in a number of leading British and European journals including *British Journal of Sociology*, *European Sociological Review*, *Sociology of Religion* and *Journal for the Scientific Study of Religion*.

MARGIT WARBURG, dr. phil., is Professor of Sociology of Religion, at the University of Copenhagen. She is author of *Citizens of the World. A History and Sociology of the Baha'is from a Globalisation Perspective* (2006) and 'Secular Rituals' in the *Research Companion to Anthropology* (2015). Her major recent articles have appeared in *Implicit Religion*, *Journal of Ritual Studies*, *Nordic Journal of Religion and Society*, *Journal of Church and State* and *Journal of Contemporary Religion*. Her special interests include Danish churches abroad, Baha'i, civil religion and religion and globalisation.